AQA Citizenship

Exclusively endorsed by AQA

AS

Duncan Watts

Nelson Thornes

Published in 2009 by:
Nelson Thornes Ltd
Delta Place
27 Bath Road
CHELTENHAM
GL53 7TH
United Kingdom

10 11 12 13 / 10 9 8 7 6 5 4 3

A catalogue record for this book is available from the British Library

ISBN 978 1 4085 1388 0

Cover photograph: Photolibrary/BrandX Pictures
Page make-up by Hart McLeod

Printed in China

Contents

Introduction iv

About the AQA specification vi

Unit 1	Identity, rights and responsibilities	1

Chapter 1 What is a citizen, and what does it mean to be British? 1

Chapter 2 How socially diverse is Britain? 23

Chapter 3 Prejudice, discrimination and disadvantage 44

Chapter 4 How can we reduce discrimination and disadvantage? 65

Chapter 5 What are rights? 81

Chapter 6 What rights do I have? 97

Chapter 7 The legal framework: protecting the citizen 115

Chapter 8 How do the courts protect my rights? 138

Unit 2	Democracy, active citizenship and participation	159

Chapter 9 Who holds power in the UK? 159

Chapter 10 The government and the citizen 208

Chapter 11 Playing your part: how to get involved and make a difference 249

Chapter 12 Citizenship in action: campaigning 283

Chapter 13 Active citizenship skills and participation 298

References 304

Index 306

Acknowledgements 313

Introduction

Nelson Thornes has worked in partnership with AQA to ensure this book and the accompanying online resources offer you the best support for your A Level course.

All resources have been approved by senior AQA examiners so you can feel assured that they closely match the specification for this subject and provide you with everything you need to prepare successfully for your exams.

These print and online resources together **unlock blended learning**; this means that the links between the activities in the book and the activities online blend together to maximise your understanding of a topic and help you achieve your potential.

These online resources are available on **kerboodle!** which can be accessed via the internet at **www.kerboodle.com/live**, anytime, anywhere. If your school or college subscribes to this service you will be provided with your own personal login details. Once logged in, access your course and locate the required activity.

For more information and help visit **www.kerboodle.com**

Icons in this book indicate where there is material online related to that topic. The following icons are used:

💡 Learning activity

These resources include a variety of interactive and non-interactive activities to support your learning.

✔ Progress tracking

These resources include a variety of tests that you can use to check your knowledge on particular topics (Test yourself) and a range of resources that enable you to analyse and understand examination questions (On your marks …).

🔎 Research support

These resources include WebQuests, in which you are assigned a task and provided with a range of web links to use as source material for research.

↘ Study skills

These resources support you in developing a skill that is key for your course, for example planning essays.

How to use this book

This book covers the specification for your course and is arranged in a sequence approved by AQA with two Units covering the AS units of the specification:

Unit 1: Identity, rights and responsibilities looks at definitions of citizenship, what it means to be British and the ways in which individuals and groups define their identities. It explores the social diversity of Britain and issues of prejudice, discrimination and disadvantage, and how their impact can be reduced. It also looks at the rights and responsibilities of citizens and the ways in which rights are protected and supported.

Unit 2: Democracy, active citizenship and participation examines the concept and nature of power in the UK - who holds it, and the relationship between the citizen and political power. It then looks at the ways in which you can become involved and make a difference, putting citizenship into action to bring about change.

Key features of this book include:

Learning objectives

At the beginning of each chapter you will find a list of learning objectives that contain targets linked to the requirements of the specification.

Key terms

Terms that you will need to be able to define and understand.

Hints

Hints on useful follow-up or study techniques.

Activities

Practical suggestions for activities to help you understand and engage with the ideas in the book and better prepare for your exams.

Further information

Further information sections look at some of these ideas in greater depth. If you have time for these they will enrich your understanding of the subject.

Case studies

Case studies help you relate ideas in the text to examples from the real world.

> A realia tinted background or a tinted sidebar indicates quoted or paraphrased material within these real-life examples.

Summary questions

These cover key ideas from each section and help you reflect on them.

AQA Examination-style questions

Specimen paper questions in the style that you can expect in your exam are provided at the end of each Unit. AQA examination questions are reproduced by permission of the Assessment and Qualifications Alliance.

AQA Examiner's tip

Hints from AQA examiners to help you with your study and to prepare for your exam.

Web links in the book

As Nelson Thornes is not responsible for third party content online, there may be some changes to this material that are beyond our control. In order for us to ensure that the links referred to in the book are as up-to-date and stable as possible, the websites are usually homepages with supporting instructions on how to reach the relevant pages if necessary.

Please let us know at **kerboodle@nelsonthornes.com** if you find a link that doesn't work and we will do our best to redirect the link, or to find an alternative site.

Online glossary

The key terms are listed alphabetically for your convenience in a glossary. To access the glossary for the book, go to www.nelsonthornes.com/citizenship_glossary.

About the AQA specification

How the specification is structured

The AS specification consists of two AS Units: Unit 1: CIST1 covering Identity, rights and responsibilities, and Unit 2 CIST2 on Democracy, active citizenship and participation.

Unit 1 is assessed through a written paper lasting 1 hour and 15 minutes that includes source-based questions and mini-essay questions; it carries 60 marks that count for 40% of the AS examination.

Unit 2 is assessed through a written paper lasting 1 hour and 30 minutes that includes a source-based question and a mini-essay, plus a structured question on active citizenship participation for which you will need to bring your Active Citizenship Profile into the exam. Unit 2 carries 90 marks and 60% of the AS examination.

Assessment Objectives

The Assessment Objectives are common to both the AS and A2 units:

Assessment Objective			Weighting		
			AS	A2	A Level
A01	Knowledge and understanding	• Demonstrate knowledge and understanding of specific citizenship issues (problems, events, concepts, ideas, processes and opinions). • Relate subject knowledge and understanding to citizenship issues using a range of real and topical examples.	15%	10%	25%
A02	Analysis and evaluation	• Analyse issues, problems and events in relation to the citizenship concepts and topics studied. • Evaluate information, views, opinions, ideas and arguments and assess their validity.	10%	15%	25%
A03	Communication and action	• Select, organise and present relevant information and arguments clearly and logically, using specialist terminology. • Construct and advocate reasoned, coherent arguments with conclusions, drawing on evidence of a candidate's own participation and actions within the study of citizenship.	25%	10%	35%
A04	Synthesis	• Synthesise knowledge, ideas and concepts from different areas of the subject in order to generalise, argue a case or propose alternative solutions.	0%	15%	15%

©AQA – reproduced with permission from the AQA specification.

Identity, rights and responsibilities

1 What is a citizen, and what does it mean to be British?

Hint

In many of the topics discussed in this book, there is one large issue that dominates debate. Make sure that you familiarise yourself with that debate, using information from television and newspapers, as well as the material presented here. Synthesise your knowledge and understanding of the relative ideas and concepts, so that you can convey this information to the examiner in a clear manner.

In this case, the key question is 'What does it mean to be British?' As you work through this chapter, ask yourself whether there is a single British identity or whether there exists a diversity of identities.

What is a citizen?

Citizenship refers to membership of a **state**. Most people identify themselves in terms of the particular country of which they are citizens. In studying citizenship, we are particularly concerned with the relationship between individuals and the state, which grants **rights** to and imposes obligations upon those individuals.

However, the concept of citizenship is a complex one, not easily capable of being reduced to a single, straightforward definition. It embraces several features that would differ according to who is listing them. They might include elements such as a common civic identity, good neighbourliness, acceptance of a core of shared democratic **values**, recognition of the country's past achievements and generally agreement on entitlements and responsibilities, including the right – some would say duty – to participate in the nation's affairs.

In Britain and elsewhere, there are many citizens who are not especially interested in, knowledgeable about or actively bothered with matters concerning public affairs. They do not wish to be involved and may in some cases be more concerned with personal advancement than with the well-being of society.

The nature of citizenship

Acceptance of the importance of citizenship as a desirable, indeed necessary part of the individual–state relationship can be dated back to the early days of **Athenian democracy** (see also pages 2 and 249–50), which flourished for a few centuries BC. In ancient Athens, those who were acknowledged as citizens were expected to:

- participate in the government and administration of their polis or city-state
- attend civic meetings and take part in debate
- vote on issues of public policy
- be active members of their community, exercising their rights and fulfilling their obligations.

Athenian experience reminds us of the need for citizens to understand the democracy in which we live and be active within it. We need knowledge if we are to make the choices that face us on an informed basis. When the choices have to be made, we have the chance to exercise our right to vote in support of one party or another. Voting may be viewed as a symbol of citizenship.

Active citizenship

Today, many thinkers and writers of whatever political persuasion unite in their desire that every individual citizen should be a full and active member of his or her political community.

■ Key terms

Citizenship: an individual's legal membership of and recognition by a state that grants mutual rights and obligations between state and citizen.

State: an organisation that possesses political power, enabling it to issue and enforce rules that are binding for the people living in a given territory. It usually has a monopoly of coercive power (force).

Rights: legal or moral entitlements that allow people to act or be treated in a particular way, for example to enjoy some form of freedom or equality.

Values: the beliefs, principles or accepted standards of individuals or particular social groups, in which they have a emotional investment, perhaps for or against something – i.e. as when a person is said to have 'liberal values'. They represent deep moral feelings about what is right or wrong, acceptable or not acceptable. Values define us both as individuals and as a society.

Athenian democracy: the form of democracy developed in the Greek city-state of Athens around 500 BC.

Active citizenship: the belief that citizens who have done well out of life have a moral duty to be active, participating members of their community, volunteering to serve others. Usually, the meaning requires more than 'good works', but some evaluation of how what is done fits into the wider picture of public policy surrounding it.

The White Paper *Excellence in Schools* (1997) saw the study of Citizenship as a necessary preparation for adult life in a parliamentary democracy. Shortly after its publication, an Advisory Group on Citizenship was established under the chairmanship of Professor Bernard Crick. Its brief was:

> To provide advice on effective education for citizenship in schools – to include the nature and practices of participation in democracy; the duties, responsibilities and rights of individuals as citizens; and the value to individuals and society of community activity.

The Crick Report discerned three elements of citizenship:

■ education in a parliamentary democracy
■ social and moral responsibility
■ community involvement and political literacy.

The programme it recommended was designed to address ideas such as democracy, community and society, so that within the statutory scheme there is scope to consider, among other things:

■ what is meant by representative democracy, and its advantages and disadvantages compared to other political systems
■ the responsibility of belonging to society, the rights and obligations involved and how these are enforced
■ an awareness of community and cultural diversity, involving a better understanding of our history and national life, and of issues concerning equal opportunity, national identity and cultural differences
■ why some groups feel excluded from society and the difficulties caused for individuals and society when this sense of alienation develops
■ exploration of topical social, moral, spiritual, political and economic issues
■ the practical skills necessary for young people to play a full part in society as they develop into adulthood. Some of these are learning skills – including discussion, communication and cooperation – while others are practical – involving knowledge of the democratic process, including decision-making and opportunities for participation, volunteering and community work.

The Crick Report made it clear that the idea of the new subject was 'to create active and responsible citizens', in particular empowering young people to 'participate effectively in society'. He illustrated the distinction between good and **active citizenship**. Professor Crick spoke of a school where pupils in a particular class – as part of their remit of participation in the community – staged a party for the old people in a nearby residential home: 'they negotiated with the matron, then purchased provisions and arranged among themselves an entertainment. A fine time was had by all.' For him, this was good citizenship in action, showing a moral motivation and perhaps providing a feel-good factor. It was not, however, active citizenship.

For Crick, the project could have been a fitting culmination or celebration of a prior process of setting out to discover something of the complicated relations and policies of the personal social services, local authorities, the NHS, government departments and the voluntary sector. In other words, the matter of caring for and about elderly people raises issues such as:

■ why the elderly people were in residential accommodation and not cared for in their own homes

- an understanding of how care arrangements worked and of their strengths and weaknesses
- the nature of public policy regarding the care of the elderly
- how provision of care could be improved
- perhaps even a representation to one of the various authorities – for instance by writing to the local Member of Parliament.

For such good works to be labelled active citizenship, a fund of knowledge is required so that the context of the situation can be fully understood. Young people need not only to acquire information, but also to have the presentation skills to be able to communicate it. By using these qualities, they may be in a position to assess needs and argue the case for or against change. In Crick's words, the difference is between 'learning for effective action' and 'simply doing something that in itself is good'.

Case study

An anti-smoking campaign

ACT!, a mixed age and gender group at Ashley School in Widnes, Cheshire, took part in a series of training sessions about the nature of active citizenship. Members formalised themselves and elected a Chair, Vice-chair and Treasurer. After discussion of various alternatives, they decided to make smoking among young people their main priority. The intention was to base their campaign within the school, but then take it out into the wider community.

Among ACT's activities, they have:

- carried out a survey to gauge students' opinions on smoking
- started a poster campaign with the opportunity for all students in the school to put forward a design
- visited the Roy Castle Lung Cancer Foundation in Liverpool for advice and information about smoking and how to run an anti-smoking campaign
- met with Lord Jack Ashley at the House of Lords to inform him about the campaign and to find out what the Government's position is on the smoking issue
- linked up with work experience students at the Roy Castle Foundation and students from a local college, to design and develop a series of education games about the effects of smoking
- piloted the games in primary schools in the local area
- been in contact with a publisher to produce the games professionally and sell them to schools to raise funds for the Roy Castle Foundation.

The ACT! project contained all of the key stages of active citizenship: *planning, doing, monitoring, evaluating*.

Subjects and citizens

There is a distinction between **subjects** and **citizens**. Subjects are people who live under regimes that place obligations upon them, but concede no rights, for example in South Africa under apartheid (where black people were denied rights) and the dictatorships of the 20th century (such as

Activities

1 Using your own words, write a paragraph to distinguish between good and active citizenship.

2 List any activities carried out in your school or college that might be termed 'good' or 'active' citizenship. Explain briefly in each case why they fall into the category you have allocated to them.

Key terms

Subjects: people under the domination of a monarch or government. They are subservient to the state in which they reside, being denied rights.

Citizens: full members of their political community who possess rights in relation to the state in which they reside.

in Hitler's Germany and Mussolini's Italy). By contrast, citizens – as members of a political community – possess rights and have a say in the manner in which government is carried out. A democracy has citizens, rather than subjects.

Differing views of citizenship

New Labour has recognised that generous social benefits are costly to the taxpayer and may no longer be affordable in the form that they were once paid. The party still favours support for social and economic rights. It strengthened protection of people's rights via the passage of the Human Rights Act. But in the Blair–Brown years, it has placed more emphasis upon the traditionally Conservative territory of duties. In this respect, it has been much influenced by **communitarian thinking**, notably that of the American academic **Amitai Etzioni** who emphasised the importance of citizens showing a sense of responsibility. Communitarians argue that the politics of rights should be replaced by the politics of the common good. They believe that by stressing **individualism** and personal entitlements, there is a danger that the needs of others are neglected. This undermines a sense of community and social belonging, leaving some people feeling 'left out' of the mainstream of society.

Activities

1. Using the internet to assist you, find out and list four or five key aspects of communitarian thinking.

2. Good Citizenship teaching is intended to combat a range of problems including:
   - widespread anti-social behaviour and a lack of concern for the feelings of other people
   - intolerance of minorities, be they racial, religious or any other disadvantaged group
   - a low standard of civic discussion, resulting from a serious deficiency in knowledge of many issues, especially relating to politics
   - a low turnout in elections
   - a lack of effective participation by citizens in their communities
   - a decline in the quality of public life.

   In the light of your own experience of statutory Citizenship lessons, how successful has it been/can it be in tackling such issues? Do such lessons present any particular problems for teachers or pupils? Can you learn how to be a good citizen at school?

Citizens' rights and duties

Traditionally, the British have been regarded as technically 'subjects of the Queen'. This was once a settled part of the British Constitution. Although they possessed important legal rights, they were not entitlements that they could claim against the state. Protection was granted by the state, rather than enforceable against it. It derived from their status as subjects of the monarch. However, in recent decades there has been increasing interest in and movement towards the development of a **rights culture**, in which individuals have become aware of the rights that they possess. Many campaigning groups have not accepted the old constitutional language and argue that they have rights against the state simply because they are citizens of a democracy. This process culminated in the passage of the **Human Rights Act (1998)**, which speaks in more modern terms of a wide range of rights as entitlements, rather than as concessions granted by the monarch. Few British people would now regard themselves as subjects subservient to the state or monarchy. One argument advanced for producing a written constitution for the UK is that it would clearly assert the status of individuals as full citizens. (At present, the UK is one of very few countries without its constitution codified in a single document.)

In addition to what may be regarded as their **human rights**, citizens have **legal rights**, which depend on their membership of a particular state. (These may be civil and political or social and economic entitlements – see pages 81–2 for further elaboration.) Their enjoyment of rights is conditional upon the performance of **duties**. No one can expect that his or her interests will be safeguarded unless he or she recognises and respects corresponding obligations towards others. Duties involve respecting the rights of others, showing the qualities of a good democrat (including tolerance, acceptance of the need for compromise and support for peaceful change) and recognising that in a democracy the majority rules and minorities have rights. Another duty is that of obedience to the law, unless there is a compelling case against such obedience. If people break the criminal law, they may lose the civil rights of the citizen and effectively become subjects in prison. Citizens are also expected to pay their taxes and, as required, perform jury service (see pages 122–3).

Social citizenship

Legally, a citizen is a member of a state, either someone who has been born in the country or who has a legal right to be there. In this sense, citizenship refers to a status conferred by law. However, the term is also associated with the idea of entitlements or rights as a consequence of membership of a community. Because citizens participate in its everyday life, they possess civil and political rights. Many would also claim that they have responsibilities, including civil and moral obligations to one another as members of that **polity**.

Among those who are accepted as full citizens, there are huge inequalities in the distribution of wealth and income, with large numbers of people living disadvantaged lives, some suffering from serious deprivation. Various political and social thinkers have acknowledged these disparities, leading to a situation in which there are several interpretations of citizenship and of rights. Shortly after the end of the Second World War, the sociologist T.H. Marshall developed the concept of **social citizenship**. He advocated the importance of positive social rights that guaranteed the individual a minimum level of basic provision and acknowledgement of their status in society. He defined positive rights as those that provided the individual with the opportunity 'to live the life of a civilised being, according to the standards prevailing in society'.

Responses to social citizenship

Liberal democracies such as those in the West have always scored strongly in any listings of acceptance of political and civil rights. However, the idea of social rights has proved much more controversial. They have been disputed by many members of the **political Right**, who have seen them not only as intrinsically unjustifiable but as potentially damaging to the performance of the economy.

However, Marshall's views were taken up by many on the **political Left**. In particular, the majority of Labour and Liberal MPs were enthusiastic about adding social and economic benefits to the other advantages that resulted

Key terms

Human rights: universal and fundamental rights that derive from people's humanity. They cannot be granted, taken away or limited, for they are inalienable and innate. They can be secured or violated.

Legal rights: the rights granted to citizens by virtue of their membership of their particular state. Their existence is necessary for individual freedom – i.e. freedom of assembly, of movement and of speech.

Duties: obligations – i.e. the responsibilities that people have towards their state and its members.

Polity: a political community, the term deriving from the Greek polis (city-state).

Social citizenship: the idea that citizenship implies social rights that guarantee an individual a minimum social status – i.e. positive rights.

Liberal democracies: seek to combine the powers of democratic government with liberal values concerning the freedom of the individual. They provide limited government, diverse sources of economic and political power (pluralism), a free media and a range of essential liberties and rights.

Political Right: (including the British Conservative Party) traditionally identified with preservation of the interests of the established, propertied classes. Supporters are wary of state intervention and seek to limit the scope of government as much as possible. They place more emphasis on personal responsibility and individual enterprise.

Political Left: (including the British Labour Party) traditionally identified with the interests of the masses. It supports the use of governmental power to create a more just society in which economic and social problems can be addressed. Accordingly, it favours political, economic and social change, and wants to promote greater equality.

Key terms

Welfare State: refers to a system whereby the state undertakes responsibility to protect the health and well-being of its citizens. Via a series of government programmes and benefits, the idea is to provide basic economic security for the population from 'cradle to grave', especially when they are unemployed, elderly or sick.

from membership of a state. In the early years after the Second World War, they strongly supported the creation of the **Welfare State**, with its range of measures on issues such as education, health and welfare.

The citizenship of duty

For several decades, citizenship was increasingly associated with the possession of rights. However, in recent years greater emphasis has been placed upon the 'citizenship of duty'. The Right has always stressed that obligations must be placed alongside rights. Its supporters have emphasised the importance of obedience to the law, hard work, provision for oneself and one's family and being a good citizen.

The Conservative governments of the 1980s attached great importance to the prosperity of the economy and creating a climate in which individuals could demonstrate an entrepreneurial spirit and make money. By the end of the decade, some more thoughtful members questioned whether in the process of liberating individual initiative and enterprise, they had neglected the needs of society at large. They began to talk of 'active citizenship'. A leading Conservative minister, Douglas Hurd, expressed the view that it was desirable for individuals who had benefited from the prosperity of the 1980s to show concern for social ills and not just be self-interested. He felt that people should get involved in their community. They might be a school governor, join Neighbourhood Watch and do various forms of charitable work, thereby becoming 'active citizens'.

Case study

Active citizenship – the Refugee Integration and Active Citizenship (RIAC) Project

Devon is a county in which refugees and migrants struggle to have their existence recognised, for it is widely depicted in the media as though it is entirely 'white'. The RIAC project supported the integration of refugees and asylum seekers in Devon and ran until 2006. The project was concerned to develop a multi-agency strategic coordination service, which included bring about a Devon Interpreter's Network, Multilingua.

Support was provided via:

- interviews with refugees, service providers and employers to identify the issues and barriers faced by new arrivals
- cooperation with public and voluntary sector providers at all levels to improve the services available to refugees and asylum seekers
- promoting active citizenship with refugees and asylum seekers – discussion of their rights and responsibilities, and of what they could expect from public services
- supporting voluntary organisations working with refugees and asylum seekers, for instance by developing partnerships.

… Multi-agency networking is an effective way of pooling resources. For example, the Devon Migrant Workers Multi-agency network has produced a Welcome to Devon Pack (not as easy as it seems!). I wouldn't say though that such initiatives necessarily support community-led initiatives, who rely on committed and driven individuals and their resources, to get relevant activities off the ground. For migrant workers who have to earn a living, finding the necessary time to work for their communities is not easy, and in one example, Exeter CVS (Community Service Volunteers) managed to help one young Polish graduate out of factory shopfloor work into paid community development, through our networking with the county council. This effort too was fraught with institutional obstacles and lack of understanding of public authority staff on how to work with community people in a sympathetic and supportive way!

Otherwise, our take on Active Citizenship has always been one of making sure that newcomers are made aware of their rights and responsibilities, as well as providing opportunities for networking and connecting with local people, mainly in the form of volunteering, informal learning or social activities.

This explains why we have had several projects which developed an Active Citizenship component to ESOL (English for Speakers of Other Languages) programmes – despite and in addition to national initiatives, resulting in such materials. The gap, we felt, was to provide a community-focused perspective to one that otherwise risks to be more 'FE-college' focused. Adapting information to the locality, from a pragmatic and cultural point of view, is also important.

In this respect, the information sessions for Eastern European migrants provided another development, insofar as a Polish native speaker organised and facilitated these, as well as ESOL materials, with the help of local providers, public, private or trade union. The following is a nice success story of how awareness of rights, provided in an interactive and accessible way, can lead to concrete results:

The session on employment law involved a local solicitor, and participants, who were asked to bring their payslips, were given advice on their pay entitlements, NI contributions etc. The solicitor also handed out his business card. The next day, one Polish woman working in a local shop (a national chain of retailers) went to her manager, pointing out that she seemed to have been paid less than the minimum wage. At the sight of the attached solicitor's card, the manager quickly said that there must have been a mistake, and the worker had her pay adjusted to the correct minimum wage and received a back payment of £800 into her account the following day.

Another session was held on equality and diversity, with a local representative of a Faith group explaining about equality legislation. The session explored the different facets of equality, discrimination, as well as common patterns of cultural differences, cultural shock and the phases that commonly newcomers go through, which can affect their mental health and well-being.

In our view, Active Citizenship is more than just about 'rights and responsibilities' and a unilateral 'integration' approach; it should be holistic, interactive, accessible, flexible and focused on the diverse needs of the newcomers. What is quite important is to value collective action, community support and self-help, but knowing that this does not materialise out of nothing and requires professional support and financial resources in order to be effective. In other words, Active Citizenship should ideally be integrated in a Community Development strategy, and be based on the principles of Empowerment.

Source: discussion with Gabi Recknagel of Exeter Community Service Volunteers

Activities

1. Make a list of 10 things that a person might do to qualify as an active citizen in Hurd's sense of the term.

2. Read this section and the case study on Exeter CSV in conjunction with the information on good and active citizenship (pages 2–3). Explain in a paragraph or so why the Exeter project is an example of active citizenship. List the features of the project that make this a good example of active citizenship in practice.

■ Key terms

Socialists: people who believe that unrestrained capitalism or free enterprise is responsible for a variety of social evils, such as the exploitation of working people and the pursuit of greed and selfishness. They favour cooperative values, which emphasise the values of community, equality and justice, and state action to promote these values.

The Left always placed more emphasis upon rights, **socialists** believing that the disadvantaged were in need of positive help. Thus it was Labour that legislated to introduce the National Health Service and end racial and sexual discrimination. Members of the Labour Party still retain their preference for righting social injustices and tackling poverty. However, the approach adopted by New Labour under Tony Blair and subsequently has been rather different to traditional Labour thinking.

■ Summary questions

1. What are the merits of being a British citizen?

2. Is it true to say that, in short, a subject does what he is told whereas a citizen has the right to be heard?

3. 'And so my fellow Americans, ask not what your country can do for you – ask what you can do for your country.' Reflect on the comment made by President Kennedy of the United States in his Inaugural Speech (January 1961). Think about the loyalty we owe to our country and what things we can or should do to serve it.

4. Perhaps using the experience of ancient Athens as set out in the lists below to guide you, make a list of the advantages and disadvantages of citizenship for citizens of the UK today:

Rights conferred
- to participate in political life within the assembly of citizens
- to vote laws
- to decide foreign policy
- to be randomly selected to serve as magistrates for the city
- to vote for policies and strategies, and political and military leaders
- to condemn a citizen to exile.

Duties expected
- to do military service
- to pay taxes.

■ Key terms

Nationality: the status of being a citizen of a particular state, by birth or naturalisation.

Naturalised: given citizenship, as can happen to a person of overseas birth. Naturalisation is the application process by which people become British. Unless they have a claim to citizenship based on ancestry, they usually have to apply for naturalisation in one of the following two categories: after six years' residence in the UK or after three years as a spouse of a UK citizen. Since 1 November 2005, they also have to have passed the Citizenship Test.

■ What does it mean to be British?

In Britain, a series of laws from the 1960s onwards have restricted the definition of British citizenship. We now operate under the terms set out in the British Nationality Act (1981), which distinguished five different categories of **nationality** entitlements. It defines entitlement to citizenship and residence in the United Kingdom, restricting citizenship (with full rights of residence) to:

- those born in the UK before January 1983 who were automatically British citizens by birth
- those born here after 1983, if one parent is a British citizen or was allowed to stay here permanently.

Where neither parent is British at the time of the child's birth, but they later become settled, they can then apply for their child to become **naturalised**. If children do not inherit any nationality from their parents and are born and remain stateless for seven years, the parents can apply for them to become British. An applicant who is married to a British citizen may acquire citizenship if he or she is settled here, has lived in Britain legally for at least three years and is of good character. For those unmarried, the citizen qualification is more onerous.

Citizens and aliens

As a result of these limited entitlements, legal entry into the United Kingdom was and remains strictly controlled. Legal citizenship was not granted to all who live in the British Isles. Non-citizens or 'aliens' were not given rights to live, work and vote here. Citizens of **British dependent territories** (who held British dependent territories citizenship) were given no right of entry. **British overseas citizens**, people who live abroad but who have no recent connection by family or residence with the UK, also have no such right. However, the Nationality, Immigration and Asylum Act (2002) modified the situation. It granted British overseas citizens and those in dependent territories the right to register as British citizens if they had no other citizenship or nationality and have not after 4 July 2002 renounced, voluntarily relinquished or lost through action or inaction any citizenship or nationality. Previously such persons would not have had the right of abode in any country and would thus have been in effect stateless.

New controls: the points-based system

Ever since the UK joined the European Union, inhabitants of other member states have been entitled to enter the UK under the regulations concerning the free movement of labour. However, temporary controls can be introduced when a new member state joins the EU, in order to prevent a sudden influx of migrants. The British government did not impose these restrictions in 2004 when 10 new countries became members of the EU, but it did so in 2007 to limit the possible entry of Bulgarians and Romanians. (Any such restrictions lapse after five years.) Otherwise there is no barrier to prevent residents of one member country from living and working in another.

New arrangements were announced in May 2008 for future immigration from outside the European Union. Ministers propose that there should be a points-based system along the lines used in Australia. The purpose is to ensure that only skilled migrants whose skills are in demand in the UK are allowed entry. Jobs will be advertised for at least two weeks to British job-seekers who have first priority before a migrant can be recruited from outside the European Union. The only exceptions will be if the job has been declared a shortage occupation or is an internal company transfer.

In future, migrants will have to show they are competent in English to a 'basic-user' standard, using familiar everyday expressions and being able to discuss basic personal details. It is expected that the new requirement will prevent 5 per cent of existing skilled migrants coming to Britain. Overall, if the regulations had been in place in 2007 then according to Home Office statistics some 85,000 skilled workers and their dependants would have moved to Britain, compared with the 97,600 who successfully secured work permits.

Becoming a British citizen

Migrants applying to become British citizens have since 2004 been required to demonstrate an understanding of life in the UK in one of two ways:

- by taking the Life in the UK **Citizenship Test** or
- by taking combined English for Speakers of Other Languages (ESOL) and Citizenship classes.

People attaining British citizenship are now required to attend a Citizenship ceremony. This is intended to give added significance to the acquisition of citizenship.

Key terms

British dependent territories: 14 territories (e.g. Bermuda and St Helena) listed in the British Nationality Act (1981), most of the residents of which were granted British dependent territories citizenship (BDTC) that did not give them a right of abode in the UK. The Labour government decided in 2002 to include these persons in the offer of British citizenship, giving them the right of entry. The total number with BDTC is around 200,000.

British overseas citizens: citizens of the United Kingdom and its colonies (CUKCs) who do not have a close connection with the UK or its dependent territories and therefore do not have full rights of abode in the UK. Several early independence Acts for Commonwealth countries did not contain provision for loss of CUKC rights by their citizens, for instance two parts of what is now Malaysia, Malacca and Penang.

Citizenship Test: launched by the British government for foreigners who wish to become British. It involves knowledge of *Life in the UK*, a specially prepared book, and sitting a 45-minute test on British society, history and culture. People take the test at one of 90 centres across the country, before taking part in a formal Citizenship ceremony.

Further information

The oath of allegiance

The oath reads: 'I, [name], swear by Almighty God (alternatively 'do solemnly, sincerely and truly declare and affirm') that, on becoming a British citizen, I will be faithful and bear true allegiance to Her Majesty Queen Elizabeth the Second, Her Heirs and Successors according to law.' It is followed by the pledge: 'I will give my loyalty to the United Kingdom and respect its rights and freedoms. I will uphold its democratic values. I will observe its laws faithfully and fulfil my duties and obligations as a British citizen.'

① Arrival in UK

② Study to improve language and knowledge of British society

③ Take a 'Britishness' test

Retake

Marry a British citizen and reside in UK for three years

Remain in the country legally for five years

④ Apply to become a UK citizen

⑤ Citizenship ceremony in which an oath and pledge of allegiance are sworn

⑥ Can apply for passport, vote, etc (subject to existing conditions)

Fig. 1.1 *The route to British citizenship*

Fig. 1.2 *A Citizenship ceremony taking place in Banqueting Hall, Whitehall, 22 July 2008, for citizens from Richmond-upon-Thames, Tower Hamlets, City of Westminster and Kensington and Chelsea*

■ The United Kingdom and its constituent parts

The term 'Great Britain' refers to the mainland countries of England, Scotland and Wales, although the term is sometimes used synonymously with United Kingdom. The UK comprises Great Britain and Northern Ireland (the British part of the partitioned island of Ireland), the Isle of Man and other small islands. However, although the UK government officially distinguishes between Great Britain and the United Kingdom, the former term (or more often simply Britain) is widely used as a synonym for the latter. When speaking of UK inhabitants, it is common to speak of the British people.

'Englishness' within the UK

A recent article in the *New York Times* (6 March 2007) illustrated that the inhabitants of the different regions of the British Isles are genetically nearly identical to each other.

Rather than each successive invasion of Celts, Anglo-Saxons and Normans pushing the former inhabitants to the margins and taking over, the core British population has instead remained more or less unchanged since the isles were originally settled many thousands of years ago. If so, and there is really no genetic difference between an Englishman and a Irishman, then perhaps all that serves to distinguish the British nations from each other are **culture** and history. But where national identity is concerned, some English worry that they are getting the short end of the stick. If Scots have kilts, and the Welsh have dragons – and both have their own languages – are the English the 'none of the above' of the British Isles?

Key terms

Culture: the way of life that people experience, referring to the sum of their inherited and cherished ideas, knowledge and values. Their beliefs, attitudes and the things they care about are based on the experiences to which they are exposed throughout their lives. They may also derive from their class, ethnic group, gender, language or religion.

Views of Englishness

So what is Englishness? When asked this question, people tend to list a variety of attachments, characteristics and interests, including bowler hats, class, cricket, not complaining, patriotism, orderly queuing, politeness, public schools, repression (particularly being uptight about one's emotions), tea and the village green.

A former Conservative prime minister of the 1918–39 era, Stanley Baldwin, attempted to define Englishness in 1924:

> England comes to me through my various senses – through the ear, through the eye and through certain imperishable scents … The sounds of England, the tinkle of the hammer on the anvil in the country smithy, the corncrake on a dewy morning, the sound of the scythe against the whetstone, and the sight of a plough team coming over the brow of a hill, the sight that has been England since England was a land … the one eternal sight of England.

Baldwin's was an idyllic representation of what England was like and doubtless even when he was speaking many town and city dwellers would not have enjoyed the rural sights and sounds of which he spoke. Yet his views were echoed many years after when a later prime minister, John Major – also of the Conservative party – spoke on the eve of St George's Day in 1993 of 'warm beer, invincible green suburbs, dog lovers and pools fillers and – as George Orwell [a novelist] said – old maids cycling to holy communion through the morning mist'.

The growth of English national identity

Because England has dominated the UK in population terms, Englishmen and women have never had to explain their identity in the way that Scottish or Welsh identity has had to be explained, or in the way that the identity of black people and Muslims is much discussed today. But today, given the pressures of **devolution** from below and moves towards a European identity from above, some people have given thought to questions of identity, whereas in the past the issue was shrugged off as some people believed that English qualities required no explanation.

In recent years, the quest for Englishness has been partially represented by the English nationalism movement. Some of its members have argued that so much attention has been paid to immigrants and their impact on the country that the needs and wishes of English people in the UK have gone unrecognised. They have also noted the concessions being gained by the Scots and Welsh in the direction of self-government. They feel that England is being neglected. To counter such feelings, former home secretary David Blunkett tried to find a glue that bonds people together. He has defined Englishness in predominantly cultural terms, as landscapes, the sea, cities, poetry, music, humour and other aspects of the way of life. But many countries have these features. They are not distinctive of England. They do not tell us what an English person is like or what that person believes.

It may be that trying to express a collective identity is doomed to failure, for collective identities are today unravelling. Many people do not have the same allegiances as their forebears to a religion, **social class** or political party. Because they have also become more mobile as a result of ease of travel, they often lack any strong sense of loyalty to a particular locality, be it to a region or a country. (For a few, home is now in more than one country.)

Table 1.1 *The four countries of the UK, by population*

Country	Population	% of UK population
England	49,138,831	83.6
Scotland	5,062,011	8.6
Wales	2,903,085	4.9
N Ireland	1,685,267	2.9

Source: 2001 census figures

Key terms

Devolution: the statutory granting of powers from the central government to government at regional or local level – e.g. to the Scottish Parliament, which has operated since 1999.

Social class: the division of the population into categories on the basis of their economic and social status, determined by their background, occupation, income and other aspects of their lifestyle. The usual distinction is into manual (working class) and non-manual (middle and upper class) groups, although there are many substrata within these broad groupings.

Activities

1. List some of the features that you associate with Englishness.

2. In a few sentences, explain whether or not you feel yourself to be English.

Key terms

Fourth of July: the day set aside by Americans to commemorate that same date in 1776 when the US declared its independence from Britain.

Activities

1. African, South American and other non-European footballers – along with other elite sports men and women – who cannot speak English will be barred from joining clubs in the Football League under the points-based system. Write a few lines to explain whether or not you agree that it is a basic requirement that they should have some command of English. (Note: entertainers and others coming to perform at one-off events and festivals will not be affected.)

2. Write a paragraph to indicate and explain your response to the 'Tebbit test' of Britishness.

On rare occasions such as sport (cricket and football matches, for example) a sense of English solidarity may seem more apparent. But these expressions of national feeling are at best intermittent. At other times, most people would find it difficult to say exactly what being English means.

The nature of British identity

In a legal sense, people who were born in Britain or who are legally recognised as citizens can be described as British. Differences of ethnic background, language or religion are irrelevant. There are black Britons and white Britons, Hindu and Christian Britons. Of the members of ethnic minority groups currently in Britain, more than half were born here.

Not everyone recognises that those born in Britain or who have acquired British citizenship are as British as the majority population. Several years ago, politician Norman (now Lord) Tebbit complained that immigrants to this country often failed to identify with it. He used the world of international cricket as his criterion. He claimed that the attitude of immigrants to Britain was easily detected by finding out which team immigrants cheered when England were playing in a Test Match, as between England and Sri Lanka or England and the West Indies. He went on to say: 'It's an interesting test. Are you still harking back to where you came from or where you are? I think we've got great problems in this regard.'

Yet of course an English person, born of English parents, might nonetheless like to see the Brazilians or the Dutch beat England at football, simply because of admiration for the way the opposing teams play. At a motor racing Grand Prix, an English person might in recent years have supported the Italian Ferrari team because the team were viewed by many sportswriters as 'simply the best'. Does support for non-English or non-British sportspersons make anyone less British or less patriotic?

As Chancellor of the Exchequer, Gordon Brown showed strong interest in developing a sense of Britishness within the community. He envisaged some sort of British Day, equivalent to the **Fourth of July** independence celebrations in the United States. He suggested that Remembrance Day and Remembrance Sunday were the nearest we had to a British day, 'unifying, commemorative, dignified and an expression of the British idea of standing firm for the world in the name of liberty'. These could evolve into a time for reflection on British history, culture and achievement. He also urged the need for a new youth community service scheme and other ways of stressing the importance of a united people.

He has stressed the importance of reclaiming national symbols such as the union flag from political groups such as the British National Party (BNP) on the Far Right. Since becoming Prime Minister in 2007, he has continued to develop the Britishness theme, urging that there should be a day of national patriotism of some kind. He defines Britishness as standing for 'liberty for all, responsibility by all and fairness to all'. He suggests that whatever the issues that divide people in the four home countries – such as growing support in Scotland for national separation from England, the feeling among some English people that Scots have preferential funding and treatment, and the loyalties of national football fans – the United Kingdom remains a force for good.

Associated with the debate about celebrating the best of Britain was the establishment of the inaugural Veterans' Day, first held on 27 June 2006.

In his speech as chancellor for that occasion, Gordon Brown spoke of the achievements of armed forces veterans, but also pointed out that:

> Scots and people from the rest of the UK share the purpose – that Britain has something to say to the rest of the world about the values of freedom, democracy and the dignity of people that you stand up for. So at a time when people can talk about football and devolution and money, it is important that we also remember the values that we share in common.

Activities

1. If you were given the task of choosing a date for British Day as a new public holiday, which date would you choose? Explain your response.

2. It has been suggested by a former government minister (who heads a review of how to strengthen a sense of national identity and promote Britishness) that all young people – on attaining the age of 18 – should take part in a citizenship ceremony in which they swear allegiance to the queen. Write a few sentences to explain your reaction to this idea.

3. Do we need a new national anthem or a revision of the existing one (perhaps to remove verses that are rarely performed)? Give reasons for your answer.

4. Can you think of a good alternative to *God Save the Queen*?

Fig. 1.3 *Gordon Brown, Labour MP from 1983, party leader and Prime Minister from 2007*

In June 2005, religious leaders debating 'Islam and Muslims in the World Today' at a London conference discussed what they believed being British was. Their views encompassed core values such as freedom of expression and religious practice, participation in the democratic system, valuing education and respect and tolerance for others. But other speakers felt that Britain had a long way to go before all its communities could be united in a common purpose. One noted the lack of national cohesion in Britain, observing that: 'People have more allegiance to football teams than they have to Great Britain. What is the glue that is going to hold society together?' The Bishop of London stressed the importance of acknowledging people's multiple identities: 'Many people are very proud of being Scottish, Welsh, as well as being Catholics and Muslims … Some kind of national story of the peoples of this Western European island has to be developed that doesn't deny people's rights or how we came to be where we are.'

The Britishness debate links together several major 'identity' questions that are often considered in isolation from each other:

- the state of the United Kingdom after devolution
- diversity
- multiculturalism and integration (see pages 37–9)
- the role of religion in a multi-faith and for many people increasingly **secular society**
- Britain's ambivalence over its place in Europe and role in the world.

What does Britishness mean?

Britishness is a term that refers to the common culture and national identity of the people of the United Kingdom, particularly those on the mainland. Today, it is used particularly in relation to the attempt to define what it means to be British.

Further information

On the London conference

Shaykh Ibrahim Mogra of the Muslim Council argued that to be British 'is being tolerant and respectful towards others, while at the same time being able to embrace and celebrate difference'. He gave a simple example: '… what many British people love is fish and chips. I think that is a great way to cook potatoes and it is a favourite with my family. Many white Anglo-Saxons like chicken tikka masala. Therefore, we have enriched our lives by taking the best from each other.'

Key terms

Secular society: a society that is not overly concerned with religion or sacred matters, in which the majority of people have no particular religious affinities.

Fig. 1.4 *Symbols of Britishness*

There is no one definition of what it means to be British. It remains an elusive concept, although some of the ideas given above tend to feature in any listing. One blogger from Switzerland pointed to the confusion of our national identity: 'Being British is about driving in a German car to an Irish pub for a Belgian beer, then travelling home, grabbing an Indian curry or a Turkish kebab on the way, to sit on Swedish furniture and watch American shows on a Japanese TV. And the most British thing of all? Suspicion of anything foreign.'

As a result of the issues surrounding **ethnicity** and to a lesser extent devolution, there has been renewed discussion of national identity and what it means to be British. There is no prescribed list of qualities or characteristics that make up 'Britishness', but a recent Commission for Racial Equality (CRE) poll found that 86 per cent of those interviewed agreed that you do not have to be white to be British. We now live in a very much more diverse society than that of our ancestors.

The debate about identity has been given another twist by a further development in the last three decades or so, British membership of the European Community, now Union. Since the signing of the **Maastricht Treaty**, British people have become citizens of the European Union, although surveys suggest that the overwhelming majority do not consider themselves to be European in the way that inhabitants of France or Holland might do.

Confused descent

Few of us can claim to be pure English or pure British. By background, we are of confused identity. As Tony Blair pointed out: 'Blood alone does not define national identity … Britain has been shaped by a rich mix of all different ethnic and religious origins.' Even members of our royal family, that most British of institutions, are of very mixed descent. In her jubilee speech to Parliament, Queen Elizabeth II recognised that she too understood the changing face of Britain, by talking about 'our richly multicultural and multi-faith society'. It is this ethnic diversity that makes it increasingly difficult to determine what makes someone British.

Key terms

Ethnicity: (from the Greek word ethnos, meaning a tribe) refers to a mixture of different social characteristics that may include common origin, culture, geography, history, language and religion, which give a social group a common consciousness and separates them from other social groups. Some countries use nationality to define ethnicity.

Maastricht Treaty on European Union: negotiated at Maastricht (Holland) in December 1991, signed in February 1992 and entered into force in November 1993. It led to the creation of the EU in its present form, after agreement had been reached on issues such as steps towards further monetary and political union.

Summary questions

1. What is the difference between Great Britain and the United Kingdom?

2. What are the qualifications of entry into the United Kingdom today?

3. Is there such a thing as Englishness?

4. What does being British mean to you?

5. Consider the views of London mayor, former Conservative MP and TV celebrity Boris Johnson, on Britishness. On his website for the London mayoral election campaign, he described himself as a 'one man melting-pot', with French, Turks and Germans among his ancestors:

> We gave the world industrialisation, democracy and football. In other words, we gave the world its economic system, its political system and its main leisure activity, and we continue to be a hugely beneficial civilising force across the planet. There is a distinctive British culture, cast of mind and set of values. It's not just tolerance, though tolerance is part of it …
>
> These are all the sort of things that you would put in the drawer and want to keep: … long sufferingness; tea – which is of course a foreign import; the habit of embarrassment; trying to get into swimming trunks on the beach by wrapping a towel around yourself and then falling over.
>
> I also think it's quite unBritish to keep bashing on about Britishness. One of the things we are most valued for abroad is our understatement and our refusal to keep asserting, the way the Americans do, that 'we are the greatest nation on earth'.

What is your reaction to his listing of characteristics of things that are distinctly British? Do you recognise the picture he portrays?

Fig. 1.5 *Boris Johnson, Mayor of London from 2008*

How do we define our identity?

There are more than 6.7 billion people in the world, each of whom is different not only physically but in other respects as well. Our individual **identity** is largely governed by our family background and upbringing, our culture (including our religious background) and our place of origin. We are all unique.

We each belong to several different communities. A community is a group of people who live or work in one locality. However, we often use the term to refer to a group of people who have cultural, ethnic, linguistic or religious characteristics in common. For instance, we speak of the Irish community in Birmingham, Glasgow or Liverpool, and of the Jewish community in Leeds or London.

We are all part of:

- our family
- our school or workplace
- our neighbourhood (street, town or city)
- the clubs, teams and other organisations of which we are members
- religious communities, sometimes known as communities of faith
- our country
- our continent, in our case, Europe; we are all citizens of the European union
- the world and its inhabitants, the whole human race. As the poet John Donne put it: 'no man is an island, entire of itself'.

Key terms

Identity: refers to the distinctive characteristics that make individuals or groups who they are and by which they are recognised – e.g. names give us an individual or national identity.

In a basic sense, the information that determines our identity is the sort of information that would feature on an identity (ID) card if we had one. A passport contains similar essential data, enabling others to recognise who we are. Among other things, it contains our names, gender, and date and place of birth.

In a wider sense, identity refers to the way we see ourselves and others see us. It goes beyond the basic distinguishing attributes such as age, height and weight and instead sees us in a social setting. Disability, ethnicity, friendships, gender, sexuality, social class and workplace are all relevant in determining the people we are.

In an individual sense, then, our identity refers to the kind of people we are and how we see ourselves, to the individual characteristics that make us distinctive. In a social sense, it concerns not just who we are but how we are perceived by others, and who others are and their understanding of themselves and one another. In a national sense, it enables us to be recognised as Britons, Chinese or Vietnamese. In a global sense, it makes us members of international organisations, whether this is the worldwide Roman Catholic Church or the European Union. As Weeks (1991) put it:

> Identity is about belonging, about what you have in common with some people and what differentiates you from others. At its most basic, it gives you a sense of personal location, the stable core to your individuality. But it is also about your social relationships, your complex involvement with others.

Factors influencing identity

Individual identity is influenced by the process of **socialisation**, which connects the different generations. Sociologists often distinguish three phases of socialisation:

- The primary stage (primary socialisation) involves the socialisation of helpless young infants into family membership, enabling them to become self-aware and familiar with the ways of the culture into which they are born. It is the first experience individuals have of social norms. In the process of primary socialisation, children have to be cared for by their elders who themselves undergo new learning experiences (as in the third stage).

- The secondary stage (secondary socialisation) is mainly carried out in school, where both teachers, teaching assistants and peer group attitudes are part of the process of learning about life and the way in which people usually behave. Other influences include those acquired from the media, which show images of how people behave and provide role models for people to emulate; membership of religious communities, acquisition of religious teachings and attendance at places of worship help to promote an insight into personal and social values; and membership of other organisations such as clubs and societies. In this stage, young people move on from understanding the world of the family to gain an understanding of **society** at large.

- The third is adult socialisation (tertiary socialisation), in which individuals take on new roles for which the two earlier stages may not have fully equipped them, as husbands, wives or partners, as parents and as employees. The process of cultural learning continues throughout life, which is why Macionis and Plummer (2005) describe socialisation as the 'lifelong process by which individuals construct their personal biography'.

Activities

1. Write down 10 statements under the heading 'Who am I?' that enable people to recognise what makes you the person you are.

2. Using the list provided in the bullet points, for each one write down your own involvement – e.g. your family or families, your clubs, teams etc.

Key terms

Socialisation: the process of learning and instilling the social attitudes and values of any community, via agencies such as the family, education, the media, etc.

Society: an extended social grouping of individuals having broadly common interests and a distinctive cultural and economic organisation. The term therefore refers to the totality of social relationships among human beings. Of society, Margaret Thatcher famously observed: 'There is no such thing! There are individual men and women and there are families.'

Changing identities

Identities are not necessarily fixed. In contemporary society, they have increasingly tended to break down or become fragmented. Some of the factors that define identity such as ethnicity, family, gender, location, nation and social class are liable to change, as in the examples below:

- Identities such as gender and ethnicity are acquired at birth and are in many cases durable, although they too can change. Trans-sexuals deliberately set out to acquire a different identity. The sexuality of people of one gender may vary: a man or woman can be bisexual, gay or heterosexual. Ideas of masculinity and femininity are no longer clear-cut.
- There is frequent geographical mobility, causing individuals to be removed from other members of their families and their original localities.
- Social class may change, given the mobility that enables people to change their position on the class ladder.
- National identity is challenged in various ways, for instance by the UK's membership of the European Union of which we are all citizens and by the forces of **globalisation** that cut across national boundaries.
- In the case of members of ethnic minority groups, migration to the UK provides them with a new set of identities.

Individual identities are increasingly based upon a multiplicity of lifestyles and become more fluid over a lifetime. In addition to the characteristics discussed above, people can be identified by their patterns of consumption, by the brand-name of the goods they purchase. Choosing an Armani suit or Dolce & Gabbana glasses can be viewed as a statement of identity.

Understanding social identities

Social identities can be understood in relation to a range of variables.

Age

Age has long been considered an important element of identity and has become an important issue in matters of citizenship and public policy. It does not provide a fixed identity, because in the nature of life people move through different phases as they grow older. They have different needs at different stages of their life and do not remain young or middle aged forever.

Commentators increasingly talk of the rights of young people or of the increasingly large numbers of old people who now constitute a significant section of the population. The elderly have a sizeable impact upon governmental policy, most obviously affecting policy on health and social care. They have the capacity to exercise considerable influence on elections (the 'grey vote'). However, both young and old might view themselves as disadvantaged groups in society.

Perceptions of age – whether or not a person is young or old – vary according to the observer. For someone under 20, 50 seems a long way off and an indication of advanced years. Children often view their parents as elderly. People of 50 may feel themselves to be in the prime of life and definitely middle-aged rather than old. Even at 70, many will see themselves as relatively young senior citizens, the more so in an age when life expectancy has increased so markedly.

Key terms

Globalisation: the increasing interdependence of people, organisations and states in the modern world, and the growing influence of global cultural, economic and political trends. It also refers to the improved access to overseas events and media in the age when modern means of communication have made the world seem much smaller.

Further information

Centenarians in the UK

- As in other advanced, industrialised countries, since the 1950s the number of people aged 100 and over has increased faster than any other age group.
- The main reason is increased survival between age 80 and 100, because of improved food, housing, hygiene and sanitation, living standards and medical treatment.
- There are proportionately more female than male centenarians, seven women for every man.

Source: www.statistics.gov.uk

The average age of the UK population in 2006 was 39.0 years, an increase on 35 years earlier when it was 34.1. Overall, the UK has an ageing population, the result of a drop in the mortality rate and in past fertility rates. This has led to a decline in the number of under-16-year-olds (currently one in five) and an increase in the number aged 65 and over (currently one in six). It is projected by the Office of Fair Trading (OFT) that the proportion over 65 will exceed that of under-16s in 2014, a development that has already occurred in four other EU countries: Germany, Greece, Italy and Spain.

Activities

1 List any ways in which a) the young and b) the elderly might seem to be disadvantaged groups in society.

2 Do you think that young people can be said to have a common sense of identity? Give examples.

3 At what age do people become old?

4 What characteristics do you associate with becoming old?

5 List the ways in which the implications of an ageing population are important for government and for all of us.

6 What special needs might be relevant to those who share an identity as centenarians?

Key terms

Stereotypes: preconceived, one-sided, over-simplified, exaggerated and usually prejudicial portrayals of groups or classes, which take no account of individual differences. They usually have a negative impact that can lead to discrimination. Those who hold such views are often resistant to any change of attitude.

Multiculturalism: a situation of cultural pluralism and the attitudes of tolerance that make this possible. It stresses the importance of different cultures, races and ethnicities, and their equitable status and harmonious coexistence within the same society.

Multicultural society: a society that comprises a diverse range of ethnic groups and cultures.

Gender and sexuality

Gender has traditionally been a key determinant of identity and the social roles played by individuals. Boys have been seen as aggressive and seekers after adventure; girls as more passive and concerned with beauty and shopping. As they move into adulthood, men have been the hunters who provide the means of support for their families. Women have had family responsibilities, running the home and breeding and rearing children. Yet these have always been generalised **stereotypes** and there have been many exceptions to the traditional pattern over many decades. Many girls have been seen as 'tomboys' and women have worked in factories to boost the income of poor families since the beginnings of the factory system in the early 19th century.

Since 1945 the pattern of family life has changed, so that women are now a large part of the workforce. Several factors combined to liberate women from their traditional role and contribute to their improved position in society. The growth of educational opportunities (especially in higher education), the need for labour in the 1950s and 60s, the increased ability of women to regulate their own fertility and the development of more domestic appliances (e.g. dishwashers and freezers) – all meant that there were jobs available and women with the time, inclination and qualifications to fill them.

As mentioned above, issues of sexuality are now less straightforward than they were 50 years ago. Whereas women were once encouraged to think of their role in terms of reproduction, today many have chosen to seek satisfaction with partners of the same sex. Those who are in same-sex relations may enter civil unions that cater for their needs for secure long-term relationships in which they enjoy the rights of married couples.

Ethnicity

British society is now socially diverse, comprising people from a range of different backgrounds. Although the merits of **multiculturalism** as a theory and way of life are today hotly contested (see pages 38–9), it is undeniably true that the UK can be labelled as a **multicultural society**.

In spite of the early introduction of controls (see page 68), the onset of **New Commonwealth** immigration led to a substantial increase in numbers of Afro-Caribbean, Asian and other immigrants. More recently, the entry of asylum seekers (whether as genuine seekers after political freedom or economic migrants in search of a better way of life) has further added to the diversity of the British population. Migrants from Ireland or Central and Eastern Europe could in many cases blend in with the way of life of the native population, whereas the negative attitudes and sometimes evident hostility experienced by New Commonwealth immigrants made it more difficult for many of them to adapt to Britain's traditional culture. Because of the discrimination and prejudice experienced by sections of the ethnic minority population, ethnicity has become a key feature of identity for many individuals and groups in the UK. Immigration has been the major reason for the growth in the number of people in the UK who subscribe to Islamic beliefs (see pages 35–6). The identity of a British Muslim has become a highly significant feature of national and global politics in recent years, given the importance of Islam as a world religion.

Social class, work and location

During the **Industrial Revolution**, Britain became a class-based society. Social class continued to be a feature of British social and political life throughout much of the 20th century, more so than in many other countries. Class divisions and identities overrode other identities, including ethnicity, language or religion.

In the UK, class is determined largely by:

- occupation and the status that goes with it
- background, education and qualifications
- **income** (personal and household)
- **wealth** or net worth including the ownership of land and other forms of property.

Other factors include style of living (e.g. where you live and how you spend your money), attitudes to life and speech. Class accents have become less distinct in recent years, in part because of the influence of mass broadcasting.

Class is most commonly determined by the occupation of the main breadwinner in the family. Occupations are categorised into groups, a frequently-used classification being that shown in Table 1.2. The distinction often made is between the working class ('blue collar' or manual workers and their families) and the middle class (the 'white collar' professional and non-manual workers). The terms are not entirely satisfactory; for many members of professions would point out that they are people who work for a living.

The terms working and middle class underpin much discussion of the subject. Such divisions are aligned to differences in income and wealth, although not entirely so. Broadly, many middle class people are 'better off', having higher incomes, greater wealth and other possessions and a more comfortable lifestyle than members of the working class. Yet some 'white collar' employment (e.g. junior clerical workers and nurses) is relatively ill-rewarded, whereas some manual tasks (e.g. plumbers and builders) earn relatively high wages.

Parental background and in particular father's occupation is the criterion of class that is normally employed, although the other criteria help determine one's place on the **class ladder**. Broadly, people within the same class tend to have similar backgrounds, the same kind of

Key terms

New Commonwealth: members of the British Commonwealth that joined as a result of decolonisation (e.g. often poor, predominantly non-white countries in the developing world, in Asia, Africa and the Caribbean). By contrast, the Old or White Commonwealth comprises more wealthy countries of the developed world (e.g. Australia and Canada).

Industrial Revolution: the transformation of British industry that occurred in the 18th and 19th centuries that turned it into an advanced industrial nation.

Income: the amount of monetary or other returns, earned or unearned, that accrues over a period of time.

Wealth: the total value of money and material possessions owned by an individual or organisation.

Class ladder: the process of social mobility. It enables people to move from one social stratum into another, there being a ladder of opportunity that may enable people to improve their position. Some evidence suggests that men's chances of rising up the social scale in Britain have stalled because of greater competition from women and a slower rate of growth for top jobs.

Further information

Determining social class

Table 1.2 *One way to determine social class*

Category (% of pop.)	Groups included
A/B (28)	Higher/lower managerial, professional and administrative
C1 (29)	White collar, skilled, supervisory or lower non-manual
C2 (19)	Skilled manual
D/E (23)	Semi-skilled and unskilled manual/residual, casual workers, long-term unemployed and very poor

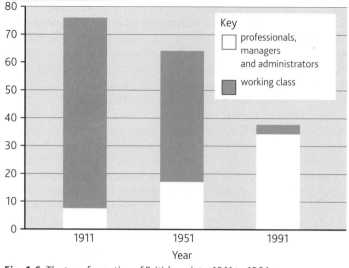

Fig. 1.6 *The transformation of British society, 1911 to 1991*

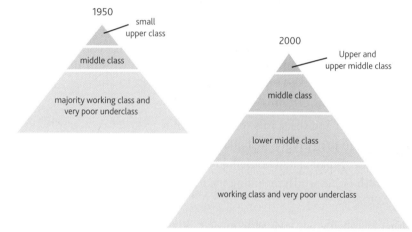

Fig. 1.7 *Britain's changing class structure, 1950 to 2000*

Key terms

Social levelling: the way in which the extremes in society – especially of income and wealth – are moderated. Increasing educational opportunity has helped to expand opportunities for all to climb the ladder of opportunity and reach senior positions. Progressive taxation and the status that comes to many people from ownership of their home, cars and visits abroad for holidays have also served to allow many people from a range of backgrounds to enjoy similar experiences.

Social mobility: relates to the extent to which people are in a different social class from the one in which they were brought up. It defines the chances of an individual climbing the social ladder and moving from a lower to a higher-income bracket as an adult. It is a barometer of how meritocratic and fair a society is; a powerful measure of equality of opportunity.

education, the same kind of spending patterns, leisure and life style. But such generalisation is less true today than it was a few decades ago. Education since 1945 has been a main cause of **social levelling**. The vast majority of children and young people go to the same sort of school, a state comprehensive. There is far more chance of offspring from working class homes going on to university than three or four decades ago. Once a student has graduated, all sorts of new occupational possibilities are opened up, in senior management and the professions. In other words, one's background may be working class, but occupation, income, home and lifestyle may be definitely middle class. For many families, there is much more **social mobility** today than in 1945. Of course, although it is usual to think of mobility upwards – from the son of a road-sweeper to a lawyer – it is possible for the son of doctor to end up driving a bus or train.

To speak of the working class as a solid grouping is much less meaningful than it was 40 or 50 years ago. There is more fluidity between classes and political commentators such as Ivor Crewe (1996) distinguish between the 'old working class' and the 'new working class'. The old or traditional working class tended to live on large council estates in the North of England, Scotland and South Wales, in areas of heavy industry (in particular, coal, iron and ship-building), be unskilled or not very skilled and be members of the traditional trade union serving their sector of employment. The new working class is often to be found in the Midlands or South of England, doing more skilled work in newer, smaller industries that are less trade unionised. They may operate in the new service economy or in hi-tech industries. They are likely to be owner-occupiers, living in their own house.

With the rapid decline of the old manufacturing industries towards the end of the 20th century, the traditional, manual working class became smaller and more fragmented. By contrast, as in most industrial economies, the new working class has been expanding and improving its position. More people are becoming more middle class in their incomes and lifestyles. Whereas in 1950 some two-thirds of the population was working class and one-third middle class, today the proportions are broadly equal but with the working class in the minority.

The patterns of employment are also dramatically different than in the 1950s. As in other European countries, as the manufacturing base has been eroded, more people have turned to working in the service sector, performing tasks ranging from cleaning to teaching and insurance, among many others. Gallie's study (1993) suggests that the percentage of the population in manual work now constitutes little more than one-third of the population, with the percentage who may be classified as 'professionals, managers and administrators' (including a vast range spanning people in the City earning a million and many teachers earning under £30,000) lagging not far behind.

Activities

1. List the characteristics traditionally associated with a) membership of the middle class and b) membership of the working class.

2. To what class would you assign the current leaders of the three main political parties in the United Kingdom? (You may need to check out some information on the internet.)

3. In which social class do you place your own family?

Summary questions

1. What is meant by socialisation?

2. How do parents, teachers and the media contribute to the process of socialisation?

3. What is meant by social class? How is it determined?

The continuing significance of class

Britain has often been viewed as a very class-bound society, with a 'them and us' division holding back our national progress. A former German chancellor, Herr Schmidt (the equivalent of prime minister) once said that we would never solve our problems in industrial relations unless we finally ridded ourselves of our 'wretched class system'. He was pointing to the 'them and us' attitudes that were said to hold back the modernisation of British industry and damage relations between management and the workforce in some firms.

Schmidt was speaking in the 1970s and in aspects of British industry old attitudes have been replaced and there is more emphasis on all employees working together. In industrial relations and some other areas such as voting (see below), class has a diminishing impact on British society today. But society is far from being 'classless' and class-conscious attitudes linger. Indeed, there is evidence that inequality is increasing (see page 52). It remains true that your **life chances** are significantly influenced by the class into which you are born and brought up. Life is easier if you are born with a silver spoon in your mouth (i.e. come from a privileged background). It is noticeable that holders of positions of influence and power in Britain (including barristers, bishops, judges, politicians, senior civil servants and top business people) are frequently

Key terms

Life chances: the opportunities each individual has to improve their quality of life. The concept, devised by German sociologist Max Weber (1864–1920), shows how access to opportunities itself depends on such things as food, clothing, shelter, education and health care.

Economic migrants: those who leave their own country in order to find a better standard of life in another one.

Asylum seekers: refugees seeking asylum in a foreign country in order to escape persecution, war, terrorism, famines and associated conditions that threaten their existence. In many cases, they may be seeking to escape from poverty and deprivation, seeing the chance of a better lifestyle elsewhere.

9/11: the attacks on the World Trade Center, often referred to as the events of 9/11, comprised a series of coordinated suicide terrorist assaults upon the United States in 2001. Two planes crashed into the World Trade Center in New York, one targeting each of its Twin Towers.

London bombings: the terrorist attacks on the capital on 7 July (52 killed) and 21 July (none killed) 2005.

Global citizenship: recognition of the fact that we are all human beings living on one planet, that current use of the world's resources is inequitable and unsustainable, that as the gap between rich and poor widens so poverty continues to deny millions of people their basic rights and that we have an obligation to treat people on the basis of universal equality.

Activity

Sociologists and others sometimes talk of 'fractured' or 'fragmented' identities to suggest that people no longer possess a single, unified concept of who they are. What do you think are the three most important challenges to traditional ideas of identity?

middle or upper class in origin, although of course there are exceptions. (See the discussion of those who exercise power on page 169–70.)

Identities and citizenship under threat

Politicians often discuss issues of identity. Different societies have their own values. As we saw in the previous section, UK government ministers have been reflecting on nationality, the British national character, what makes us British and what immigrants need to do to become recognised as having these characteristics. National identity is being used as a means of creating solidarity among citizens of different backgrounds and characteristics. This is seen as the more important as the country has become increasingly multicultural and as the emphasis on regional identities has increased.

Politicians are keen to create a sense of social harmony and belonging. They understand that various factors have combined in recent years to revive and perhaps confuse the issues of identity and citizenship. Among them are:

- Britain's membership of the European Union
- the consequences of devolution to Scotland, Wales and Northern Ireland, with the creation of the Scottish Parliament, the Welsh National Assembly and the Northern Ireland Assembly
- the controversy surrounding **economic migrants** and **asylum seekers**
- the social disturbances in some inner-city areas
- the consequences of the **9/11** attacks on the World Trade Center (11 September) and the **London bombings** (7 and 21 July 2005).

In particular, riots in the northern English towns of Bradford, Burnley and Oldham (2001) and the outrages in the capital suggest that social solidarity is not as strong as had been thought. New Labour's attempt to create strong communal bonds has failed to convince some members of society of the importance of uniting around common values and support for each other's points of view. Some commentators fear that alienated minorities have excluded themselves from citizenship through choice rather than circumstance. They do not identity with any sense of Britishness or belonging.

European and global identity and citizenship

The notion of citizenship increasingly has an international dimension. In several countries of the European Union there is a strong sense of national and of European identity. Dutch, French and Italian citizens tend to regard themselves as Europeans, without this in any way compromising the fact that they are loyal to Holland, France or Italy respectively. In Britain (see page 240–1) there is much greater coolness to the idea of belonging to Europe, hence the label sometimes applied to the British of being 'reluctant Europeans'. Nonetheless, whatever their feelings, they are legally Europeans. The Maastricht Treaty (1992) establishes 'citizenship of the European Union' (Article 8) for every legal citizen and worker in any member state.

Beyond European citizenship, some commentators argue the need for people to accept the idea of **global citizenship**. They are aware that developments in communication have made us all much more aware of what is happening in other countries around the world. Many residents of Planet Earth today accept that our identities and citizenship now transcend geographical and political boundaries.

How socially diverse is Britain?

Learning objectives:

■ to be able to define the concepts of diversity, multiculturalism, stereotype and labelling

■ to know the patterns of migration affecting the UK

■ to know the current demographics of the UK and the extent of diversity in the UK

■ to understand the debates surrounding multiculturalism and integration

■ to understand the role of the mass media in stereotyping and labelling social groups.

Key terms

Birth rate: the number of births per thousand of the population.

Death rate: the number of deaths per thousand of the population.

Net migration: the difference between immigration (the number of people coming into a country) and emigration (the number leaving the country) over a given period of time.

Life expectancy: the average age a person can be expected to reach, as determined by statistics.

A country's population is determined by its **birth rate**, **death rate** and **net migration**. Annual population growth therefore is the result of natural increase (births minus deaths) and more immigrants coming into the country than emigrants leaving it.

Increasing **life expectancy** affects the number of deaths each year. It results from improved diet, accommodation and especially medical care. The number of births is influenced by the availability of contraception, the trend to later child-bearing and in some cases of childlessness. Migration is influenced by a range of factors, with some people seeking new life opportunities overseas and residents of other countries hoping to have a better existence elsewhere.

Further information

The UK birth rate

■ In 2001, the total fertility rate (TFR) in the UK dropped to a record low. It has increased each year since then in all four home countries.

■ The current level of fertility is relatively high compared with that seen during the 1990s. But it was considerably higher during the 1960s 'baby boom', peaking at 2.95 children per woman in 1964. In 2006, Northern Ireland continued to have the highest fertility rate with 1.94 children per woman.

Activities

Examine the table below and then answer the questions that follow:

Year	No. of live births	Total fertility rate	% of births to non-UK born mothers
1996	649,485	1.74	12.8
1997	643,095	1.73	13.1
1998	635,901	1.72	13.6
1999	621,872	1.70	14.3
2000	604,441	1.65	15.5
2001	594,634	1.63	16.5
2002	596,122	1.65	17.7
2003	621,469	1.73	18.6
2004	639,721	1.78	19.5
2005	645,835	1.79	20.8
2006	669,601	1.86	21.9

Source: Office of National Statistics, UK Snapshots

1 How do you account for the low TFL rates of recent years, as compared with the high figures for the 1960s?

2 Suggest reasons for the increase in the TFR in recent years.

3 Why might you expect the recent trend to continue over the next few years?

■ The UK population

The UK is densely populated and highly urbanised. The most densely populated areas are Kensington and Chelsea in London, the least the Highlands of Scotland. Ninety per cent of the population live in urban areas, almost 40 per cent in seven large **conurbations**. Almost one-third live in the predominantly urban and suburban south-east of England, with about 7.7 million in the capital of London. Only about 20 per cent live in rural areas.

At the time of the 2001 census, the UK had the third-largest population of the countries in the European Union (behind Germany and France) and was the 21st largest in the world. In 1971, the UK population was 55,928,000. By mid-2006, it was 60,587,000, of which 50,763,000 lived in England. This represents a rate of growth of 8 per cent. However, growth has been faster in more recent years. Between mid-1991 and mid-2006, the population grew by an average annual rate of 0.4 per cent, after mid-2001 by 0.5 per cent. It grew by 349,000 people in the year to mid-2006 (0.6 per cent), the equivalent of adding a city larger than Cardiff.

In every year since 1901, with the exception of 1976, there have been more births than deaths in the UK and the population has grown due to natural change. Until the mid-1990s, this natural increase was the main engine of population growth. Since the late 1990s there has still been natural increase (in the year to mid-2006, natural change accounted for 45 per cent of total change), but net internal migration into the UK from abroad has been an increasingly important factor in population change. The UK is unusual in the EU in having large migratory flows, both into and out of the country, not least because of the relative ease with which some groups have been able to enter the country and then their subsequent disillusion when things have not turned out quite as well as they might have anticipated.

In figures released in October 2007, the Office of National Statistics revealed expected population growth of nearly 17 million to 77.2 million by 2050. If the current growth rate were to be maintained, the UK would have 100 m inhabitants by the end of the 21st century.

According to the 2001 census, the most numerous age groups were those who were born in the years 1946–51 (the post-Second World War baby boom): those born in a second boom a generation later in 1961–6 (the largest group of all): and those born in the more modest boom a generation after that, born in 1986–91. The 1946–51 group began to reach retirement age from 2006 onwards (women from 2006 and men from 2011). The sudden increase in the number of people who will be claiming the state pension has led many politicians, political commentators and social analysts to speak of a 'pensions crisis'.

■ Factors influencing migration

Migration is the movement of people from one place to another. It can be permanent or temporary, voluntary or forced, international or internal.

Emigration involves leaving one's native country or region to live in another. Immigration is when an individual arrives in a new country to live, in other words the act of moving into one country from another. Emigration and immigration are therefore two sides of the same coin, the former being viewed from the perspective of the country of origin, the latter from the perspective of the country of destination.

People may choose to emigrate for a variety of reasons, which include **push and pull factors**. Usually, the factors are economic, social, political or environmental, although they may be personal:

◼ *Economic, social, political and environmental motives:* Many migrants move together with their families to a different country in search of a better way of life. They hope to find improved job opportunities or pursue a particular career path, a better income, improved education, better health provision and other facilities that might improve their lifestyle. Sometimes, the reasons may be social, perhaps the wish to be closer to family or friends. Whatever the reason, such emigration may be long term, a permanent uprooting of the family from one country or continent to another. It may be short term, the idea being that those affected will return to their homelands once they have earned enough money to give them a better standard of life. Political motives might involve the search for peace or freedom, as when people currently live under a government they dislike or even find unacceptable. Armed conflict, civil war, natural or environmental disasters, political disagreement and religious fundamentalism might encourage people to flee abroad to find a more secure and stable life elsewhere for themselves and their families. This may be voluntary emigration, where migrants despair of their chances of ever being allowed to live life as they would like to be able to do, for they feel that the existing regime is too intolerant or threatening to the group to which they belong. Sometimes, it is a case of involuntary migration, where the process of **ethnic cleansing** or population transfer means that they have no choice.

◼ *Personal motives:* People sometimes migrate to seek or be with a partner. In the case of those approaching retirement in more affluent nations such as the UK, they may opt to settle in a country with a milder climate. Sunny Cyprus and Spain have proved to be magnets for British ex-patriots.

Most people who leave their country of origin are motivated by the search for better opportunities. But millions have been forced to migrate for fear of persecution. Often those who are forced to migrate become **refugees**. They do not carry many possessions with them and do not have a clear idea of where they may finally settle. United Nations figures showed that at the end of 2002, 8.4 million people had refugee status worldwide, the lowest figure since the 1980s.

Net migration into the UK from abroad has been an increasingly important factor in population change.

Trends and patterns in migration

Migration is not a recent phenomenon. Most people in the UK and elsewhere do not need to go back more than two or three generations in their family tree to find a migrating ancestor. The majority of British people are white, but they are not of common stock. The ancestry of contemporary Britons has been much affected by a series of invasions and migrations. They are descended mainly from the varied ethnic stocks that settled in Britain before the 11th century. The pre-Celtic, Celtic, Roman, Anglo-Saxon and Norse influences were blended in Britain under the Normans, who had lived in Northern France. Subsequently, other groups have entered the UK, having fled from persecution or poverty abroad. Among them were **Huguenots** fleeing from 17th-century France, Irish escaping hunger in 19th-century Ireland and Jews fleeing from **pogroms** in late 19th-century Russia.

◼ **Key terms**

Push and pull factors: push factors are those circumstances that encourage or force a person to move, such as civil war, drought and lack of employment. Pull factors are those incentives that encourage a person to move, including the improved prospects that derive from a better job, better education and a better standard of living in the country they are moving to.

Ethnic cleansing: the various policies and practices designed to bring about the mass expulsion or extermination of people from a minority ethnic or religious group within a certain area.

Refugees: people who flee from some danger or problem, especially persecution. They leave their home without having a new home to go to.

◼ **Activity**

Look at the further information on page 31. Write a few sentences suggesting any explanations for
a) the net outflow in migration in the period to 1985 and
b) the net inflow in the last few years.

◼ **Key terms**

Huguenots: some 2 million French Protestants who suffered persecution in 16th and 17th-century Roman Catholic France. Many went into exile, some 50,000 fleeing to England, of whom about 10,000 moved on to Ireland.

Pogroms: organised massacres of an ethnic group, particularly of Jews.

Small numbers of people from other countries have been resident in the UK for centuries. Probably the first Africans to arrive came during the reign of Queen Elizabeth I, as a result of John Hawkins's expeditions between Africa and the New World. By the 18th century, it had become fashionable to have black domestic servants, so that an advertisement such as the following was not uncommon:

> *A healthy Negro girl, aged about fifteen years, speaks good English, works at her needle, washes well, does household work, and has had the small pox.*

Public Ledger, 1761

From the end of the 19th century until the 1940s there was further immigration, with new arrivals settling in the dock areas. These were mainly men who in some cases were recruited to serve in chemical and munitions factories in the First World War, were demobilised in the UK at the end of the war or volunteered for work in the Second World War to work in factories at a time of labour shortage. Many of these immigrants came from the Caribbean, although between the wars there were also many students from India and West Africa, as well as the West Indies.

Another source of immigration to the UK was Germany in the build-up to the Second World War. Many Germans, in particular those minority groups who were suffering persecution under Nazi rule, sought to emigrate to the UK, some 50,000 being successful. Many of them were Jews.

Immigration since the 1950s

After 1950 immigration increased rapidly. Most migrants looking for work after 1945 came from the Caribbean, the process beginning with the arrival of *SS Empire Windrush* in 1948. It brought 492 passengers (mostly Jamaicans), the majority of whom were skilled or semi-skilled and quickly found work. Shortage of manpower in Britain and opportunities for advancement were widely publicised in the West Indies, resulting in the arrival of more than 3,000 per year in the early 1950s. Whether they were recruited directly in their native countries (as were many nurses and Barbadians who worked for London Transport) or obtained jobs on arrival, the majority of West Indians occupied vacancies not filled by British workers. A substantial number of early West Indian immigrants were women.

Fig. 2.1 *The arrival of* SS Empire Windrush *at Tilbury Docks, Essex, 1948*

Indian and Pakistani immigration started with small groups of seamen in ports, who began to move to inland cities to seek work in factories. Those who did well sent for family members and fellow-villagers, mainly men. Following the partition of India and Pakistan in 1947, there were large upheavals along the frontier. Many Sikhs lost their farmlands in the Punjab and came to Britain looking for work. Gujeratis (mostly Hindus) migrated to seek better opportunities in work and education than they could find in their densely populated home state. Pakistanis (mostly Muslims) came from poor hill districts in the east and west of their country.

Nearly all the immigrants who left these various districts of the Indian sub-continent in the 1950s were young men. Some would return to their place of origin, to be replaced by a son or brother who might seek to boost the family income. Few brought their wives and families. The number of immigrants rose sharply from the mid-1950s, through to the 1970s, when restrictive measures introduced by British governments began to make an impact on the rate of arrival. During those boom years for entry into the UK, there is evidence to suggest that the numbers coming in at any given time varied according to the demand for labour in the host country. When demand fell away (e.g. between 1957 and 1959), there was a corresponding decrease in West Indian immigration.

Those who arrived in the years after 1945 were overwhelmingly from the New Commonwealth, from the non-white majority countries that had once been part of the British Empire. However, after the Second World War, some German and Italian prisoners of war remained, the rest being repatriated. As well as Germans and Italians, work-permit schemes recruited Austrians, Ukrainians and Poles, although not all remained. In 1951 there were 162,339 Polish-born people in Britain, many of whom had arrived in the war and subsequently settled. Their number had dropped considerably 20 years later.

Immigration since 1990

Refugees and asylum seekers

As a signatory to the United Nations Convention Relating to the Status of Refugees (but not to the International Convention on the Protection of the Rights of All Migrant Workers and Members of Their Families), the UK has a responsibility not to return refugees to a country where they would face hunger and/or persecution. Some immigrants of the last decade or so have fled from war zones in which the British have been fighting, in particular Afghanistan, Iraq and the Balkans, following the particularly brutal wars after the break-up of Yugoslavia in the 1990s.

Asylum seeking has become highly controversial, for many journalists and commentators – as well as many British people – suspect that many of those who claim asylum are in reality economic migrants who want a better life in Britain. They sometimes point out that as the British Isles are a long way from the countries from which refugees are fleeing, it could be that they are choosing it more by preference than from dire necessity.

Immigration from Europe

One of the Four Freedoms of the European Union is the right to free movement of people. Since the expansion of the EU from 15 to 25 countries in May 2004, the UK has accepted immigrants from several new member states. There were already Maltese and Greek/Turkish Cypriot communities in the UK, via their Commonwealth connection. What was new was the arrival in vast numbers of immigrants from Central and Eastern Europe. Most member states exercised their right to introduce temporary immigration control (due to end in 2011) over entrants from these **accession countries**, although some are now removing them. The UK introduced no such controls.

Figures published in August 2007 indicated that 682,940 people from the eight new countries on the continent applied to join the Worker Registration Scheme (WRS) between May 2004 and June 2007. But of course those who were self-employed or not working (including students) did not need to register in this way, so that the figure underestimates the number of arrivals. Some subsequently returned to their country of origin or moved elsewhere, but for 2005 there was a net inflow of 64,000 newcomers. In particular, Poles (who constitute the majority of those who registered under the WRS) have made a big impact on the composition of several towns and cities.

Further information

Asylum seekers and non-EU economic migrants

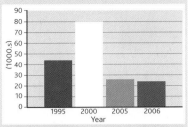

Fig 2.2 *Number of people entering the UK*

Main sources of entrants in order (2006): Afghanistan, Iraq, Somalia, Sri Lanka, Turkey, Iran, Serbia/Montenegro, Pakistan, China and Zimbabwe

N.B. In 2006, the UK was 16th in the league table of industrialised countries for the number of asylum applications per head of population

Source: Home Office figures

Activities

1. If necessary using the internet to assist you, think of any reasons why substantial numbers of people have entered the UK from each of the countries mentioned in this section.

2. List the ways in which immigration from the New Commonwealth has had an impact on the UK.

3. List the ways in which the immigration from Central and Eastern Europe of recent years has a) helped and b) posed problems for British society.

Key terms

Accession countries: accession is a term that strictly refers to those that join an international organisation, but is usually employed in the context of the enlargement of the EU. In this case, it refers to countries that have joined the EU, namely the eight Central and European countries, plus Cyprus and Malta, that entered in May 2004.

When Bulgaria and Romania joined the EU in 2007, the Labour government did introduce some restrictions to limit immigration to students, the self-employed, highly skilled migrants and agricultural/food workers.

Case study

Immigration from Central and Eastern Europe since 2004

- A total of around 1 million people had moved from the new EU member states to the UK by April 2008, but approximately half of them have since returned home or moved on to a third country.
- There was a net inflow of 64,000 people from the eight Central and Eastern European accession states in 2005, the first whole year of post-2004 immigration.
- Poles (who make up the majority of those registered with the WRS) currently represent a substantial proportion of the population of some UK cities.
- Slovakia, Lithuania and (in much smaller numbers) the Czech Republic, Hungary, Latvia, Estonia and Slovenia have been the other main sources of European immigration.
- Restrictions imposed upon the entry of Bulgarians and Romanians (2007 entrants to the EU) indicate that just under 16,500 registered on the various schemes and thereby gained a right of entry in the first six months of that year.

Table 2.2 *Recent arrivals in the UK: top 10 countries of origin for overseas workers, 2006–7 (000s)*

Poland	222.8	Lithuania	24.1
India	49.3	France	20.2
Slovakia	28.8	South Africa	16.9
Pakistan	25.3	Germany	15.2
Australia	24.4	China	13.2
		Total	**713.5**

Illegal immigrants

In addition to the groups referred to above, there are also illegal immigrants who have entered the UK without authority (perhaps using false documents) and those who have overstayed their visas. By their very nature, they are difficult to quantify. The Home Office has a more limited view of the likely number than do some research bodies, but many sources place the number at between 500,000 and 600,000.

Case study

Immigration from Poland: its impact on Crewe

In the 2001 census, 60,708 people living in the UK were recorded as having been born in Poland. The Polish community had one of the oldest age profiles in the UK, with 54% of those born in Poland being of pensionable age or over.

Because the British government imposed no restrictions on entry from the Accession countries of the EU, Polish citizens were able to come to the UK after May 2004. More Poles – and inhabitants of the other new member states – arrived than ministers anticipated. As a consequence, several parts of the country have been much affected by a new tide of Polish immigration. Such was its suddenness and scale that in some cases those charged with planning local services found themselves overwhelmed by the unprecedented social change affecting their communities.

The situation in Crewe

Crewe was one such town. In 2001, members of ethnic minorities constituted just 2% of its population. By the end of 2006, the percentage had increased to 6%. Some 3,000 East European incomers had arrived – all from Poland.

In previous years, staff at the town's biggest recruitment agency – Advance Personnel – had detected a local labour shortage. The level of unemployment in Crewe was very low and few people seemed to be interested in low-wage, part-time jobs. In particular, packing, distribution and food-processing plants couldn't get enough workers.

Six months before EU enlargement, Advance Personnel's managing director, Jason Canny, opened an office in Poland, where unemployment neared 20%. Aware that only two other countries – Ireland and Sweden – had not imposed restrictions on entry, he anticipated a good response, but even with his knowledge of the situation he was amazed by the number of Poles who wanted to come to the UK. His company was involved in recruiting workers for firms in several parts of Britain, but he knew the situation in Crewe personally, for there the majority of Polish migrants passed through his agency. He related his experience and feelings in a BBC television programme, in which he told the presenter about the effects in the UK generally, but more specifically upon the town:

' … the migrating workforce that has come into the UK is far bigger than people realise. Not just in our area, but nationally … I've seen a lot of changes in Crewe, and I've been personally responsible – or at least my company has. It's quite mind-blowing the changes we've gone through …'.

Too much too soon?

Initially, most of the workers who arrived in Crewe were single men living in rented houses provided by recruitment agencies such as Advance Personnel. But within a year or so, they began to bring their families. The Crewe and Nantwich Borough Council started organising advice sessions and a community association for the incomers. But it provided the services on the basis of no advance warning, experience or additional resources. Some councillors resented the fact that they had not been alerted by central government and disputed the ministerial claim that the impact of Polish immigration on any one individual area would be very modest.

The local authority suddenly found itself in receipt of an influx of Polish children into its schools, in some cases without any warning. Another interviewee in the programme, Christine Garbett, the head of St Mary's Catholic Primary, explained what happened: ' … I assumed initially that the handful who'd contacted us would be the only ones we'd be assimilating into the school. That it would stop. But it didn't stop'. She went on to point out that the 23 Polish children in St Mary's had integrated well – and already learned a lot of English.

Of the newcomers interviewed, Adam Kolasinski – trained in Poland in maths, administration, computing and teaching – had been unable to find work in his home country. In Crewe, he found a job on a production line, making oven-ready pizzas. Earning five or six times the average Polish wage, he was convinced that he and his family would remain in England: ' … Life is good, kids grow up normally. I have more time to spend with my family that I don't have to spend struggling for money'.

Fig. 2.3 *A UKIP poster captures some people's feelings about immigration*

Hint

See also pages 30–1 for details of emigration by Poles who arrived following the 2004 influx.

Activities

1. Using the case study of Crewe to help you, list the main effects of Polish and other Central/Eastern European immigration into the UK.

2. In the light of the information given and your own observations, do you think that there is a problem of numbers, as far as immigration is concerned? Can the UK absorb the current number of immigrants?

Some of the information above has been adapted from an edition of Newsnight, *20 January 2006*

Emigration

Emigration was a major force in the world in the 19th and 20th centuries. Millions of poor people and their families left the European continent to seek a better life in the Americas or parts of the British Empire. Thousands of British people left to give themselves a new start and acquire fresh opportunities in the countries of the Old Commonwealth (Australia, Canada and New Zealand), around 200,000 per annum at the turn of the 20th century.

More British people have been emigrating in the new millennium than at any other time since the 1970s, according to official figures. Estimates produced by the Office of National Statistics (ONS) revealed that some 190,000 British citizens left in 2003.

The rate of departure from the UK has been so great in recent years that population falls are only masked by immigration. For instance, the ONS calculated that in 2007 207,000 British citizens – more than half of the 400,000 moving abroad and amounting to one every three minutes – left the country, while 510,000 foreigners arrived to stay for a year or more. In both cases (total immigration and total emigration), the figures were the highest ever recorded.

The return of East Europeans to their homeland

In addition to British citizens who have moved abroad, there has in the last few years been a strong tendency for East Europeans of the post-2004 era to return to their original homeland. According to *The Independent* (27 February 2008), almost half of the million Central and Eastern European immigrants who arrived in the UK have either returned home or seriously contemplated the matter. Poles in particular are returning to their native country in large numbers. The trend has come as no surprise to the London-based Institute for Public Policy Research (IPPR), whose website explains that some other EU member states are now relaxing their employment rules: 'Migration from Poland is very unlikely to continue at the levels we have seen in the first few years of [EU] enlargement. It has always been a question of when these flows started drying up, rather than whether they would'.

Fig. 2.4 *Occupations of UK Emigrants 2004/International Passenger Survey, Office of National Statistics*

■ Case study

The return of many Poles to Poland

Many members of the Polish community have returned home, a trend that seems likely to continue according to IPPR research. They are attracted by one particular pull factor (the strengthening of the Polish economy and the higher salaries now available in Poland) and push factors such as job shortages and a fall in the value of the pound in the UK.

The Independent quoted the example of one returnee, twenty-three-year-old Maciek Imiolczck. He arrived in England in early 2007, anticipating a stay of several years: 'I thought I could make much more money there and that it would be an easy life, but it wasn't like I expected.'

Maciek has a business degree and hoped to find a well-paid job in London, but after struggling to find work he eventually took a post as a receptionist in a hostel: 'I couldn't find anything that paid more than the minimum wage and it was really hard to live off that. I realised life in London was much tougher than I'd been led to believe.'

Maciek went back to Poland after six months, to work as a tour guide in Krakow: 'The work I do now is better paid, interesting and my qualify of life is infinitely better.'

Other emigration destinations

The *Brits Abroad* project conducted for the BBC in 2006 by the IPPR suggested that more British people than ever before want to turn dreams of a foreign life into reality. Almost one in 10 British citizens are currently living overseas:

Table 2.3 *British people currently living abroad: 10 countries with the largest British population*

Country	Full time	Full and part time	Pensioners
Australia	1,300,000	1,310,000	45,311
Spain	761,000	990,000	74,636
United States	678,000	685,000	132,083
Canada	603,000	609,000	157,435
Ireland	291,000	320,000	104,650
New Zealand	215,000	217,000	46,560
South Africa	212,000	214,000	38,825
France	200,000	261,000	33,869
Germany	115,000	126,600	33,034
Cyprus	59,000	65,000	11,742

Source: IPPR research

N.B. The study found that there were 5.5 m expat Britons. Part-time Britons are classified as those who spend three months or more of the year in the country listed.

In an ICM poll for the study, 1,000 people were questioned for the survey and 54 per cent said they had considered emigrating, little change from a similar 2003 poll. However, the number hoping to move in the near future has almost doubled.

When asked why they would go, the most important reasons were a better quality of life, better weather and a feeling that the UK is too expensive. Some 12 per cent said they did not like what the UK had become, while one in 10 said they already had friends or family overseas.

Summary questions

1 How was much of the New Commonwealth immigration of the 1950s onwards distinctive from that which had gone on before?

2 Why has immigration from Central and Eastern Europe been a key feature of the last few years?

3 Why have large numbers of Central and Eastern European immigrants returned to their place of origin?

4 Why do large numbers of Britons leave the UK each year?

How far is Britain a multicultural society?

A century ago, the United Kingdom seemed to be a broadly united and cohesive society, lacking in many of the problems of identity that were

Further information

UK net migration by five-year intervals, 1950–2005 (000s)

Five-year period	Net migration
1950–5	– 500
1955–60	– 70
1960–5	220
1965–70	–250
1970–5	–185
1975–80	– 50
1980–5	– 250
1985–90	30
1990–5	170
1995–2000	490
2000–5	945

Source: Population Division of the Department of Economic and Social Affairs of the United Nations Secretariat, World Population Prospects: The 2006 Revision and World Urbanization Prospects

Activities

1 In the light of the countries listed as top locations for the British abroad, what do you think are the main factors that have encouraged British citizens to leave the UK?

2 List the main hopes of Central and Eastern European immigrants on arrival in the UK. What do you think has been the most important reason for the return of a substantial number of them?

a feature in other countries. In recent decades, this **homogeneity** has come under challenge. There is greater social diversity than there was 50 years ago.

British society since the 1960s

In a description of the social fabric in the Britain of the 1960s, a French political scientist Blondel described Britain as a relatively homogeneous society. The British were portrayed as an integrated community in which values did not differ radically between different social groups, whatever their **race**, ethnicity, religion or language.

Since then, British society has been transformed in several respects:

- **Social class is less important** and there is greater social mobility than ever before.
- **An urban–rural divide has become more important** in recent years. The issue of fox-hunting and its abolition focused attention on the gap between the attitudes expressed by many country people to those living in towns and cities, not least because country-dwellers felt that 'townies' did not understand the rural way of life. Fox-hunting was part of a wider feeling that the countryside was being neglected, bearing the brunt of post office and small school closures, and inferior transport provision.
- **The ethnic minority population has significantly increased**. Overall, the million or so non-white population of 1970 has become some 5 million today. More than half of the present non-white population was born in Britain. Four out of five Afro-Caribbeans under 35 began their life here and there are as many Afro-Caribbean Britons under 30 with a white parent as there are with two black parents. Immigration has had a particular impact upon some towns and cities. A multicultural and **multi-ethnic society** has developed and is here to stay.

Ethnic minorities in the UK

The labels used to describe Britain's ethnic minority population have changed over recent decades. It was usual back in the 1950s and 1960s to refer to 'immigrants' or 'coloureds', but the terms are less common today. 'Immigrant' seems less relevant now that more than half of the members of ethnic minority groups were born in the UK. 'Coloured' is often viewed as a condescending and rather meaningless term, the more so as many of those involved have intermarried with the native population. Often ethnic minorities have been known as 'blacks', but this too has disadvantages. No one is literally black, just as no one is literally white. In the last census (2001), the term 'Black and Ethnic Minority' (BEM) was employed and this remains the language used in governmental statistics.

Here, it is convenient to speak of 'ethnic minorities'. It is a convenient all-embracing term for people of many different origins. However, to see those so labelled as in any way homogeneous (having the same characteristics) would be very misleading. We are talking about peoples of very diverse cultural backgrounds, each ethnic group having its own traditions and lifestyle. All of the 5 million or so involved are individuals, with their distinctive personal characteristics.

Who do we mean by 'ethnic minorities'?

There is also some debate as to which groups should be considered part of that group, but using the last (2001) census as a guide we are including all groups except the categories of white people. Of the UK population

92.1 per cent described themselves as white (though not necessarily British). The remaining 7.9 per cent (4.6 million) belonged to non-white ethnic minority groups. Around half of the non-white population in 2001 were Asians of Indian, Pakistani, Bangladeshi or other Asian origin. A further quarter of the population were black and 15 per cent of the non-white population were from the mixed ethnic group. About a third of this group were from white and black Caribbean backgrounds.

The census findings on the distribution of the UK's ethnic minorities were as follows:

■ Nearly half of Britain's non-white population lives in Greater London. Forty-five per cent of the UK's entire minority ethnic population lives in Greater London. The area of the country with the second largest proportion of the minority ethnic population is the West Midlands (with nearly 14 per cent), followed by West Yorkshire (8 per cent). The English regions with the lowest proportions of the minority ethnic population were the North-East and the South-West. In each case, ethnic minority people made up only 2 per cent of the population.

■ In fewer than 30 local authorities do ethnic minorities make up more than 15 per cent of the population. Leicester has the highest proportion of any city, with 22.3 per cent (mainly Indian).

Table 2.4 *The UK population by ethnic groupings, 2001*

Category	Number	% of whole population	% of ethnic minority population
White	54,153,898	92.1	n/a
Mixed	677,117	1.2	14.6
Asian or Asian British			
Indian	1,053411	1.8	22.7
Pakistani	747,285	1.3	16.1
Bangladeshi	283,063	0.5	6.1
Other Asian	247,664	0.4	5.3
Black or Black British			
Black Caribbean	565,876	1.0	12.2
Black African	485,277	0.8	10.5
Black Other	97,585	0.2	2.1
Chinese	247,403	0.4	5.3
Other	230,615	0.4	5.0
All minority ethnic population	4,635,296	7.9	100
All population	58,789,194	100	n/a

Source: National Statistics Online *(www.statistics.gov.uk)*

N.B. The 2001 Census figures quoted above represented a 53% growth in the minority ethnic population between 1991 and 2001 (from 3.0 m in 1991, to 4.6 m)

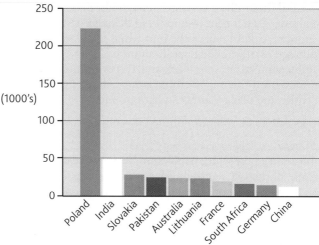

Fig. 2.5 *Country of origin for overseas workers*

Activity

Write a paragraph to distinguish race and ethnicity. List 10 ethnic groups living in the UK today. Tick any that are well represented in your locality.

Fig. 2.6 *A shop front in Selly Oak, Birmingham, illustrates the diversity of its clientele*

- More than half of black Caribbeans and more than three-quarters of black Africans live in Greater London.
- More than half of the Indian community lives in the South-East, more than half of the Bangladeshis in Greater London and nearly half of Pakistanis live in the West Midlands or Yorkshire and Humberside.
- The Chinese population is more dispersed than other non-white groups.

Age and employment

Because of the high net birth rate and the demographics of international migrants, the ethnic minority population is on average younger than the white population. Its median age was 27, compared to 40 for the white population. As a consequence, the ethnic minority share of the working age population is disproportionately large, 9.3 per cent of the 35.2 million people of working age in 2004. However, in general, members of minority groups have lower levels of economic activity than white people. In that same year, 65.3 per cent of the working age ethnic minority population were economically active, compared with 79.6 per cent of the UK's working age population as a whole.

The jobs of ethnic minorities are still largely concentrated in those sectors of the economy to which they were attracted in the 1950s and 1960s. In many cases, these are the sectors of the economy with greater risk of low pay, doing shift work with longer hours of work and with less access to training. The decline of manufacturing as the basis for the economy and the growth of 'new' hi-tech industries located away from town centres (where ethnic minorities are concentrated) may have made things worse for their work prospects. The introduction of the minimum wage has given a boost to the wage levels they experience.

Some groups, such as the Chinese and Indians, have experienced upward mobility, often by establishing their own businesses, whether they be corner shops, restaurants or in professions such as accountancy. Of the more recent Central and Eastern European immigrants, many work in the service industries (e.g. in hotels and eating places), although the Poles have been able to fill many gaps in the market for electricians and plumbers.

In 2001, the then home secretary (David Blunkett) set out the need for extra migrants on two grounds. The first was the extra growth this would provide in an economy with serious shortages of labour in the agriculture, construction, hotel and hospitality sectors. The second was as a means of curbing the activities of gang-masters, who run illegal immigration rackets. A special *Guardian* series on asylum and immigration in 2001 showed that 50 per cent of seasonal agricultural workers, such as fruit pickers, are brought to Britain by gang-masters.

Religious diversity

Religious rivalry has not been a traditional feature of the United Kingdom, except as part of the complex of problems associated with Northern Ireland. In countries ranging from Canada to France, it has been an important factor in political life, but in Britain tolerance of religious differences – often based on indifference to the topic – has traditionally been the norm. However, religion has been a cause of diversity in recent years.

In particular, immigration has been a key factor associated with religion, leading to a rapid increase in support for Islamic beliefs (see Table 2.5 for an indication of the multi-faith society that Britain has become). This has had political repercussions. On the one hand, there have been demands from some Muslims for their own schools, raising issues about the desirability of allowing or encouraging separatist tendencies. On the other, the events of 9/11 2001 have had an impact, at the very least alerting British people to changes that had already taken place in society.

Table 2.5 *The UK's religious mix, 2001*

Religion	UK total	UK %
Buddhist	151,816	0.3
Christian	42,079,417	71.6
Hindu	558,810	1.0
Jewish	266,740	0.5
Muslim	1,591,126	2.7
Sikh	336,149	0.6
Other religions	178,837	0.3
Total all religions	45,162,495	76.8
No religion	9,103,727	15.5
Not stated	4,288,719	7.3

Table 2.6 *Muslim Europe and Muslim Britain*

Percentage of Muslims living in some European countries

France	10.0 %
Netherlands	5.5%
Germany	3.7%
UK	2.5%
Italy	2.4%

The population by numbers – 1.6 m total no. in UK

43%	originate from Pakistan
17%	originate from Bangladesh
9%	originate from India
36%	Tower Hamlets in Muslim (highest concentration in UK)
20%	Pakistani/Bangladeshi women active in job market, compared with 70% white and black Caribbean women
30%	pupils of Pakistani origin leave school with 5 or more A–C grades at GCSE, compared with 50% of pop. in general
33%	have no qualifications, the highest fig. for any UK ethnic group
13%	male unemployment rate, highest in UK
£150	is average. (monthly) amount which Pakistani and Bangladeshi men earn less than white men

Source: The Times, *4 July 2006*

■ **Activity**

Consider the following figures (%):

	agree	disagree
The 7/7 bombers should be considered martyrs	13	87
The Muslim community needs to do more to integrate into mainstream British culture	65	21
It is acceptable for the police to view Muslims with greater suspicion, in the light of 7/7	16	81
Suicide bombings can be justified in the UK against military targets	16	79

Source: adapted figures from a Populus *poll, June 2006*

In the light of the above, write a paragraph to explain whether you agree with *The Times* headline (4 July 2006) about the UK's Muslim community:

A COMMUNITY DIVIDED ON TERRORISM AND SECURITY

A few months before the attack on the World Trade Center, disturbances in the North of England had laid bare the grievances of British Muslims, forcing recognition of the fact that community relations were no longer just about race relations, but about faith as well. The post-Iraq war situation has led to developing antagonism among some Muslims for the actions taken by Britain and America against their fellow believers in that troubled country. In the 2005 general election, some Muslim associations advised their followers not to support the Blair government that took Britain into war. Again, in this respect, diversity and tension characterise aspects of the social scene.

The influence of minorities on the national character

It is important to distinguish between a multicultural society and multiculturalism as belief and policy. As a statement of fact, Britain is a multicultural society, markedly more so than it was some 50 years ago. In a country that is multicultural, all ethnic groups should feel that they have a place and that they are accepted and included.

As we have seen on pages 25–9, Britain has always had minority populations and successive bouts of immigration have modified the national character and shaped national development. But until around 50 years ago, this did not significantly challenge broad social cohesion or ethnic unity. Since the early 1950s, the situation has changed considerably. The onset of New Commonwealth immigration and, more recently, the entry of asylum seekers and migrants from Central and Eastern Europe has in some cases been associated with negative attitudes and on occasion evident hostility from the host population.

British society reflects, on a cultural level, the many different ethnic groups that have made their home in the UK, not just because each group can celebrate its own customs and traditions but that all members of society can join in and benefit from the cultural diversity that has been created. However, although society has become multicultural, most people do not live in multicultural communities. Much of the growth in the ethnic minority population has been in traditional areas of settlement.

Multiculturalism is an **ideology** advocating that society should comprise, or at least allow and include, distinct cultural groups of equal status. It involves the political accommodation by the state and/or dominant

Key terms

Ideology: a system of assumptions, beliefs and values about public issues, which are part of a comprehensive vision of society. The concept is central to politics, as almost every political tendency has some degree of ideological backing. Ideologies help us to explain the political world and point towards what form of political action should be taken in particular circumstances.

culture of all minority cultures, as defined first and foremost by reference to race or ethnicity. The accommodation of minorities now poses a challenge in many parts of the world.

Multiculturalism emerged as an official policy in English-speaking countries in the late 1960s, in relation to the cultural needs of non-European migrants. The term was quickly adopted as official policy by most member states in the European Union. However, it is currently an extremely divisive issue in the UK and in several other Western democracies. Spokespersons from many walks of life – including politicians and leading members of the clergy – have pointed to the dangers of multiculturalism in the UK and found it wanting as the model for race relations in Britain. They suggest that it is based on an article of faith; that all men and women of goodwill can live together contentedly, celebrating their differences, each community preserving its own culture while respecting those of others.

Three models of race relations in the UK

Policy on race relations is a divisive issue that tends to generate an emotional response. Broadly, there are three models of how such relations might be handled.

Assimilation

Assimilation is the approach traditionally favoured by the political Right. MPs such as John Townend (in the House from 1979–2001) claimed that immigration had undermined Britain's 'homogeneous Anglo-Saxon society'. He argued that members of ethnic minorities born in Britain should consider themselves British and not look to the country of family origin for their identity. This is a similar view to the approach adopted by Lord Tebbit, in his 'cricket test' (see page 12).

Assimilation was the expectation of many politicians when many immigrants came to Britain from the New Commonwealth, often at the behest of ministers who wanted to fill labour shortages. The idea was that new arrivals would leave their traditional habits and lifestyle behind them and adopt British customs and the British way of life instead.

The assimilatory model resembles the US metaphor of the '**melting-pot**', via which immigrants and their families surrender their traditional values. As remarkable as US diversity may be, the existence of a strong and widely shared sense of national unity is even more remarkable. Its existence was highlighted several decades ago by the reporter John Gunther (1947):

> Homogeneity and diversity – these are the stupendous rival magnets ... Think of the United States as an immense blanket or patchwork quilt, solid with different designs and highlights. But, no matter what colors burn and flash in what corners, the warp and woof, the basic texture and fabric is the same from corner to corner, from end to end.

Critics see assimilation as unnecessary and unfair, arguing that members of ethnic minorities are entitled to retain the customs and lifestyles of their culture. At worst, it borders on a belief in 'white supremacy', all incomers accepting that the British way of life is best. Whatever view is taken of assimilation, it never happened, in part because of marked cultural differences but also because the ethnic minorities faced discrimination in many areas of their daily routine.

■ **Key terms**

'Melting-pot': the process – particularly noted in the United States – whereby persons of different ethnic background are blended or assimilated into mainstream society.

■ **Further information**

Public attitudes to multiculturalism

Findings of MORI survey

62% believe multiculturalism makes Britain a better place

32% agree multiculturalism threatens the British way of life

58% agree people who come to live in Britain should adopt British values/traditions

28% say people who come to live in Britain should be free to live by their own values/traditions

Source: BBC/MORI poll, August 2005

Key terms

Integration: the process of absorbing people belonging to different ethnic, religious or other groups into an existing community. There is a dispute as to whether this should allow people to retain their cultural identities or whether it should lead to assimilation. A former Labour home secretary, Roy Jenkins, defined it 'not as a flattening process of assimilation, but as equal opportunity, accompanied by cultural diversity, in an atmosphere of mutual tolerance'.

Elite: refers to a small, privileged group that tends to dominate government and society.

Ghettoes: densely populated slum areas of a city inhabited by a socially and economically deprived minority.

Integration

There is a clear distinction between the British pursuit of **integration** and French efforts to achieve assimilation. Integration is not assimilation. An integrated society aims to respect cultural diversity, widen understanding between communities, reduce racial hatred and give people a sense of belonging. It provides for the coexistence of minority cultures within the majority one. Assimilation goes much further, attempting to absorb differences and make the minority culture part of the majority one. The problem with the melting-pot is that it is the predominant culture that dominates. In the eyes of many people, a self-confident democracy should ideally be able to celebrate diversity.

Under the integrationist model, there is evidence of distinctive – but not segregated – cultures. Importance is attached to the need for glue to bind us all together, via the use of the English language and devices such as the Citizenship Test. The requirement laid down in 2005 that all new arrivals have some basic competence in English is seen as a way of making sure that they can find employment, support themselves and gain widespread acceptance.

Integration implies that there should be a sense of belonging, without this meaning that cultural traditions have to be sacrificed. All ethnic groups will retain their distinctive identities and customs, but they will nonetheless take pride in being British and respect British values.

Multiculturalism

Multiculturalists believe that in a multi-ethnic society, cultural difference should be preserved and celebrated. Each ethnic group should tolerate the different cultures in society, but not seek their full integration. They stress that people of goodwill can work together, benefit from their diversity and in their communities preserve their traditions, while at the same time respecting the rights of other cultures.

Such a vision sees diversity as a positive force, increasing the richness of communities and actually encouraging tolerance. In practice, it implies the creation of more single-faith schools that preserve different cultures and the strong protection of minority rights against discrimination and antagonism by use of the law.

The challenges of living in a multicultural society

Supporters of multiculturalism often portray it as a self-evident entitlement of cultural groups, as a form of civil rights grounded in equality of cultures. They embrace diversity as a positive force, encouraging and enabling different cultures to learn about each other's art, literature and philosophy, and influence each other's cuisine, fashion and music.

Opponents tend to see multiculturalism as an unwanted vision that has been imposed on them by a liberal, progressive **elite**, which has not sought their consent. They fear it will lead to cultural **ghettoes** and undermine a sense of national identity and unity. In particular, they dislike the way that in practice it means the creation of more single-faith schools and an undue emphasis upon minority rights.

Peaceful coexistence between members of different communities requires a high level of mutual respect for and toleration of each other. The difficulty is that if families continue to speak their native language, this excludes them from the rest of society and encourages extremist whites to adopt racist attitudes.

The recent debate on multiculturalism

Labour has traditionally been sympathetic to multiculturalism, placing much emphasis on the rights of minorities to preserve and celebrate their culture whilst encouraging their participation as citizens – that is, integrating without assimilating. Indeed, during the periods of Labour rule in the 1960s and 1970s there were many commentators in Europe who regarded Britain as an inspiration in formulating their own policies. However, in recent years the policy has come into question. The existence of poor social conditions and **racism** have – particularly in some highly polarised towns and cities in the North of England where there is an absence of shared values – become barriers to the integration of minorities, so that multiculturalism has not functioned as it is supposed to do. In the light of events such as the riots of 2001 and the London bombings, some Labour politicians have seen a need to stress social cohesion and inclusion, rather than diversity.

Lord Ouseley, a former chairman of the **Commission for Racial Equality** and his team were asked by the government to examine the nature of Britain's multiracial, multicultural society. In their report, Community Pride, Not Prejudice (2005), members of the inquiry urged the need for members of ethnic minority groups to be allowed to practise their customs and traditions without fear or prejudice, but spoke also of the desirability of them doing their best to integrate into the mainstream British culture. They noted how many Muslims felt excluded from society, but criticised them for their isolation into 'Islamic ghettoes'. They had shunned wider contact with the rest of the community, as part of a self-imposed segregation. Also, they had been too willing to turn a blind eye to the increasing levels of criminal activity among a minority of their younger members, to the extent that some gangs were becoming 'untouchable'. The Ouseley vision was of a country in which each community felt a responsibility to promote full integration and from which none were excluded.

Ruth Kelly, the communities minister in the last Blair government, responded to such contributions by expressing her wish to open up an 'honest' debate about multiculturalism. Tony Blair himself stated that Britain had certain 'essential values' and that there was a duty upon all groups and individuals within society to uphold them. He did not reject multiculturalism as such, but emphasised the importance of preserving the British heritage and way of life because they represented essential principles and standards.

Key terms

Racism: the belief that human races have distinctive characteristics that determine their respective cultures. It usually involves the idea that one's own race is superior and has the right to rule over or dominate others. It often leads to discrimination and sometimes race hatred.

Commission for Racial Equality (CRE): a non-departmental public body set up under the terms of the Race Relations Act (1976) to tackle racial discrimination and promote racial equality. It now forms part of the Commission for Equality and Human Rights.

Winterval: a fusion of the words winter and festival, this is a term coined to describe all of the festivities that take place around the end of the year. It was first used in Birmingham (1998) to cover the three-month collection of multi-faith and secular events running from October to January, including Bonfire Night, Diwali and the New Year and other seasonal events, as well as Christmas itself.

Summary questions

1 Is it preferable to seek to integrate members of ethnic minorities rather than to encourage cultural diversification? If integration is the better option, how might it be promoted?

2 Has the past preoccupation with multiculturalism created a situation in which the majority has had to make too many concessions to appease the minority? Among other things, you might consider the celebration of a range of religious festivals associated with minority groups and the 'Winterval' issue.

3 Would race relations in Britain be improved if the distinctive identities of immigrant families were to be cast into the melting-pot and absorbed into the mainstream?

4 In its race relations policy, should Britain strive towards a combination of respect for diversity with a commitment to shared common values?

Key terms

Labelling: classifying people using an easy word or phrase that represents a generalisation about them and their characteristics. It involves defining or describing people in terms of their behaviour, e.g. someone who may appear not to be fully open or straightforward when talking about an occurrence may be labelled as a 'liar'.

What is stereotyping?

Stereotypes tend to be generalisations about a group to which we do not belong, to which we attribute a defined set of characteristics, usually based on minimal or limited knowledge. Persons may be grouped according to their ethnicity, gender, sexual orientation or any number of other categories.

Stereotypes may be positive or negative in tone. Many people who are prejudiced stereotype those whom they victimise. Stereotyping involves **labelling** people as though they are all the same, making assumptions that may be based on inaccurate ideas and misinformation. At best, stereotyping can be a way of summarising groups and making general statements about them. However, more often it is used negatively to devalue individuals and groups of people. Such stereotypes are hard to change, even in the face of strong evidence to counter them.

The purpose in stereotyping is not necessarily unworthy. It may derive not from any malevolent intent, but from a wish to ease and move along a conversation, by simplifying the picture. It is a means of understanding and streamlining our thoughts about the social world, for it enables us to reduce the amount of 'processing' or thinking about any new person we meet. We attribute to that person a whole range of characteristics and abilities that we assume all members of that person's group possess, our stereotyped picture enabling us to 'fill in the blanks' about the individuals concerned.

Stereotyping can be subconscious. We innocently create pictures about people. This influences our opinions in subtle ways without us actually wishing to label people unfairly. For instance, if we walk through a park late at night and meet a group of elderly people, we are unlikely to feel alarmed or endangered, whereas if we meet a group of teenagers wearing hoodies, we may feel threatened.

Stereotypes often arise out of fear of members of particular groups. Many people find it hard to cope with mentally sick people, perhaps associating mental illness with individuals who are prone to violence. Violence committed by mentally sick people is actually no more common than that committed by the general population, but it may be that occasional stories or experience of an emotionally disturbed individual going on the rampage have created a deep-seated myth, which is passed on from one person to another.

An advantage of stereotyping is that it enables us to respond to situations with some speed, if we have come across similar situations before – as when we meet new people belonging to a different group. A disadvantage is that it is unfair to generalise, rather than to treat people as individuals with their own identities and characteristics. Such impressions may be unjust, untrue and long-lasting. They:

- reduce a wide range of differences in people to simplistic categorisations
- transform assumptions about particular groups of people into 'realities'
- can be used to justify the position of those in power
- can perpetuate social prejudice and inequality.

Our stereotypes remain unchanged or change only infrequently, even if there is evidence to suggest that our beliefs about others are misguided or wrong. When we do alter them, it is done in one of three ways:

- As we acquire new information and hear it often repeated, we adjust our stereotypes incrementally, to adapt to the new situation. Usually,

Activity

List the ways in which stereotyping of people can be helpful or harmful.

it requires more than one piece of evidence to bring about change, for a single argument or item of factual information is dismissed as an exception that proves the rule.

- We reject and discard our traditional stereotype and think afresh about the category of people concerned. This is generally done only when there is a bulk of evidence that conflicts with the stereotype.

- We create a new stereotype that incorporates the new information, making it a sub-type of our general picture of the group concerned. For example, if we visit California, we may view Californians as being rather different from our image of Americans as a whole.

The generalisations we have may be reasonably accurate in many cases, but the danger is that by stereotyping we make assumptions that may be inaccurate and based on inadequate knowledge and understanding. We often have stereotypes about groups with which we are quite unfamiliar, having never actually had first-hand contact with members of them.

Those who are stereotyped can find the experience perturbing, as they experience an anxiety or stereotype threat of being on the receiving end of unfair treatment. This is because stereotypes can often lead to discrimination and persecution, if the stereotype is unfavourable.

The nature of stereotypes

Psychologists' have been fascinated with stereotypes since the early part of the 20th century. Walter Lippmann (1922) spoke of stereotypes as 'pictures in our heads' and proposed that they have an important role in our mental processing. A decade or so later, social psychologists began to survey people to examine their stereotypes. The most renowned of these studies remains that conducted by Katz and Braly (1933). Students at Princeton University in the USA were presented with a list of attributes from which they selected five that most strongly characterised 10 different ethnic and national groups. Katz and Braly's research addressed two important questions: What do people believe about different social groups? And, how strongly do they believe it?

The two writers found that those interviewed – mostly white Americans – had no difficulty in responding to their questionnaire. They held clear stereotypes of particular communities. For instance, Jews were seen as shrewd and mercenary, Afro-Caribbeans as lazy and happy-go-lucky, and their own group as industrious and intelligent.

Members of most ethnic groups probably have images of other groups. This is a natural feature of human behaviour, which helps people to identify themselves with and feel secure in their own communities. In their study, Katz and Braly identified a point widely commented on ever since, namely that racial stereotypes always seem to favour the race of the observer rather than the observed. They tend to belittle other cultures and ethnicities. In this way, they can become a means of justifying racist attitudes and forms of behaviour.

The role of the mass media

Some stereotypes have their roots in situations we have experienced or in tales related by friends and family, which inform our views. Alternatively, we may have read magazines or books, or watched films or television programmes. For much of its history, the American film industry portrayed Afro-Americans as lazy, unintelligent and/or prone to violence. Physically attractive women have often been portrayed as unintellectual (e.g. the 'dumb blondes'), unintelligent and sexually promiscuous.

Activities

Thinking of racial and female stereotypes:

1. Do you think that the portrayal of members of ethnic minority groups and women in magazines, newspapers and the movies is unflattering? List any examples.

2. Are such groups well represented in media output?

3. How are women portrayed in video games? Give some examples.

■ Further information

Female stereotypes

Meehan (1983) distinguished 10 common female character types:

- ■ *the imp*, the rebellious tomboy
- ■ *the good wife*, domestic, attractive, home-centred and content
- ■ *the harpy*, the aggressive single woman
- ■ *the bitch*, the manipulative, scheming and dangerous sneak and cheat
- ■ *the victim*, the passive female who suffers accident, disease or violence
- ■ *the decoy*, the heroine disguised as a victim, apparently dependent and helpless but actually endowed with strong inner reserves
- ■ *the siren*, who uses her sexuality to lure her victims to a sticky end
- ■ *the courtesan*, the near-prostitute who appears as a cabaret hostess or saloon owner in US Westerns
- ■ *the witch*, who has extraordinary and seemingly unlimited power which may be used to fulfil the aims of a man who dominates her
- ■ *the matriarch*, who has authority, power and prestige, and is something of a heroine.

Meehan also found that women tend to be portrayed as either good or evil, not both: good women are submissive, sensitive and domesticated: and bad women are independent, rebellious and selfish. In addition, she found that fewer women than men are portrayed in the media, whether in advertisements, cartoons or soaps, and that middle-aged and older women whose looks may be fading find it particularly hard to get 'meaty' roles.

Media stereotypes are probably inevitable, especially in the advertising, entertainment and news industries, which need as wide an audience as possible to understand information as quickly as possible. Stereotypes fulfil the function, for they act as codes that give audiences a quick, common understanding of a person or group of people.

Anyone who examines the entertainment and news media will notice that members of ethnic and visible minorities are inadequately represented. This lack of diversity behind the scenes in newsrooms and film studios makes it more likely that portrayals of minorities are often stereotypical and – on occasion – demeaning. By either ignoring minorities or casting them in the role of villain, editors and journalists unconsciously tell us stories about who is important, who is trustworthy and who is a troublemaker. As these stories are repeated in the news, they can become the accepted view among those to whom alternative interpretations are not evident.

The portrayal of women

Television and other mass media have traditionally portrayed women in a limited number of roles, for instance the sex object, the mother-in-law or the nagging wife. Rarely are they portrayed as successfully combining marriage and a career. The most obvious example of this one-dimensional portrayal is in pornography, in which women are treated as flesh rather than as human beings.

Television advertisements on commercial channels tend to use stereotyped images. Trowler (1999) quotes research, which shows that:

- ■ women are seven times more likely to appear in ads for personal hygiene products than not to appear
- ■ 75 per cent of ads using women were related to bathroom or kitchen products
- ■ 38 per cent of women were pictured inside the home (14 per cent for men, who were more likely to be shown in business or outdoor settings)
- ■ twice as many women were shown with children than were men
- ■ 56 per cent of women in ads were judged to be only housewives
- ■ women's bodies are 'exploited shamelessly and quite unscrupulously in advertisements as sexual commodities to sell anything from aftershave to motor cycles'.

■ Activity

Using the information about the Meehan study, do you recognise these stereotypes, or are they out-of-date? Do you agree with Trowler who claims that television today is 'more feminised, with the increased programming of talk shows, quiz shows and soap operas'?

Try illustrating the types by reference to popular television programmes, listing an example or two for each. Are there any types with which you strongly disagree?

The portrayal of ethnic minorities

As with women, members of ethnic minorities are often portrayed in stereotyped roles. For instance, coverage of conflict situations between the police and the black community in some towns and cities is often unflattering to those engaged in protest about their conditions. Black people are also still liable to be on the receiving end of what some people would see as racist humour.

As with women, members of ethnic minority groups have long been under-represented in television soaps and drama. Coronation Street and other similar series are today more likely to include the occasional non-white person in the cast, although in many cases non-whites are the bit players who pass through the local pub or grace a crowd scene.

Case study

Lenny Henry on the British broadcasting media

Comedian and actor Lenny Henry has warned there are too few black and Asian people occupying senior roles in the UK media and called for a 'huge seismic shift' in recruitment.

Henry said there had been a concerted effort to increase the number of black people in front of the camera but they would continue to feel unrepresented until they held more management positions.

'I think there's been a concerted effort to up the ante as far as presenters and broadcasters from the ethnic minorities are concerned. But it is not enough,' he said during a live chat on the Guardian's arts website this afternoon.

'Until there are more people of colour involved in the decision-making pro-cesses both on mainstream commercial TV and on the BBC, black and brown people in this country will never feel they are represented fairly on television.

It has changed significantly in the last ten years but I think our problem is we are impatient for change.' ...

The BBC director general, Greg Dyke, famously declared he was going to end the 'hideously white' ethos of the corporation. However, there is 'little evidence so far that the BBC is attracting more people from ethnic minorities to its output', according to the 2002/3 annual report ...

BECTU, Britain's biggest broadcasting union, recently branded UK television 'institutionally racist', accusing programme-makers of excluding ethnic minorities and ghettoising them away from mainstream shows.

Channel 4 newscaster Jon Snow has also claimed that when black and Asian trainees enter the newsroom they are encouraged to become reporters so they can be seen by viewers. This gives the impression that the media employ more people from ethnic minorities than is really the case.

Source: Media Guardian, 25 November 2003

Further information

Racial stereotypes

Trowler's study includes a list of regular stereotypes that have traditionally appeared in television programmes and in tabloid newspapers. They are:

- parasites, 'those who have come to the UK to live off social security'
- athletes and musicians, a positive stereotype undermined only by the suggestion that Afro-Caribbeans are only good at particular sports and interested in specific varieties of music
- criminals, the muggers responsible for 'black crime'
- Sambo types, 'the happy, laughing, dancing imbeciles with rolling eyes and widespread empty grins' who have now largely departed from the small screen but were once common at the movies
- brute savages, the characters who at one time appeared in televised versions of children's adventure stories
- pidgin English speakers, people who only seem to speak in what seems like a caricature of English.

Activity

Do you recognise the stereotypes listed by Trowler concerning the presentation of members of ethnic minorities on television? Again, for each one mentioned, see if you can think of a couple of examples to illustrate them in present or recent programming. Are any of the stereotypes no longer applicable?

Summary questions

1 Are the media biased against members of ethnic minority groups?

2 Are stereotypes necessarily harmful?

3 Sterotyping – useful shorthand or an ally of prejudice and discrimination? Discuss.

3 Prejudice, discrimination and disadvantage

Learning objectives:

- ■ to be able to define the concepts of prejudice and discrimination

- ■ to understand the different forms prejudice and discrimination can take

- ■ to have knowledge of the differential life chances of people in the UK

- ■ to understand the relationship of life chances to gender, social class, age, disability, sexuality and ethnicity

- ■ to understand the different definitions of poverty, explanations of causes and consequences of poverty.

■ Key terms

Prejudice: an opinion – especially an unfavourable one – formed without adequate information and facts.

Discrimination: the unfair treatment of a person or social group, based on prejudice.

Roma peoples: commonly known as Gypsies, a traditionally nomadic people who originated in Northern India but are today particularly concentrated in parts of Europe.

Racial prejudice: the belief, without reasoned evidence, that members of other racial groups are different and inferior. It is therefore an important constituent of racism.

The word **prejudice** literally means 'prejudgement', making one's mind up prior to being aware of the full facts of the situation. Prejudice against a particular group of people – for instance, members of an ethnic minority – involves prejudging members of that community before understanding its habits and lifestyle or becoming acquainted with them as a result of shared experiences. Prejudice can be positive or negative, in favour of or against individuals or circumstances. Usually, it is negative. It often results in **discrimination**, which involves a negative response to other people. This discrimination in turn disadvantages those people in various ways.

■ Forms of prejudice

Many groups have been the victims of negative attitudes, including the **Roma peoples** of Eastern Europe and the Jews in late 19th-century Russia. In Britain, prejudice has been at various times directed against disabled people (disablism), against women (sexism) and against Jews and the post-1945 immigrants, particularly those from the New Commonwealth (racism).

Racial prejudice against the new arrivals from the 1950s onwards may be explained in several ways. Some people have suggested that prejudiced attitudes originated with missionaries in the late 19th century who returned to England with stories of seemingly strange and unfamiliar customs and practices of local people. More usual explanations are that prejudice is based on ignorance of the unknown, of people who are different. People in the majority community have a natural suspicion of minorities who come into their country, of whom they know little, who have a different lifestyle, who speak, dress and act distinctively. When those newcomers form a close-knit group in a locality and do not choose to mix with the wider community, such suspicion is strengthened. When they look different, again this feeds prejudice. Differences are interpreted as threatening (see the verse of Kipling's poem in the Activity on page 45).

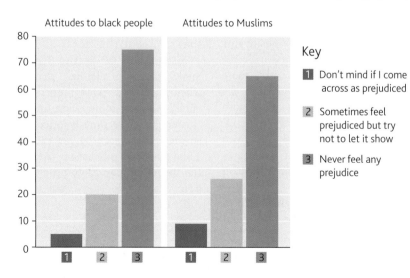

Fig. 3.1 *Levels of prejudice in British society*

Case study

Levels of racial prejudice in the UK, 1987–2002

After several years of decline, prejudice began to increase again in 2002:

- 1987 39 per cent admitted to being prejudiced
- 2001 25 per cent
- 2002 31 per cent (2 per cent admitted to being 'very prejudiced').

The authors of the survey, Catherine Rothon and Anthony Heath, claimed that 'overall, there's been a gradual move away from prejudice over the last few decades'. They found no link between the number of people settling in the UK and the level of prejudice. Instead, they said it was 'noticeable that there was a huge increase in articles relating to immigration from 2000 onwards'. This, the report suggested, 'could well be linked with the reversal in 2002 of what had until then been a downward trend in levels of prejudice'. They suggested this was linked to the increase in prejudice on media reports about immigration and a possible reaction to the September 11 attacks.

The report said that people were more likely to become racially prejudiced as they grew older, although the effect of this would be 'very small'. It predicted a return to increasing tolerance in the years to come. It suggested this would happen as more people went to university: 'People with degrees are less likely to describe themselves as prejudiced than are other educational groups'. Fewer than one in five graduates (18 per cent) admit to being prejudiced, compared with over a third (35 per cent) of those with no qualifications.

Source: 'Trends in racial prejudice', in Park, A., Curtice, J., Thomson, K., Jarvis, L. and Bromley, C. (eds), British Social Attitudes Survey (20), Sage, London, December 2003

Another factor might involve **scapegoating**. Scapegoating theory is usually relevant to prejudice at times of economic decline or social tension. It was easy for members of the **Nazi Party** in interwar Germany to whip up anti-Jewish feeling at a time when there were Germans without employment and many well-paid professional positions were occupied by Jews. Scapegoating involves projecting the blame for one's own misfortunes on some other individual or group, instead of examining fundamental causes. It is easy for white people to scapegoat black people by claiming that they would be in work were it not for those immigrants who have taken available jobs. In times of recession, this can be a powerful feeling.

Much prejudice is ultimately rooted in fear of the unfamiliar. That fear might also be based on the expectation that newcomers will disproportionately make demands on public services such as education and health, or on unemployment benefits. Women might fear that maternity beds will be unavailable to them because of the higher birth rate among members of some ethnic minorities. Parents may fear that their children's opportunities at school will be impeded because teachers have to spend much of their time on youngsters who have little or no command of basic English.

Racism and racist feelings are resistant to change and can result in discrimination towards and the disadvantage of minority groups. This illustrates the dangers of making general statements about communities and their inhabitants, and failing to recognise that communities are made up of individuals with their own personal qualities. The combination of prejudice and stereotyping makes it all too easy to label large groups of people as dishonest, lazy or in some way undesirable.

Activity

Father, Mother and Me
Sister and Auntie say
All the people like us are We,
And everyone else is They.

1 What point do you think was being made by the poet Rudyard Kipling?

2 How does it apply to the issue of prejudice against immigrants?

Hint

As you read through this chapter, the emphasis is on whether or not we are all equal citizens. The existence of prejudice, discrimination and disadvantage all suggest that we are not as equal as we might like to think we are. Be on the look-out for evidence that illustrates the three characteristics, for example, latest reports on the news or instances in people's conversation.

Citizenship is a subject that flourishes on an up-to-date understanding of British society. Examiners will be keen to see that you possess a fund of useful examples to enliven your answers.

Key terms

Scapegoating: refers to attempts to make a person or group bear the blame for the difficulties and failings of others.

Nazi Party: the popular name of the National Socialist German Workers' Party, which was formed in 1919 and elected to power in Germany in 1933 under the leadership of Adolf Hitler.

■ Forms of racial discrimination

Racial discrimination describes unequal treatment on the basis of race or ethnicity. It was widely practised in the early days of New Commonwealth immigration.

Discrimination has been illegal in Britain since the legislation of the 1960s, which defined it as 'treating a person less favourably than another person on grounds of colour, race or ethnic or national origin'. Prior to that legislation, discrimination in the area of employment was common. On occasion, the discrimination was very explicit, taking the form in some cases of notices such as 'No black bastards here' or 'We don't want any more Indians'. Discrimination in the private letting of rented accommodation was also a frequent occurrence, with advertisements in shop windows often including the phrase 'No coloureds'.

Both **direct** and **indirect discrimination** are banned. In other words, obvious discrimination is not allowed (very offensive speech or action and 'incitement to racial hatred'). Neither is a more subtle form, in which conditions are laid down that no member of an ethnic minority could ever meet. A 'No blacks' notice is direct discrimination; whereas a 'No people whose grandparents were born outside Britain' rule is indirect discrimination.

Direct discrimination occurs when you are able to show that you have been treated less favourably on racial grounds than others in similar circumstances. To prove this, it will help if you can give an example of someone from a different racial group who, in similar circumstances, has been, or would have been, treated more favourably than you. Racist abuse and harassment are overt forms of direct discrimination.

Key terms

Direct discrimination: occurs when someone is treated less favourably than another on grounds of his or her perceived or actual age, disability, gender or ethnic background. For instance, it is unlawful to decide not to employ, deny promotion to or dismiss someone because of his or her religion or beliefs.

Indirect discrimination: occurs where the effect of certain apparently neutral requirements, conditions or practices imposed by an employer or education provider have a disproportionately adverse impact on one group or other. For instance, a rule that employees or pupils must not wear headgear could exclude Sikh men and boys who wear a turban in accordance with practice within their racial group.

■ Case study

Indirect discrimination in practice

An example of indirect discrimination occurred in the case of *Aina v Employment Service* (2002). A black African employee applied for the post of equal opportunities manager and was assessed as having the skills and ability for the job. However, his application was rejected because, unknown to him, the post was open only to those within the organisation who were permanent staff at higher grades than his. The employment tribunal held that there was no justification for the requirement. This therefore was indirect discrimination on racial grounds.

Extract based on one provided on the Equality and Human Rights Commission website

■ Activities

1 List the various explanations that might be offered to explain racial prejudice. Write a few sentences to say which you find the most convincing. (In the process, you might consider your own feelings and in particular whether or not you feel or have experienced prejudice.)

2 A number of surveys have found that racial prejudice and discrimination still exist in Britain today. Can you think of any examples of such prejudice or discrimination?

3 Write a paragraph in your own words to distinguish between direct and indirect discrimination.

Bases of prejudice

In addition to the areas of immigration and race relations, debate about the rights and merits of equal treatment has focused on the issues surrounding other groups in society, in particular the treatment of Muslims, gays and lesbians, as well as gender discrimination. In this section, we also briefly mention **ableism** and **ageism**.

Many of the terms used to describe strong dislike of or discrimination towards particular groups end with the suffix 'phobia', meaning fear or loathing. For instance, xenophobia refers to individual or cultural hostility to foreigners or outsiders.

Islamophobia

Immigration and race have been key factors associated with religion, leading to a rapid increase in support for Islamic beliefs in the UK (see the table on page 35 for an indication of the extent to which Britain has become a multi-faith society).

Islamophobia refers to demonisation, dislike or fear of or prejudice against Muslims or Islamic culture. In 1997, the Runnymede Trust produced a widely accepted definition of Islamophobia, describing it as the 'dread or hatred of Islam and therefore, leading to the fear and dislike of all Muslims', stating that it also refers to the practice of discriminating against them by excluding them from the economic, social and public life of the nation. Runnymede noted that it includes the perception that Islam has no values in common with other cultures, is inferior to the West and is a fanatical, fundamentalist and violent creed, rather than a true religion.

Specifically, Runnymede detected eight key characteristics of Islamophobia:

1 Islam is seen as a monolithic bloc, static and unresponsive to change.
2 Islam is seen as separate and 'other'. It does not have values in common with other cultures, is not affected by them and does not influence them.
3 Islam is seen as inferior to the West. It is seen as barbaric, irrational, primitive and sexist.
4 Islam is seen as violent, aggressive, threatening, supportive of terrorism and engaged in a 'clash of civilisations'.
5 Islam is seen as a political ideology and is used for political or military advantage.
6 Criticisms made of the West by Islam are rejected out of hand.
7 Hostility towards Islam is used to justify discriminatory practices towards Muslims and exclusion of Muslims from mainstream society.
8 Anti-Muslim hostility is seen as natural or normal.

Islamophobia in the UK is associated with the increased presence of Muslims in the Western world and in Britain in particular. It gained considerable impetus from the 9/11 attacks on the World Trade Center and the London bombings four years later.

Homophobia

Homosexuality refers to the sexual orientation of a person who is sexually and romantically attracted to others of their own gender. Homosexual men are often referred to as 'gay'. So too are women with same-sex leanings, although more often they are referred to as 'lesbians'.

Key terms

Ableism: discrimination in favour of able-bodied people and against those who are disabled.

Ageism: discrimination based on chronological age, especially against the elderly. The assumption made is that a person's age should determine their social status and their roles in society.

Key terms

Homophobia: refers to an irrational fear and hatred of homosexuals and homosexual activity and behaviour based upon that fear or contempt.

Further information

Homophobia and bullying

I came out to friends in school about a year and a half ago. It was between me and a few good friends but of course the whole school knew within a couple of days.

I came out to my best friend first and she said she had already thought so anyway and she didn't mind. So I felt great and I thought that everyone else would be fine about it. I was bullied for over five years; the worst was in year 10 when I started my GCSEs. People kind of outed me and then it was hell for months. It got so bad, I was put on anti-depressants and had to see a psychologist.

Extracts from two case studies on the Stonewall website

Activity

Consider the illustration in Fig 3.2. Do you consider the protest to be homophobic?

Explain your answer.

There is no single definition for the term **homophobia**, as it covers a wide range of different viewpoints and attitudes. Homophobia often describes hostility to or fear or hatred of gay people and homosexuality, but it is not limited to this specifically. It may refer to the attempt or desire to discriminate against homosexuals. Someone who dislikes gay people or is violent towards or who has distaste for the actions they perform might be described as homophobic.

Homophobia has a long history and although the law on homosexuality has been amended in recent decades it continues to exist among some people. Prior to 1967, consenting relations between men of the same sex were forbidden by law. However, in recent decades, there has been a near-revolution in attitudes. Many people with gay or lesbian preferences have felt sufficiently confident to 'come out'. Politicians, entertainers and others prominent in public life have declared themselves to be gay. Even institutions such as the armed services and the Church of England have been forced to reconsider their traditional attitudes. Whereas a previous archbishop of Canterbury argued that God loves homosexuals but not the sin they commit, more liberal bishops have managed to reconcile homosexuality with religious belief.

Attitudes towards same-sex relationships between consenting adults have become notably more tolerant, with political opinion gradually accepting the notion of gay rights. Yet in spite of the changes in popular attitudes, homophobia can cause extreme harm and disruption in the lives of young gay and lesbian people. A homophobic climate forces them to decide whether to declare their sexual orientation and face possible discrimination from their family and society, or conceal their sexuality. Having a concealed identity can cause great anxiety and the dilemma of whether to 'come out' can cause severe personal distress. Equally, for young people who have been brought up to believe that homosexuality is wrong, the realisation that they might be gay can cause them to feel immoral, and lead to feelings of low self-esteem.

Fig. 3.2 *A protest by a member of Westboro Baptist Church, 19 April 2006*

Case study

Stonewall – popular attitudes to and treatment of the gay community

Stonewall is a gay rights organisation. It was founded in 1989 by a small group of women and men who had been active in the struggle against Section 28 of the Local Government Act. It has campaigned actively in recent years to:

- secure a new criminal offence of inciting hatred against lesbian, gay and bisexual (LGB) people
- gain statutory protection for LGB people from discrimination in the provision of goods, facilities and services
- achieve full partnership rights for same-sex couples
- secure full legal recognition for same-sex parents
- tackle homophobia and homophobic **bullying** in schools
- make the public aware of the new employment equality legislation.

Stonewall's *The School Report: The Experiences of Young Gay People in Britain's Schools*, produced in 2007, found that homophobia was experienced more often and in a more extreme form by young people than by adults. It noted that 92 per cent of homosexual, lesbian and bisexual pupils had been subject to verbal abuse; 67 per cent had experienced overt bullying in school; and 41 per cent had been physically assaulted.

Stonewall's 2008 survey, *Serves You Right: Lesbian and Gay People's Expectations of Discrimination*, found that 66 per cent of gay and lesbian people would expect to face barriers due to their sexuality if they wanted to run as an MP in the UK. One in five lesbian and gay people in the UK said they had experienced bullying in the workplace as a result of their sexual orientation.

Key terms

Bullying: refers to the act of intentionally causing harm to others, through verbal harassment, physical assault or other means of coercion such as manipulation. It takes many forms, but the UK has no legal definition to say exactly what it includes. It is done to coerce others by fear or threat.

Sexism

Sexism is a type of prejudice or discrimination based on gender. It involves dislike of or discrimination or hatred towards people based on their sex. It can also more widely refer to the belief that one gender is superior to the other; hatred or distrust towards the opposite or same sex as a whole; and imposing stereotypes of femininity on females or masculinity on males. For the most part the term is particularly employed to refer to discrimination against females, though it is possible for males to be discriminated against on account of their gender as well. People who actively engage in this type of discrimination are called sexists.

Sexism manifests itself in a number of ways, including:

- the use of offensive terms and language
- making prejudiced statements about the other gender or members of the other gender
- paying someone less or promoting them less often based on their gender
- believing that you are better than someone of the other gender
- any discrimination based solely on someone's gender.

Fig. 3.3 *Moira Stewart (1949–) was the first African-Caribbean newsreader on BBC television and the winner in 2004 of a Global Diversity Award for being such an effective role model. Her long career was brought to a halt when the director-general decided early in 2007 that 'her skills as a newsreader have become redundant in the modern age'. He denied 'sexism, racism or ageism' in making his decision*

Activities

1 Does the fact of being 58 years old mean that a newsreader's skills 'have become redundant in the modern age'? Discuss.

2 Make a list of the possible advantages and disadvantages of employing a person over 60 as part of a workforce.

Sexual discrimination can arise in a wide range of social situations. At school or college, girls might claim that they are being excluded from a particular opportunity or that they are being sexually harassed. At work, employees may be asked discriminatory questions during a job interview. For instance, in seeking promotion young women might be asked about their intentions of interrupting their careers to get married and/or have children. Or again, they may have to put up with sexual harassment from their employer or those above them in the management hierarchy.

Ageism and age discrimination

Ageism is any prejudice or discrimination against individuals or groups on account of their age. The term derives from the United States and was coined to denote discrimination against elderly people. However, the term has also been used in reference to discrimination against children and young adults, to describe ignoring their ideas because they are young or assuming that they should behave a certain way because of their age. Age discrimination is rarely about active dislike (unlike racism, for example), but is based on stereotyped prejudices and myths. For example, the generalisations that younger workers are less committed and older workers more loyal could be construed as ageist assumptions. In employment, it applies when someone's age is used as the basis for employment decisions, for example not recruiting someone because they are perceived to be too young or old.

Age discrimination is the latest type of discrimination to be tackled after race and sex discrimination. However, it has not had the high profile of the others, both of which have been outlawed for many years. According to the unions, it is the most widespread type of discrimination in the workplace and takes different forms. It can be overt and deliberate, or it can be subtle and perhaps even unintentional. Overt discrimination may involve someone being made redundant because they are considered too old for the job. Indirect discrimination might involve making ageist comments. In some industries, such as media and advertising, age discrimination has been endemic, almost accepted fact of life for decades.

Ableism and disability

Ableism involves discrimination or prejudice in favour of able-bodied people and against people with disabilities, especially physical ones. Disability refers to medical conditions that leave those who suffer from them significantly impaired, relative to members of the rest of society. The term is often used to refer to individual functioning, including cognitive, intellectual, physical or sensory impairment. It covers a variety of forms of mental illness, as well as various types of chronic and often degenerative disease. Nearly 2 million people fall within the broad category of 'disabled people'.

Rauscher and McClintock (1997) define ableism as 'a pervasive system of discrimination and exclusion that oppresses people who have mental, emotional, and physical disabilities'. They note that:

> Deeply rooted beliefs about health, productivity, beauty, and the value of human life, perpetuated by the public and private media, combine to create an environment that is often hostile to those whose physical, emotional, cognitive, or sensory abilities fall outside the scope of what is currently defined as socially acceptable.

Examples of ableism include inaccessible public buildings, unusable transportation systems and segregated education.

The hierarchy of prejudice

Allport's *The Nature of Prejudice* (1954) noted that negative attitudes tend to express themselves in actions. Prejudice and discrimination may take several forms. Allport distinguished a hierarchy of five forms of prejudice, of ascending seriousness:

1 **Antilocution** means that a majority group freely make jokes about a minority group. Speech is in terms of negative stereotypes and negative images. Commonly seen as harmless by the majority, antilocution itself may not be harmful but it sets the stage for more severe outlets for prejudice. It is sometimes known as 'hate speech', which includes speech intended to degrade, intimidate or incite violence or prejudicial action against a person or group of people based on such things as their race, gender, age, ethnicity, national origin, religion, sexual orientation, gender identity, disability, language ability, moral or political views, socio-economic class, occupation or appearance (such as height, weight or hair colour). Examples include telling ethnic jokes or making statements such as 'all blacks are lazy' or 'Jews are cheap and rich'.

2 *Avoidance* refers to situations where prejudice is more intense. Those belonging to a minority group are actively avoided by members of the majority group, even at the cost of considerable inconvenience. No direct harm may be intended, but harm is done through isolation. Examples include never socialising with a particular group or walking on the opposite side of the street.

3 *Discrimination* applies when a minority group is discriminated against by denying them opportunities and services and so putting prejudice into action. Discriminatory behaviour has the specific goal of harming the minority group by preventing them from achieving goals, getting education or jobs etc. The majority group is actively trying to harm the minority.

Discrimination is a more active form of prejudice. It covers detrimental distinctions and choices that have an adverse impact on the group in question, as when all members of a group are excluded from certain types of employment or educational opportunities.

Case study

Harassment in the workplace
Anisetti v Tokyo-Mitsubishi International plc (1998)

The Indian-born head of credit derivatives at an international Japanese bank in London resigned, claiming he had been made to feel like a 'second-class citizen' by his Japanese employers. He said he had been humiliated, excluded by workers speaking Japanese and underpaid, simply because he was not Japanese. The bank argued that it was 'natural' for Japanese staff to use their own language among themselves.

An employment tribunal upheld the complainant's claim that he had been discriminated against unlawfully, not because of his Indian national origins, but because he was not Japanese. The tribunal noted that the bank had maintained a practice which had effectively excluded the complainant from various activities, and treated him less favourably than others. The complainant was awarded around £1 million in compensation.

Key terms

Antilocution: simply means 'bad-mouthing'. People who have prejudices talk about them with like-minded friends. Often referred to as hate speech, it involves the making of hostile verbal remarks about a group of people or a community.

Activity

Do you agree with Dr Allport that there is a natural progression that leads from antilocution to much more grave offences?

Key terms

Lynching: hanging carried out by a mob without a trial, an act that is often racially motivated.

Pogroms: organised persecution (often officially encouraged) of a minority ethnic group, especially that of the Jews by the Russian authorities in the late 19th century.

'Tarring and feathering': a form of physical punishment that involves smearing tar and feathers over someone, as a form of enforcing a kind of justice by ritual humiliation.

The Troubles: the period of conflict from the late 1960s to the mid-1990s in Northern Ireland in which there was communal violence, rioting and the threat of disorder involving Republican and Loyalist paramilitary organisations, the Royal Ulster Constabulary (RUC), the British army and others.

Ethnic cleansing: refers to the various policies and practices designed to bring about the mass expulsion or extermination of people from a minority ethnic or religious group within a certain area.

Genocide: the systematic killing and ultimately destruction of a civilian population, as in the case of the Jews, Poles or Gypsies in the Second World War. The intention is to eliminate particular political, cultural or religious groups.

Institutional (or structural) racism: a form of racism that occurs in public bodies, such as universities and in private corporations. Coined by a black power advocate in the US some 40 years ago, the term describes the racism that resides – covertly or overtly – in the policies, procedures, operations and culture of such institutions.

4 *Physical attack* occurs when members of the majority group vandalise minority group things, burn property and carry out violent attacks on individuals or groups. Physical harm is done to members of the minority group. Particularly severe and well-documented examples are **lynchings** of black Americans in Southern states, **pogroms** against Jews in Europe, and '**tarring and feathering**' carried out by members of some sectarian groups in Northern Ireland, in the era of **The Troubles**. Other activities might involve throwing rocks or other missiles, burning crosses, destroying property and rape or beatings.

5 *Extermination* is where the majority group seeks the total extermination of the minority group, on the grounds of their race/ethnicity. In these cases, the intention is to eliminate the entire group of people (e.g. in Hitler's Final Solution of the 'Jewish Problem', **ethnic cleansing** in former Yugoslavia, and the **genocide** practised particularly against the Tutsis in Rwanda). Lynching, murder and genocide are commonplace.

Antilocution can easily lead to various forms of discrimination that are found acceptable by the general population or society. Once derogatory verbal remarks become acceptable to a society, this may lead to other damaging forms of behaviour. Research about hate crimes and genocide usually finds that the person or group committing the hate crime or genocide must first hold negative views of the person, group or community.

Racial attacks

As Allport observed, prejudice and discrimination can advance to the level of attacks. In recent years, much attention has focused on the state of race relations in Britain's large cities. The murder of Stephen Lawrence in South London (1993) by a group of white youths proved to be a key event in a number of ways. It seemed to be a crime with no motive other than racial hatred, pointing to the want of understanding of individuals and groups for others who were different to themselves. It led to suggestions that the police had not investigated the crime as carefully and thoroughly as they might have done, fuelling demands by the Lawrence family and other campaigners for a full inquiry. The resulting Macpherson Inquiry drew attention to '**institutional racism**' within the police force, a situation where racist attitudes were part of the culture of many officers, including some occupying important positions in the hierarchy. It drew attention to the breakdown in trust between the community and the police.

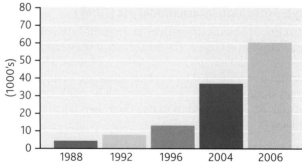

Fig. 3.4 *Racial attacks in England and Wales.* Note the higher figures in the British Crime Survey (based on people's experiences and perceptions of crime), which dropped to 139,000 in 2006 compared with 179,000 the previous year. According to the Institute of Race Relations, there have since 1991 been over 65 murders in mainland Britain with a suspected or known racial motive

Source: Home Office figures of crimes handled by the police

Police forces have collected information on racial incidents from 1986 onwards. They employ a definition that covers: 'Any incident in which it appears to the reporting or investigating officer that the complaint involves an element of racial motivation: or any incident which includes an allegation of racial motivation made by any person'. As a result of the Macpherson review, the definition was amended. Today, 'a racist incident is any incident which is perceived to be racist by the victim or any other person'.

Disadvantage: how are life chances distributed?

The nature of life chances

Inequality in the distribution of wealth and income has long been a feature of most countries including Britain. For many centuries, the division between the rich and the poor was regarded as an unalterable fact of life. Usually, the former constituted a tiny minority, which exercised substantial power. In contrast, poverty was commonly the lot of the majority who were denied much say in the way their societies were governed.

Many would see these differences as being largely inevitable, as some people use their talents and flourish whereas others – with less talent and/or opportunity – trail behind. In their view, the important thing is that everyone should have adequate means to lead a comfortable life. In their view, inequality is inevitable in a capitalist society, in which the bulk of industry and other forms of property are in private hands.

Others feel that differences in wealth and income are too marked. These differences are too influential in determining people's living standards, their ability to enjoy good education, health, holidays and other things that make life enjoyable, and that some measure of redistribution is desirable. In their view, the stranglehold of the wealthy and influential over senior positions in British public life is undesirable.

Inequality today appears to be as marked as it ever was. The sources of wealth may have changed over time and there has been significant **social mobility**. Yet the gulf between rich and poor stubbornly remains. It has a clear impact on life chances and the opportunities available to individuals to improve their quality of life by having access to societal resources such as education, health care and shelter. These opportunities are influenced by the inequality in society. Specifically, the German sociologist, Max Weber (1864–1920), identified three elements that determine a person's life chances: economic factors, power and status.

Life chances can be illustrated by reference to two areas of policy that impact upon us all.

Life chances in relation to education and employment/income

Education

According to National Statistics, the gap in GCSE attainment levels by parental socio-economic group increased in the 1990s. In 1992, 60 per cent of children with parents in managerial or professional occupations attained five or more GCSEs, grade A* to C. This was 44 per cent more than the proportion for children with parents in unskilled manual occupations. In 1999, the gap had risen to 49 per cent. By 2002, it had dropped back to 45 per cent (77 per cent, as against 32 per cent).

On the basis of ethnic background, whereas children born into Indian families achieve highly, out-performing any other social group, those of Afro-Caribbean or Bangladeshi/Pakistan origin fare less well.

The underachievement of black children in schools, 1971

In a study published nearly four decades ago, Bernard Coard identified five factors that limited achievement:

- The racist policies and practices of the education authorities of that period.

- Racism within the curriculum itself; the actual reading materials that the children were obliged to use. The poor self-image, self-esteem and self-belief which the vast majority of the black children experienced.

- Low teacher expectations, and how destructive a force these could be.

- Inadequate black parental knowledge of and involvement in what was happening to their children at school in that period.

- The lack of black parental organisation to tackle the situation faced by their children; including especially the need for more black teachers in the schools, and the need to set up black supplementary schools in the black community.

Source: Bernard Coard, How the West Indian Child is Made Educationally Subnormal in the British School System, New Beacon Books, 1971

Raising black performance

Highlighting the issues facing one particular group of school children is always a tricky matter.

It is sensitive enough if you are highlighting gender or class. But when you start to talk about the particular needs of one ethnic group you are tiptoeing into a minefield. Yet this is exactly what Saturday's conference on 'London Schools and the Black Child' is doing. Its organiser, the Labour MP Diane Abbott, says she has had to fight hard to get government, schools and parents to recognise that children of African and African-Caribbean descent have particular needs which are not being met by the school system. The biggest obstacle is what is known as the 'colour blind' approach. This …is rooted in the best of intentions, namely to counter conscious or unconscious prejudice. But perhaps we have now got to the point where a simple 'colour blind' policy is not only not helping those it is meant to protect, but may be putting them at a disadvantage.

Children of African and African-Caribbean origin show a distinctively different pattern of progress in schools. At age five, so-called 'baseline' testing has shown they are performing as well as, if not better, than other groups.

But by the start of secondary school they are starting to fall behind and statistics show that black African-Caribbean pupils are between three and six times more likely to be expelled from school.

Although there is an absence of detailed statistics, GCSE results also show that African-Caribbean pupils do less well than other ethnic groups in formal examinations.

Source: Mike Baker (BBC education correspondent), BBC News, 16 March 2002

The impact of tuition fees

TUITION FEES FAVOUR THE RICH (headline in The Guardian, *14 February 2008)*

The article suggested that teenagers from poorer families are turning their backs on a university education, because of fears they will be saddled with thousands of pounds worth of debt. It also claimed that:

- the number of students planning to study at institutions nearby has risen from 18 per cent in 1998 to 56 per cent 10 years later

- those from independent schools are more likely to move to a university in a different city, opening up the option of Oxbridge and other leading institutions: their decisions were made on the basis of reputations, rather than costs

- students seemed to be confused by the complex system of bursaries and grants for which they might be eligible

By contrast, Government figures suggest an overall 7 per cent rise in university applications to a record level, including a modest rise in the number from lower socio-economic groups.

Beyond GCSE, middle-class children are more likely than working-class children to stay on at school for study in the sixth form or in further education. In 2002, 87 per cent of 16 year olds with parents in higher professional occupations were in full-time education. This compares with 60 per cent for those with parents in 'routine occupations' and 58 per cent with parents in 'lower supervisory' ones.

The same picture is true of access to higher education. The numbers who proceed from school to college or university have substantially increased over the last 40 years, from some 5 per cent in the early 1960s to more than 40 per cent today. This has provided many children with an opportunity to acquire high qualifications and move up the class ladder. However, the rapid expansion has primarily been of benefit to middle-class pupils, while still offering access for only a small minority of the children of the poorest. Recent evidence suggests that the introduction of tuition fees and student loans has changed the thinking of would-be undergraduates as to whether and where they undertake further study. Full-time undergraduates are liable to pay tuition fees of up to £3,000 a year, but the poorest students (where parents earn less than a combined total of £17,500 per year) are eligible for non-repayable support of up to £3,000 year.

Activity

Write a few sentences to explain what you think are the main reasons for the greater attainment levels of females rather than males at GCSE, GCE and degree level. Think about the ones listed below, although you may include any others that come to mind:

■ Girls find it easier to focus on study.

■ Boys have not improved their performance at the same rates as girls in the early years. They never recover, especially in language-related subjects.

■ The demand for high levels of female labour since 1945 has raised expectations of girls and fuelled the feminist campaign for gender equality.

■ The efforts of government and policy-makers to encourage girls to boost take-up of science and technical education.

Employment and income prospects

School attainment strongly influences employment prospects. The likelihood of being employed is greater for those with higher qualifications. In 2003, 88 per cent of working age adults with a degree were in full-time work, compared to 50 per cent with no qualifications. Moreover, there is a clear relationship between higher qualifications and higher earnings, particularly for those in possession of a degree. The average gross weekly income of full-time employees with a degree was £632 in 2003. This was more than double the weekly income of £298 for those with no qualifications.

Life chances in relation to health

Socio-economic class has long been linked to inequalities in healthcare provision. A report in 1842 showed that the average age at death in Liverpool was 35 for members of the gentry and professionals and 15 for labourers, mechanics and servants. Much more recently, in 1980 the Black Report pointed to the relationship between social class and health inequalities, by making particular reference to varying infant mortality rates, levels of cancer and heart disease, access to facilities in the National Health Service (NHS) and life expectancy. Any such study now would also need to include figures for obesity. Then and today,

Activities

1   Suggest reasons that may account for the relative school success of Indian children in comparison with those of African-Caribbean background.

2   Do you think that any of the barriers faced by black children of a few decades ago are still relevant today? If so, which ones?

3   List points that can be made for and against the introduction of tuition fees.

4   Does it matter if young people from poorer backgrounds feel they need to apply to a local centre of higher learning (so that they can live at home), rather than apply to a range of locations further away from home?

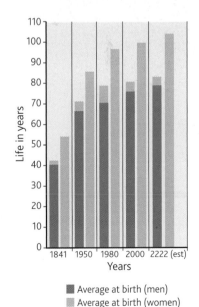

Fig. 3.5 *Life expectancy (LE) in England and Wales*

Source: Office of Health Economics

Further information

Health in Blackpool

... Poor health manifests itself within the context of social deprivation.

When compared to both the North West and England as a whole, the health of the people of Blackpool is relatively poor with reduced quality of life and early death.

Life expectancy in Blackpool for males has shown little improvement over the last 10 years ... For women the picture is similar ... and unlike for men, no recent improvement. Of the 374 Local Authorities in England and Wales, Blackpool has the second worst life expectancy for men.

There are also significant inequalities within Blackpool itself; people residing in some areas, live substantially longer than those from adjacent areas.

An analysis of the causes of early death in Blackpool compared to the national average highlights the reasons for poor life expectancy, as being digestive disorders which are related to alcohol, injuries and poison, coronary heart disease and cancer. The latter diseases are caused by poor nutrition, low levels of physical activity and smoking.

Source: Health and Well-being Improvement Plan, *Blackpool Council, 2006*

Activities

1 Suggest and list reasons why in general women outlive men. You may need to look up the subject on the internet.

2 Suggest reasons why a working-class man living in Newcastle upon Tyne is likely to have a shorter life than a working-class man living in Surrey.

3 Using the example of Blackpool to help you, write a few sentences to explain the link between health, life expectancy and poverty.

there is clear evidence that economic deprivation is a key factor in poor public health. When asked about health inequalities on *BBC Breakfast* Tony Blair said 'It is to do with poverty. It's to do with diet; it's to do with exercise. It starts at school and it starts with what parents feed their children.' He was speaking as the new *Health Profile of England* was unveiled by the Department of Health (October 2006).

Among the findings of the *Health Profile*, there were some positive indicators, notably:

■ life expectancy continues to rise and is now at its highest ever level

■ substantial recent falls have occurred in mortality from the major targeted killers – circulatory diseases and cancer

■ infant mortality is now at its lowest ever level.

However, the report shows that many challenges remain, for example:

■ persistence of long-standing health inequalities

■ increasing rates of obesity in children

■ rising rates of diabetes

■ high rates of teenage pregnancies.

The report suggested the need to address both the more immediate determinants of health and health inequalities such as smoking, sexually transmitted infections, alcohol consumption and poor diet, and the more fundamental determinants such as poverty, education and housing. It illustrated various inequalities according to age, ethnicity, gender, geography (within England and Europe) and socio-economic group. The inequalities were being reduced between disadvantaged groups and areas and the national situation in killer diseases, but was widening between rich and poor in figures for infant mortality, in life expectancy between advantaged and disadvantaged areas of the country and between social classes in obesity trends.

■ On obesity, the report indicated that without dramatic action millions more children and adults would on existing trends be obese by 2010. A third of adults and a fifth of all children would be obese, leading to greater suffering from cancer, heart disease and type 2 diabetes. Women in the West Midlands were the most likely to be obese, while those living in the South-East and South-West were the least likely. For men, the greatest prevalence of obesity was in the Yorkshire and Humber region, while the least was in London.

■ On life expectancy, the findings were that men and women in northern counties die on average two years and one year earlier than their southern equivalents. Broadly, life expectancies diminish as one moves from the South to the North of England and to Scotland. However, there are distinct areas of lower life expectancies in local authorities in South-East Wales, Central London and Manchester. Figures for Glasgow are well below the UK average, men are likely to die 6.5 years earlier, and women 4.3 years earlier than the average.

Summary questions

1 What sort of measures should the government be taking to promote the life chances of all citizens?

2 Should we be concerned if a) white children fare better than African-Caribbean, Bangladeshi and Pakistani children and b) girls fare better than boys?

Life expectancy

According to the Office for National Statistics (2007), the variations in life expectancy among social classes persist. While it has risen for all social classes over the last 30 years, people in professional occupations have the longest expectation of life and those in the lowest class categories the shortest expectation.

Between 2002–5:

- life expectancy for all social groups improved
- males in the professional classes had a life expectancy at birth of 80.0, compared with 72.7 for those in the manual unskilled class, while for females, the figures were respectively 85.1 and 78.1
- unskilled men aged 65 could expect to live a further 14.1 years, approximately the same figure for professional men in the early 1970s.

Comparing the early 1970s to 2002–5, the increase in life expectancy at birth improved more significantly for men than women (8.0 years for non-manual and 6.8 years for manual employees, as against 5.2 and 4.8).

Poverty in Britain

Assessing **poverty** is complex and controversial, but by any absolute standards the people defined as poor in the UK are better off now than when the Welfare State began in the late 1940s. However, since the 1960s, there has been continuous debate among sociologists, pressure group activists and politicians about the extent of poverty and who should be counted within the category of 'the poor'.

Relative and absolute poverty

The definition of poverty adopted by the United Nations in 1995 referred to:

> … a condition characterised by severe deprivation of basic human needs, including good, safe drinking water, sanitation facilities, health, shelter, education and information. It depends not only on income but access to services.

Most writers would agree that in the UK this kind of **absolute poverty** is very limited in extent and that in comparison to underdeveloped countries such as Bangladesh or Ethiopia, poverty in the UK is a relative concept.

By **relative poverty**, we mean those who are deprived, feel poor and – judged by the standards of our own time and our own society – are poor. They lag seriously behind the rest of society and cannot afford the lifestyle of the average person. It is little consolation to the person experiencing deprivation in modern Britain to know that the British poor may certainly appear well placed when judged against the position of Bangladeshis or Ethiopians, for their plight cannot be judged by the absolute standards of the past or by experience elsewhere. Their survival may not be in doubt, but the fact is that they feel poor and, judged by the standards of their own time, are poor. As they look around at their contemporaries in society, they are only too aware of the greater prosperity enjoyed by some groups and how far they themselves lag behind these groups. They feel at a serious disadvantage.

Relative poverty does not allow for merely biological and basic environmental needs. People have social needs if they are to play a full part in society. If pensioners cannot afford to see their friends because they cannot afford to buy a round of drinks, are they not relatively

Key terms

Poverty: defined within the EU as household income below 60 per cent of the median disposable income level in that year. It is common to distinguish between absolute and relative poverty. The EU employs the relative concept.

Absolute poverty: the lack of sufficient necessities and resources with which to keep body and soul together.

Relative poverty: defines income or resources in relation to the average. It is concerned with the absence of the material needs that enable people to participate fully in accepted daily life.

Fig. 3.6 *Absolute poverty in Ethiopia*

poor? They similarly want to be able to buy toys and other gifts that their grandchildren might expect. If children at school lack the clothes, common-place possessions (such as computers or mobile phones) and opportunities to participate fully in social relationships, are they not also relatively poor?

Activities

1 Write a couple of sentences giving your reaction to the statements below:
- 'Poverty is not being able to afford the pair of new trainers that you would like to possess.'
- 'Poverty means not being able to go on an annual holiday.'
- 'Not being in work means that you are living in poverty.'
- 'Poverty in Britain is an urban and largely inner-city phenomenon.'
- 'There is no absolute poverty in Britain.'

2 Write a paragraph to explain your understanding of the nature of poverty in Britain.

Case study

Poverty in Blackpool

… Crime, disorder, anti-social behaviour and the misuse of drugs, cannot be viewed in isolation. The experience of these issues can vary from town to town and community to community.

Blackpool:

- ranks 24th in the Indices of **Multiple Deprivation**
- has a predominantly white population (98.4%)

The 2001 census showed that 25.5% of the town's population was aged 65 or over compared with 15.9% for England and Wales as a whole. It asked people to describe their health over the preceding 12 months:

- 13.8% said their health was not good in comparison to the national figure, which was 9.2%
- 25.4% had a long-term illness, in comparison to 18.2% nationally
- 9.8% considered themselves to be permanently sick or disabled, in comparison to the national figure of 5.5%.

Source: Crime, Disorder & Drugs Audit, A Profile of Blackpool, 2004: for further information, see www.bsafeblackpool.com

… For decades the coastal town of Blackpool, on the Irish Sea, was a favourite summer resort in England. However, with charter tourism the number of people travelling to foreign countries for their holidays increased, the town lost some of its appeal and gained some familiar symptoms of economic decline: reduced numbers of visitors; declines in seasonal trade, guest houses, hotels and other tourist facilities; and services closing down. The resident population of 153,000 still notices a difference between the quiet winter season and the buzz of high summer, but the new experiences of poverty and deprivation tell the story of the decline in the local tourist industry – the backbone of the town's economy. Many of the inhabitants have moved to Blackpool from other parts of the

Key terms

Multiple deprivation: the occurrence of several forms of deprivation concurrently, such as low income, poor housing and unemployment. The indices of multiple deprivation is based on six indicators: income deprivation, employment deprivation, health deprivation and disability, housing deprivation, education, skills and training deprivation, and geographical access to services such as a GP, post office and schools.

United Kingdom, still seeking seasonal work, but there are far fewer opportunities than there used to be. According to John Dempsey, who is a General Practitioner Project Worker at the Blackpool Citizens Advice Bureau, the town also attracts a lot of unemployed people. 'It's more pleasant to be unemployed here by the seaside, rather than somewhere else in a less attractive environment,' he says. But this means that Blackpool is attracting the social problems attached to unemployment, such as drug abuse and alcoholism, as well as poverty and deprivation.

Source: Sigrún Davídsdóttir, report entitled Combined Social Support and Health Care in Deprived Areas, *Citizens Advice Bureau in Blackpool, 2007*

… Seasonal employment in the town's tourist industry and the large stock of low-cost, privately rented accommodation mean there is a constant flow of people moving into and out of Blackpool. Poverty levels are high: Blackpool is the twelfth poorest area in the country. The number of children on Blackpool's child protection register who are vulnerable to, or experiencing, sexual abuse is, at 16%, almost twice the natural average, as is the number of children living in care homes or foster families. It is one of the only places in the country where girls do worse at school than boys. The suicide rate among the 15 to 19 age group in Blackpool is eight times higher than the UK average. Under-age and unprotected sex is rife. HIV cases rose by 50% between 2001 and 2004; one in twelve girls is pregnant before the age of 18.

Children are attracted to the bright lights of Blackpool, so the town receives its fair share of runaways. And there are always plenty of sexual predators waiting for them to arrive, knowing they will be cold, hungry and homeless; probably already victims of abuse. On average, two more young children are found to be homeless in Blackpool every month …

Source: The Guardian G2, 30 May 2008

Fig. 3.7 *Some 10 million visitors flock to Blackpool every year. Many of them probably fail to appreciate the scale of deprivation in the town*

Activity

Using the information in the case study and that on health and life expectancy (pages 55–7), write an account entitled 'Poverty and its impact in Blackpool'.

Comment on the Rowntree findings

Out of sight, out of mind. That is the predicament of Britain's poor, at least if yesterday's report ... is right. It charts a widening economic chasm between communities. Neither affluence in Surrey's stockbroker belt nor hardship in the Gorbals is new. But looking across the country as a whole, Rowntree finds that in the last three decades of the 20th century, those below the breadline came to be clustered in pockets of deprivation; at the same time, rising property prices saw comfortable localities become exclusive. That matters, and not just because the dwindling chances of an actuary [a person who keeps accounts] rubbing shoulders with a struggling single mother make it less likely that they will understand one another's perspectives. For economic apartheid works to entrench low expectations among poorer communities, undermining the social mobility that politicians of all stripes have been arguing is essential to ensure a strong economy, with the best people in the right jobs.

Source: The Guardian, *18 July 2007*

■ Key terms

Joseph Rowntree Foundation: a social policy research and development charity, seeking to better understand the causes of social difficulties such as poverty.

Cycle of poverty: the way in which poverty recurs in families from generation to generation, unless there is outside intervention to break the pattern. The idea is that seriously disadvantaged people lack the resources of education, money and coping skills necessary to break out of poverty.

The social distribution of poverty in Britain

There is today a huge gulf in wealth and the lifestyle it can support between the most successful and fortunate members of society and the rest. Poor and wealthy households are becoming more and more segregated from the rest of society, for according to the **Joseph Rowntree Foundation** the UK faces the highest inequality levels today for more than 40 years. Its analysis of the geographical changes in the distribution of wealth over time suggest that:

- the UK is becoming an increasingly divided nation
- rich areas such as the South-East of England have become disproportionately wealthier over recent decades
- in some cities more than half of all households are now 'breadline poor', on a level of relative poverty with enough to live on but without access to opportunities enjoyed by the rest of society, yet above the level of absolute poverty or 'core poor'
- urban clustering of poverty has increased, while wealthier households have concentrated in city outskirts.

According to the survey, *Poverty, Wealth and Place in Britain, 1968–2005*, the Rowntree researchers found that between 1991 and 2002 the personal wealth held by the richest 1 per cent of the population rose from 17 to 24 per cent.

The political debate about poverty

Since 1945, governments of both main parties have accepted in general terms that a redistribution of resources from the better-off to the poor should be a guiding principle of social policy. Tax revenues were used to finance a welfare state, with free health care and other benefits, including free primary and secondary education. The benefits would be financed disproportionately by the better off and drawn disproportionately by the least well off. This would reduce the impact of poverty. As we have seen, it became apparent that this approach had not eliminated poverty, which was increasingly recognised as a serious problem from the 1960s onwards. In particular, there was anxiety about the levels of child poverty as uncovered by the Child Poverty Action Group (CPAG).

By the 1970s, there was a widely held acceptance that poverty existed and that governmental measures were necessary to tackle its particular causes, such as low pay, old age, the invalidity or death of the main wage-earner and unemployment. There was also an understanding that many people were born into a **cycle of poverty** from which they found it difficult to escape. Families from a deprived area are more likely to produce children who may fare less well in a difficult inner-city school, gain low qualifications, be unable to command a steady job, and go on to have a family whose prospects are little different. Of course, not all suffer in this way. Some break out from the limitations of their upbringing.

By the end of the 20th century it was widely accepted that many people in Britain were poor. There was much more contention over the size of this minority, the groups that were included and about what poverty really meant. Poverty is defined by the European Union and by British ministers today as being below the line of 50 per cent of average income.

Academic analysts, campaigning activists and politicians of the Left tended to emphasise the social causes of poverty, such as low pay, unemployment, old age and the changing pattern of family life. Politicians on the Right tended to stress individual causes, some seeing the poor as inept or blameworthy.

In 1989, the then Conservative secretary of state for social security, John Moore, expressed a widely held Conservative feeling when he attacked the poverty lobby for failing to make it clear that absolute poverty had been wiped out. He suggested that those labelled as 'the poor' were simply 'less equal' and that the notion of relative poverty was simply a statement about inequality in society. In his view, however rich society became, use of the concept of relative poverty would undermine the overall impression, because by definition those considered to be relatively poor would drag 'the incubus of relative poverty' with them as most people moved up the income scale. As he put it, there would be 'poverty in paradise'.

Moore was also concerned that there was a developing **dependency culture** in the UK, with too many people coming to rely on state benefits. His critics said that he was trying to define the poor out of existence. They preferred to concentrate on Conservative measures that in their view had made the situation worse, among them the introduction of the **community charge**, the failure to increase levels of child benefit for three consecutive years and the introduction of the **Social Fund**.

Activities

1. Using the internet to assist you, find out more about the community charge and the hostility its introduction aroused. Write a few sentences saying why many people felt it was unfair.

2. Write a couple of paragraphs to explain the Conservatives' approach to poverty in the Thatcher/Major years.

New Labour in office after 1997

Political author and columnist Will Hutton wrote *The State We're In*, an influential study of British society in 1995, in which he argued that the changes in British society did not amount simply to a case of the rich getting richer and the poor getting poorer. They were more complex, for he noted that even among the better off there were signs of growing insecurity and stress in their lives. He advanced the idea of a 40:30:30 society, with 40 per cent in permanent full-time employment, 30 per cent 'insecurely self-employed, involuntarily part-time or casual workers' and the most disadvantaged 30 per cent at the bottom either unemployed or working for poverty wages.

New Labour was influenced by Hutton's writings, which informed some of its **communitarian thinking**. Leftish politicians argued that Thatcherism had created widespread deprivation, by cutting social security benefits, abolishing council house subsidies and presiding over high levels of unemployment. The result was increased social inequality and the emergence of a powerless and deprived '**underclass**'. This posed a threat to communities.

Labour had long spoken of the need to break out of the '**poverty trap**'. Where no member of a family was working and all were reliant on state benefits, there was little incentive for anyone to seek employment. If they did try to find work and earn money, the value of their earnings would be immediately eroded by taxation. In addition, they would begin to lose those benefits that were means-tested. With some income coming in, such entitlements as housing benefit and income support would be lost. The family could be worse off by working than by not working.

Key terms

Dependency culture: the way of life that develops when significant numbers of people become dependent on state benefits.

Community charge (or 'poll tax'): a form of funding for local government, introduced by the Thatcher administration. Every adult living in a particular area paid a flat charge to the local council and thus made a contribution to the costs of maintaining local services. Occupants of tiny council flats now paid the same as those who lived in stately homes.

Social Fund: a means of making payments (mostly loans, not grants) to cover the costs of 'exceptional needs' of poor claimants, introduced by the Thatcher administration. Payments were discretionary rather than entitlements.

Communitarian thinking: refers to a school of philosophy that is critical of individualism and stresses instead the importance of community interests and values. Communitarian ideas were popularized by Etzioni (see page 5).

Underclass: the lowest societal stratum, comprising the most economically and socially disadvantaged members of the community, who are often portrayed as living outside society's norms and values.

Poverty trap: a situation in which families find that there is no incentive to seek work. The double effect of paying tax and losing benefits when they start work may result in a reduction in net earnings.

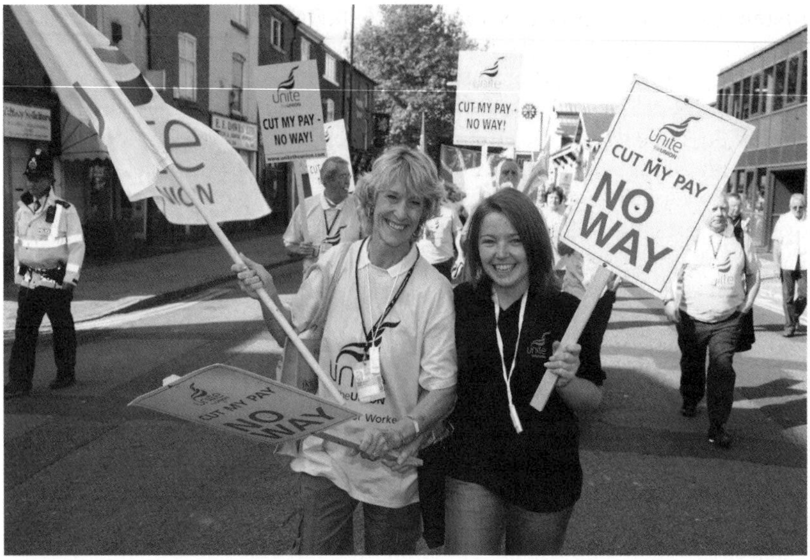

Fig 3.8 *London University staff and students support the cleaners in a May Day protest for better wages, 2007*

The trap could be addressed in three ways. Earnings at the lower end of the wage scale could be increased, via a minimum wage; taxation at lower earnings levels could be reduced or eliminated; and a system of **tax credits** could be introduced to compensate families for the loss of benefits, thereby ensuring that their effective income levels would be increased. This was designed to ensure that anyone would gain by seeking, finding and remaining in full-time employment. Labour was to act on all three solutions, soon after obtaining office.

Key terms

Tax credits: a system where the tax authorities actually pay back taxes to poor families. This improves their financial status and can reduce poverty.

Selective universality: the name sometimes applied to New Labour's social security policies. It refers to the idea that, although all benefits have been reformed, there is a focus on those groups who are especially in need through no fault of their own.

Activity

Write a short letter from a Conservative MP who is a member of the New Right to a national newspaper, to explain the problems associated with the underclass in Britain.

Governmental measures

Among the measures introduced by New Labour over the last 10 years or so have been:

- encouragement for single parents to return to work as soon as possible, helped by the provision of free and universal nursery care for three-year-olds
- the 'fair deal' for the unemployed and a series of measures to make it easier and worthwhile for those out of work to find employment
- help for the disabled to find work rather than remain on benefit, as part of a broad 'welfare to work' approach
- increased assistance for elderly people, such as the winter fuel allowance
- increased support for families with young children, via a range of benefits (e.g. much-improved child benefit levels) and other targeted forms of relief
- the introduction of a national minimum wage (NMW).

Almost all UK workers of 16 or over have a legal right to a minimum level of pay, set by the government each year and based on the recommendations of the independent Low Pay Commission (LPC). This is regardless of the kind of work they do or the size and type of company. The rate is reviewed every year. Any increases take place in October. There are different levels of national minimum wage, depending on the age of the worker.

Labour's approach to social security policy has sometimes been referred to as **selective universality**, an apparently odd phrase that refers to a system that is designed to be of general benefit, but which targets action upon poor families – especially those with children. It has resulted in some progress in tackling the poverty and insecurity of the most disadvantaged. But for critics within the Labour Party, its weakness has been the failure to use the tax system to redistribute income from rich to poor. The role of welfare in bringing more people into the workforce and in reducing poverty can only go so far unless it is prepared to raise taxes at the highest levels.

Social exclusion is a relatively new term in British policy. It refers not only to poverty and low income, but to some of their wider causes and consequences. It describes what happens when people are excluded from essential services or everyday aspects of life that most of us take for granted. Socially excluded people or places can become trapped in a cycle of related problems such as unemployment, poor skills, low incomes, poverty, poor housing, high crime, bad health and family breakdown. They are not just about money, although a decent income is clearly essential to any solution. The government's current definition of social exclusion is:

> ... a complex and multi-dimensional process. It involves the lack or denial of resources, rights, goods and services, and the inability to participate in the normal relationships and activities, available to the majority of people in a society, whether in economic, social, cultural or political arenas. It affects both the quality of life of individuals and the equity and cohesion of society as a whole.

Social exclusion involves the failure to keep all groups and individuals within reach of what most of us expect in order that we can realise our full potential. It can result in the alienation of the disadvantaged from the rest of society, so that they become in effect an underclass, a group of people who have limited life chances and who are becoming increasingly detached from the rest of society. It is often connected to their social class, educational status and living standards, and how these affect their access to various opportunities.

The Blair and Brown governments have been committed to social inclusion, which involves a coordinated response to the very complex system of problems posed by social exclusion. Focusing on social inclusion means emphasising things such as access to services, good social network, decent housing, adequate information and support, and the ability to exercise basic rights.

Key factors contributing to social inclusion are:

- adequate income
- good mental and physical health
- low risk of crime and low fear of crime, good quality neighbourhood
- provision of appropriate care
- mobility and access to transport
- good social networks
- good access to suitable local services
- opportunities for civic participation and cultural activities
- use of basic financial services
- employment, learning and skills opportunities
- opportunities to use digital technology
- suitable, well-maintained housing

Activity

List and briefly explain in your own words four methods by which New Labour has attempted to tackle the problem of poverty.

Key terms

Social exclusion: a term widely used by the Blair and Brown governments to refer to those who are seriously deprived and have a range of social problems with a variety of causes. Tony Blair described it as ' ... a shorthand label for what can happen when individuals or areas suffer from a combination of linked problems such as unemployment, poor skills, low incomes, poor housing, high crime environments, bad health and family breakdown'.

■ suitable information, advice, advocacy and redress

■ use of common consumer goods.

Case study

Child poverty in the UK today

I feel people look at us differently to other friends or family – they feel sorry for us and say not to buy presents or bring food for family events.

Parent, quoted in Hooper et al., Living with Hardship 24/7, *The Frank Buttle Trust, 2007*

A couple of months ago Shekira was ill, and because we all sleep together, we all became ill.

Parent, as quoted in Child Poverty and Housing, *End Child Poverty, 2007*

Some facts:

■ 3.8 million children are living in poverty in the UK (after housing costs)

■ the proportion of children living in poverty grew from 1 in 10 in 1979 to 1 in 3 in 1998; today, 30 per cent of children in Britain are living in poverty

■ since 1999, when the current Government pledged to end child poverty, 600,000 children have been lifted out of poverty

■ the UK has one of the worst rates of child poverty in the industrialised world

■ the majority (54 per cent) of poor children live in a household where at least one adult works

■ 43 per cent of poor children live in a household headed by a lone parent, but the majority of poor children (57 per cent) live in a household headed by a couple

■ 42 per cent of children in poverty are from families with three or more children.

Poverty can have a profound impact on the child, their family, and the rest of society. It often sets in motion a deepening spiral of social exclusion, creating problems in education, employment, mental and physical health and social interaction.

Source: Information taken from the End Child Poverty website www.endchildpoverty.org.uk

Activity

Read the case study on child poverty and then write a couple of paragraphs to explain what you regard as the main reasons for child poverty in the UK.

How important an issue do you regard child poverty? Give reasons for your response.

Summary questions

1 Why does economic inequality matter? What might be done about it?

2 In what respects, if any, do those who live in poverty have themselves to blame for their disadvantage?

3 How effectively has New Labour tackled the issues surrounding poverty in Britain?

4 'The very rich are getting richer; the very poor have in the last few years fallen further behind.'

Is inequality a) inevitable and b) currently excessive?

4 How can we reduce discrimination and disadvantage?

Hint

In this chapter we are seeking to find out how discrimination and disadvantage can be tackled and how effectively governments handle the issues. Remember also that individuals and groups within society can be change-makers. Active citizenship implies that people working together can effect improvements within their community. The roles and actions of individuals working alone or in groups are a key theme of the course.

Key terms

Equality of opportunity: an approach intended to provide a social environment in which people have an equal chance and are not excluded from the activities of society or from achieving personal advancement in areas such as education, employment or health care on the basis of any social disadvantage, such as their family background.

Equality of outcome: a form of equality that seeks to lessen or eliminate differences in material conditions between individuals, for instance by equalising their income or wealth. Some would suggest that genuine equality of opportunity cannot be achieved without greater equality of outcome, for an advantaged background provides a good starting point in life.

In the American Declaration of Independence (1776), the ringing phrase 'All men are created equal' did not mean that its authors felt that everyone was alike or that there were no differences between human beings. Indeed, several of its authors believed that African-Americans were genetically inferior to whites. However, it went on to speak of 'inalienable rights' to which all were equally entitled. A belief in equal rights has often led to a belief in **equality of opportunity**. In other words, everyone should have the same chance. What individuals make of that equal chance depends on their abilities and efforts.

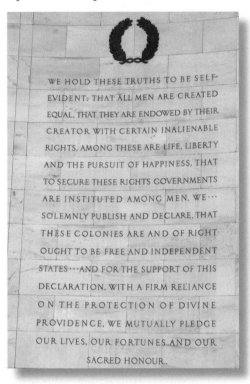

Fig. 4.1 *The US Declaration of Independence*

The concept of equality

Perfect equality has not yet been achieved in any country or society. Depending on their position in the social or class hierarchy, people have differential access to power and influence in society. While the small stratum at the top has a disproportionate share of resources in terms of income, housing, information, food, education, job opportunities, prestige and status, the poor have far less than an average share of resources, whether for ordinary living or for defending their interest. In contrast, the wealthy can use their resources to preserve their position.

Many people would agree on the ideas of equality of worth, equality before the law and political equality (one person one vote, each vote to count equally). They would also in theory support equality of opportunity. Few advocate absolute **equality of outcome**. Indeed, freedom in the economic sphere has commonly resulted in marked inequality of income and wealth.

So what do we mean by these forms of equality?

Equality of worth

All men (and women) are not equal in any descriptive sense. For instance, they are not equal physically or intellectually. In a prescriptive sense, we might say they should be treated equally, as long as there are no grounds for treating them differently. In other words, people with identical tax returns should be treated equally; people suffering from different ailments should not. The entitlement of all people is therefore to equal consideration. They should be treated equally, unless there are good reasons for not doing so. Understood in this way, the principle of equality does not say that all human beings must be treated alike. We presume that they should be, unless there are grounds for making distinctions.

Equality before the law

All humans have certain fundamental rights and should be treated equally unless there are special circumstances making for an exception. The spirit of the idea is that these fundamentals apply to all people because of their common humanity. Equals in law should be treated equally by the law.

Of course, the law is not equally accessible to all. **Legal aid** is only available to the very badly off, whereas the rich can hire the services of a prestigious barrister. In beginning court proceedings, education, social standing and wealth can have an influence. The ignorant or poor do not always have the means to establish their rights, whereas privileged people can take action to clear their name and win large damages.

Although the presumption is that the law should treat people equally, some argue for 'positive discrimination' in favour of those who have for years suffered disadvantage – such as women, members of minority races and disabled people. They suggest such groups should be given an increased opportunity enabling them to 'catch up' and gain positions hitherto denied to them. 'Equality before the law' is enshrined in the Race Discrimination and Sex Discrimination Acts, but positive discrimination can give disadvantaged people an extra push. The two ideas may seem to be in conflict.

Equality of opportunity and equality of outcome

Equality of opportunity means that everyone has the same starting point or equal life chances. It can be used to justify inequality, because talent and hard work are unequally distributed.

Equality of outcome, the most controversial form of equality, means that there is movement towards a more equal distribution of income, wealth and other social goods. Few favour absolute equality, but they do find existing inequalities unacceptable. Supporters claim that greater equality promotes social justice and community cohesion. Everyone has a stake in society and an incentive to contribute. If, by contrast, we accept gross inequality, there is the danger that an underclass is created, with all of the problems this can present for society. Social exclusion is the breeding ground for criminality and other forms of social unrest.

To its detractors, equality of outcome represents a form of 'levelling downwards', as part of a policy of '**social engineering**' designed to eliminate differences in society. It is economically damaging, in that redistributive policies such as higher levels of taxation impede enterprise and risk-taking. According to this view, the free market is the best means of promoting prosperity and ensuring a better standard of life for everyone. The poorest section of the community will benefit from the **trickle-down effect**, for they will receive a small proportion of what may become a much larger cake.

Activity

Write a couple of paragraphs explaining the differences between equality of opportunity and equality of outcome, and the relationship between the two concepts.

Differing political views about equality

Equality has traditionally been a political issue at the heart of the Left–Right divide. Socialists dislike the degree of economic inequality in society and point to the vast discrepancies in wealth and income. They note the extent to which affluence confers social advantage in education, health and other forms of social provision. For many years, the Labour Party emphasised the importance of equality of outcome. Most supporters did not favour absolute economic equality, but rather wanted to see their party work towards the creation of a more equal society in which the distinctions of rich and poor were less apparent. New Labour has laid less emphasis upon the traditional party belief in working towards greater equality of outcome. It embraces equality of opportunity as a desirable outcome, implying that everyone should start on a level playing-field, so that they have the same life chances. Because of individual differences in ability and talent, it is likely to result in economic and social inequality.

Conservatives stress that men are born unequal. They have different abilities, and some will flourish.

Summary questions

1. Is equality of opportunity a precondition of a fair society?

2. Will equal opportunity guarantee equality of outcome?

3. In the light of the information in this unit on identity and race relations, reflect on and list some of the ways in which New Labour in office has made Britain a more equal society?

4. Consider these two comments and then write a couple of paragraphs to describe your vision of an equal society in the UK:

'An equal society protects and promotes equality, real freedom and substantive opportunity to live in the ways people value and would choose, so that everyone can flourish.'

'An equal society recognises people's different needs, situations and goals and removes the barriers that limit what people can do and be.'

Source: Department of Communities and Local Government publications

Anti-discrimination policies

Faced with the problems of immigration, racial disadvantage and discrimination, and poor race relations, post-1945 governments have responded in three ways:

1. They have restricted entry of newcomers (the '**numbers game**'). It was usually argued that if there was to be an improvement in race relations and an end to discrimination, then the numbers of newcomers must be controlled to manageable proportions.

2. They have offered special assistance to priority areas where conditions have been particularly problematical, and attempted to build more harmonious and cohesive communities via education and community initiatives.

3. They have used the law to tackle prejudice, discrimination and racially motivated harassment and violence (see measures listed on pages 70-1).

Key terms

Numbers game: refers to the way in which post-1960 governments of all colours have portrayed improving race relations in terms of restricting entry to the UK – i.e. they have been keen to emphasise that strict controls enable other, more constructive policies to work.

Controls on entry into the UK

The issue of large-scale immigration from the New Commonwealth first received the attention of government ministers in 1962. Numbers had been building up in the mid to late 1950s and by the end of the decade there was pressure for political action to curb entry into Britain. As a result of a series of restrictive measures since then – most recently, the introduction of a points system in 2008 – it is today difficult for non-EU citizens to be legally allowed into Britain on a permanent basis. The position of EU citizens is different (see page 9).

The emphasis of Labour and Conservative immigration and asylum policy when the parties have been in office has been on restriction. For some politicians the underlying assumption was that it was the immigrant presence which provoked discrimination and racial tension. Others felt that it was the white reaction to that presence which created the difficulty. Either way, curbs on entry were seen as necessary, for without action on numbers it was felt that there was little hope of maintaining even reasonable race relations.

Special assistance: building cohesive communities

Governments have acknowledged the need for help to areas where social problems have been aggravated by immigration. It is understood that where social deprivation and over-crowding occur, then racial protest and rioting, as well as right-wing extremism, are more likely to feature. At times, the policy has received a new impetus (e.g. after the Brixton riots in the early 1980s, with the publication of the **Scarman Report**, and after the Oldham riots in 2001 in the form of investment in community–amenity improvements in the town).

Fig. 4.2 *The Honeywell Centre, in the New Deal for Communities (NDC) area of Hathershaw and Fitton Hill – an example of new community facilities in Oldham, following the riots of 2001*

Other measures can and have been taken. Ministers have assisted the employment of ethnic minority women by offering support to all women with the cost of childcare and early learning. Schools in which many children need help with the English language have been given special priority for funding. The emphasis within urban policy of improving local economies and creating jobs has been a relevant part of the policy of encouraging the unemployed into employment. The post-1997

Labour government would see its Fair Deal and anti-poverty measures as essential to improving the position of members of all communities.

Those who work in the area of race relations also stress the need for government to make it a priority to tackle racism in early years education, in order to encourage young people to appreciate ethnic diversity.

Case study

Regeneration and the promotion of community cohesion following the 2001 riots in Northern towns

The urban disturbances in Oldham, Burnley and Bradford in the North of England in summer 2001 were dramatic in their impact on the towns and cities involved They also proved to be very significant for the UK as a whole, for they marked a watershed in 'race relations' policy approaches. The lack of 'community cohesion' became the fashionable 'explanation' for the disturbances. Consequently, attempts to create it became the dominant principle for government's approach to issues of racial tension and ethnic integration.

Rebuilding the communities

Various schemes were recommended and in several cases introduced:

- the recycling of the old textile mills to make new workshops, along the lines of the **Dean Clough** project in Halifax
- revitalising the public realm, the schools, hospitals and security services
- the construction of middle-income housing, cultural and leisure centres to attract a mix of social classes and racial groups
- achieving these renewal goals, by ensuring that planners and policy-makers placed collective local participation at the heart of every programme of urban regeneration.

Promoting community cohesion

Measures taken included:

- issuing detailed guidance to local authorities and other public bodies as to how they should both promote and measure cohesion
- introducing a new legal duty on schools under the Education and Inspections Act (2006) to 'promote cohesion'
- making cohesion the key focus for discussions around issues such as ethnic and national identity, integration, multiculturalism and racial equality (see the debate over multiculturalism on pages 38–9).

Unlike the various inquiries following the 1981 Brixton riots (e.g. Scarman, 1981), those produced at a local level in Oldham and Burnley did not focus on the actual events and what sparked the troubles. Instead, the disturbances were portrayed as an accident waiting to happen, symptomatic of deeper lying problems existing across the UK's 'multicultural' towns and cities. In particular, it was argued that deep-seated physical and cultural ethnic segregation in the UK had led to a profound lack of shared values, or of mutual respect and understanding between ethnic groups, with ethnic conflict the inevitable outcome.

Key terms

Dean Clough: a complex of multi-storeyed granite buildings in the centre of Halifax built in the mid-19th century for carpet manufacturing. Closed in 1983, they were later turned into an industrial park in a regeneration scheme that created space for some 200 firms, including many new small businesses.

What policies have been instituted?

There is a range of legislation relating to equal opportunities.

Legislation to improve race relations

In office – with Liberal/Liberal Democrat support – Labour governments have passed four race relations Acts, as well as a series of other measures. The Conservatives have traditionally been uneasy about the use of the law in this field, many MPs arguing that you cannot make people behave better by legislation. The use of the law is still controversial, some still seeing it as undesirable, some as impractical and some as ineffective. However, it has been an important part of the package of measures designed to reassure members of ethnic minorities that protection is available for them. It has also helped to bring about gradual change in long-term attitudes.

The most recent laws introduced in this area are as follows:

- *Race Relations Act (2000)*, a Labour measure that tightened earlier legislation in 1965, 1968 and 1976 that had defined and outlawed discrimination, whether direct or indirect. Now, its scope is extended to the police, those working in the prison service and some other groups.
- *Racial and Religious Hatred Act (2006)*, again a Labour measure, created the offence of inciting hatred against a person on the grounds of their religion.
- *Equality Act (2006)* created a single Commission to handle issues formerly dealt with by the Commission for Racial Equality (CRE) and other anti-discriminatory commissions. This single commission is known as the Commission for Equality and Human Rights (CEHR).

The law and racial harassment

Racial harassment is a serious and continuing problem. According to the Commission for Racial Equality (CRE) it meant 'verbal or physical violence towards individuals or groups on grounds of their colour, race, nationality or ethnic or national origin, where the victims believe the aggression was racially motivated and/or there is evidence of racial motivation'. Harassment includes attacks on property as well as people, but it is racial attacks on people that cause the greater concern.

The majority of victims are members of ethnic minority groups, particularly Asians. Pakistanis are the most vulnerable, many of the threats and crimes they experience having some form of racial motivation. Such crimes are committed overwhelmingly by white people (98 per cent against Pakistanis; 93 per cent against Indians), and the perpetrators are predominantly male (80 per cent). Assaults are covered by various criminal laws, most of them covered by existing legislation and some by newer laws. Measures taken to tackle harassment include the following:

- *Public Order Act (1986)* tightened the law on racial incitement, so that it is an offence to act in such a way as to 'stir up hatred against any racial group in Great Britain'.
- *Crime and Disorder Act (1988)* created nine new racially aggravated offences. For these crimes (e.g. assault, criminal damage), the guilty person is liable to get two years added on to the existing offence because of the racial factor.

Left and Right approaches to tackling race relations and promoting equal opportunities

The Left has been more willing to act on race relations and some of its supporters would like to see more use made of American-style **affirmative action programmes**, better known in the UK as forms of **positive discrimination**. These positively discriminate in favour of disadvantaged minorities. Their supporters feel that the only way to redress the balance and secure equal opportunity in a relatively short time is to enforce careful ethnic monitoring and use quotas in areas such as employment. Those on the Right usually dislike any form of positive discrimination, claiming that it creates a backlash among the white population who feel that there is reverse discrimination and does nothing for the self-esteem of those who gain advancement not on merit but purely because of their ethnic origin. Many have also been uneasy about race relations legislation, believing that you cannot change human nature by passing laws. It is about education and persuasion.

Summary questions

1. Is it necessary to limit the number of arrivals in Britain in order to establish good race relations and promote opportunities for all?
2. Which measure introduced by any government in recent decades has been the most useful in improving British race relations? Give reasons.
3. Is further legislation necessary? If so, what form should it take?
4. What else could be done to promote equal opportunities in the field of race relations?

Tackling ageism and discrimination against disabled people

The Employment Equality (Age) Regulations, in force since October 2006, implement the EU Framework Directive on Equal Treatment in Employment and Occupation and make discrimination on the grounds of age unlawful in employment and education. Employers are no longer permitted to use age as a criterion for recruitment, promotion, training and termination, and significant changes have come into force that affect retirement, pay and benefits and pension schemes.

The new law recognises that differences of treatment on the grounds of age can sometimes be justified. For example, it may be necessary to make special provisions for younger or older workers in order to protect their safety and welfare. However, employers need to 'objectively justify' exemptions to the regulations, by providing clear evidence to support any claim.

Older people experience most age discrimination. However, it can also be targeted at young people. It is now unlawful for an employer to impose a lower age limit when recruiting, unless this restriction can be objectively justified or is imposed by law.

Helping people with disabilities

The disability rights movement began in America in the late 1960s, encouraged by the example of the African-American civil rights and women's movements. Various individuals and groups in the UK joined together in 1981 to set up an umbrella organisation of some 130 independent agencies, the United Kingdom's Disabled People's Council

Key terms

Affirmative action programmes: programmes designed to increase the chances of minorities and women being selected for positions in public life, such as on university courses or in management positions. Their usefulness and fairness became a topic of fierce debate in the 1990s.

Positive discrimination: refers to a system that actually favours members of ethnic minorities or women because they are considered to have been long disadvantaged, for instance when it comes to such things as job recruitment and prospects. The Good Friday Agreement (1998) requires the Police Service of Northern Ireland to recruit equal numbers of Catholics and Protestants.

(DPC). It campaigns for the civil rights and social inclusion of disabled people and promote full equality and participation in UK society for them. The DPC represents through its member bodies around 350,000 disabled people.

The UK DPC and others lobbied government for recognition of the rights of disabled people. Over the last decade or so, important legislation has been introduced, notably the Disability Discrimination Act (1995), which was intended to tackle the discrimination that many disabled people faced. The Act required businesses to make 'reasonable adjustments' to their policies or practices, and to physical aspects of their premises, in order to avoid indirect discrimination; established the Disability Rights Commission (DRC), which closed in September 2007 (see page 74) to monitor treatment of disabled people and make recommendations; and gave disabled people significant rights in the areas of:

- employment
- education
- access to goods, facilities and services
- buying or renting land or property, including making it easier for disabled people to rent property and for tenants to make disability-related adaptations.

It became unlawful for organisations to treat a disabled person less favourably, for reasons related to the person's disability, without justification.

The 1995 legislation has been significantly extended, notably by the Disability Discrimination Act (2005). In its amended form, it now requires public bodies to promote equality of opportunity for disabled people. It also allows the government to set minimum standards so that disabled people can use public transport easily. It applies to all employers and everyone who provides a service to the public, except the Armed Forces.

Other more specific measures have included the following:

- *Special Educational Needs and Disability Act (2001)* made it unlawful for education providers to discriminate against disabled pupils, students and adults. They now have a statutory duty to ensure that disabled people are not disadvantaged in comparison to those who are not disabled.
- *Private Hire Vehicles (Carriage of Guide Dogs etc.) Act (2002)* prevented operators of such vehicles from refusing to take or charging for assistance dogs.

Activity

Using the internet to help you, look up details of the Civil Partnership Act to see what rights have been secured. Find out any figures relating to the popularity of the new arrangements. Note that far more couples have entered into such partnerships than ministers ever anticipated.

Key terms

European Court of Human Rights: an international court based in Strasbourg, comprising a number of judges equal to the number of member countries of the Council of Europe that have ratified the Convention on Human Rights. It applies the Convention, ensuring that states respect its rights and guarantees. Its judgments are binding, the countries concerned being under an obligation to comply with them.

Activities

1. List some of the special needs of disabled people.

2. List three ways in which governments of recent years have tried to make improved provision for disabled people.

Providing equal rights for gays and lesbians

Attitudes towards same-sex relationships between consenting adults have become more tolerant, with political opinion gradually accepting the notion of gay rights. In this it has been aided by decisions taken in the **European Court of Human Rights**.

In office, New Labour has:

- *repealed Section 28 of the Local Government Act (1988)*, which banned the 'promotion' of homosexuality in schools and colleges
- *lowered the age of consent* so that it is the same as in different-sex relationships
- *passed The Adoption and Children Act (2005)*, which for the first time granted unmarried and same-sex couples in England and Wales the right to adopt children
- *introduced the Civil Partnership Act (2004)*, which provides same-sex couples with the same legal entitlements as married couples.

The treatment of women: progress towards equal rights

All contemporary societies remain male-dominated. Men have traditionally been the bread-winners and wage-earners, whereas women were expected to remain at home. Today, men have more chance of reaching the top in their chosen profession. A **glass ceiling** makes it less likely that women will do so. They do – in many cases – go out to work, as well as fulfilling the traditional child-bearing and nurturing roles. Many have found good opportunities in the professions, such as medicine, accounting and the civil service. They now account for approximately half of Britain's labour force, but they tend to receive less promotion and career advancement than men. In many sectors, they are also paid less, as employers seek ways of evading the regulations on equal pay for equal work. Moreover, it is notable that most of the part-time, unskilled and lowly paid jobs are filled by women. These tend to be vulnerable to the impact of new technologies in the workplace.

The role of government in advancing the position of women

In recent decades, a series of measures have improved the rights and extended the opportunities of women in society. These include the Equal Pay Act, the Sex Discrimination Act and the **Equality Act**, all of which were introduced by Labour governments.

- *The Equal Pay Act (1970)* established the principle of 'equal pay for equal work'. This was the first major piece of legislation on women's rights for many years. The intention was to prohibit discrimination in employment practices, with regulations covering pay, allowances and benefits, holidays and hours of work. The Act helped to advance the position of working women, although there were many ways in which employers could redefine jobs in favour of men, so that they could be paid more.
- *The Sex Discrimination Act (1975)* supplemented the law on pay. It was introduced to outlaw discrimination in recruitment, training and fringe benefits, among other things. An Equal Opportunities Commission (EOC) was set up to monitor the workings of this and the Equal Pay Act, as well as to investigate allegations of discrimination. The emphasis of the EOC was on conciliation rather than confrontation, but its approach became more forceful over the next decade.
- *The Employment Protection (Consolidation) Act (1976)* introduced the statutory maternity rights scheme, whereby employers were required to make statutory maternity payments to female employees who went on maternity leave. These rights allowed a woman employee to return to the same job or suitable alternative work after the maternity period. The Act provided that a woman on maternity leave could not be made redundant.

Fig. 4.3 *Elton John and David Furnish: among the first couples to take advantage of the introduction of civil unions*

Key terms

Glass ceiling: a term that is commonly used to describe the unacknowledged discriminatory barrier preventing women and minorities from rising to leadership positions in an organisation, such as a private corporation. There is a limitation blocking upward progression, a glass (transparent) one because the limitation is not immediately apparent and is normally an unwritten and unofficial policy.

Equality Act (2006): amends the Equal Pay Act (1970) and the Sex Discrimination Act (1975) and places a statutory duty upon public authorities to ensure that they eliminate unlawful discrimination and harassment of their employees and promote equality of opportunity between men and women. Among other things, it created the new Commission for Equality and Human Rights (CEHR).

Activity

List and briefly explain what you think were the three most important reasons for women achieving greater equality with men in the post-1945 era.

Try to find out about some of the factors that contributed to the improved position of women in the late 20th century. You might consider why those listed below were significant:

■ increased opportunities to work in the professions

■ the development of labour-saving devices and more domestic appliances (e.g. freezers)

■ the growth of educational opportunities (especially in higher education)

■ the need for labour in the 1950s and 1960s

■ the increased ability of women to regulate their own fertility.

Fig. 4.4 *Trevor Phillips, head of EHRC*

Labour and the other opposition parties were generally sympathetic to the cause of gender equality in the 1980s and 1990s, but the Thatcher governments were not noted for their commitment to female opportunities and rights. Having shown that women could break through and succeed in a man's world, the prime minister of the day seemed unwilling to use her considerable influence to help other women by showing sympathy for the provision of nursery education and crèche facilities, among other things. In the Conservative years (1979–97), there was an emphasis within the party on family values.

■ Equal opportunities: the role of government bodies

Ministers have emphasised that in their view equality is not a minority concern. It matters to all of us. At some point in our lives, we are all liable to face barriers that may prevent us fulfilling our potential or participating fully in society.

The Equality and Human Rights Commission

The new Equality and Human Rights Commission (EHRC) began its work in October 2007. Established by the Equality Act 2006, it represents a merger of three separate equality commissions, which no longer function. These were the:

■ Disability Rights Commission

■ Commission for Racial Equality

■ Equal Opportunities Commission.

Why a single Commission?

Ministers argued that a single Commission has many benefits, including:

■ bringing together equality experts and acting as a single source of information and advice (instead of the previous separate organisations)

■ being a single point of contact for individuals, businesses and the voluntary and public sectors

■ helping businesses by promoting awareness of equality issues, which may prevent costly court and tribunal cases

■ tackling discrimination on multiple levels – some people may face more than one type of discrimination

■ giving older people a powerful national body to tackle age discrimination.

The purpose of the Equality and Human Rights Commission

The fundamental objective of the EHRC, as summarised in section 3 of the Equality Act 2006, is to support the development of a society where:

■ people's ability to achieve their potential is not limited by prejudice or discrimination

■ there is respect for and protection of each individual's human rights

■ there is respect for the dignity and worth of every individual

■ every individual has an equal opportunity to participate in society; and there is mutual respect between groups based on understanding and valuing diversity and on shared respect for equality and human rights.

A key element in the Commission's brief is to end discrimination and harassment of people because of their disability, age, religion or belief, race, gender or sexual orientation. It is expected that it will take an active role in helping to achieve change to benefit some of the most vulnerable and least well-represented people in society.

The Government Equalities Office

In July 2007, on becoming prime minister, Gordon Brown announced the establishment of a new Government Equalities Office. It has assumed responsibility for the government's overall strategy and priorities on equality issues. It will handle:

- reviews of discrimination issues
- policy on gender equality, including the minister for women's priorities
- matters surrounding sexual orientation
- integrating work on race and religion or belief equality into the overall equality framework.

Case study

The role of charities in bringing about improvement – the Manchester Refugee Support Network (MRSN)

MRSN is a refugee-led charity based in Moss Side, Manchester. MRSN works to build strong and independent refugee organisations and to give people the information they need to settle and build new lives.

MRSN aims to:

- support and empower Manchester's refugee communities to establish strong organisations
- increase public awareness around issues of asylum and media representation
- give refugees and asylum seekers a voice and the chance to express themselves and represent the needs and aspirations of their own communities
- reduce levels of stress, unemployment, poverty and isolation for asylum seekers and refugees.

MRSN provides the Refugee and Migrant Forum Manchester with an organisational base.

Refugee and Migrant Forum Manchester (RMFM)

The Refugee and Migrant Forum Manchester is a network of refugee community leaders who aim to express the needs and aspirations of their communities and to influence policy and service delivery in Manchester.

Between August and November 2007, the Forum identified a number of objectives which would enable them to meet their strategic goals which included the following:

- To raise awareness of the work of RMFM and to increase the involvement of existing members
- To identify/audit existing skills, experience and qualification of existing members

---

Further information

The EHRC

Our vision

A society built on fairness and respect. People confident in all aspects of their diversity.

[The EHRC ...]

... aims to reduce inequality, eliminate discrimination, strengthen good relations between people, and promote and protect human rights

... challenges prejudice and disadvantage, and promotes the importance of human rights

... enforces equality legislation on age, disability, gender, race, religion or belief, sexual orientation or transgender status, and encourages compliance with the Human Rights Act

... uses influence and authority to ensure that equality and human rights remain at the top of agendas for government and employers, media and society. We will campaign for social change and justice.

Source: EHRC website

Activity

Using the internet to help you, find out about other community action projects designed to improve the quality of life in a town or city. You might start by looking up the CSV (Community Service Volunteers) to become aware of its campaigning activities and help in training volunteers, at www.csv.org.uk.

■ To provide information about the RMFM to enable members to make informed decisions about getting involved

■ To have up to date information on members' interests and skills so that relevant training and development opportunities could be made available to them.

The report outlined the findings and evaluation of a piece of research carried out by 12 members of the RMFM into the existing skills, experience, qualifications and interests of refugee, asylum seeker and migrant community members. They wanted to audit the skills, qualifications and areas of expertise of refugees and asylum seekers who have some involvement with the activities of the RMF.

Source: extracts from a report of the Manchester Refugee Support Network, The Skills Audit Community Project, by Shahida Sidduqe and Zoë Speekenbrink

■ How effective have government policies been?

The laws against racial discrimination at work today cover every part of employment. This includes recruitment, terms and conditions, pay and benefits, status, training, promotion and transfer opportunities, right through to redundancy and dismissal. However, in spite of the laws to prevent discrimination, many members of ethnic minorities find that their chances of advancement are impeded at a particular level by a glass ceiling.

Opportunities and problems

The present situation was summed up by Jane Kennedy MP and former minister of state for work and chair of the Ethnic Minority Employment Task Force (2004):

> People from a wide range of ethnic backgrounds are achieving success in business, public service, sports and the arts. They are contributing to the social and economic growth of the nation.

Fig. 4.5 *The home of the Indian billionaire Lakshmi Mittal in Kensington – previously owned by Formula 1 magnate Bernie Ecclestone*

Nonetheless, ethnic minorities continue to face discrimination that is preventing them from reaching their potential. Despite great improvements in race relations over the past 20 years, there is a long-term and potentially very damaging gap between the employment rates for ethnic minority people and the rest of the population. This gap – which has persisted almost unchanged for two decades – indicates not simply that some ethnic minorities are being denied the opportunity to achieve and sustain employment, but that we are wasting a vital pool of talent.

If we fail to tackle the barriers to employment that some ethnic minorities face, we will also fail to make the most of the potential represented by those ethnic minority people who are unable to find work.

How equal are women today?

Today, women make up more than 50 per cent of the British population and some 45 per cent of the workforce. As we have seen, on average girls leave school with better qualifications than boys, more of them study at university and they gain higher degrees. Employment opportunities are greater than ever previously. Although many women still work in education, healthcare, offices and the retail sector, others have achieved success in the business world and in professions such as accountancy and the law. The old assumption that women should stay at home and look after the children has been widely discarded. More than three-quarters of women with school-age children are in paid employment.

In most households, women still perform the traditional domestic roles of child-rearing and housework, as well as going out to work. In some homes, men have taken more responsibility in family life, a trend helped by recent legislation on paternity leave. But there is not equality within the allocation of home duties. In other areas, too, there is discrimination against women. The glass ceiling prevents many high-flyers from gaining access to the highest-paid jobs and the average hourly rate of pay for women is 20 per cent below the male level.

Many people still often complain of the way women are portrayed in the media. Some magazines and many advertisements tend to emphasise the desirability of glamorous, alluring females, often with thin, model-type figures, even at the very time when the bulk of the population is becoming larger. They neglect middle-aged and more mature women for whom there are few good roles. In other words, the allegation is that the portrayals of women are often of physically near-perfect examples, whose attractiveness can be used to enhance viewing figures, sell a variety of products or promote the sale of newspapers.

Fig. 4.6 *Images of women are still a commodity*

Activities

1. Using the internet to help you, find out examples of any individual members of the ethnic minority community who have been successful in business or the professions – e.g. Lakshmi Mittal (see Fig. 4.5).

2. List the ways in which women do and do not get a fair deal in today's society. Suggest any ways by which the position of women could be improved.

Women in politics

Table 4.1 *Women in political office in the UK*

Political institution	Number of members	Number of men	Number of women	Percentage of women
European Parliament: British MEPs	78	58	20	25.6
Westminster: House of Commons*	646	518	128	19.6
Westminster: House of Lords	748	605	143	19.1
Cabinet (first Gordon Brown-led one)	22	17	5	22.7
Scottish Parliament	129	86	43	33.3
Welsh National Assembly	60	32	28	46.7
Northern Irish Assembly	108	90	18	16.7
London Assembly	25	16	9	36.0
Local authorities: England (2004 data)	19,689	13,645	5,774	29.3
Local authorities: Wales (2004 data)	1257	983	274	21.8

Source: Government Equalities Office
*With women making up 19.6 per cent of our MPs, the UK is ranked 14th within the EU. (For more on women in politics, see page 256–7.)

According to the website of the Government Equalities Office, there are clear benefits in having greater female participation:

> An increase in the number of women elected would lead to a higher quality of decision-making, reflecting the greater diversity of experience of those making the decisions.
>
> There is evidence in the newly devolved institutions in Scotland and Wales that the relatively high number of women have had a discernible impact on shaping their policy agendas. In both bodies, women parliamentarians have championed issues such as childcare, the social economy and equal pay.
>
> In addition, the UK faces a serious problem of lack of interest in the political system from the electorate. If politics looks old, white and male, it can seem irrelevant and dull to many people, and lead to lower participation rates and a reduction in democracy. Research published by the Electoral Commission suggests that having more women elected representatives actually encourages greater participation rates amongst women more generally.

Source: equalities.gov.uk

Representation also plays a symbolic role. It is important for decision-makers to be effective role models and to be truly representative of their electors.

The use of the law to promote equal rights and opportunities: a reflection

The Commission for Racial Equality (the most long-lasting successor of the Race Relations Board), advanced five reasons why the law can be beneficial in the area of race relations:

1 it is necessary to offer an unequivocal declaration of public policy

2 a law supports those who do not wish to discriminate, but who feel compelled to do so by social pressure

3 a law gives protection and redress to minority groups

4 a law provides for peaceful and orderly adjustment of grievance and release of tensions

5 a law reduces prejudice by discouraging the behaviour in which the prejudice finds expression.

The arguments concerning anti-discriminatory legislation are similar, in whatever the area under discussion. If we take the example of the role of the law in promoting good race relations and promoting ethnic minority rights, several of the points can be applied in the cases of other forms of discrimination and denial of civil rights.

In favour of using the law to combat racial discrimination

Those who support legislation take the view that by legislating much can be done to improve racial harmony, reduce levels of discrimination and gradually create a climate in which most people respect the rights of others and treat them with civility. Admittedly, this cannot be achieved quickly. But at the very least if you cannot change attitudes overnight by use of the law, then at least you can modify the most objectionable aspects of human behaviour and stop most people from behaving in an unfriendly or hostile manner, dangerous to social stability.

Many people see the law as a marker of the sort of society that Britain wishes to be. It shows a desire for tolerance, fair-mindedness and decent behaviour.

The case against using the law to tackle discrimination

Some people take the view that legislation cannot successfully combat discrimination, whether it concerns disabled people, women, gays or any other group in society. They may deny the extent of discrimination in the first place. If they concede that there is discrimination, they are likely to use the argument that you cannot make people like each other or change the way they feel by passing laws. It takes time to change attitudes in regard to racism, sexism and other forms of discrimination and prejudice. This can only be done by using bodies such as the Equalities and Human Rights Commission, which can focus on education, public campaigning and the practical experience of people living together. In the case of race relations, social harmony can be promoted by keeping the numbers involved down to reasonable proportions via curbs on immigration.

Another argument is that using the law creates a 'privileged' section of the population, offering special legal protection to a particular group of people while denying rights to the majority. It is white people who are most likely to be judged to be falling foul of the law, by uttering comments that are unflattering or cruel about those of a different ethnic origin. Such people can be placed at a disadvantage in what they see as their own country. Supporters of this view might go on to point out the possibility that this will create a backlash against minority groups, thereby making race relations worse.

A final argument employed against anti-discriminatory legislation is that it is too often associated with '**political correctness**'. Opponents see it as a form of cultural coercion by liberal-minded people who are limiting the rights of people to say and do what they think, for fear of saying or doing something that the law says is 'offensive'.

Key terms

Political correctness: refers to speaking and writing about socially sensitive matters such as culture, gender or race in a way that avoids the use of potentially offensive terminology, which is seen as inappropriate in a tolerant and multicultural society. Much condemned on the political Right, the implication is that such language is not only in itself absurd, but also involves censorship and social engineering.

Can more be done to end discrimination and promote equal rights?

Members of ethnic minorities, women and other minority groups still suffer some discrimination, though not always of the overt kind, for example by finding that the glass ceiling prevents them from being promoted above a certain level, particularly in some of the professions. Some campaigners for equal rights suggest that the answer to the glass ceiling is positive discrimination, perhaps involving quotas to ensure that a minimum number of women or members of minority groups are appointed to higher levels. But as we have seen, this is highly controversial as it is claimed that employees of 'inferior' quality are likely to be promoted simply to fulfil a target. Supporters argue that quotas would change the culture in many organisations. With better opportunities, more able women will be encouraged to enter such professions at the lower end so that the quotas for 'top' positions will increasingly be reached by the advance of equally able people.

Case study

How individuals can campaign for equal treatment

Disabled 'denied' post office rights

A severely disabled woman yesterday challenged contentious government plans to shut up to 2,500 local post offices, claiming ministers failed to consider the impact on handicapped residents. Judy Brown, who uses her branch in Hastings at least twice a week, is seeking a judicial review of the closure programme, which is designed to stem the network's losses of £3.5m a week. She claimed the government's failure to carry out a full assessment of how large-scale closures would affect disabled people breached anti-discrimination legislation. The government has said it acted lawfully and is contesting the application.

Report by Megan Murphy, Financial Times, *13 May 2008*

Summary questions

1. Have a) members of ethnic minorities and b) women come near to achieving full equality with men in the UK today?

2. Can the law help to promote good race relations?

3. Is anti-discriminatory legislation fair?

4. Do we need an Equality and Human Rights Commission?

5. Government action has made Britain a more tolerant country in its attitude to the elderly, disabled people and the gay community in recent years. Is this an appropriate role for government?

6. What can individuals do to help ensure that they gain equal recognition?

5   What are rights?

Learning objectives:

- to be able to define the concept of human rights, and duties and responsibilities
- to understand the debate surrounding rights and responsibilities.

Key terms

Inalienable rights: entitlements that should never be denied or taken away, because they derive from people's common humanity.

Human rights are those entitlements that allow us the minimum necessary conditions for a proper existence. In other words, they enable us to develop as individuals and achieve our potential irrespective of the class, race, religion or nationality to which we belong.

The concept of human rights is an elusive one and is interpreted differently by different politicians and by different governments. Some place the emphasis on one type of right, while others stress the importance of another type. Many writers would distinguish the following:

- *Legal rights:* Liberties the law allows us and which are recognised by the judicial machinery in any state – e.g. freedom of speech/assembly.
- *Moral or natural rights:* Sometimes described as **inalienable rights**, these are entitlements that cannot or should not be removed for they derive from people's common humanity – a person ought to be granted them, because he or she has a morally compelling claim. They are inherited at birth, being the sole property of the citizen who decides how and to what ends they are used. For centuries, political thinkers have discussed the existence of such rights, arguing over how they can be recognised and made effective.

The Universal Declaration of Human Rights (UDHR), adopted by the United Nations in 1948, states in Article 3 that everyone 'has the right to life, liberty and the security of the person'. The spirit of the document is clearly set out at the beginning, in Article 1, which observes that: 'All human beings are born free and equal in dignity and rights. They are endowed with reason and conscience, and should act toward one another in a spirit of brotherhood.'

The adoption of the UDHR reflected a mood of idealism in which people of the world community felt that the horror and devastation of the Second World War must be no more. The commitment to human freedoms was an indication of this concern for a better future.

Rights accorded by law

Legal rights derive from our membership of a particular society, rather than from our status as human beings. They will vary from country to country and there is no limit to their number. Different governments concede different rights. At any time, they can be amended/removed by a change in the law. A useful distinction is between:

1 *civil and political rights,* often based on moral or natural rights, these are the minimum ones necessary for full citizenship
2 *economic and social rights,* which concern the living standards/ lifestyle of people who live in the community.

Writers often go further and distinguish civil liberties from civil rights. Civil liberties are negative freedoms, freedoms from some form of restraint or limitation upon their behaviour. They require non-interference from government. They enable individuals to carry out certain actions that enable them to participate fully in the political system, for instance freedom of speech and of assembly. Civil rights are positive freedoms. They make demands of government in terms of the provision of resources and thus expand governmental responsibilities. They provide basic requirements of a good life, such as the right to work and to enjoy health treatment. They represent a set of protections that greatly affect people's lives (e.g. anti-discriminatory legislation to combat adverse treatment that individuals might suffer on grounds of ethnic background, gender or religion).

The rights that people can enjoy are usually outlined in the **Constitution** or Fundamental Law of a state. Some are of the moral/natural variety; most are civil/political. They are essential entitlements if legal, political and social life is to operate effectively.

Activities

1. Write a paragraph to explain the difference between legal and moral/natural rights.

2. Which of the following rights are legal/political ones and which are moral/natural ones?
   - The right to life
   - Freedom of assembly
   - Freedom of worship
   - The right to happiness
   - The right not to be subjected to cruel or degrading punishment
   - The right to vote
   - Freedom from slavery, servitude or forced labour
   - The right to food and shelter
   - The right to privacy
   - Freedom of expression
   - Freedom of assembly
   - The right to protest

The importance of rights in a democracy

The existence or absence of individual civil liberties and civil rights is the litmus test for a country that claims to be democratic. There may be disagreement over the freedoms to which citizens are entitled, but the following would command general assent:

- the right to life and personal security
- **equality before the law** and other legal freedoms such as freedom from inhuman or degrading punishment
- the right to vote in free elections, on the basis of political equality
- freedom of expression, including the rights to speak and write freely, freedom of assembly and of movement, as well as freedom of information
- freedom of conscience, including the right to worship or not to worship.

Others would claim freedom from discrimination, which is associated with the idea of equality before the law. In more recent years, the **right to privacy** in the home (during recreation and in respect of correspondence) is often asserted, as are a range of social rights. The South African Constitution introduced a novel right, the right to human dignity (see page 87).

There is only minor controversy concerning the main civil and political rights in most democracies. However, economic and social rights are a more contentious area.

Rights consciousness

Since 1945 there has been a growing interest in the area of human rights and **rights consciousness**. Whereas for a long while the rights emphasised tended to require the government not to act (e.g. permitting freedom of expression and assembly), in recent years more importance has been attached to the passage into law of entitlements that do need positive government intervention. Depending on the regime, government was expected – at the very least – to be concerned about safeguarding the right to work and the right to enjoy an adequate standard of living, decent accommodation, a fair income, educational and health opportunities. Many have seen it as the duty of government to promote such standards and opportunities by active intervention. Again, since 1945 there has been a growing consensus that measures should be taken to enhance freedom from discrimination in many fields, on grounds such as disability, gender and race. In other words, in many societies thinking has moved on from concern with negative liberty – freedom from state interference – to a concern for positive liberty, the actual promotion of policies to advance people's rights.

In general, people have become much more aware of the rights they possess and more determined that neither government nor other citizens should limit them. Individuals as well as groups have been keen to protect their existing rights and in some cases demand new ones. They have been willing to go to court to assert claims about those rights, leading to what some describe as a 'litigation explosion' and 'hyperlexis' (excessive law). In other words, rights consciousness has been accompanied by action to achieve the entitlements thought to exist, leading to litigation consciousness.

Rights consciousness worldwide

This emergence of a growing concern for rights and for new types of rights has been reflected in many of the international conventions that have been devised dealing with the topic. The Universal Declaration of Human Rights stands as an ideal to which member nations should aspire, though the document has no legal status. By contrast, the **UN International Covenant on Civil and Political Rights (ICCPR)**, which came into effect in 1966, is supposed to be binding on countries that have ratified it, as is the **European Convention on Human Rights** drawn up by the **Council of Europe** and in operation since 1953. The European Convention has done much to expand the liberty of the individual and the rights of minorities in member countries. It has served as a benchmark for many activists concerned with rights across the world. In 1959, in New Delhi, an International Commission of Jurists urged all governments to seek inspiration from its contents and operation.

Other than in conventions, the emergence of 'rights consciousness' has been apparent in the development of new constitutions and/or of special provisions for the protection of rights. Several countries have introduced some form of charter or bill of rights. Countries that had previously been satisfied with the old Westminster model of democracy began to contemplate new forms of protection (e.g. Canada and New Zealand). Almost all countries granted independence by Britain in the post-1945 era opted for a written constitution with a bill of rights to operate in tandem with it. In addition, in the United States, which has had such provision throughout its relatively short history, the Supreme Court has in the post-1945 era been noted for its '**judicial activism**', seeing the protection and advancement of individual and minority rights as a major function.

Key terms

Rights consciousness: refers to the general awareness of rights to be claimed or asserted against others, particularly the government.

UN International Covenant on Civil and Political Rights (ICCPR): a theoretically legally binding document devised by the United Nations, which commits countries that have ratified it to report periodically on their record of compliance with its provisions (pages 101–2).

European Convention on Human Rights: drawn up by the Council of Europe in 1950 and came into force three years later. It is an international legal instrument devised in the belief that the freedoms to which individuals are entitled are best protected by a system of democratic government. Britain helped draft the Convention and was the first country to sign it.

Council of Europe: established in 1949 as the first European political institution of the post-1945 era. Its aim was 'to achieve greater unity between its members for the purpose of safeguarding and realising the ideals and principles which are their common heritage and facilitating their social and economic progress'. Its other key goal was to work for the 'maintenance and further realisation of human rights and fundamental freedoms'.

Judicial activism: the idea that the courts should be active partners in shaping public policy. Supporters see the courts as having a role in looking after groups long denied political influence or clout. Opponents portray them as being excessively liberal, pro-criminal and soft on crime.

Activity

List and briefly explain three indications of the greater interest in and respect for rights in the post-1945 era.

Discussion of rights has been – and continues to be – much in the air. The developments that were noted above have been closely followed by enthusiasts for human rights throughout the world. In some regimes, respect for basic liberties is often lacking, and there are many instances of individuals being appallingly abused.

Summary questions

1 Do rights matter?

2 Is the development of rights consciousness in Britain and across many other parts of the world a good thing? Give reasons.

3 Non-Western political leaders sometimes criticise the concept of human rights as being a product of Western thinking. They suggest that it fits less comfortably with the outlooks and values of several Asian and Middle Eastern countries. For instance, the Saudi and Iranian approaches to rights bear little resemblance to that prevailing in liberal democracies, with flogging and torture being regular forms of punishment. Can we expect the same support for human rights in these parts of the world as we would expect in our own country?

4 What is the most important right that you enjoy? You might choose one moral and one legal right. Explain your response.

The relationship between rights and duties

Different ideologies place greater emphasis on some rights and freedoms than on others:

Further information

See also pages 4–6 in for information on Left and Right attitudes to duties.

1 *Traditional socialists* have stressed the importance of collective rights that enable groups to work together to improve their position. For them, rights such as freedom of assembly and the right to strike are particularly important. *New Labour* places less emphasis on the importance of collective rights than some socialists would wish. However, along with Liberal Democrats and others committed to extending civil rights, ministers do argue the case for positive freedoms such as freedom from sexual or racial discrimination. In these cases, government is specifically removing disadvantage suffered by one section of the community.

2 *Conservatives* place much emphasis on widening the area of choice available to individuals. They argue for an extension of home ownership, the right to determine the type of education available for one's children, the right to opt for private health provision, the right not to join a trade union, and particularly for the right to own and bequeath property. They prefer to see the government of the day doing less, passing fewer laws and not unduly interfering with people as they pursue their lives. According to this view, the activities of government are limited. A traditional Conservative refrain is that 'the best government is that which governs least'.

Attitudes to the relative importance of rights and duties

In Chapter 1, we saw that there were also differing attitudes between Left and Right regarding the importance attached to duties. The Left has generally stressed entitlements rather than responsibilities, whereas the Right has talked more about obligations. In the late 1980s, as the debate on Citizenship acquired new impetus, some Conservatives began to emphasise the need for citizens to play an active role in their communities, by becoming more involved in local organisations. 'Active citizenship' became a common theme, with talk of how people could think more about what they could contribute to society rather than what they might get out of it. There were echoes of the language used by President Kennedy of the United States in his Inaugural Address in 1961: 'And so, my fellow Americans: ask not what your country can do for you, ask what you can do for your country.'

New Labour too became committed to the language of citizenship. Tony Blair and Gordon Brown were early enthusiasts for communitarian thinking (see page 4). Both acknowledged the importance of duties as well as rights, recognising that in the past the Labour Party had been more willing to accept the latter rather than the former.

The relationship between rights and duties has a long history. In the 18th century, writing of *The Rights of Man*, the radical Thomas Paine observed that:

> When we speak of right we ought always to unite with it the idea of duties: rights become duties by reciprocity. The right which I enjoy becomes my duty to guarantee it to another, and he to me; and those who violate the duty justly incur a forfeiture of the right.

In other words you have a duty to ensure the rights you enjoy may also be enjoyed by others. If, for example, you enjoy freedom of speech you have the duty to ensure others enjoy it also. If you enjoy freedom from arbitrary punishment, you have a duty to ensure others that freedom.

The Universal Declaration of Human Rights (UDHR) similarly expressed the link between rights and duties. Article 3 extends the right to life, liberty and security of person to everybody but also obliges those same individuals not to deny the rights of others. Article 29 outlines a similar point:

> Everyone has duties to the community in which alone the free and full development of his personality is possible ... In the exercise of his rights and freedoms, everyone shall be subject only to such limitations as are determined by law solely for the purpose of securing due recognition and respect for the rights and freedoms of others and of meeting the just requirements of morality, public order and the general welfare in a democratic society.

Fig. 5.1 An Electoral Commission poster urges people to vote in local elections

The concepts of obligation and reciprocity in relation to rights

Citizens have rights as members of their community. If these rights and freedoms are to be recognised, certain limitations must be placed upon the freedom of others who will have corresponding duties and responsibilities. Here are some examples:

- The ownership of property by one person implies that others will observe their obligation not to tamper with it or in any way damage it.

■ The right of all people to live without fear implies that we all have a duty to say or do nothing that might cause distress to individuals or groups. This might mean curbing any personal prejudices about people of a different ethnic group or religious inclination, in the interests of social harmony. US Justice Oliver Wendell Holmes Jr once argued against people having an absolute right to do as they pleased. As he put it, 'no one is free to shout "Fire" in a crowded theatre'.

Moreover, if the rights of individuals deserve recognition, a case can be made that so do those of governments in a democracy. Governments acquire legitimacy by their election. Among other things, they can expect that citizens will normally obey the law and be fully participating members of society, exercising their right – some would say duty – to vote.

Obedience to the law

Broadly speaking, if laws are seen to be just and fair, there is scant justification for breaking them. Most people, for most of the time, do not break the law in any major way, partly out of fear that they will be apprehended and punished if they break society's rules. They may also wish to be seen as respectable, peaceful and law-abiding citizens who behave in the appropriate manner.

Various kinds of non-legal sanctions also influence people to act in the approved manner, so as to avoid such things as gossip, ridicule or social ostracism. For some people, the fear of public reproach or loss of friends may count for more than the fear of prison. The social penalty constitutes a part of the total that society imposes for offences against the law. There are also certain religious and moral sanctions that encourage citizens to obey the law, in particular the concepts of 'sin' and 'immoral behaviour'.

Is it ever right to break the law?

People may break the law because of ignorance of what the law is or because in minor cases there is a fair chance that they will not be caught or (if they were unlucky) in the hope of lenient treatment, for example by exceeding the statutory speed limit perhaps by a marginal amount.

Some people would suggest that the tendency to be law-abiding is only worthwhile if the laws are good, just and enforceable. Many famous people have challenged the law if it is seen to be unjust and if opportunities do not exist for them to express their opposition to authority. Mahatma Gandhi and Dr Martin Luther King are two well-known examples of individuals who were prepared to use **civil disobedience** to confront what they regarded as unjust laws.

Civil disobedience is law breaking that is justified by reference to some higher morality. It is a considered and public act designed to make a point to those in authority. Its moral force is dependent to some extent on the willingness of the person who commits the act to accept the punishment that follows from law-breaking. This is the point of the action. It is an overt measure determined to demonstrate to the rest of society the strength of one's ethical, religious or political feeling.

Voting

Elections are the main channel for popular participation. Voting in them is often viewed as a civic duty, in the way that in Ancient Athens (see page 1) all adult males were expected to attend open meetings and take an active role in the discussion of public affairs.

■ Key terms

Civil disobedience: non-violent law-breaking that is justified by reference to some higher moral or political principle. It is an overt and public act of protest, designed to gain publicity and 'make a point'.

■ Activity

Find out more about the circumstances in which Gandhi and King felt it necessary to resort to civil disobedience.

Should people vote?

Voting might be considered important for several reasons:

- A central idea is that those who exercise power should be accountable to the people. Elections give us a chance to hold those who rule us to account. If we do not think much of their performance, they can be thrown out at the next opportunity.

- Elections also give us a chance to choose between different people, policies and priorities, so that we can have a say in decisions about the way the country/organisation is run.

- Elections are really a badge of citizenship. They are our main opportunity to be involved and help to shape our lives.

- People in the past struggled to ensure that they could vote, and we should not therefore devalue their efforts.

- A single vote can make a difference. Consider the US Presidential election, 2000, an incredibly close contest in which everything depended on the outcome of recounted votes in a few Florida counties.

Examples of legal rights in society

There is some disagreement over the freedoms to which citizens are entitled, but the following would command general assent:

- the right to life and personal security
- equality before the law and other legal freedoms such as freedom from inhuman or degrading punishment
- the right to vote in free elections, on the basis of political equality
- freedom of expression, including the rights to speak and write freely, freedom of assembly and of movement, as well as freedom of information
- freedom of conscience, including the right to worship or not to worship.

Others would claim freedom from discrimination, which is associated with the idea of equality before the law. In more recent years, the right to privacy in the home (during recreation and in respect of correspondence) is often asserted, as are a range of social rights. In the South African Constitution (1996), specific social and economic rights are not spelt out, but the inclusion of the wide-ranging Article 10 is potentially significant (see Further Information).

There is only minor controversy concerning the main civil and political rights in most democracies. However, economic and social rights are a more contentious area.

Civil rights concerning the criminal justice system

Many legal rights are concerned with the system of criminal justice and involve the protection of personal freedoms. They allow everyone to act and behave as they would wish to do, subject to not breaking the law. The right of personal freedom is a long recognised and fundamental one. As far back as 1215, **Magna Carta** laid down the principles that: 'No man shall be taken or imprisoned or disseised [dispossessed], nor will we go upon him nor will we send upon him except by the lawful judgement of his peers or [and] the law of the land.'

Freedom from arbitrary arrest is protected by the ancient writ of **Habeas Corpus**, by which any detainee must be brought before a court within a specified time. Anyone held for a 'serious arrestable offence' must be

Further information

Rights in the South African Constitution

- Devised after the country had endured years of systematic oppression of individual and group rights, the South African Constitution is a remarkably liberal document.

- It emphasises anti-discriminatory provision, laying down that 'the state may not unfairly discriminate directly or indirectly against anyone on one or more grounds, including race, gender, sex, pregnancy, marital status, ethnic or social origin, colour, sexual orientation, age, disability, religion, conscience, belief, culture, language and birth'.

- Article 10 states that: 'Everyone has inherent dignity and the right to have their dignity respected and protected.'

Key terms

Magna Carta: a charter granted by King John at Runnymede in 1215, recognising the rights and privileges of the barons, Church and freemen.

Habeas Corpus: a writ which requires that a person detained by the authorities should be brought before a court of law so that the legality of the detention may be examined. The writ has historically been a key instrument in safeguarding individual freedom against arbitrary state action.

Check on the fate of Labour's anti-terrorist legislation (2008) to see in what form it was passed and what impact it is currently having.

■ Key terms

Right to silence: refers to the legal protection given to people undergoing police interrogation or trial in certain countries from any adverse consequences of remaining silent. If they choose to remain silent, no inference may be made as to their likely guilt. The right to silence is not specifically mentioned in the European Convention, although the European Court has ruled sympathetically to the rights of defendants on the issue.

Electorate: all qualified voters.

Franchise (or suffrage): the right to vote for representatives in a legislative body.

produced before a magistrate after 36 hours. Given the authorisation of the magistrates, detention can be continued for up to a maximum of four days. The recent anti-terrorist legislation (2008) would – if passed in its present form – enable the authorities to keep a person in custody for a maximum of 42 days. Once held in custody, the right to a fair trial, the presumption that a person is innocent until proven guilty and – give or take recent changes – the **right to silence** are accepted features of our legal system.

The range of other civil and political rights

The right to vote

Probably the most commonly listed civic right is the right to vote. A country is democratic if the people have the means and opportunity to effectively participate in the way that it is run. Citizen participation is basic to the democratic system. People may not be able to make decisions directly, but those who do make them are accountable to the **electorate** at election time. All adults have gained the **franchise** or right to vote, sometimes as a result of prolonged struggle.

Freedom of expression

Freedom of expression is not viewed as an absolute right in any country, but it is a highly prized concept in many. In the First Amendment to the US Constitution, it is explicitly declared. Article 19 of the International Covenant on Civil and Political Rights affirms the right of all people to seek, receive and impart information and ideas of all kinds, regardless of frontiers, 'either orally, in writing or in print, in the form of art, or through any other media of his choice'. Article 10 of the European Convention expresses a similar guarantee, though it does not specifically include references to seeking information and ideas.

In Britain, freedom of expression and particularly free speech are thought to be part of our heritage. As the poet John Betjeman put it:

Think of what our nation stands for

Books from Boots and country lanes

Free speech, free passes, class distinction

Democracy and proper drains.

The British attachment to free speech and free assembly is symbolised by Speakers' Corner, Hyde Park in London. On Sunday afternoons a variety of people including political extremists, representatives of minority ethnic groups and religious zealots, among many others, advocate their views to anyone who will listen. Such activities, showing the maximum tolerance of dissident opinions, indicate a mature democracy. The French philosopher and satirist Voltaire recognised their importance when he famously said: 'I disapprove of what you say, but I will defend to the death your right to say it.'

Limits on freedom of expression

For those who would limit freedom of expression, the case needs to be a powerful one. The more that restrictions would lessen the transmission of knowledge and undermine recognition of people's right to choose the lifestyle that suits them, the more convincing the argument needs to be. Not all materials carry the same weight, of course. In cases where accurate news reporting is involved or members of the public feel

Fig. 5.2 *Speakers' Corner, a symbol of British free speech*

entitled to see governmental documents, the defence of free expression is especially important for prohibition would seriously limit people's chances to develop their own opinions in the light of the available evidence. On the other hand, the justification for permitting the right to fabricate sensationalist stories, to make films or display material about sado-masochism, racism or support for terrorist violence may seem relatively less fundamental or actually damaging to society.

In the case of *James v the Commonwealth of Australia* (1936), the judgement declared: 'Free speech does not mean free speech; it means speech hedged in by all those laws against defamation, blasphemy, sedition and so forth. It means freedom governed by law ...'. As with other freedoms, there was then no special protection enabling people to speak freely, but there were no restrictions to interfere with established rights unless citizens fell foul of particular laws.

In the UK, the main legal limitations on freedom of expression remain:

- The law of **sedition**
- The law of **blasphemy**
- The law of **defamation**
- **Race relations legislation**
- [In the case of the press] the **Official Secrets Act (1989)**, **DA-Notices**, **Contempt of Court** and the **Obscene Publications Act (1959)**.

However, in a free society even if some issues seem more important than others, there is a need to defend all forms of expression and communication, except where those activities actually cause harm to other groups or individuals. Some are easy to justify simply because they appear to cause much good and pose little threat. However, even actions that are harmful to individuals and groups may still be justified and necessary as part of the price we pay for living in a free society.

Case study

The offence of blasphemy

The law against blasphemy was successfully invoked in a private prosecution against the then editor of *Gay News*, Derek Lemon, in

Key terms

Sedition: illegal speech or behaviour that undermines lawful authority and is intended to cause the disruption or overthrow of the ruling regime. It used to be widely defined to stifle debate involving any criticism of government policy. The modern interpretation is narrower. In 1909 (*The King v Aldred*), Justice Coleridge defined it as language 'intended to incite others to public disorder, to wit [that is to say], rebellions, insurrections, assassinations, outrages or any physical force or violence of any kind.'

Blasphemy: using language disrespectful of the Christian religion, which exposes it to 'vilification, ridicule or indecency'. In the 20th century, blasphemy has been interpreted much more narrowly and is therefore an uncommon offence. In 2008 the government published legislation to end the laws against blasphemy and blasphemous libel.

Defamation: technically divided into slander (defamation by word or gesture and therefore a temporary attack) and libel (defamation by printed word or in broadcast form, and because it is recorded a permanent form).

Race relations legislation: this has made it an offence to publicise views likely or intended to have the effect of provoking racial disharmony. The prosecution does not any longer have to prove an intention to incite racial hatred, only that this was the consequence of what was said or done (see page 73).

Official Secrets Act (1989): intended to reform the 1911 Act of the same name. Within a narrower area concerning vital areas of information it tightened the rules, especially concerning the right of search and seizure of material. Even a disclosure involving fraud, neglect or unlawful activity cannot now be defended as being in the public interest.

1978. He had published a poem, *The Love that Dares to Speak its Name* and an accompanying drawing, both of which were held by the complainant 'to vilify Christ in His Life and His Crucifixion'.

The judgment suggested that 'anything concerning God, Christ or the Christian religion' was covered, if it is written 'in terms so scurrilous, abusive or offensive as to outrage the feelings of any member or sympathiser with the Christian religion'.

Some other civil freedoms

Freedom of association involves the right of people to combine (meet together) freely, without fear of arbitrary interference. It is the basis of the right of people to join a political party, a pressure group or a trade union, and to publicise their common concerns. Allied to rights of association is freedom of assembly. The right is exercised every time that young people visit a cinema, club or pub. More controversial are those occasions in which they meet in rallies and festivals, for purposes of political discussion or protest. Meetings such as the anti-war protests in several European countries in early 2003 are a vital part of life in any democratic country. The right to express discontent in marches and demonstrations allows 'people power' to find an outlet, providing an opportunity for views to be put forward, sometimes of a kind that do not get much coverage in the media or via other institutions such as Parliament. Free association and assembly ensure that citizens have a chance to participate fully in civil life.

Labour relations are an important aspect of rights of freedom of association. The right to join a trade union (or not to join one) and to pursue labour objectives through collective action is one acknowledged in the Universal Declaration of Human Rights. It is well established in international law, the UN Covenant explicitly recognising it.

Freedom of religion and conscience is another important civil right allied to freedom of expression. Any religion or cult has the right to hold a service and practise its rituals, although there have been occasions when the definition of a religion or the nature of a group's behaviour have caused problems. Believers in scientology claim to be members of a religion devised by L. Ron Hubbard that is practised in the Church of Scientology; some opponents portray it as a dangerous cult. They deny that their behaviour is harmful or exploitative, but in Britain and elsewhere their status has sometimes been a cause of controversy.

Some other rights

In addition to the civil/political and economic/social rights listed, citizens have rights as consumers (see pages 92 and 112). They have also acquired new rights in the area of privacy (see pages 92 and 102), although their extent is still uncertain. In addition, they have rights in relation to information, concerning both access to documentation concerning government policy and the storage of data about themselves (see pages 105–11).

Social rights

Among the social, economic and cultural rights that might be asserted are the following:

- the right to an adequate standard of living – food, clothing, accommodation etc.
- the right to work

- the right to reasonable conditions of labour – including fair hours and rates of pay
- protection against unemployment
- the right to free education and access to higher education
- the right to health care
- special assistance for mothers and children.

In the area of social rights, there is much scope for disagreement. Many would assert the right to work, to housing, to health care and to decent educational opportunities. But difficulties abound. The right to work may be seen as a fundamental one, but what if – perhaps for sound reasons – the priorities of government policy concern the defeat of inflation and curbs in state spending? This runs the risk of greater unemployment, so that the right to work is then one denied to many people. The right of access to good healthcare and education is accepted as crucial, in that both help to determine life opportunities. But does that include the freedom to pay for private provision that may confer an extra advantage on those who have the means available? And what about housing? Everyone clearly needs shelter, but is it the responsibility of every individual to make his or her own arrangements or is there an entitlement to some form of public accommodation for those in need of a home?

The range of possible social rights is almost limitless. Some 30 years ago, the Institution of Professional Civil Servants agreed at its annual conference that the provision of a pension scheme that was inflation-proof and therefore guaranteed purchasing power was a basic human right and a principle of elementary justice.

Particularly controversial is the issue of abortion, a matter on which some alleged rights conflict with others. The right of a woman to have total control over her own body and thus have an abortion should she so wish is asserted by the 'pro-choice' lobby. This is not consistent with the wishes of 'pro-lifers' who argue for the right to life of the unborn foetus, a potential human being.

There are many examples in which competing rights may be advanced. For instance, the freedom to strike in pursuance of an industrial dispute may conflict with the rights of those who wish to work. In areas such as anti-discriminatory legislation, the rights of important minorities to protection may be at variance with the rights of other people to speak and act as they wish. In so many claims and counter-claims concerning social rights, the difficulty lies in balancing the desire for personal liberty and the need for measures widely perceived as being for the general good.

Further information

Problems with social rights

The right to work

- The right to work is often considered to be a basic human right.
- It is established under Article 23.1 of the Universal Declaration of Human Rights, which states: 'Everyone has the right to work, to free choice of employment, to just and favourable conditions of work and to protection against unemployment.'
- The Indian Constitution acknowledges the difficulty of fulfilling the right of all to work, via its qualification that the right is secured 'within the limits of economic capacity and development'.

Activity

Choose the three social rights that you consider to be the most important. Write a couple of sentences on each to explain why you think they are important.

Table 5.1 *The range of traditionally claimed rights in the UK*

Rights	Details
Legal rights	Protection of personal freedom, including freedom from detention without charge and the right to silence. There are police powers to stop and search on suspicion
Civil and political rights	
Freedom of association and bodies assembly	Includes the right to meet, march and protest freely. There are some restrictions made by the police and other public on public order grounds
Freedom of conscience and worship	Includes the right to practise any religion, the right of parents to withdraw children from religious education lessons in schools
Freedom of expression	Includes the right of individuals and the media to communicate information and express opinions. These are subject to the laws mentioned on page 93
Freedom of movement	Includes the right to move freely within and the right to leave Britain. The police are empowered to stop and search on suspicion. Suspected terrorists can be held
Right to privacy	A developing right, not previously acknowledged until the passage of the HRA. General right outlined in European Convention, subject to needs of state security
Political rights	The right to vote, as guaranteed for all people of 18 and over by the Representation of the People Act (1969)
Economic and social rights	
The right to own property	Includes the right to hold property as one wishes and not be deprived of it without due process. Compulsory purchase orders infringe rights of ownership
Rights at work	Includes protection against unfair dismissal, maternity rights, right to a satisfactory working situation and freedom from discrimination
Social freedoms	Includes a range of freedoms: to marry, divorce, practise contraception, seek abortions and – in the case of consenting partners – practise homosexuality
Consumer/ information rights	Sale of Goods Act, Advertising Standards legislation etc. Rights of access to personal information and information regarding governmental documentation

Further information

Problems with social rights

The issue of smacking

- Under the UN Convention on the Rights of the Child, ministers are expected to outlaw smacking by parents.
- A body of informed opinion agrees that there should be such a prohibition (including a House of Commons select committee, 2003), in order to prevent physical punishments being used as an excuse for child abuse.
- The committee wanted to rule out the defence of 'reasonable chastisement', which is often used by abusers in court to explain the serious injuries suffered by their children.
- Ministers took the view that the recommendations were unenforceable; no limitation has been introduced.
- Some claim that a ban would represent an intrusion into parents' legitimate rights and duties.

Conflicting rights

Rights can conflict with each other. On page 91 we noted the clash that can arise between the rights of the mother and of the unborn child in discussion of abortion. The rights of parents and children can come into conflict, for instance on the issue of smacking. There is much potential for conflict in the area of social rights, such as the right of employees to strike or not to strike. So, too, some of the limitations on free speech (see page 88–9) such as the law of defamation and the legislation on race relations deny the rights of individuals in order to promote the greater good of society by securing the rights of the bulk of the community.

The areas of freedom of speech, of association and of protest are all contentious, for they raise the question of whose rights are paramount – the individuals or groups of individuals who wish to exercise their right to air their views or the wider rights of society to go about their lives in a peaceful and secure manner, without feeling in any way threatened.

Limitations on free speech

Where restriction is necessary, it is important that citizens can easily find out what the limits are so that they can adjust their behaviour accordingly. It must be demonstrated that restriction is necessary in any democratic society in that it fulfils some pressing social need, and is proportional to the aim of responding to that need. It is not enough merely to assert that some restriction is necessary for national security and public order, but evidence must be provided that there is a genuine and serious danger to which the state is not over-reacting.

Pluralism and tolerance are democratic virtues that suggest a maximum emphasis on freedom of expression. But there are conditions under which limitations are acceptable. Where there is a perceived and dangerous terrorist threat, there may be good grounds for restriction. Again, the European Convention and the International Covenant actually require restrictions on the advocacy of national racial and religious hatred.

Reasons for regulation include such issues as:

1 national security
2 public safety – the prevention of public disorder/crime
3 protection of the rights and freedoms of others
4 public health and morals (a more controversial one).

It is the relationship between the theoretical principle of freedom of expression and the practical limits imposed by state restrictions that determines how much freedom of expression an individual actually has. The emphasis must be on freedom of expression, so that restrictions have to be exceptional cases, the need for which is convincingly demonstrated.

Limitations on the associated rights

Limitations on freedom of association

British law has traditionally allowed maximum freedom of association, in line with international obligations. There is provision under the Prevention of Terrorism legislation to ban certain bodies throughout the United Kingdom and it is illegal for people to seek to become a member of them. However, such proscribed (banned) organisations are relatively few in number.

The civil position is less clear cut. For instance, in the protest at **Twyford Down** in the early 1990s, peaceful motorway protesters were categorised in the same way as those among them who committed damage to vehicles used by building firms. All were restrained by an **injunction** from further protest, and made to pay a proportion of Department of Transport court costs.

Limitations on freedom of assembly

Under the allied freedom of assembly, people may come together in a public meeting provided that they can hire premises or meet on private property. To use a public facility, such as a park or shopping centre, they need permission. There is no general right to stage a gathering in Trafalgar Square, even if it has often been seen as a haven for those who wish to register their disapproval of government policy.

Activity

Write a paragraph or two to explain your thinking on whether or not parents should ever be allowed to smack their children.

Key terms

Twyford Down: the location for Britain's first major anti-motorway protest. A group of protesters set up a camp at a site through which the M3 was to pass. The section of road was opened in 1994, in spite of strong protests from various environmental organisations and activists.

Injunction: an equitable remedy in the form of a court order, whereby a party is required to do or refrain from doing certain acts – e.g. to prevent the continuation of a nuisance.

Limitations on the right to march in procession

It is traditional for British people to wish to demonstrate their feelings on a political issue via a procession or protest march, and in so doing they are behaving lawfully if they are not breaking a particular law. There are limitations on where they can exercise this freedom, however. They may do so on the public highway as long as they keep moving and react in an orderly manner. If they stop, they may be guilty of obstruction under the 1980 Highways Act, for roads are designed for the movement of traffic from one place to another. They may also be causing a public nuisance.

The issue of demonstrating along the highways may seem relatively unimportant, at most an inconvenience. However, it became a live one during the **Miners' Strike** when the courts found that 'unreasonable harassment' of workers seeking to get to their place of employment was a form of 'nuisance' that was unacceptable.

More threatening to society is a situation in which political activists of an extremist kind wish to march. The Public Order Act (1936) was designed to deal with the rise of the '**Blackshirts**' in the 1930s. It gave the police the right to change the route of a proposed march, and to impose conditions on the way it was organised. In particular, the carrying of weapons and wearing of uniforms were banned. Today, the same issues arise. The freedom of the National Front to hold a rally may well conflict with the right of local residents who do not wish to have provocative marchers passing near their houses, so that the right to carry out the activity has to be balanced against the concerns of other citizens.

The law has been updated in recent years, because of the number of rallies that have led to some degree of violence. The Public Order Act (1986) removed some offences present under the old law and created new ones. The law on racial hatred was clarified and tightened, and the law on riot, violent disorder and affray was also amended. Riot is the most serious offence under the Act, for it carries a threat of up to 10 years' imprisonment. A riot involves the activities of 12 or more persons who use, or threaten to use, unlawful violence.

The rights to assemble and protest were not guaranteed by law in Britain until the passage of the Human Rights Act (see page 101–4). However, in the European Convention and the International Covenant they are seen as key elements in a democratic society. In the Convention, the freedom is clearly proclaimed and then exceptions follow.

The need for state security

There is sometimes conflict between the rights of the state and the rights of the individual. The attacks on the World Trade Center have had a highly significant impact on discussions of state security, alerting politicians on both sides of the Atlantic to the dangers presented by terrorist activity, and leading to the creation of anti-incitement and anti-terrorist legislation.

The Racial and Religious Hatred Act (2006) created the offence of inciting (or 'stirring up') hatred against a person on the grounds of their religion. 'Religious hatred' was defined as hatred against a group of persons on account of their religious belief or lack of it. A person who uses threatening words or behaviour, or displays any written material that is threatening, is guilty of an offence if that person intends thereby to stir up religious hatred.

Measures to counter terrorism on a UK-wide basis were contained in legislation already passed in 2000 and in an emergency measure passed in 2001. Among other things, the legislation created new offences of inciting terrorist activity from within the UK and specific ones relating to the training of terrorist activists. A new and more controversial measure was introduced in 2005 and passed the following year, the Prevention of Terrorism Act. Among its controversial features was the creation of an offence of '**glorifying terrorism**' in the UK or abroad, new ground-rules for proscribing certain extreme organisations and powers of closure over places of worship used to foment (incite) extremism.

Case study

Inciting and/or glorifying terrorism – some cases involved

Glorification is the offence committed by a person who 'glorifies, exalts or celebrates' a terrorist act. In 2005, Tony Blair made it clear that 'the sort of remarks made in recent days should be covered … this will also be applied to justifying or glorifying terrorism anywhere, not just in the United Kingdom'. 'The sort of remarks' was taken to be a reference to Omar Bakri Muhammad who had received much media attention for his reaction to the London bombings. There had been other statements, made by a number of controversial figures, including Muslim clerics such as Abu Qutada and Abu Hamza al-Masri. Muhammad, said to be a spiritual leader for Al-Qaeda, had led an Islamist organisation based in the UK until its disbandment in 2004. (Subsequently, he voluntarily travelled to Lebanon and was denied re-entry into Britain.)

The arguments over the offence of glorification were prolonged. For instance, universities and professional associations had feared that any history lecturer who quoted statements by revolutionaries or teacher of a politics class who showed an Osama bin Laden video could face jail for glorifying terrorism. They received assurances that the question of intent was all-important and that such cases would not fall foul of the law.

Some critics said that existing laws were adequate and were already being used to prosecute individuals such as Abu Hamza (who preached at Finsbury Park Mosque in London) and other likely targets of the glorification charge. The first conviction of a Muslim preacher – that of Abdullah el-Faisal in 2003 – was brought under the Offences Against the Person Act (1861) for soliciting murder without a specific victim. (He called for the killing of Jews, Hindus, Americans and non-believers.)

In November 2007, Samina Malik became the first person to be convicted under the Terrorism Act (2006). The self- described Lyrical Terrorist, a 23-year-old Heathrow Airport shop clerk from Southall, West London, was found guilty of 'possessing records likely to be used for terrorism', but was earlier acquitted on the more serious charge of 'possessing an article for terrorist purposes'. The jury heard how she posted poems on the internet supporting Bin Laden and martyrdom and that a variety of terrorist literature was found when her house was searched, including poems she had written, terrorism manuals and other written terrorist material.

The conviction of Abu Hamza

In October 2004, Abu Hamza was charged with 16 crimes (one of which was dropped) under the provisions of various British statutes, including encouraging the murder of non-Muslims and intent to

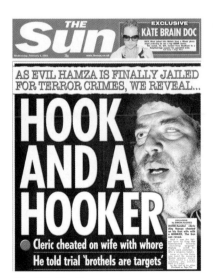

Fig. 5.3 *Abu Hamza*

Activities

1 Explain whether you think that ministers were right to create an offence of glorifying terrorism. Give your reasons.

2 Consider the case study and then write a couple of paragraphs to explain your reactions to the use of the law against Muslim clerics and others who seem to be in some way supporting terrorism. Think about their rights to freedom of expression and the governmental priority attached to maintaining security.

3 When state rights and those of individuals or groups conflict, where do you place the emphasis? Think about issues such as ASBOs and ID cards, and their relevance to the discussion.

stir up racial hatred. In February 2006, he was found guilty on 11 charges, which were:

- six charges of soliciting to murder under the 1861 legislation; not guilty on three further such charges
- three charges related to 'using threatening, abusive or insulting words or behaviour with the intention of stirring up racial hatred' under the Public Order Act (1986)
- one further charge of owning recordings related to 'stirring up racial hatred'
- one charge of possessing a 'terrorist encyclopaedia' under the Terrorism Act.

Abu Hamza was sentenced to seven years' imprisonment to run concurrently for eight counts and 21 months for the others. He has already been in jail since May 2004. In delivering his verdict, the judge declared that Abu Hamza had 'helped to create an atmosphere in which to kill has become regarded by some as not only a legitimate course but a moral and religious duty in pursuit of perceived justice'.

Summary questions

1 Do we have genuine freedom of speech in the UK today?

2 Which do you think are the three most important rights described in this chapter? Give reasons for your selection?

3 Should there be any limitations on the freedom of the individual?

4 'Freedom of expression is a defining characteristic of a democracy.' Do you agree?

5 Can it be right to curb religious incitement in a democracy?

6 Should radical Islamic or terrorist organisations be banned in the UK?

7 Should radical Muslim clerics be denied the chance to express their views in the UK?

8 Consider the quotation below. Do you agree with it?

To be able to defeat terrorism we need more debate, not less. Violence becomes endemic when governments suppress uncomfortable or challenging points of view. This government is now charging very fast down that road. The best way to stop people encouraging violence is to defeat them in argument, not to prevent them explaining why they are angry. This legislation goes much too far down the route of inhibiting freedom of speech and may yet be found by the courts to have breached article 10.

Source: comment column, Making bad law worse, The Guardian, 16 February 2006

6 What rights do I have?

Learning objectives:

- to have knowledge of human rights and the ways in which they are protected through the European Convention on Human Rights, the Human Rights Act, the Freedom of Information Act and the Data Protection Act

- to have knowledge of other rights of UK citizens, e.g. welfare rights and the debates surrounding those rights

- to be able to define the concepts of welfare rights.

Key terms

Geneva Conventions: adopted or revised in 1949 as a series of international rules designed to limit the barbarity of war. They chiefly concern the treatment of non-combatants and prisoners of war. A total of 194 countries have now signed the conventions.

International Labour Organisation (1919): originally an international body with a wide remit in matters of employment welfare and workers' rights. Since 1945, it has developed as an important piece of human rights machinery. The Conventions of the ILO on Human Rights cover issues such as 'Freedom of Association and Protection of the Right to Organise' (87) and 'Equal Remuneration for Men and Women' (100).

Organisation for Security and Cooperation in Europe: primarily concerned with the promotion of international security, but it also stresses human rights and the rule of law, for breaches of democratic standards can undermine international relations and therefore endanger security.

The barbarism of the Second World War inspired many people to think that measures should be taken to prevent such brutality from ever recurring. Accordingly, in the post-1945 era, procedures for the protection of rights have been elaborated under the auspices of several international agencies. These include the **Geneva Conventions**, the **International Labour Organisation**, the **Organisation for Security and Cooperation in Europe**, the European Union and the Council of Europe. Britain is a member of all of these bodies and has commitments under the agreements into which past governments have entered.

Here we are primarily concerned with the protection afforded to British citizens by membership of the United Nations, of the European Union and of the Council of Europe, via the European Convention and the Court of Human Rights.

The protection of rights: the United Nations

The United Nations was destined to play a leading role in the protection of rights. In the **UN Charter**, there was a commitment to the promotion of human rights and emphasis was placed on the need for nations to respect them. The most important and well-known steps taken were proclamation of:

1 the Universal Declaration of Human Rights; and
2 the two International Covenants agreed in 1966 (one on civil and political rights, the other on cultural, economic and social rights).

The Declaration is non-binding, but it has considerable moral standing. There were those who from the outset wished to turn it into a covenant, with the intention that those states which ratified it would be legally committed. But this effort was lost in the atmosphere of the **Cold War**, which was then developing. Countries were unenthusiastic about agreeing to any machinery that might endanger their national sovereignty and encourage interference in their internal affairs.

In 1966 agreement was reached on two documents, although it was another 10 years before they became operative. Of the two covenants, the International Covenant on Civil and Political Rights (the ICCPR) and the International Covenant on Economic, Social and Cultural Rights (ICESCR), the Western states were more sympathetic to the former and the **Soviet bloc** to the latter. It was open to countries to ratify either or neither, but many opted to support both of them. Given the atmosphere of the times, it was unlikely that there would be strong enforcement machinery, although in theory the covenants are binding.

Those countries that have ratified either document are committed to little more than to report periodically on their record of compliance with its provisions. They may also (in the case of the ICCPR) have opted to allow the Covenant's Human Rights Committee to listen to complaints from other states and their own nationals about their failure to adhere to the terms of the agreement. In the case of complaints by other states, a friendly settlement may be encouraged. In the case of individuals, the Committee may adjudicate upon the petition. Britain has not signed the optional protocol that allows this right of individual petition, arguing

Key terms

UN Charter (1945): committed signatories to the promotion of human rights and the need for nations to respect them. After establishing a Commission on Human Rights (1946), the UN devised its Universal Declaration of Human Rights (1948).

Cold War: the state of constant rivalry, suspicion and sometimes extreme tension between communist Eastern Europe and the Western nations (led by the US) from the mid-1940s until the early 1990s.

Soviet bloc: refers to the countries of Eastern Europe that were dominated by the Soviet Union (USSR) in the days of the Cold War – e.g. Hungary, Poland and Romania.

Treaty of Rome (1957): the agreement signed by six Western European countries to establish the European Economic Community, now known as the European Union (EU).

Single European Act (1986): implemented several objectives of the Rome Treaty, among them the removal of trade barriers and customs duties between member states, thereby creating a single market; and the introduction of free movement of goods, persons, services and capital.

that individual rights are better protected by the European Convention. Therefore, Britain merely makes occasional reports to the Committee and undergoes questioning by its members about its performance.

The Universal Declaration of Human Rights

Article 1.

All human beings are born free and equal in dignity and rights. They are endowed with reason and conscience and should act towards one another in a spirit of brotherhood.

Article 2.

Everyone is entitled to all the rights and freedoms set forth in this Declaration, without distinction of any kind, such as race, colour, sex, language, religion, political or other opinion, national or social origin, property, birth or other status. Furthermore, no distinction shall be made on the basis of the political, jurisdictional or international status of the country or territory to which a person belongs, whether it be independent, trust, non-self-governing or under any other limitation of sovereignty.

Article 3.

Everyone has the right to life, liberty and security of person.

Article 4.

No one shall be held in slavery or servitude and the slave trade shall be prohibited in all their forms.

Article 5.

No one shall be subjected to torture or to cruel, inhuman or degrading treatment or punishment.

Fig. 6.1 *Extract from the UN Declaration of Human Rights*

The protection of rights: the European Union

Although the European Convention is by far the most impressive piece of European law to ensure that rights are respected, the treaties involved in the development of the European Union also confer important rights. Certain categories of people benefit from aspects of EU policy, such as French agricultural workers whose standard of living has been protected by the Common Agricultural Policy. Again, the **Treaty of Rome (1957)** – many of the objectives of which were fulfilled via the **Single European Act (1986)** – ensures freedom of movement and the transferability of professional qualifications throughout the EU. Prohibitions against sexual and nationality discrimination have a long standing in the treaties. In other ways, the EU has developed a role in protecting and advancing human rights. For instance, all EU states have abolished capital punishment for all crimes and the EU has been active in the campaign for its global abolition.

Sometimes, problems have occurred either because national laws are different or because of the absence of specific legislation in some areas. Past issues have included the non-recognition of qualifications, the unequal treatment of men and women, or matters of pensions and social security where the claimant has worked in more than one state. In these and other cases, petitions may be made to the appropriate European machinery, be it the **European Commission**, the **European Parliament** or the **European Court of Justice**.

Few approaches are made directly to the European Court, for this is an exceptional facility and one available only at considerable expense. Most petitions are made to the European Parliament, which established a Commission on Petitions, comprising 28 Members of the European Parliament (MEPs) who are interested in the question of citizens' rights.

The European Parliament has been a strong defender of women's rights. It has a permanent committee to examine matters in which these are not being fully acknowledged. Many issues have arisen out of a requirement of the Treaty of Rome that 'men and women should receive equal pay for equal work' (Article 119).

The promotion of human rights within the EU

For more than two decades, there has been occasional discussion of the ways in which the Community should advance in the area of human rights. The signing and implementation of the Maastricht Treaty on European Union was a significant development. It established that those fundamental rights guaranteed by the European Convention must be respected by all signatories to the Treaty of Rome.

Since the Treaty on European Union (TEU) came into force, a number of new rights have arisen. It was accepted at Maastricht that it was an important objective of the new Union 'to strengthen the protection of the rights and interests of the nationals of its Member States through the introduction of a citizenship of the Union'. Accordingly, people living in member countries have now become citizens of the EU. As a result, they have acquired additional voting rights. European citizens living in Britain are entitled to vote or be a candidate in Euro-elections. In the same way, British nationals are allowed to do the same elsewhere in the Union. Also, since 1994, all European citizens are entitled to take part in municipal elections in a country in which they have residence, though formal arrangements for this change have yet to be made.

A further development of considerable importance was the consideration given to what was originally known as the Social Charter and at Maastricht became the **Social Chapter**. Eleven states were prepared to sign this *Protocol and Agreement on Social Policy*, which was not part of the main treaty. The British Conservative government saw the Social Chapter as an insidious form of socialism that would impose shackles on British industry and thereby limit competitiveness. The Labour Party and trade unionists adopted a more pro-European stance. Once in office, Tony Blair quickly signed up to the Protocol. This involved the creation of new social rights for British people.

Finally, in the draft Amsterdam Treaty (June 1997), it was agreed that the Union would respect not only those rights guaranteed by the European Convention, but also those set out in the **European Social Charter**. In addition, it was decided that the institutions of the EU would take action to promote the needs of persons with a disability. In addition,

Key terms

European Commission: a hybrid organisation that makes decisions in some areas and carries out decisions made by the Council of Ministers in others. Among other things, it has powers to initiate policies and represent the general interest of the EU.

European Parliament: meeting in Strasbourg, receives reports from Commissioners and holds debates and a question time. Its legislative role was initially only advisory, but in every major EU treaty (e.g. the Single European Act, Maastricht, Amsterdam and Nice) its powers have been increased.

European Court of Justice: rules on matters of EU law as laid down in the treaties and can arbitrate in disputes between major states and in those between the Commission and Member States. Based in Luxembourg, it can levy fines on those states in breach of EU law and on those that do not carry out treaty obligations.

Social Chapter: a protocol of the Maastricht Treaty committing Member States to a range of measures concerned with the social protection of employees. It was subsequently incorporated into the Treaty of Rome at the Amsterdam summit (1997). Britain originally had an opt-out, but the Blair government soon signed the Chapter, under which rights such as paternity leave and the 48-hour week were granted.

European Social Charter: drawn up by the Council of Europe to fill a gap left by the European Convention, which mainly covers civil and political rights. Signed originally in 1961, it was revised in 1996. Among other things, it protects the rights to work, to safe, healthy working conditions, to strike, to social security and to benefits from social welfare services. The European Committee of Social Rights (ECSR) is the body responsible for monitoring compliance in the states party to the Charter.

Key terms

Council of Ministers: officially now the Council of the European Union, this is the primary decision-making body of the EU, comprising a representative of each Member State with responsibility for whatever policy area is under consideration, e.g. environment ministers when the environment is being discussed.

Charter of Fundamental Rights: sets out in a single text, for the first time in the EU's history, the whole range of civil, political, economic and social rights of European citizens and all persons resident in the EU. It is organised into six units, dealing with dignity, freedoms, equality, solidarity, citizens' rights and justice. Of the more recent rights, it includes the prohibition of reproductive cloning of human beings (Article 3).

Lisbon (Reform) Treaty: intended to provide the EU with streamlined, modern institutions and improved working methods, as befits an organisation of 27 members. It seems unlikely that it will be implemented in its original form following its rejection by Irish voters in a referendum held in June 2008, even though it has been ratified by most Member States.

the **Council of Ministers** was empowered to take appropriate action to combat discrimination based on sex, racial or ethnic origin, religion or belief, disability, age or sexual orientation.

Any country wishing to join the EU today has to be a signatory to the European Convention on Human Rights. However, the EU was unable to sign it in its own right, without a treaty change. Accordingly, it devised the **Charter of Fundamental Rights**, which not only included the rights contained in the Convention but also drew upon various UN and EU agreements, covering economic, political and social rights. It includes 'new' rights such as good governance and a clean environment. Proclaimed in 2000, it was included in the proposed constitution for Europe, which was rejected by the voters in France and the Netherlands in 2005. It has no legal force at present, but should the **Lisbon (Reform) Treaty** be ratified the Charter would become legally binding and the EU would accede to the ECHR. The European Court of Human Rights, currently totally separate from the EU, would become the highest court in the EU for Human Rights, above the EU's Court of Justice.

■ The European Convention and the European Court of Human Rights

The European Convention was a document drawn up mainly by British lawyers in the Home Office. The bodies responsible for its implementation (the European Commission on Human Rights and the European Court of Human Rights) began their work in 1953. They predate, are not part of and should not be confused with the European Union, which has just been described. However, the relationship between the organisations is set to become much closer, should the Lisbon Treaty be ratified.

Britain was an early signatory of the document and from 1965 its citizens had the right of access to the European machinery. This meant that although the Convention was not part of British law, citizens who felt that their rights had been denied could take the long road to Strasbourg to gain redress and possibly compensation.

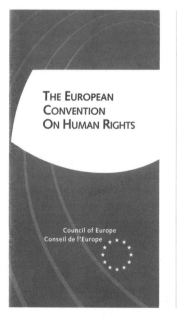
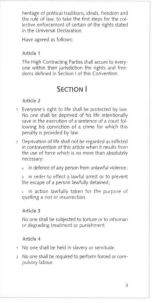

Fig. 6.2 *Extract from European Convention on Human Rights*

The Human Rights Act

The case for incorporation of the Convention was accepted by Labour back in the early 1990s, when John Smith was leader (1992–4). Along with many centre-Left politicians, he and his successor, Tony Blair, recognised that the status of the Convention in Britain was unsatisfactory. Britain was ultimately bound by it, yet citizens had difficulty in using it. Ministers were tempted to play for time and not give way when infringements of rights were alleged. This was because they knew that Strasbourg justice was slow, sometimes taking five to six years to get a court decision. Many people were tempted to give up the struggle, rather than wait for a European verdict.

Tony Blair and his ministers, having overcome their party's long-term hostility to 'Tory judges', argued that the courts would provide an essential check upon the might of an overweening [unduly powerful] executive.

> ### Further information
>
> #### The contents of the European Convention
>
> Of the 66 articles, the most well known are the first 10:
>
> 1 commitment of all signatories to secure the rights set out in the Articles below
>
> 2 right to life
>
> 3 freedom from torture, inhuman or degrading treatment
>
> 4 freedom from slavery or forced labour
>
> 5 right to liberty and security of person
>
> 6 right to a fair trial by an impartial tribunal
>
> 7 freedom from retrospective criminal laws
>
> 8 right to respect for private and family life, home and correspondence
>
> 9 freedom of thought, conscience and religion
>
> 10 freedom of expression.
>
> For each entitlement, the basic statement is set out in one paragraph, followed by a series of qualifications that list the exceptions to it.

The introduction of the Human Rights Act

In October 1997, New Labour produced a White Paper showing how for the first time a declaration of fundamental human rights would be enshrined into British law. The detail of the proposals showed that the courts were not being empowered to strike down offending Acts of Parliament, as happens in Canada. Instead, judges would be able to declare a particular law incompatible with the Convention, enabling government and Parliament to change it if they so wished, and providing a fast-track procedure for them to so do. In this way, the proposed Act would not pose a threat to the principle of **Parliamentary Sovereignty**.

The resulting Human Rights Act (HRA) (passed in 1998) became operative from October 2000. It provides the first written statement of the rights and obligations of British people, by incorporating most – but not all – of the European Convention on Human Rights into British law. It allows them to use the Convention as a means of securing justice in the British courts. Judges are now able to apply human rights law in their rulings. The Act also totally abolished the death penalty in UK law.

The Convention Protocols to which the UK signed up

The UK has ratified Protocols 1, 6 and 13. The UK has not yet ratified the other protocols containing substantive rights (Protocols 4, 7 and 12). These are under review.

> ### Hint
>
> The European Convention and the Human Rights Act have become massively important in the protection of rights within the UK. Be sure that you know the contents of the Convention and Act, and understand how the Articles they contain are qualified. Be in a position to quote two or three examples from the document. Know at least a few examples of cases brought under the Act and be in a position to piece together a picture of how successfully it is extending the rights of the citizen.
>
> **N.B.** It is important to recognise the difference between the European Court of Justice, which meets in Luxembourg and is the highest court of the European Union and the European Court of Human Rights, which meets in Strasbourg and was established under the European Convention on Human Rights. The Convention was adopted by the Council of Europe, which itself is completely different from the European Union.

> ### Activity
>
> Look up the contents of the European Convention, to find examples of how different rights are qualified – e.g. Articles 5 and 10.

> ### Key terms
>
> **Parliamentary Sovereignty:** the constitutional principle that Parliament theoretically possesses and exercises unlimited power to make, repeal or amend any law, without challenge from any other UK body or institution. It is the supreme law-making authority in the UK. It has traditionally been viewed as a key element of the British constitution, although its impact has been modified in recent years by membership of the EU.

■ Key terms

Judiciary: the branch of government responsible for interpreting and applying the laws in particular cases, e.g. the British judges.

■ Activities

1. Read the section on judges and judicial power (see pages 145–157). Write a couple of paragraphs to say in what ways it might be regarded as perturbing if the introduction of the HRA does tilt the balance of power from Parliament to the judiciary, as Bogdanor claims? Give an explanation of your answer.

2. Using the internet to assist you, find out about how the HRA has helped develop a law of privacy in the UK. You might look up cases such as those concerning:
   - Gordon Kaye, the British television actor who wanted to block publication when a tabloid photographer and reporter entered his hospital room shortly after emergency brain surgery
   - Catherine Zeta-Jones and Michael Douglas and their suing of *Hello!* magazine for publishing unauthorised photographs of their wedding
   - Naomi Campbell's complaint against a tabloid, which published details of her treatment for cocaine addiction at Narcotics Anonymous
   - FIA president Max Mosley's battle with the *News of the World*, in which the motor-racing supremo vigorously denied the newspaper's allegation that there was a Nazi element in his sado-masochistic practices.

Life under the Human Rights Act

The Human Rights Act makes it unlawful for any public body to act in a way that is incompatible with the Convention, unless the wording of an Act of Parliament means they have no other choice. It requires UK judges take account of decisions of the Strasbourg court and to interpret legislation, as far as possible, in a manner compatible with the Convention. An individual can still take a case to the Strasbourg court as a last resort.

From 2000, the British courts have had more power than ever before to hold the government and public bodies to account for their actions. Much of the discussion of the new Act has surrounded the question of the extent to which the judges will embrace their new opportunity with enthusiasm and flex their muscles at the expense of Parliament. Accustomed to poring over the precise wording of British statutes, judges are now required to interpret what the law is in a particular situation when a citizen brings a case under the 'broad-brush' phraseology of the European Convention. Many precedents [earlier cases] that previously influenced their legal judgments have lost some of their former relevance.

The HRA does appear to tilt the balance of the Constitution in favour of the judges. As political scientist Bogdanor (2003) puts it, the measure 'considerably alters the balance between Parliament and the **judiciary** … for in effect the Human Rights Act makes the European Convention the fundamental law of the land'. Not all academics and commentators agree with his judgment. Morris (1999) doubts that major social and political change will in future be driven by judges rather than legislators, noting that 'there is little evidence of this in those countries in which the Convention has long been domestically incorporated'.

The impact of human rights legislation

The effect of incorporation of the Convention is to introduce a new human rights culture into British politics. In general, decisions by Parliament, a local authority or other public body must not infringe the rights guaranteed under the Act. Where rights conflict, such as privacy versus freedom of information, the courts will decide where the balance should lie. Judges have the task of deciding cases as they come before them.

There were some concerns that the Act would clog up the courts (particularly in the early stages) and that the chief beneficiaries would be lawyers. It was expected that the courts would be deluged with all kinds of cases, some of them extreme. In Scotland, where the European Convention was already in force, 98 per cent of the cases in the first year failed. In the event, there was no legal free-for-all. Between 2000 and 2002, of 431 cases involving human rights heard in the high courts, the claims were upheld in 94. Keir Starmer (2003), a barrister much involved in such cases, has concluded that 'hand on heart, the Human Rights Act has changed the outcome of only a very few cases'.

Three early rulings under the HRA

1 Self-incrimination

In 2000, two men photographed by a speed camera, Amesh Chauhan and Dean Hollingsworth, were sent a form by the police asking them to identify who was driving the vehicle at the time. They protested under the Human Rights Act, claiming that they could not be required to give evidence against themselves. The initial judgment in Birmingham Crown Court was in their favour, the judge arguing that the police requirement was in breach of the Convention, due to become law in England and Wales later that year. However, this ruling was later reversed.

2 Romas

In *Connors v UK* (2004), the court had declared that travellers who had their licences to live on local authority-owned land suddenly revoked had been discriminated against compared to the treatment of mobile-home owners who did not belong to the traveller population and thus their Article 14 (protection from discrimination) and Article 8 (right to respect for the home) had been infringed. Under Article 41 (just satisfaction), the court awarded the applicant €14,000 for non-pecuniary damage and €21,643 for costs and expenses.

There has never been a case where the Human Rights Act has been successfully invoked to allow travellers to remain on greenbelt land. Such an outcome seems unlikely, following a House of Lords ruling, which severely restricted the occasions on which Article 8 may be invoked to protect someone from eviction in the absence of some legal right over the land.

3 Afghan rulings

The case concerned nine Afghan men who hijacked a plane to escape the Taliban and forced the crew to divert to Stansted, north of London. They were convicted of hijacking in 2001, but the convictions were later quashed in the Court of Appeal (2003). In 2004, a panel of adjudicators ruled that returning the men to Afghanistan would breach their human rights under the Convention. They were granted temporary leave to remain, but this placed them under restrictions that would not have enabled them to choose where they wished to live or to obtain work.

In May 2006, an Immigration Tribunal ruled under the Human Rights Act that the hijackers could remain in the UK. A subsequent court decision in *S and Others v Secretary of State for the Home Department* ruled that the government had abused its power in restricting the hijackers' right to work. The series of judicial rulings provoked widespread hostility in the UK, particularly in the tabloid press and in the Conservative Party. Labour ministers too were affronted; Prime Minister Blair calling one judgment 'an abuse of common sense'. Home Secretary John Reid, whose department had brought the case, expressed his alarm and frustration: 'There is a very serious threat – and I am the first to admit that the means we have of fighting it are so inadequate that we are fighting with one arm tied behind our backs. So I hope when we bring forward proposals in the next few weeks that we will have a little less party politics and a little more support for national security.'

Anti-terrorist legislation and the HRA

Governments are able to derogate [opt out] from the Convention in times of dire emergency. The terrorist threat caused ministers to derogate in November 2001, a derogation that lasted until May 2005. There are other countries that have applied such a derogation, for example Greece in 1969, Ireland in 1978, Northern Ireland in 1988 and Turkey in 1996.

Although it had passed permanent counter-terrorism legislation only a year earlier, the British government's response to the attacks on the World Trade Center (9/11) was to rush through emergency legislation to increase governmental powers to deal with individuals suspected of planning or assisting terrorist attacks within the UK. The Anti-Terrorism Crime and Security Act (2001) passed by Labour in response to the perceived terrorist threat fell foul of the judges. In a case involving the detention without trial of nine foreigners at HM Prison Belmarsh, the judges found that the detention of foreign terror suspects without trial was incompatible with European – and therefore domestic – law, being

---

Further information

The Conservatives and the Human Rights Act

- At the time of the passage of the Human Rights Act, Conservative Party leader William Hague echoed many recent Conservative criticisms of allowing power to pass from an elected Parliament to judges who could not be dismissed.

- In the Conservative 2005 election campaign, Michael Howard vowed to 'overhaul or scrap' the Human Rights Act, saying: 'The time has come to liberate the nation from the avalanche of political correctness, costly litigation, feeble justice, and culture of compensation running riot in Britain today ... the regime ushered in by Labour's enthusiastic adoption of human rights legislation has turned the age-old principle of fairness on its head.'

Belmarsh 2004

Belmarsh – Britain's Guantanamo Bay?

You don't have to go to Cuba to find terror suspects controversially imprisoned. Nine foreigners have been held in London's Belmarsh Prison for almost three years without charge or trial. So is it the UK's Guantanamo Bay? ... The nine ... were not able to see the intelligence against them ... under charges brought under anti-terrorist legislation.

Source: extract from BBC News, 6 October 2004

The real threat to the life of the nation, in the sense of a people living in accordance with its traditional laws and political values, comes not from terrorism but from laws such as these. That is the true measure of what terrorism may achieve. It is for Parliament to decide whether to give the terrorists such a victory.

Source: Lord Hoffman, December 2004 ruling

■ Activity

Write a few sentences to explain on which side your sympathies lie in the dispute between the government and the judiciary in the approach to anti-terrorist legislation.

■ Summary questions

1 Compare Labour and Conservative attitudes to the Human Rights legislation.

2 Has the Human Rights Act been a force for good?

both disproportionate (in that less-restrictive measures were available) and discriminatory (since UK nationals suspected of terrorism were not liable to indefinite detention).

Ministers tried to amend the original legislation, via their Prevention of Terrorism Act (2005). This introduced 'control orders' that applied to both UK and foreign nationals suspected of involvement in terrorism. Human rights groups argued that these were incompatible with both Article 5 (the right to liberty) and Article 6 (the right to a fair trial), a position again upheld by the courts in April 2006. A High Court judge issued a declaration that Section 3 of the Act was incompatible with the right to a fair trial under Article 6 of the European Convention on Human Rights. Mr Justice Sullivan described the Act as an 'affront to justice'.

Fig. 6.3 *Protest outside Belmarsh prison in south-east London*

■ The right to know

The United States and several liberal democracies in Europe acted to provide individuals with access to information contained in government records before the United Kingdom went down that route. However, three measures have 'opened up' United Kingdom government and made it easier to find out what is going on 'behind closed doors':

1 *The Local Government (Access to Information) Act (1986)* made local council records available within a short period after they were documented.

2 *The Data Protection Act (1998)* gave individuals a right of access to their personal information held on file by all private and public institutions. They are entitled to have mistakes in any data corrected.

3 *The Freedom of Information Act (2000)* provided the public with a broader statutory right to information from government and public authorities.

The Data Protection Act (DPA)

The Data Protection Act gives you **the right to know** what information is held about you and sets out rules to make sure that this information is handled properly. It is the main piece of legislation that governs the protection of personal data in the UK. It provides a legal basis for the handling of information relating to living people, in practice creating a means by which individuals can enforce the control of information about themselves. Most of the Act does not apply to domestic use, such as the holding of a personal address book. However, subject to some exemptions, organisations in the UK are legally obliged to comply with this Act.

The Act makes new provision for the regulation of the processing of information relating to individuals, including the obtaining, holding, use or disclosure of such information. Often, the information that causes concern refers to that held by credit rating agencies, but it also includes character references about students and job applicants that are provided by teachers and employers. For the first time, the Act also tackles the rapidly spreading technology of surveillance by closed circuit television (CCTV), providing means of legal control. The Information Commissioner is responsible for a code of conduct governing the use of CCTV, for those who establish and operate such systems. The Commissioner also has responsibility for implementation of relevant EU regulations concerning access to telecommunications traffic and guaranteeing a 'right to privacy' in respect of the telecommunications traffic of individuals.

The Act gives individuals rights to:

- gain access to their data
- seek compensation
- prevent their data being processed in certain circumstances
- 'opt out' of having their data used for direct marketing
- 'opt out' of fully automated decision-making about them.

Key principles of the legislation

Personal data:

1 shall be processed fairly and lawfully
2 shall be obtained only for one or more specified and lawful purposes
3 shall be adequate, relevant and not excessive in relation to the purpose or purposes for which they are processed
4 shall be accurate and, where necessary, kept up to date
5 shall not be kept for longer than is necessary for that purpose or those purposes
6 shall be processed in accordance with the rights of data subjects under this Act.

In addition:

- appropriate technical and organisational measures shall be taken against unauthorised or unlawful processing of personal data and against accidental loss or destruction of, or damage to, personal data
- personal data shall not be transferred to a country or territory outside the **European Economic Area** unless that country or territory ensures an adequate level of protection for the rights and freedoms of data subjects in relation to the processing of personal data.

Key terms

The right to know: refers to the belief that in a liberal democracy people should have an appreciation and understanding of the facts and implications of any governmental action. They can then vote at election time on the basis of informed consent.

European Economic Area: an organisation that enables three of the four members of the European Free Trade Association (Iceland, Liechtenstein and Norway) to benefit from the single market created by the EU, without actually being members of the Union.

Case study

What is covered by the DPA

Q: My neighbour has CCTV cameras overlooking my property. Is this in breach of the Data Protection Act?

If your neighbour is a private individual e.g. the cameras are on their residential property, it is unlikely that they will be breaching the Data Protection Act because there is an exemption for domestic/household processing of personal data as long as this does not involve putting personal information on a website or otherwise disclosing it to the world at large without good reason. They may however be breaching other legislation, such as the law about harassment or voyeurism, and so may be referred to another body such as the police to investigate.

Q: I think a data controller has breached the Data Protection Act. What can I do?

Under Section 42 an individual has the right to make a complaint to the Information Commissioners Office.

Q: What protects my personal information when it is being passed to overseas companies and call centres?

The Data Protection Act prohibits the transfer of personal information from the UK to other countries unless those countries can ensure the same level of protection. Organisations can also set up contracts with overseas organisations receiving personal information. This ensures that a higher standard of protection is in place than there might have been in the receiving country.

Organisations in the UK which have personal information processed on their behalf overseas are responsible for the security of your information. The UK organisation is required to make sure the company overseas complies fully with the UK Data Protection Act.

Q: I was refused credit, is there anything I can do?

Under the Data Protection Act you can request a copy of your credit history file, which lists the loans, mortgages and credit cards you have and whether these have been paid on time. It will also show if the payment has gone into default or been satisfied. You can apply to one or all of the main credit reference agencies (Equifax, Experian or Call Credit). If any details on your file are incorrect you should go back to the person or organisation who has put this on your record and ask them to update their records.

Q: I think my personal information is wrong. Can I correct it?

Under the fourth principle of the Data Protection Act, information must be accurate and up to date. If you feel that your information is not factually accurate (this is information that can be proven to be inaccurate and not an opinion of the person or organisation) you must contact the person or organisation that is holding this information and tell them you believe your information needs updating to be factually accurate under the Data Protection Act. If they fail to do this and your information still remains factually inaccurate you can contact the ICO.

Source: questions and responses taken from the office of the Information Commissioner website, www.ico.gov.uk

Activities

1 List circumstances under which information on a person's credit status might become important to them.

2 Why are some people concerned over the operation of CCTV cameras?

Powers of the Information Commissioner over data protection

The data protection powers of the Information Commissioner's Office are to:

- conduct assessments to check organisations are complying with the Act
- serve information notices requiring organisations to provide the Information Commissioner's Office with specified information within a certain time period
- serve enforcement notices and 'stop now' orders where there has been a breach of the Act, requiring organisations to take (or refrain from taking) specified steps in order to ensure they comply with the law
- prosecute those who commit criminal offences under the Act
- conduct audits to assess whether organisations' processing of personal data follows good practice
- report to Parliament on data protection issues of concern.

Freedom of Information Act (FOIA)

Freedom of information legislation, known as 'sunshine laws' in the United States, establishes rules on access to information or records held by government bodies. In many countries there are constitutional guarantees covering the right of access to information, often backed up by more specific legislation. Sweden was the first country to introduce such legislation. Today, in excess of 70 countries around the world have implemented some form of laws on access to information. A basic principle behind many of them is that the burden of proof falls on the body *asked* for information, not the person *asking* for it. The requester does not usually have to give an explanation for their request, but a valid reason has to be given if the information is not disclosed.

The passage of freedom of information legislation reflects its importance to liberal democracy. However, there are differences in national practice, reflecting competing views of what liberal democracy entails and disagreement over what freedom of information is supposed to achieve.

In England and Wales (separate legislation exists for Scotland) the 2000 Act makes provision for the disclosure of information held by public authorities or by persons providing services for them. These include:

- central and local government
- the health service
- schools, colleges and universities
- the police
- several other non-departmental public bodies, committees and advisory bodies.

The public has the right of access to information held by such authorities, which are normally required to make this information available. However, some information might be withheld to protect various interests that are allowed for by the Act. If this is the case, the public authority must tell the person requiring it that it has withheld information and why. The intention of the Act is stated as being 'to increase visibility into the work of public bodies, to ensure that policy-making processes are fair, democratic and open'.

Most requests for information are free. A person might be asked to pay a small amount for making photocopies or postage. However, if the public

Further information

How the Freedom of Information Act operates

- The Act provides access to a wide range of documentation held by public authorities.
- Requests must be clear and specific enough for it to be evident what is being sought; this discourages 'fishing' expeditions for information.
- Refusal to supply information can be appealed to the Information Commissioner, who has power to investigate and adjudicate, but not enforce.
- Responsibility for freedom of information has passed from the Department for Constitutional Affairs to the Ministry of Justice.

authority thinks that it will cost them more than £450 (or £600 for a request to central government) to find the information and prepare it for release, then they can turn down the request. They might ask for it to be narrowed down and made more specific.

The Act in practice

The passage of freedom of information legislation was in defiance of a long-standing preference for secrecy in British government and politics. Indeed, in some respects the 2000 Act is no exception, in that it contains several blanket exemptions, including commercial security, defence, international relations, national security and the advice given in government policy-making processes. Given the traditionally restrictive British approach to the release of information, many commentators doubted whether the Act would allow significant disclosures. Indeed, disclosure is specifically limited by the terms of the **Official Secrets Act (1989)** and other measures. Furthermore, the Act does not extend to public bodies in the overseas territories or crown dependencies. Some of these have contemplated implementing their own legislation, though none is currently in force.

In spite of these constraints upon its effectiveness, the Act has been used to extract a wealth of information, some of it on matters of public rather than personal interest. The Information Commissioner who is responsible for matters relating to its operation has interpreted his brief in a relatively liberal manner, most notably in February 2008 when the Brown government was ordered to release the minutes of Cabinet discussions in which ministers discussed military action against Iraq (see the case study below for the ministerial response).

The Information Tribunal, which hears appeals from notices issued by the Information Commissioner under the DPA and FOIA, has backed the Commissioner in his interpretation of the FOI legislation. He has ordered disclosure of some material relating to officials' advice to ministers after only a few months, a position upheld in two High Court challenges brought by the government. The Tribunal has accepted that the public interest normally favours confidentiality while policy is being developed and that ministers and officials need 'time and space … to hammer out policy … without the threat of lurid headlines'. But once the decision has been taken and announced, in its view the case for disclosure becomes stronger.

In key decisions, the Tribunal has:

- ordered the Department of Work and Pensions to disclose a 2004 assessment of the benefits of introducing identity cards
- required disclosure of officials' advice to the then deputy prime minister on granting planning permission for a tower block near Westminster; they wanted it refused, but John Prescott granted it
- ordered the release of high level Department for Education and Skills board minutes regarding a schools funding crisis in 2003.

Key terms

Official Secrets Act (1989): intended to reform the 1911 Act of the same name. In some respects, it liberalised the old law by removing the blanket ban on disclosure under the old 'catch-all' Section 2, but in the narrower and more vital areas of information it tightened the rules. Even a disclosure involving fraud, neglect or unlawful activity cannot now be defended as being in the public interest.

Case study

Report of the release of Cabinet records on the proposed military action against Iraq

Richard Thomas, the Information Commissioner, said the papers should be released under the Freedom of Information Act because of the 'gravity and controversial nature' of the discussions. Ministers said that they had not yet decided whether to appeal against the decision.

It marks the latest stage of a battle over the March 2003 meetings, where ministers discussed the advice by Lord Goldsmith, then the Attorney-General, on the legality of the war in the run-up to the invasion which toppled Saddam Hussein's regime.

The Cabinet Office has refused to make the details public on the grounds that the papers were exempt because they related to the formulation of Government policy and ministerial communications.

However … 'the Commissioner considers that a decision on whether to take military action against another country is so important that accountability for such decision-making is paramount,' a statement said.

Comment on the above: Michael Evans, Defence Editor

No Government likes to have its inner thoughts broadcast to the outside world, especially when the subject matter is as sensitive as the invasion of Iraq. This latest foray into the Freedom of Information Act is more serious for the Government. Its lawyers will no doubt have been confident that the minutes of a Cabinet meeting would be sacrosanct, and that Section 35 of the Act which provides an exemption against disclosure, would suffice.

However Richard Thomas, the Information Commissioner, has never regarded Section 35 as a blanket exemption, and in this case, he believes the argument for disclosure in the public interest outweighs the Government's desire to keep secret, for good Whitehall traditional reasons, the musings of ministers around the Cabinet table.

Source: Times Online, 26 February 2008

Activity

In the case of the 2003 disclosures concerning Iraq, do you support the action taken by the Information Commissioner? Give reasons.

N.B. The Justice minister, Jack Straw, went on to use a clause in the Freedom of Information Act to prevent publication in defiance of the Commissioner. He claimed that release threatened the confidentiality essential to the proper functioning of government.

The impact of the FOIA

Keeping costs down

In October 2006 the government announced proposals to make it easier for public authorities to refuse requests under the legislation on cost grounds. Firstly, authorities would be able to include the cost of the time spent *reading* the information, *consulting* others about it and *deciding* whether it should or should not be released. Secondly, it was proposed that the cost of unrelated requests made by the same individual or organisation to an authority could be aggregated [added together] and refused if their combined cost exceeded the £450 or £600 limits.

The effect of the proposals would be seriously to restrict the amount of information that can be obtained under the Act. The first would make it difficult to get information that was complex, sensitive or raised public interest issues of considerable importance, for these tend to be time-consuming. The second would again severely ration usage by campaigning organisations, the media and others, for often they do put in multiple requests for information.

When Gordon Brown became prime minister in 2007, it was suggested that he may drop the proposed changes, as the Constitutional Affairs Committee of the House of Commons urged him to do. So far no decision has been announced.

Exempting MPs and Peers

In 2007, the Freedom of Information (Amendment) Bill was introduced by a Conservative MP as a private members bill to the Commons. Initially, he did not expect it to pass:

> If someone approached me and asked for a letter sent to the police or a council about a constituent, I would tell them to go away. But there have been cases where the other body can be approached and things slip through the net. I want to make sure this cannot happen. The move would protect constituents and MPs. If an MP writes to their chief constable trying to get off a driving ban – that is totally different. I am flagging up the issue but I expect nothing will happen.

The proposal won wider support than was anticipated, both within the Labour and Conservative Parties. Critics suggested that ministers and shadow ministers were giving tacit approval as a means of watering down the effectiveness of the 2000 Act and avoiding embarrassing disclosures such as detailed information about MPs' expenses. If it became law, it would have the effect of exempting MPs and Peers from its provisions. This ensures that MPs' correspondence could not be monitored and that details relating to the way they conduct their work would not be available.

The fears expressed by critics reflected their mounting concern that many MPs and those in government office regarded the FOI legislation as an unnecessary nuisance. They felt it was wrong that MPs and Peers alone should be excluded in this way from legislation, which they themselves applied to the whole public sector. They also made the point that if MPs feel they do not need to comply, this might have the effect of encouraging other authorities to withhold information as well.

The Bill was passed by the House of Commons in May 2007, but did not find a sponsor in the House of Lords. A report by the Lords' Select Committee on the Constitution (June 2007) said that the Bill 'does not meet the requirements of caution and proportionality in enacting legislation of constitutional importance … we have been sent no evidence indicating a need for such an exemption or that existing protections for constituents' correspondence were inadequate '. The proposal was resurrected by ministers in early 2009 but it ran into substantial opposition.

Case study

Ministerial attempts to block the freedom of information legislation

Labour's flagship freedom of information laws are being blocked by ministers who are increasingly refusing to answer routine inquiries about government policy. New figures show that:

■ Seven government departments, including the department in charge of monitoring the new powers, are identified in a Whitehall report as refusing to give answers to more than half of all requests made by the public.

■ The Foreign Office has the worst record by claiming exemptions for 70 per cent of all requests it has received. In total, of the 62,852 requests made to central government since 1 January 2005, 26,083 have not been granted. And of those questions the

Government considers properly resolved many have not been answered to the questioner's satisfaction.

◼ Public requests for information have fallen to the lowest number since the laws were implemented.

◼ The Department for Constitutional Affairs, which has responsibility for implementing the 'right to know' laws, has the second worst record, by only providing full answers to 39 per cent of all requests.

◼ While Labour has been happy to release documents embarrassing the previous Tory administration over its handling of 'Black Wednesday', Britain's forced withdrawal from the ERM. Ministers have been less willing to let the public use the Act to shed light on Labour's own political controversies.

The same article drew attention to requests not answered by government departments.

Requests, officially denied in the first year of operation

Can you please disclose the public cost of guarding Charles and Camilla?

The Royal Family is exempt from the Freedom of Information Act. It would not be in the public interest to reveal information not covered by this exemption because of the potential threat to royal security.

Would you reveal the discussions relating to the Home Office's original decision to reclassify cannabis?

We believe that disclosure would lead to reluctance on the part of officials, ministers and others to provide frank advice in future.

Can we see the documents and briefing papers for Lord Levy's meetings with American diplomats over the Middle East crisis?

It is not in the public interest to disclose any of this material. Such a revelation would also harm international relations.

Please disclose the correspondence between the Food Standards Agency and Cadbury Schweppes in respect of the chocolate bar salmonella scare earlier this year.

Disclosure of some of the information held would prejudice any possible prosecution and may prejudice the commercial interest of Cadbury's.

Can we see the report into the links between MRSA rates and bed occupancy written by the Department of Health's chief economic adviser?

This would be detrimental to the future formulation of government policy.

How about Tony Blair's Christmas card list?

Many of the addressees are foreign dignitaries. This information would be harmful to international relations.

Could you send us all the written evidence given by police forces to the Government's 2004 public consultation on prostitution?

Disclosure might harm police efforts to prevent and detect crime.

Please disclose the minutes of Margaret Thatcher's last cabinet meeting.

It is important that ministers' discussions in cabinet are full and frank. To arrive at agreed policy positions and plans for actions, discussion needs to be free and uninhibited.

Summary questions

1. Is there a public 'right to know'?

2. Why might it make government more difficult to conduct if the details of Cabinet discussions are generally made available during the lifetimes of those involved in making decisions?

3. Has the Freedom of Information Act on balance been a success or a failure?

4. Why might effective freedom of information legislation be regarded as a key tool of active citizenship?

5. Can you justify the exemptions for MPs' allowances and expenses?

Source: extract from The Independent, *What freedom of information?: Ministers are accused of scuppering right-to-know legislation, 28 December 2006*

The EU and consumer protection

The EU's first consumer programme was issued in 1975. Since then, there have been directives requiring national action to protect consumer rights in areas such as:

- the safety of cosmetic products
- the labelling of foodstuffs
- advertising aimed at children
- the selling of financial services
- guarantees and after-sales service
- the safety of toys
- the safety of building and gas-burning services.

Activities

1 What rights do individuals have as e-consumers? Look up www.internetrights.org.uk/factsheets and list any protection available.

2 What protection is available under the UK Consumer Protection (Distance Selling) Regulations 2000?

■ Other rights of UK citizens

Other rights of UK citizens not covered by the HRA include consumer rights, welfare rights and the right to defend oneself.

Consumer rights

Much of the protection available to British consumers derives from five fundamental rights:

- *The protection of health and safety*, involving banning the sale of products that may jeopardise them.
- *Protecting the consumer's economic interests*, involving regulation of misleading advertising, unfair contractual agreements and unethical sales techniques such as those used in selling time-share properties.
- *Granting the right to full information about goods and services offered*, including the labelling of foodstuffs, medicines and textiles.
- *The right to redress*, involving the rapid and affordable settlement of complaints by consumers who feel they have been injured or damaged by using certain goods or services.
- *Consumer representation in the decision-making process*, via consumer associations such as *Which?*.

Much legislation on consumer affairs is the responsibility of the British government. However, some of the protection derives from membership of the European Union, although the guideline for EU legislation in this area is 'as little regulation as possible, but as much as is necessary to protect consumers'. EU legislation either fills in gaps left by national laws or covers areas where the consumer in one member state has a complaint concerning another member state, as when a British consumer is the victim of dubious time-share sales in Spain.

Welfare rights

Welfare rights refer to entitlements to benefits under the legislation that created and sustains the Welfare State. In many modern, developed economies, most state welfare benefits are provided on a selective basis, that is, eligibility is determined by individual circumstances. Income, disability and age are the usual criteria employed when potential recipients' eligibility is tested. Benefits may be selective both in terms of the social group eligibility and in terms of the level of support. For example, state pensions are obviously only available to the old and their partners who survive them and the amount of pension may vary according to circumstances and past employment record.

In other systems, benefits are provided on a universal basis. All social groups may be eligible and the benefits may be distributed on a flat-rate basis, which means that the same benefit is given to everybody irrespective of circumstances.

Elements of both systems prevail in most countries. The Welfare State in Britain, as created by the post-1945 Labour government, was based more on universal than selectivist principles. Everybody was entitled to health care. Public housing was for 'general need' and rents were unrelated to income. Family allowances were at a flat rate, as was the old age pension.

Today, elements of universalism still persist, for instance in usage of the National Health Service and in the entitlement to an old age pension and child benefit. Many other benefits are however means-tested, as with entitlement to measures of income support and pension credits.

The right to defend oneself

The word 'reasonable' is basic in any discussion of the right of self-defence. The defence exists both in common and statute law. In common law, it has existed for centuries and permits a person to use reasonable force to:

1 defend himself from attack
2 prevent an attack on another person
3 defend his property.

In addition to the common law defence, Section 3(1) of the Criminal Law Act 1967 (the statutory defence) provides that: 'A person may use such force as is reasonable in the circumstances in the prevention of crime, or in effecting or assisting in the lawful arrest of offenders or suspected offenders or of persons unlawfully at large.'

Case study

The conviction of Tony Martin (2000)

Tony Martin lived in an isolated farmhouse in Emneth Hungate, in Norfolk, nicknamed 'Bleak House'. On the night of 20 August 1999, two burglars, 29-year-old Brendon Fearon and 16-year-old Fred Barras entered the residence. When confronted by Martin, they attempted to flee through the window but he shot them; Fearon in the leg and Barras in the back. Barras died while trying to escape the house and was later found dead in the grounds by a police dog. Fearon managed to escape and seek aid from a couple living nearby. Martin left the farm that evening, hid the firearm in his mother's house and spent a night at the local inn. In January 2000, Fearon admitted to conspiracy to burgle and served more than half of a three-year prison sentence.

On his arrest, Martin told the police that he had already been burgled on several occasions and met with police inaction, stories doubted and denied respectively by the police. He claimed to have been acting in self-defence when he shot the two burglars. On 23 August, Martin was charged with the murder of Barras. In his trial (April 2000) he was found guilty of murder and given a life sentence. On appeal, his conviction was reduced to manslaughter on grounds of diminished responsibility, for the court accepted that he suffered from paranoid personality disorder.

The Martin case became a *cause célèbre*, attracting huge media coverage and the interest of several prominent politicians. It polarised opinion in the UK to a greater extent than usual. Some saw him as a trigger-happy and rather weird person, who wilfully killed a fleeing boy using an illegally held shotgun. Others saw him as a wronged man and an example of how the British legal system tilts towards protecting criminals rather than victims. Some of his supporters pointed to an increase in rural crime, claiming that people in the countryside such as Tony Martin felt vulnerable and exposed.

Local opinion in the Fenlands of Norfolk was divided too. Some believed Martin to have been weird, but harmless. Others were already familiar with his hatred of burglars and Gypsies, and his comments about what he would do if he ever caught them. They gave him a wide berth. He was said in court to have talked of putting

Fig. 6.4 *What the police found at 'Bleak House'*

Gypsies in the middle of a field, surrounding it with barbed wire and machine-gunning them. Barras was both a thief and a Gypsy.

When the jury visited the Martin home, the police had to clear sackloads of rubble from the floor, point out booby traps and cut back swathes of dangerous hogweed to make it safe for them to enter. It was in these circumstances that Martin lived with his three rottweilers. He always slept with a shotgun by his side.

Activities

1 Consider these two responses to the Martin case:
   - 'His actions were those of an irrational man and to that extent one must sympathise with him, whilst recognising the dangers inherent in firearms. But when is loss of a life ever equal to loss of property? Anyone who suggests that material property has greater value than human life is warped in their judgement.'
   - 'The burglar got exactly what he deserved. The law seems to be on the side of criminals and not of those who seek to defend themselves and their property. We have got our priorities all wrong.'

   With which verdict – if either – do you agree? Give reasons for your response.

2 Write a couple of paragraphs in answer to these questions:
   - Should people take the law into their own hands in order to protect their property?
   - Should they have the right to protect it whatever the consequences?

Summary questions

1 How well are consumers protected in the UK?

2 What is the difference between universal and targeted social benefits?

3 Was Tony Martin fairly treated?

7

The legal framework: protecting the citizen

Learning objectives:

- to be able to define the concepts of civil law and criminal law

- to understand the debate surrounding equality of access to the law and equality before the law

- to have knowledge of the English legal system, the legal profession and other providers of legal advice

- to have knowledge of alternative methods of resolving disputes.

Key terms

Natural or God-given law: a moral system to which humans do – or should do, in the view of those who subscribe to it – conform. It lays down universal standards of conduct. It rests on the idea that by virtue of their humanity or their status as children of God, men and women have certain inalienable entitlements. There is no general agreement about what these natural laws are, which is why philosophers have argued about their existence and range throughout history.

Rule of law: the theory that government must be based on the supremacy of law, which must be applied equally to all and through just procedures. The law governs the actions of individual citizens to one another and also controls the conduct of the state towards them. Nobody is above the law, regardless of their status or position.

Without law, there would be no basis for people living together peacefully in their communities. On the one hand, the law maintains social control, enabling the government to maintain order and introduce changes that they believe to be in the interests of everybody. On the other, it protects the rights of individuals and groups, by establishing the legal relationships between citizens and between citizens and the state.

Law: a set of human-made enacted or customary rules, enforceable by the courts, which regulate the relationship between the state and its citizens and the conduct of citizens towards each other. The community generally recognises the law as binding.

Law, morality and justice

By *law*, we mean a set of public rules that apply throughout the community and are usually considered by everybody as binding. Law determines what can and cannot be done. It is a form of control that is backed up by means of enforcement.

Morality involves conforming to conventional standards of moral conduct. In other words, it is concerned with whether human behaviour is right or wrong, with what should and should not be done. It involves listening to the voice of conscience. It derives from the concept of **natural** or **God-given law**. Natural law theories, dating back to Plato and other Ancient Greeks, suggest that law should be rooted in a moral system and based on the idea of God-given, natural rights.

Justice implies ideas of fairness and impartiality in judgement or actions; the principle that like cases should be treated alike. The exercise of fairness and impartiality in devising and applying laws is a hallmark of a just system.

Something is legal if it is in accordance with the law of the land. It is just if it is seen to be fair and equitable. It is moral if it is ethically right and proper. The idea of the **rule of law** is to bring together the ideas of law, justice and morality, hence its key principles of legal equality, consistent law, innocence until proof of guilt and judicial independence and impartiality.

Activities

1 Write a paragraph to demonstrate your understanding of the distinction between law and morality.

2 Write a few sentences to comment on the view that: 'Justice is concerned with ethical considerations, prescribing what the situation should be, whereas law has an objective character rather than being a matter of opinion or judgement.'

■ Civil and criminal law

Law is made by Parliament (**statute law**) or the courts (**case law**), although today the majority of legislation is EU law that derives from Brussels. **International law**, deriving from accepted principles, legal authorities and treaties, is the system of rules that states usually regard as binding in their relations with one another.

More commonly, law is subdivided into **criminal**, **civil** and administrative law (see pages 135–7):

■ *Criminal law* concerns offences against individuals (e.g. assault or rape), against property (e.g. malicious damage or robbery) or the state (e.g. public order or treason), the aim of proceedings being punishment of individuals who transgress (i.e. commit the crime). Crimes are regarded as being so serious that the state is obliged to take action against the person accused. The Crown Prosecution Service decides whether or not to proceed with charges, irrespective of the wishes of the victim. A successful prosecution leads to punishment, perhaps by imprisonment or a community sentence, rather than just paying some form of compensation. The terminology 'criminal law' reflects the gravity of the situation. It is regarded as more serious than civil law. It has repercussions for the accused's reputation and may end in deprivation of their liberty.

■ *Civil law* concerns disputes between persons or groups in society (e.g. **defamation** cases), the aggrieved person (the plaintiff) deciding whether or not to sue (bring charges against) a defendant. The aim of the proceedings is to extract damages, often in the form of compensation. Whereas criminal cases have to be proved beyond reasonable doubt, civil cases are adjudicated on 'the balance of probabilities'.

The aim in civil cases is to compensate the victim who has suffered from the actions of another person. It is not so much a matter of being guilty or innocent, for the person who is in the wrong may not be aware that he or she is doing wrong. For instance, if someone forgets to apply the handbrake in a car park and the car rolls into another vehicle, there is no deliberate intention to cause damage. But the car is the responsibility of the owner who is regarded as being at fault or showing **negligence**. The court finding would not be one of guilty, but of liability for compensation to the aggrieved owner of the damaged car. As we have seen, the balance of probabilities determines liability or otherwise. Once all the evidence is considered for both sides, it seems likely that the owner of the first car was in this example responsible for the outcome.

Where the wrong is committed by a child, there is no specific reason why the child should not be deemed accountable. But in most cases there would be little chance that children could afford to make financial restitution for any negligence on their part. There is continuing debate as to how far parents should be held responsible for their children's behaviour. Under English law, a parent is usually only liable if it can be demonstrated that the parent is at fault, for example by providing a child with a potentially dangerous implement without showing him or her how to use and maintain it properly.

The case of *Mullins v Richards* (1998)

Teresa and Heidi had a sword fight with plastic rulers, one of which snapped. A piece of plastic flew into Teresa's eye. The trial judge decided that Heidi had a duty of care to Teresa, that the injury was foreseeable and that Teresa was therefore entitled to compensation. However, in the Court of Appeal, the ruling was that there was no negligence on the part of Heidi, for this was a case of two young girls participating in a children's game that on this occasion sadly went wrong.

Punishment or compensation?

Whether a case is civil or criminal, the aim is to ensure that there is an effective outcome. But as we have seen, the judgement as to what is an effective outcome will be very different in the two forms of law:

- in a civil case, the aim to compensate for harm done as a result of negligence
- in a criminal case, the aim is to punish the offender and prevent any repeat of the offence.

Remedies in civil cases

Three main types of remedy are available:

- On occasion, there might be an *order for specific performance*, which requires a party in a contract to do something that he or she has promised to do – e.g. carry out work promised or move out of a home that someone else has purchased.

- An *injunction* is a court order to the defendant requiring individuals or organisations to modify their behaviour or actions. If a firm's factory belches out fumes into the neighbourhood, the aim may be to stop the process from recurring, rather than to offer compensation. Both might be relevant. The injunction in this case would not be to require the factory to cease production (which would, of course, stop the fumes altogether) but to get the owner/manager to modify the production process in such a way that the fumes would no longer be emitted. Failure to comply with an injunction is contempt of court, which involves a liability to be sent to prison.

  On occasion, the aggrieved party may seek an interlocutory injunction, which prevents the defendant from doing something that he or she was intending to do. If someone is intending to build on land where the ownership is disputed, the aggrieved party might ask for this type of injunction to prevent building from going ahead until the court has adjudicated on the matter of ownership.

- *Damages*, the payment of money as compensation, are the usual outcome for a claim of negligence, the aim being to compensate the claimant and in some way put them back in the position in which they would have been should the wrong never have been committed. *General damages* are paid to compensate for any loss of amenity, pain or suffering. Judges make their award in the light of up-to-date information provided by the Judicial Studies Board, which offers detailed guidance about awards made in similar types of cases. *Special*

1 Using the newspapers or internet to help you, seek out any examples of actions concerning negligence. Remember the three elements necessary in such cases: the duty of care; breach of that duty; and damage of some sort caused as a result.

2 Write a few sentences to say whether you think children should be made to assume full responsibility for their own actions. In the case of Heidi, did the Court of Appeal get it right? Say whether or not you think that parents should be held responsible for the wrong-doing of their children.

damages are payable for loss of earnings in the pre-trial period, for medical expenses and for any damage to property. They are easier to quantify than general damages. For instance, if any injury prevents a person from working again, the award will be for future loss of earnings. They can be paid as a lump sum or as a regular payment. Similarly, in a negligence action following a road traffic accident, it is possible to calculate the exact cost of repairing the car, hiring another vehicle, replacing damaged clothes and the amount lost in earnings.

In cases where the claimant wins the case but is unable to demonstrate that there has been any actual loss, the court may decide to award a small amount of damages in recognition that there has been some infringement of the claimant's rights.

Activities

1 Look up on the internet various cases in which an injunction has been made or damages awarded in high profile cases. Do you see any common threads in the ones that you have discovered?

2 How do English and Scottish courts differ in their approach to defamation cases?

Case study

The Sheridan case of defamation against the *News of the World*

Tommy Sheridan, a Scottish socialist politician, was alleged to have visited swingers' clubs in Manchester and engaged in an adulterous affair with another woman. He brought a successful libel action against the *News of the World* in August 2006. As this was a Scottish case, it went before a jury in the Court of Session, Scotland's highest court. The jury's task in a defamation action is to decide 'issues' that are put to them by the court.

In the Sheridan case, there were four issues, covering the following questions:

- Had the *News of the World* proved that Tommy Sheridan committed adultery?
- Had it proved that Tommy Sheridan took part in sex orgies at swingers' clubs?
- Was the paper correct in saying he had taken cocaine?
- Were claims that he drank champagne also fact?

As the questions indicate, the onus of proof in the case was on the *News of the World*. The newspaper had to defend itself by trying to prove that its story about Mr Sheridan was true. In Scotland, this is called a plea of *veritas*, while in England the term 'justification' is used. The standard of proof in a civil case is based on 'the balance of probabilities'. The judge directed the jury that, if they believed any one of the newspapers' 18 witnesses, that would be enough to make them give a verdict to the *News of the World*.

Scottish courts have traditionally awarded lower sums by way of defamation damages than English courts, although recently, at the same time as English courts have been striving to reduce high libel awards, awards in Scotland have been increasing. In Scotland, only compensatory, rather than punitive, damages are allowed. The jury felt that the full £200,000 claimed by Mr Sheridan was needed to compensate him.

Case study

Types of cases involving payment of damages:

Cases involving personal injury

According to the Citizens' Advice Bureau, 70 per cent of people who could make a valid claim for personal injury compensation don't do so, perhaps because they believe they aren't entitled or because they don't think it's worth the effort. However, the website www.whatsmyclaimworth.com quotes various cases in which its lawyers have made successful claims, including:

- Factory worker Mr W from Doncaster who was accidentally run over by a fork-lift truck at work, receiving multiple leg injuries, which kept him off work for several months. He made a claim and received £300,000 damages.
- Mr D from Wiltshire had his ear pierced at an approved tattoo and piercing parlour. Within two days, the ear had inflamed and became infected. The pain and suffering led Mr D to pursue a claim and he ended up receiving £22,000 in damages.

In all cases, the claim is calculated according to the nature and severity of the injuries, considered together with previous recent cases and personal injury guidelines.

Defamation cases involving terrorism

The number of reported defamation cases brought by people alleged to be involved in terrorism has almost tripled since last year, according to statistics from Sweet & Maxwell. Terrorism-related cases made up 13 per cent of the total number of reported claims in the year to the end of May 2007, compared to just 4 per cent the previous year and 6 per cent the year before.

Although this increase comes from a low base, these findings are still likely to be a particular concern for the media.

David Price of David Price Solicitors & Advocates has represented both claimants and newspapers in relation to terrorism claims. He says: The increase in terrorism-related claims reflects the increase in media coverage of terrorism. Inevitably with a large amount of material in the media mistakes will be made and these will lead to claims. And where a mistake is made it is likely to be seriously defamatory …

A particular risk area for the media relates to the reporting of alleged terrorist plots such as the one last August. The news is fast moving and there are often a large number of people arrested or otherwise connected. A mistake made by one newspaper can be replicated in a number of others, before the truth emerges, thereby giving rise to serial claims by the wronged party.

Defamation cases involving celebrities

Sweet & Maxwell's research also reveals that there has been no let up in the number of celebrities suing for defamation, following a significant jump in the number of reported cases. Claims brought by celebrities accounted for 30 per cent of the total number of reported defamation cases in 2006/7. In 2005/6, the proportion was 28 per cent, compared to 17 per cent in 2004/5.

Activities

1. See if you can find out the scale of awards for damages for different parts of the human body.

2. Write a few sentences to explain why terrorism-related cases of defamation have increased in number in recent years.

Sweet & Maxwell says that 'forum-shopping', where foreign celebrities choose to sue in the UK rather than in their own country, could be one reason why the proportion of celebrity claimants remains high. This is because British defamation laws are more favourable to claimants than, for example, American ones. In the US, claimants have to prove malice in order to be successful, and in addition, the right to free speech is actually part of the American constitution. UK courts will consider the right to freedom of expression more carefully against the individual's right to their reputation.

For example … Cameron Diaz sued America's *National Enquirer* in the High Court in London, as did Kate Hudson in 2006. Actor Vince Vaughan threatened to initiate legal proceedings in Britain last year against the *New York Post*.

Source: Sweet & Maxwell research, July 2007, available at their online legal information service, www.sweetandmaxwell.co.uk

Sanctions in criminal cases

Why punish?

There are four motives for punishing offenders, the first of which is difficult to measure but reflects a strong feeling among many people that wrong-doers should suffer for their wrong-doing. The other three goals can all be measured. In the UK, as in several other advanced societies, they have not been strikingly successful in combating crime when taken over the last few decades.

1 *Retribution* (or revenge) by society on those who have transgressed its code. This perhaps fulfils more of a psychological than a material need. It leads some people to demand **capital** and/or **corporal punishment**, even if these could be demonstrated to be ineffective in influencing the amount of crime. It involves looking at the crime and punishing offenders for it.

2 *Protection of society* is a fundamental aim of punishment. As long as people are in prison they cannot continue to commit crime. 'Prison works' in the sense that those imprisoned lack the opportunity to re-offend.

3 *Deterrence* is concerned to ensure that that the individual never commits the same offence again and that others do not engage in similar criminal conduct. Deterrent sentences are not widely held to have a significant impact on crime levels, other than in inverse proportion to the gravity of the offence – e.g. they may have some influence on motoring offences, but not on carrying out bank robberies, for in the latter case those involved do not commit the crime in the expectation that they will be caught.

At the most extreme end, in some countries deterrent sentences can involve grotesque or very severe punishments that physically prevent people from recommitting the crime of which they are guilty – e.g. by chopping off the hand of a thief. More usually it involves long sentences that are designed to make individuals think carefully before breaking the law again.

4 *Reformation or rehabilitation* is an aim that has been stated in many laws dealing with criminal justice. The emphasis here is on preparing prisoners for their eventual release, by making them better people via a programme of education and support for new inmates in the hope that they do not then re-offend. It is felt that rehabilitation is particularly important with young offenders, the hope being to reform the behaviour of the young person and break the cycle of offending.

Key terms

Capital punishment: refers to the penalty of death for the commission of a capital crime such as planned murder or multiple murders.

Corporal punishment: a form of physical discipline that is intended to cause pain and fear in the offender who is beaten ('flogged'), probably in public.

Activities

1 Write a paragraph or two to explain what you think we should be aiming to achieve by the sanction imposed for criminal offences.

2 Can offenders be reformed? List what you think are the most important ingredients of any programme of rehabilitation.

The range of alternative punishments

Various views about alternative punishments exist. Opinions differ widely on the most appropriate sentence for particular crimes, much depending on thinking about the purposes of punishment. Imprisonment and fines meet the goals of retribution and denunciation, protection of society (in the short term, in the case of prisons) and deterrence of the criminal and of others who might commit similar crimes. They express society's profound disapproval of those who transgress.

Community sentences or other approaches are designed to make the offender do something useful to society, confront the wrong that he or she has done and ultimately improve his or her feelings of self-esteem. Community sentences provide for some loss of liberty, without recourse to imprisonment. They range from **community rehabilitation orders** (formerly probation orders) to **community punishment orders** (formerly community service orders). The two forms may be combined in a community order punishment and rehabilitation order. This involves an offender reporting to a probation officer for advice and support to help fulfil the aim of character reform and performing community service, which has a retributive goal. There are also exclusion orders to keep offenders from certain areas, drug abstinence orders to prevent those involved in serious drug offences from taking specified Class A drugs and **ASBOs**.

A *conditional discharge* allows the offender to be released on condition that he or she does not re-offend. The period may be up to three years.

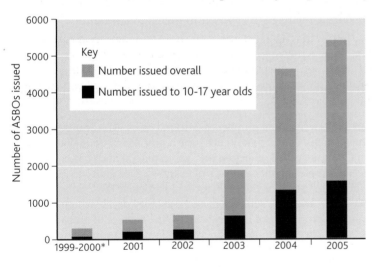

* this figure for a 20 month period

Fig. 7.1 *ASBOs issued April 1999 to December 2005*

Source: Home Office figures

Activities

1 Look through national and especially local papers for reports of sentences passed in local magistrates' courts and Crown Courts. List the main types of offences committed and the sentences given for them. See if any patterns emerge. Think about any factors that might have been involved in determining the sentence.

2 Write a couple of paragraphs explaining the merits and disadvantages of ASBOs and your verdict upon them.

Key terms

Community rehabilitation orders: involve a person being placed on probation, with possible restrictions on where he or she can live and other additional requirements. The probation officer monitors the defendant's progress, providing help in finding accommodation, a job and with family difficulties. Some critics see a conflict between the aspect of punishment and that of being responsible for helping a person to change his or her life.

Community punishment orders: involve ordering an offender to carry out between 40 and 240 hours of work, unpaid, on projects designed to be of value to the community. The orders combine punishment with the element of rehabilitation and making redress.

ASBOs: (anti-social behaviour orders) court orders applied for by local authorities and police forces (including the British transport police), which target forms of anti-social behaviour such as abandoned cars, harassment, graffiti, litter, noisy neighbours and vandalism. Under the terms of an ASBO an individual can be ordered not to go to a certain place or not to take part in certain activities for a minimum of two years.

Further information

Five highest areas for issuing ASBOs – numbers issued to 2008

▪ Manchester 1,237

▪ Greater London 1172

▪ W Midlands 787

▪ W Yorks 696

▪ Lancs 362.

Hint

Keep up-to-date on prison statistics. You can find out the number of people in custody by consulting www.hmprisons.gov.uk.

Citizenship and the law

Members of the public ('lay people') have no legal training, yet they play an important part in the legal system. Their involvement demonstrates that the law is not just a matter for lawyers and specialists, but something of importance and relevance to ordinary people too.

Apart from those individuals whose transgression of the law lands them in court, the majority of the population can participate in the legal system as active citizens in various ways. They can serve on a jury as required, they may become lay magistrates, they can be part of a system of restorative justice or they can merely attend court and see what goes on.

The jury system

Juries have long been portrayed as bastions of British liberty. Trial by jury dates back to the period after the Norman Conquest and became customary during the reign of Henry II in the late 12th century.

The role of the 12 members of a jury is to decide on matters of fact. They listen to the evidence presented and decide who did what, in order that they can arrive at their collective verdict. Usually, the verdict must be unanimous, but the judge may be willing to accept a majority verdict of 10 or 11 jurors if their deliberations have gone on for more than two hours.

Juries sit in a relatively small number of criminal cases. Most cases start and finish in magistrates' courts that do not have a jury. Many cases due to reach the Crown Court are called off before they get to judgment day, because the accused decides to plead guilty. In cases of acknowledged guilt, no jury is required. Juries are used in a few civil cases, in particular those concerning defamation or involving the state. In these cases, they decide whether or not the claimant has proved his or her case within 'the balance of probabilities' and where necessary determine the size of any damages awarded.

For and against the jury system

The jury system is widely regarded as a cardinal feature of justice that the guilt of those charged with a criminal offence should be determined by their peers (fellow citizens), bringing the law closer to the people. This is seen as a bulwark against oppression, particularly valuable when the decision involves a consideration of how actions or remarks would be interpreted by the everyday man or woman. Juries are chosen randomly from society and therefore are thought likely to be representative of the population at large, so that the system is really 'trial by one's peers'. They provide ordinary people with an opportunity for active participation in the affairs of government. If jurors make an error, it is more likely to be on the side of the accused. For these reasons, the public have faith in the jury system. Moreover, lay representation counteracts the image of the law as remote from ordinary people and is the more desirable because local people selected are likely to understand local circumstances. Finally, of course, there are 12 people making a decision rather than one judge, which seems fairer and more likely to yield an appropriate verdict.

Critics allege that juries are inappropriate to deal with highly technical cases and some civil cases involving the awarding of damages. ('Considerable' damages may mean different things according to the standards of living of those sitting in a particular court.) Sometimes, trials last over several days or weeks. This means that the whole process is expensive and that jurors, equipped with no special training, have to follow numerous arguments and a mass of evidence that can be highly complex. Others suggest that juries can be too easily swayed by skilful and eloquent advocates (legal representatives) and they are liable to intimidation.

Case study

Trial by jury in complex and technical cases

Don't scrap jury trial – top judge

Jurors in the Tony Prudhoe fraud case have been praised by the trial judge. He said plans to remove the right for alleged fraudsters to be tried by jury have been disproved by their handling of the complex case.

The Government's Fraud (Trials without a Jury) Bill aims to allow judges to decide on highly complex or lengthy fraud cases.

Ministers claim major trials put too much pressure on jurors, following the collapse of several high-profile fraud trials, including the Jubilee Line extension case which collapsed after 21 months and cost the taxpayer £60m.

Prudhoe, the charismatic conman, formerly of Corbridge, Northumberland, was jailed for seven years earlier this week for his part in a £7.5m false invoice scam which cheated three banks in the US, Italy and the Netherlands.

At an early stage of the proceedings the 60-year-old, who was chairman of Wallsend-based Engineering With Excellence Holdings, even boasted he would be acquitted of any charges because juries find fraud cases complicated.

He never got the chance to test his claim as he changed his plea to guilty before a trial at Leeds Crown Court was due to begin.

But his former lover and PA Linda Straughan and the company's former commercial director Mark Grainger denied their involvement in a scam which saw them enjoying the trappings of corporate success while creditors and workers went unpaid.

After a trial lasting just under five weeks and deliberating for 12 hours, a jury convicted Straughan, 60, of Lyndhurst Grove, Low Fell, and Grainger, 42, of Kew Gardens, Stockton, of six counts of fraudulent trading.

Source: Paul McMillan, Chronicle Live, The Evening Chronicle, 19 May 2007

Activities

1. In the White Paper, Justice for All (July 2002), Home Office ministers argued that there should be trial by judge alone a) where defendants wanted it in the Crown Court and b) in 'serious and complex fraud trials, some other complex and lengthy trials or where the jury is at risk of intimidation'. Write a paragraph or two to say what you think of such possible inroads into the jury system. Does the evidence of the trial judge in the case study in any way modify your opinion?

2. Look up details of the 2004 statute to see in what circumstances the right to trial by jury has been restricted.

Recent legislation, such as the 2004 Criminal Justice Act, has restricted the right of jury trial in some cases.

Lay magistrates

Magistrates' courts are usually made up of three people from the local community who have no professional legal qualifications and are unpaid. They are known as lay magistrates or justices of the peace (JPs). They hear well over 95 per cent of all criminal cases in England and Wales. They also decide many civil matters, particularly in relation to family work, hear licensing applications and deal with requests for warrants for arrest and search.

Lay magistrates are appointed on the advice of advisory panels in each area. Sometimes, vacancies are advertised, sometimes people are recommended by individuals or local bodies. Names are sent to the Ministry of Justice, the Lord Chief Justice now being the person with responsibility for making the final decisions.

Unpaid, magistrates give up at least 26 days a year for service in court, plus training and preparation time. Many of them work for much longer than the bare minimum. They are legally entitled to time off work, but employers are under no obligation to pay for the loss of working hours.

Candidates under consideration as lay magistrates are normally aged between 21 and 60, but most are over 40. The aim is to ensure an age, ethnicity and gender balance. They should come from within 15 miles of the court area, be of sound character, have a mature outlook and good judgement and reliability (this also involves having no criminal convictions), be able to assimilate information with ease, understand reasoned argument and be capable of reaching a reasoned decision, and sensitive to the circumstances and problems in their communities.

Key terms

BME (black and minority ethnic): first employed in the 2001 census, as an alternative to 'ethnic minority', which includes both cultural and racial characteristics. BME is seen by the Home Office as a better way to describe ethnic diversity. Other agencies use the term 'minority ethnic group'.

Table 7.1 *Appointments to the lay magistracy in the five years to 2005–6*

Year	2001/2002	2002/2003	2003/2004	2004/2005	2005/2006
Men	763	714	777	909	1,132
Women	711	696	701	857	1,080
Total	1,474	1,410	1,478	1,766	2,212
% Women	48.2%	49.3%	47.4%	48.5%	51.1%
% BME	8.5%	8.2%	8.5%	8.09%	10.17 %

Source: Department of Constitutional Affairs, Eighth Judicial Appointments Report, *2007*

The 30,000 or so magistrates receive training to give them sufficient knowledge of the law and of the nature and purpose of sentencing. A court clerk advises them on law and procedure. However, in some circumstances, district judges – formerly called stipendiary magistrates – preside over magistrates' courts instead of JPs. Legally qualified and salaried, they tend to deal with longer and more complex cases and also have jurisdiction to hear cases involving extradition.

Table 7.2 *For and against lay magistrates*

Advantages	Disadvantages
They provide a less expensive form of justice than using professional judges	Sentences passed by magistrates across the country tend to be inconsistent – people who have been guilty of similar crimes can therefore be treated differently
They ensure that the legal system does not fall into the hands of the professionals, lay representation helping to maintain confidence in the fairness of the judiciary – as laypersons, they are more in touch with the everyday life of the community and can bring broader experience to bear in their judgements than judges	They are more likely than juries to convict, for they may be more subject to local attitudes and pressures and may see their role as being to take a strong stance on any threat to community order – a judge and jury would provide greater fairness to the defendant
They have a knowledge of their area, which enables them to take particular issues and problems into account – this means that they can relate the administration of justice to local conditions	Much use is made of middle-aged, self-employed and retired persons, so that they are socially unrepresentative of their communities in which the bulk of crime is committed by young people
Although they are often middle class and late middle-aged to elderly, they are more socially representative than judges	Because of their lack of legal expertise, magistrates tend to be too reliant on their more professionally qualified clerks

Activities

1. The best activity is again to visit a court, in this case the magistrates' court. Watch the cases under consideration. Come to a judgement about who appears to be running things. Is it the clerk, the chief magistrate or the three magistrates together?

2. In the light of the evidence presented, has the Ministry of Justice (formerly the Department of Constitutional Affairs) achieved a good ethnic and gender balance 'on the bench' (i.e. within the ranks of lay magistrates)?

3. Do you like the system of lay magistrates? In your response, consider that the likely alternative would be the use of professional magistrates, now known as district judges (magistrates' courts).

Restorative justice

Restorative justice involves

a process whereby:

i) all the parties with a stake in a particular conflict or offence come together to resolve collectively how to deal with the aftermath of the conflict or offence and its implications for the future and

ii) offenders have the opportunity to acknowledge the impact of what they have done and to make reparation, and victims have the opportunity to have their harm or loss acknowledged and amends made.

Source: Restorative Justice Consortium

Restorative justice gives victims of crime the chance to tell offenders about the real impact of their behaviour, to get answers to their questions and to receive an apology. This enables them to get on with their lives. It gives offenders the chance to understand the real impact of what they have done and to do something to repair the harm. It also holds offenders directly and personally to account for what they have done.

Key terms

Restorative justice: an approach to criminal justice based on reconciliation, restoration, healing and rehabilitation. It focuses on restoring the losses suffered by victims, holding offenders accountable for the harm they have caused and building peace within communities.

Hint

Take a look at the website of the Restorative Justice Consortium (www.restorativejustice.org.uk) and keep up-to-date on the latest findings and cases.

Restorative processes are also being used successfully outside the criminal justice system, for example in schools, workplaces, care homes, health services and communities. Use of restorative justice is now becoming more widespread in the youth justice system. It is gradually being introduced in attempts to deal with adult offending.

How restorative justice operates

Offenders and victims are brought into contact through:

- direct mediation, where victim, offender, facilitator and possibly supporters for each party meet face to face
- indirect mediation, where victim and offender communicate through letters passed on by a facilitator
- conferencing, involving supporters for both parties
- wider community – this is similar to direct mediation, except the process focuses on the family as a support structure for the offender (this is particularly useful with young offenders).

Examples of restorative justice approaches include:

- getting offenders to remove graffiti and repair property they have damaged
- bringing shoplifters face to face with store managers to hear how shop theft affects others
- getting offenders to write letters of apology.

Case study

Home Office research on the impact of restorative justice projects, June 2007 (as summarised by the Restorative Justice Consortium)

Research published by the Ministry of Justice shows that 85% of victims and 80% of offenders were satisfied with their experience of a Restorative Justice conference – a meeting between the victim and offender with supporters of each present.

The Report also showed that:

- 78% of victims who took part in Restorative Justice conferences said they would recommend it to other victims
- 90% of victims who took part in an Restorative Justice conference received an apology from the offender in their case, as compared with only 19% of victims in the control group
- Only 6 victims and 6 offenders out of 152 offenders and 216 victims interviewed were dissatisfied with the conference after taking part
- Around 80% of offenders who took part in the conference thought it would lessen their likelihood of re-offending
- Victims who had been through a Restorative Justice conference were more likely to think the sentence the offender had received was fair, than victims in the control group who did not participate in Restorative Justice
- This research compares with just 33% of victims who think the criminal justice system meets their needs and 41% of victims who think the system brings offenders to justice (*British Crime Survey*, April 2005).

Activity

The case for restorative justice is that it provides victim satisfaction (in the sense that victims feel that their voice has been heard) and a chance for the accused to be aware of the harm and hurt that he or she has caused.

Write a few sentences in response to each of the following:

- How might you attempt to counter these two claims for restorative justice?
- Do you think that it does work as well as it is supposed to do?
- What problems might be involved in its use?
- Should the system be extended?

Source: Restorative Justice: the views of victims and offenders *(3rd evaluation report),* Ministry of Justice, 2007

Summary questions

1. The distinguished judge, Lord Denning, claimed that 'whenever a man is on trial for serious crime ... then jury trial has no equal'. A former commissioner of the Metropolitan Police, Sir Robert Mark, suggested that confidence in the jury system is 'based on practically no evidence whatsoever' and that juries sometimes 'get it wrong'. With whom are you inclined to agree? On balance, do the benefits outweigh the dangers inherent in the system?
2. What criticisms can be made of lay magistrates?
3. In what respects is restorative justice better than the traditional court system?

Legal representation

Citizens who have a legal problem need help. They want to be told whether or not they have a good case, how to go about obtaining a remedy and about their chances of success in gaining redress. Be it a civil or criminal matter, they require access to the criminal justice system. Whether they are rich or poor, there are times when legal advice and protection are necessary.

Access to the law

In theory, everyone should have equal access to the law. In practice, this does not always apply. In some cases, people do not pursue legal action when it might be appropriate. There might be several reasons for this:

- They do not understand the law, are unfamiliar with the legal system and do not know about the rights it gives them in particular circumstances.
- They fear that legal protection – particularly if a court case is likely to be involved – would be costly and beyond their means.
- They find it difficult to get time off work to see a solicitor or attend a court hearing during their working hours.

In cases of personal injury, far more people are entitled to compensation than ever pursue the legal route for redress. This might be because they feel that the issue is not that important, because the harm caused is relatively trivial. It may be because they fear the costs involved. Or it may be that they feel it would be difficult to get to a solicitor, given the usual opening hours of their practices. Whatever the reason, it remains true that most of those who do make a claim get a successful outcome. But it is reckoned by many firms specialising in personal injury claims that only 20 per cent or so of claimants ever get to the stage of seeking advice.

In recent years, more has been done to make access to the law more equitable (fair):

- *Advertising by legal firms for trade: Yellow Pages*, magazines and local newspapers list numerous legal companies that compete for trade; television too often carries adverts designed to attract personal injury business.
- *Opportunities to benefit from free or cheap advice:* The various sources of help are dealt with below (see pages 130–2).

Money has been the traditional barrier to equal access and equality before the law. Wealth was always seen as an advantage and it remains so

JUST COMPENSATION

Have you been injured?

- Whiplash
- Slips/trips
- Medical negligence
- Workplace accidents

You need help to win the compensation you deserve.

It couldn't be easier to claim.

Win or lose, you pay absolutely nothing!

Claims can be dealt with over the phone.

Call ***Just Compensation*** now on

0872 641968

Fig. 7.2 *The sort of advertisement for personal injury claims commonly seen in national and local newspapers* today. In cases of defamation, it is the rich and famous who can afford to acquire the services of the leading barristers in their field. They have the means and of course also have reputations to lose so that they see action in the courts as being worthwhile or even necessary to clear their good name. People with more modest incomes may be defamed frequently in their lives, but they live with it rather than approach a lawyer to defend them. Money is a factor, but so is the fact that they do not have a professional or business standing to uphold.

Case study

Bill Roache and his battle with the *Sun*

In an article in the *Sun* (1992), it was stated that Bill Roache (the long-serving actor in Coronation Street) was as dull and boring as Ken Barlow (the character he portrays in the 'soap').

It is legally impossible to libel a fictional character (e.g. the statement 'Ken Barlow is boring' is not libellous, be it true or otherwise). However, it is technically possible to libel a real person by comparing their character to that of a fictional character (e.g. the statement 'Bill Roache is as boring as Ken Barlow' can be libellous, if it is found to be untrue).

Bill Roache won his case and was awarded £50,000 damages. In the event, however, his 'victory' literally bankrupted him (1999), because of a legal loophole of which he was not aware. In the run-up to the trial, the newspaper paid £50,000 into court as 'an offer to settle', an offer that was refused. The effect was that if the trial proceeded and the jury awarded damages of £50,000 or less, then Roache would be liable for the costs for both sides of the proceedings beyond the point when the offer was made.

Roache then added to his personal difficulties by suing his solicitors for failing properly to advise him of the effect of the paper's payment into court. He lost this action, piling yet more legal costs onto his mountainous debt.

Key terms

Advocacy: means advancing an argument on someone else's behalf.

Queens Mews Chambers

Queens Mews Chambers is a leading barristers' chambers on the Western Circuit.

Every barrister at Queen Square is committed to providing the highest standards of advice and representation on matters including:

- Clinical Negligence
- Employment
- Family
- Housing
- Immigration

Direct Access
Members of Chambers normally accept instructions from solicitors. However, we have a team of Barristers who are willing to accept instructions in relation to advisory work, drafting and advocacy directly from the public under the Direct Public Access Scheme.

Tel: **0872 641968**

Fig. 7.3 *A typical advertisement for a barristers' chambers, showing the areas of work in which they specialise*

The legal professions: solicitors and barristers

Lawyers are people who have studied and practise law. They are divided into two main branches, barristers and solicitors who represent the interests of the disputing parties in a civil or criminal case. Each division has its own area of expertise and its own governing body. These bodies lay down the education, training and professional conduct required of their members. The basic training involved for each branch of the profession is broadly similar and there are today areas of overlap between their work. However, barristers have always been regarded as the more senior and prestigious of the two groups.

■ Most of the 11,000 or so barristers are self-employed, practise in a set of chambers and make their living from **advocacy**. In the higher courts, they provide a specialist advocacy service on behalf of clients who need representation. They are also involved in providing specialist opinions on complex matters of law. They usually act on instruction from solicitors and have little or no direct contact with members of the public. Members of the public in need of legal advice contact a solicitor.

Most judges are appointed from the ranks of barristers, who are often criticised as being too upper-middle class. (Their wealth enables them to cope with the lack of financial support in the first few years of their careers.) Members of **The Bar** are also often portrayed as being remote from and out-of-touch with the bulk of the population.

Some solicitors work for multinational City firms with hundreds of staff, but the majority operate from small private practices on the High Street, often in partnership with a handful of others. Solicitors may also be found working for the civil service, in commerce and industry, in law centres and in local government. Most offer general legal advice to those who need it, on matters ranging from making a will to buying a home, from dealing with a difficult neighbour to selling a firm. This is why they are sometimes referred to as the 'general practitioners' of the legal profession. They are the first people consulted when legal advice is required. Indeed, until the passage of the Courts and Legal Services Act (1990), an approach to a solicitor was the only means of gaining access to a barrister. Some specialise in a particular area, such as **conveyancing**, compensation claims, divorce law or matters of **probate**.

Solicitors perform various tasks for their clients, depending on the circumstances of the case. They write letters and make calls on their behalf, devise contracts, write wills and offer advice on any matter within their orbit. Much of their work is carried out at the pre-trial stage. This involves establishing the facts of a case, ensuring that documents and witnesses are available. They also represent their clients in court. This is a long-standing function in the lower courts, but since the 1990 legislation they have gained the right of advocacy in higher courts, where they can now present a case and question witnesses as barristers do. However, only around 1,000 or so have qualified as solicitor-advocates, out of a total of almost 80,000. Sometimes, solicitors are required to handle any post-judgment disputes surrounding any costs awarded.

Case study

The progress of Tony Blair's legal career

After his education at the prestigious independent Fettes College in Edinburgh, Tony Blair went to St John's College, at the University of Oxford, to read **jurisprudence**. He gained an upper second-class degree and then was called to The Bar at Lincoln's Inn and enrolled as a trainee barrister. He met his future wife (Cherie Booth, later herself to become a Queen's Counsel) at the chambers founded by Derry Irvine, who was to become Blair's first Lord Chancellor in his premiership after 1997.

As a barrister at the Irvine chambers, Tony Blair acted predominantly in matters of trade union and employment law. He often worked on behalf of employers and wealthy clients, as in the case of *Nethermere v Gardiner* where he unsuccessfully defended employers who had refused holiday pay to employees at a trouser factory.

Key terms

The Bar: comprises lawyers who are qualified as barristers or advocates. They are collectively known as 'members of The Bar'.

Conveyancing: the legal work carried out in connection with the sale and purchase of property. It was the sole domain of solicitors, until the 1990 Act. They were compensated for this loss of monopoly by being allowed to qualify as solicitor-advocates and appear in higher courts.

Probate: refers to the legal work involved in resolving assets and property issues after a person's death.

Jurisprudence: the branch of philosophy concerned with law and the principles that lead courts to make the decisions they do.

Hard working solicitors on your side
Naylor, Tonk and Posstlethwaite

- Divorce
- Conveyancing
- Personal injury and accident claims
- Probate and estates
- Wills and trusts
- Powers of Attorney
- Commercial and private Court work
- Debt collection
- Call now for a fast, friendly and efficient local service

Tel: **07793 161166**

email: **www.naylortonkposstlethwaite@valucon.com**

Fig. 7.4 *A typical advertisement for a solicitor's firm, showing the areas of work in which they specialise*

Activity

For each of the following types of case, decide whether you would normally expect the issues to be handled by a barrister or solicitor:

- Breach of contract
- Conveyancing
- Defending a murder charge
- Divorce
- Taking a case to the European Court of Human Rights.

Funding civil and criminal disputes

In the past, the wealthy paid their own legal expenses, the poor received help and many of those in between were unable to gain access because of the costs of recourse to the law. The poor were eligible to receive legal aid.

The Access to Justice Act (1999) was intended to meet what was often called 'the unmet need' of those who did not qualify for funding. It replaced legal aid with two new schemes:

- the Community Legal Service, which deals with civil cases
- the Criminal Defence Service, which deals with criminal cases.

Financial help in civil cases

The Legal Aid Board was replaced in 2000 by the Legal Services Commission, which operates the Community Legal Service Fund. It is empowered to negotiate contracts with solicitors and other firms in order to provide services. However, it is often alleged that there are too few such contracts and that remuneration levels are so modest that the relevant agencies are often uninterested in making contracts.

The Community Legal Service provides legal assistance, help in resolving disputes over legal rights and responsibilities and general information of use to those who seek its aid. It has a website (www.justask.org.uk), which offers wide support to those in need of advice. The assistance available via its fund does not cover cases of personal injury (which were within the orbit of the old legal aid scheme), unless medical negligence is involved. Neither does it cover issues such as conveyancing, defamation, and wills and probate. It does review cases on matters such as credit/debt, divorce, housing, immigration and nationality or asylum.

Entitlement to help depends upon disposable income and capital, the amount of assistance being determined according to a sliding scale up to a point where no funding is provided at all. The criteria for offering aid include:

- the importance of the matter to the individual and in particular the benefit that may be obtained from pursuing the claim
- the availability of other sources of funding
- the prospects for success
- the public interest
- the need to operate within the fixed budget of the Community Legal Service Fund.

The amount of the fund imposes a serious limit on what money can be made available. In real terms, less funding is available than was the case before 2000.

Alternatives are available and accessible to people who do not qualify under the Community Legal Service:

- Some of the bodies mentioned on pages 131–2 are willing to assist in making claims; for instance, the Law Society has an Accident Help-Line that deals with personal injury claims and operates a **conditional fee scheme**.
- There are also young barristers – often working in law centres – who are willing to accept cases free of charge or on a **pro bono publico** basis.
- Some people take out legal insurance, in the same way that they might take out health or motoring cover. Premium costs are recoverable from the other party or by winning the case.

■ Key terms

Conditional fee scheme: the system that originated in the US through which lawyers take on a case on the basis that there will be no payment unless they win. If they win, they will gain a proportion of the award. It has operated in the UK since 1995.

Pro bono publico: literally translates as 'for the general good'. It here refers to work carried out for which no charge is made.

■ **Activity**

Write a couple of paragraphs to say whether or not you think that enough help is now available to ordinary people in need of advice and representation. Should such aid be limited to those below a certain income level or should the scheme be universal?

Financial help in criminal cases

The Criminal Defence Service guarantees that people under police investigation or facing criminal charges can get legal advice and representation. It is run by the Community Legal Service in partnership with criminal defence lawyers and representatives.

Salaried state defenders are employed by the government. These Public Defender Service (PDS) lawyers have an uncapped budget for their services. They are available 24 hours a day, seven days a week to:

- give advice to people in custody
- represent clients in magistrates', crown and higher courts where necessary.

There is also the duty solicitor scheme, which means that a person detained in custody has access to speedy legal help.

Demand, rather than tight budgetary controls, determines the level and amount of assistance that is available to those who are arrested, detained in custody and brought to trial.

Other sources of advice and representation

Advice and practical help are available via agencies including:

- Citizens Advice Bureaux
- law centres
- arms-length government-created organisations such as the new Equality and Human Rights Commission
- pressure groups such as the AA and RAC in motoring matters, the Consumers Association in consumer-related queries and the Law Society, with its Accident Legal Advice Service (including the help-line mentioned).

■ Hint

Using their websites to help you, find out how the AA/RAC, the Consumers Association and the Law Society provide a service to those in need of legal advice and support.

■ Activity

Using the websites to guide you, find out and make a note of specific campaigns and cases that illustrate the work of the bodies mentioned above.

■ Case study

The impact of various organisations on the community

Citizens Advice Bureau

The Citizens Advice service helps people resolve their legal, money and other problems by providing free information and advice from over 3,000 locations and by influencing policymakers. Every Citizens Advice Bureau (CAB) is an independent charity reliant on funds raised locally and the commitment of trained volunteers from their local communities.

Last year, we helped people deal with over five million problems covering everything from benefits and housing to asylum and employment. If you need to chase a benefit claim, sort out your money problems or make a complaint about the NHS – a CAB can help.

Our trained advisers can help at all stages of the problem from negotiating with service providers right up to representation at courts and tribunals. Free, confidential and independent advice really makes a difference to the lives of individuals, their families and the communities they live in.

Source: www.citizensadvice.org.uk

Law Centres

The Law Centres Federation encourages the development of publicly funded legal services for those most disadvantaged in society and promotes the Law Centre model as the best means of achieving this. To improve access to justice, we promote good Law Centre practice and innovation in the delivery of high quality legal services to the Community.

Law Centres provide an independent legal advice and representation service. They employ specialists in areas of 'social welfare' law and help individuals and local groups with problems.

Law Centres involve the local community in their work to make sure that their services are those most needed and they raise awareness about people's rights and about how the law operates.

Source: www.lawcentres.org.uk

The Equality and Human Rights Commission

The independent advocate for equality and human rights in Britain, the Equality and Human Rights Commission aims to reduce inequality, eliminate discrimination, strengthen good relations between people, and promote and protect human rights.

The commission challenges prejudice and disadvantage, and promotes the importance of human rights.

The commission enforces equality legislation on age, disability, gender, race, religion or belief, sexual orientation or transgender status, and encourages compliance with the Human Rights Act.

Source: www.equalityhumanrights.com

Summary questions

1. How much similarity is there between the work performed by barristers and solicitors?
2. From what sources might you hope to gain good legal advice?
3. What alternatives exist to obtaining state funding for legal action?

■ Alternative disputes resolution (ADR)

Many legal disputes do not reach the courts. They are handled by other means. In recent years, these alternative methods of dispute-resolution have become more significant, largely because of the cost, delays and formality of court proceedings, and also because of the bitterness that can result from a polarised confrontation in the adversarial court system. In addition, some rather technical conflicts are more conveniently and easily handled by those who specialise in the particular field, rather than by judges.

Mediation, conciliation and arbitration

In civil proceedings, judges may often advise mediation, which is an informal process where the parties are brought together in the hope that some common ground can be reached. The processes of mediation are less confrontational than court proceedings, for there is an attempt to reach an agreed solution. Commercial and personal disputes are more likely to be resolved effectively and quickly, if a better personal relationship between the parties can be maintained.

Since 1997, mediation has increasingly been used in some matrimonial cases. Husbands and wives contemplating separation are advised to contact Relate to see if any reconciliation can be effected. If they are still contemplating divorce, they are advised to use mediation services to handle ancillary issues such as the position of children involved and the division of financial assets. Mediation can help to remove some of the trauma in cases where deep emotions are concerned. However, warring spouses are not always willing to participate and if they do so are liable to see it as a further opportunity to confront and perhaps humiliate their partner.

Case study

The role of Relate

Relate is the UK's largest provider of relationship counselling and sex therapy. We also offer a range of other relationship support services.

All sorts of people come to Relate and find it helps them to understand what's going on in their relationships and change things for the better. We saw 150,000 clients last year.

Feedback from those coming to Relate counselling shows that 66% come to save their relationship with their partner, or improve it. Only 9% attend to come to terms with the ending of a relationship. Our experience in the counselling room tells us that the vast majority decide to work on with the relationship.

A year after completing counselling 58% of our clients felt that their relationship was better than it had been before they went to Relate; 82% were glad that they had gone to counselling and 80% were satisfied with the service that they had received.

Source: www.relate.org.uk

Key terms

ACAS (the Advisory, Conciliation and Arbitration Service): an organisation devoted to preventing and resolving employment disputes.

Like mediation, conciliation involves an attempt to seek agreement. It is done by inviting the disputing parties to an informal meeting in order to seek a solution. It is sometimes done to resolve disputes between neighbours over potentially contentious matters such as fencing, noise and shared access. Better known perhaps is the work of **ACAS** in conflict resolution in issues concerning industrial relations. It is widely respected for its unbiased approach and specialist skills. It handles disputes between workers and their employers and more general issues in its field of expertise.

Case study

The approach of ACAS to dispute resolution

ACAS stands for Advisory, Conciliation and Arbitration Service. We aim to improve organisations and working life through better employment relations. We help with employment relations by supplying up-to-date information, independent advice and high quality training, and working with employers and employees to solve problems and improve performance.

Although largely funded by the Department for Business, Enterprise and Regulatory Reform (BERR), ACAS is a non-departmental body, governed by an independent Council. This allows us to be independent, impartial and confidential. Founded in 1975, we have over 30 years' experience of working with people in organisations of every size and type ...

The ACAS Arbitration Scheme is an alternative to employment tribunal hearings. Only cases of alleged unfair dismissal or claims under flexible working legislation may be decided. ACAS was given powers to draw up the Scheme in the Employment Rights (Dispute Resolution) Act 1998.

The Scheme was introduced as a speedy, informal, private and generally less legalistic alternative to an employment tribunal hearing. It's designed to provide a final outcome more quickly and one which mirrors the outcomes available in an employment tribunal. There are few grounds for challenging the arbitrator's award and appeals can only be made in limited circumstances.

Source: www.acas.org.uk

Activity

List the qualities that make ACAS useful in settling industrial disputes.

Where techniques of negotiation, mediation and conciliation do not work, arbitration may be the last resort. Indeed, some legal contracts contain a clause stating that in the event of an unresolved conflict the matter will be referred to arbitration, which may or may not be binding. The process is normally handled by someone with expertise in the field. He or she will ensure that each side has the chance to air its case and then issue a verdict based on his understanding of the issues put forward and the need to reach a fair outcome. Again, arbitration enables disputes to be handled informally and in a way that does not endanger the relationship between the two sides in the dispute. It is widely used in disputes ranging from those concerning unsatisfactory dry-cleaning to those concerning clients dissatisfied with the service they have experienced from travel companies in the leisure industry.

Tribunals

Tribunals are like court hearings, but much more informal. They attempt to resolve issues speedily and efficiently. They are also less expensive than court proceedings.

Tribunals may be domestic or administrative. Domestic tribunals are those that operate within a particular profession or industry. For instance, the Bar Council, the Law Society and the General Medical Council all have tribunals that have powers to fine, suspend or even disbar those within their professions who transgress against the required rules of conduct.

■ **Case study**

The General Medical Council

The General Medical Council (GMC) registers doctors to practise medicine in the UK. It regulates doctors and has the powers to either issue a warning to a doctor, remove the doctor from the register, suspend or place conditions on a doctor's registration.

Before the GMC can stop or limit a doctor's right to practise medicine, it needs evidence of impaired fitness to practise. This might be, for example, because they:

■ have not kept their medical knowledge and skills up to date and are not competent;

■ have taken advantage of their role as a doctor or have done something wrong;

■ are too ill to work safely.

We can also issue a warning to a doctor where the doctor's fitness to practise is not impaired but there has been a significant departure from the principles set out in the GMC's guidance for doctors, *Good Medical Practice*. A warning will be disclosed to a doctor's employer and to any other enquirer during a five-year period. A warning will not be appropriate where the concerns relate exclusively to a doctor's physical or mental health.

Source: www.gmc-uk.org

Administrative tribunals are concerned with resolving disputes between the individual and the state in cases involving **administrative law**. They have been established by legislation and exercise a range of functions, especially in the welfare field. There are tribunals for education, housing, immigration, industry (e.g. in industrial disputes, and for cases of redundancy and unfair dismissal), insurance and pensions, among many other sectors.

Tribunals are often used in cases where the argument concerns the discretion exercised by an official, perhaps by refusing to grant a licence or pension. Comprising a chairman with legal qualifications and two lay members with relevant interests and experience, they are independent and not subject to political or administrative interference. Tribunals make an award rather than offer a judgment.

As quasi-judicial bodies, they meet in public and seek to establish the facts and apply the relevant rules. They provide a cheap and speedy solution for many cases, having greater expertise than the ordinary

■ **Key terms**

Administrative law: as defined by the constitutional legal authority Wade – is 'the body of general principles which govern the exercise of powers and duties by public authorities'. It refers to the whole package of laws that apply to government and other public bodies. The courts may decide that a minister or department has acted *ultra vires* (beyond its powers) because of what was done or the manner in which it was done.

Table 7.3 *Workload of the Asylum and Immigration Tribunal (AIT)*

Issue	Number of verdicts given
Asylum	14,735
Immigration	85,401
Visit visas	66,190
Human rights	573

Based on statistics to be found on the AIT website

Activities

1 List any advantages and potential weaknesses of the methods described under the headings Mediation, Conciliation and Arbitration.

2 What can be said for and against the use of tribunals to resolve particular kinds of disputes? Does the statistical information on the Asylum and Immigration Tribunal influence your view of them? Could such cases be realistically handled by the UK's formal court system?

Key terms

Maladministration: the way in which decisions are made and can include bad administration, biased application of rules, failure to follow procedures, general high-handedness, harshness, neglect, plain incompetence or the improper use of powers, among other things.

courts. In the words of the Franks Report on Administrative Tribunals and Enquiries (1958), their operations are supposed to be characterised by 'openness, fairness and impartiality'. Legislation in 1971 and 1992 has controlled the operation of tribunals via the introduction of the Council on Tribunals, which ensures that they operate effectively.

Case study

The Asylum and Immigration Tribunal

We are a tribunal that hears appeals against decisions made by the Home Secretary and his officials in asylum, immigration and nationality matters. The main types of appeal we hear are made against decisions to:

- Refuse a person asylum in the UK.
- Refuse a person entry to, or leave to remain in, the UK for permanent settlement.
- Deport someone already in the UK.
- Refuse a person entry to the UK for a family visit.

Appeals are heard by one or more immigration judges who are sometimes accompanied by non legal members of the tribunal. Immigration judges and non legal members are appointed by the Lord Chancellor and together form an independent judicial body. We hear appeals in a number of hearing centres across the United Kingdom.

Source: www.ait.gov.uk

Ombudsmen

Ombudsmen are responsible for dealing with certain types of dispute. In particular, they deal with complaints against government and its agencies, overseeing aspects of legal application. They are mainly concerned with issues of **maladministration**, rather than matters of equity or inequality. Their concern is the manner in which decisions are made and covers any abuse by government departments and agencies that falls into the

Further information

The Parliamentary Commissioner for Administration (PCA)

- The office of the Parliamentary Ombudsman has been rebranded as the Parliamentary and Health Service Ombudsman (PHSO), for the same person occupies the position of Parliamentary Ombudsman and Health Service Ombudsman for England.
- The PHSO has the power to call for relevant papers from the department and compel the attendance of witnesses.
- Those seeking the assistance of the PHSO often find the process difficult. Firstly, all complaints have to go through an MP (the 'MP filter'). Secondly, the ombudsman rejects nearly 50 per cent of filtered applications at first instance. Finally, the ombudsman will not investigate complaints where recourse to an alternative remedy (tribunal, internal complaints etc.) exists.
- The restrictions have led some writers to make the claim that the institution is more of an 'ombudsmouse' than an ombudsman. It is less often heard now, not least because of the way in which discretionary powers have been interpreted by incumbents of the office.

categories mentioned in the margin. Referrals to them are made via an MP, local councillor or MEP, depending on the issue involved.

Other than the first ombudsman, known as the Parliamentary Commissioner for Administration, there is also in UK government:

- a Health Service Commissioner whose powers derive almost wholly from the Health Service Commissioners Act (1993)
- a group of Local Commissioners of Administration to deal with complaints against local authorities
- a Pensions Ombudsman, created under the Pensions Schemes Act (1993)
- a Prison Ombudsman (1994)
- the Ombudsman for Conveyancing, who deals with the Council for Licensed Conveyancers, whose main brief is to deal with complaints against conveyancing agencies but who can award compensation
- the Legal Services Ombudsman, who deals with complaints handled by the Bar Council and Law Society
- a Banking Ombudsman
- a Building Societies Ombudsman
- an Insurance Ombudsman
- the European Ombudsman, a creation of the European Union.

Ombudsmen are established to ensure that high standards of administration prevail. In general, they lack effective power, their role being to investigate and produce a report on cases, rather than determine the outcome of individual cases. However, they can make recommendations and their reports carry considerable status and may lead to changes in future procedures.

Activities

1. Look up details of any three of the ombudsmen listed, in order to find out more details of what they do and how they operate.

2. Find out more about the PHSO (and some examples of cases in which the PHSO has been involved) and then decide whether or not you think the incumbent can now fairly be described as an 'ombudsmouse'.

Summary questions

1. What are the possible benefits of resolving a dispute via alternative disputes resolution (ADR) rather than by going to court?

2. What do you understand by the term 'administrative law' and what are the main forms of redress available to citizens who feel that they have suffered ill-treatment from some public institution?

3. Are the powers of the Parliamentary Ombudsman too weak?

8

How do the courts protect my rights?

Learning objectives:

■ to have knowledge of the judicial process and court powers including the European Court of Human Rights

■ to be able to define the concept of judicial review

■ to understand the debates surrounding the effectiveness of our judicial system.

Guiding principles

The rule of law

The rule of law is the principle that the law should 'rule' in the sense that it establishes a fair framework to which all conduct and behaviour conform, applying equally to all members of society, whether they be private individuals or government personnel. No person is above the law. As proclaimed by the constitutional theorist A.V. Dicey in the late 19th century, the rule of law involves several key principles:

■ *Legal equality:* Everybody should be subject to the same laws and have equal access to the law. The granting of legal aid in the form of financial help and legal advice is available for the poorest and solicitors are on hand to assist those detained by the police who are themselves – like judges – also bound by the law.

■ *Law and justice:* The rule of law seeks to equate law and justice, the two terms often being used interchangeably, as though they have the same meaning. Legal procedures and penalties should be fair and just, consistent and open, in order that justice is not only done but seen to be done. The accused are represented by a lawyer, often tried by a randomly selected jury and able to call their own witnesses. An appeals procedure is available to remedy miscarriages of justice.

■ *Legal certainty:* There should be a clear statement of everybody's rights and obligations and of the limits to power, especially that of the state and government. The law should not be arbitrary, contradictory or unclear.

■ *Innocence until proven guilty:* It is up to the prosecution to prove guilt rather than for the defence to establish innocence. This is why there has – until recently – long been a 'right to silence' and the need in court for those prosecuting to establish guilt 'beyond reasonable doubt'.

■ *Judicial independence and impartiality:* Judges and others who apply the law need to be free from external political pressure and personal bias, in order to ensure that justice is an end in itself and not merely a political tool.

In addition to the rule of law, the courts, tribunals and public authorities are obliged to act in a judicial way, which ensures that justice is obtained for all parties. This is achieved by following the precepts of *natural justice*. These require that the machinery of justice must not be biased and that all involved in a dispute shall have their viewpoint acknowledged and heard. The fact that every subject has a right to appear before a judicial authority and have his or her say before an impartial judge is an essential safeguard of the liberties and freedoms of the individual.

The lack of bias

No one who is acting in a judicial capacity must have a stake in the outcome of the matter being determined. The Latin principle *nemo judex in causa sua* applies, meaning that no one can judge his or her own case. It was back in 1812 in the case of *Regina v Sussex Justices* that the famous and oft-repeated phrase was first employed: 'that justice should

Hint

This chapter contains important case studies on matters ranging from the European Convention and Human Rights Act to the increasingly important doctrine of judicial review. A knowledge of the cases will help you understand what they can and cannot do. Try to synthesise the findings of these studies, so that you end up with a clear picture of how the courts can protect the individual.

not only be done, but be manifestly and undoubtedly seen to be done'. In a modern setting, this means that if only one person sitting as a magistrate or in a tribunal hearing is an interested party (e.g. has a financial stake), then the outcome will be invalid because of a presumption of bias.

All views to be heard

Another Latin maxim is also relevant. *Audi alteram partem* means 'hear the other side'. This requires that any body (or organisation) that is acting in a judicial setting must listen to the evidence of all parties, with all relevant people having an opportunity to express their point of view. It is then up to the judge, magistrate or presiding official to assess the evidence and ensure that justice is done in matters where there are conflicting viewpoints and interests.

Court proceedings

Guilt or innocence is established in criminal cases via an adversarial system. This involves representatives of the two sides arguing their case and each being given a chance to cross-examine the other. The defendant pleads 'guilty' or 'not guilty'. In the event of a not guilty plea, the prosecution endeavours to prove guilt 'beyond reasonable doubt'.

> ### ■ Summary question
>
> Why is the doctrine of the rule of law regarded as an essential component of a free society?

■ Balancing conflicting interests

The law is concerned with balancing interests and rights. Sometimes, it does so by imposing a corresponding duty on another person not to interfere with our rights. Often, it is impossible to exercise a right or interest without this infringing on someone else's right or interest. The interests of the majority and those of individuals may conflict. In these situations, the law seeks to provide fair remedies such as damages and injunctions in civil cases and in criminal ones provides different sentences for different categories of crime and grading sentences according to the circumstances involved.

Examples of the balancing role of the law arise in situations where:

■ exercising a right may interfere with another person's freedom – the laws on abortion have to balance the rights of women to control their own bodies with the right of the unborn child, for instance in determining the time-period in which an abortion is permissible

■ our individual rights to do as we want with our own land or property are balanced by the obligation to avoid harm to other people, such as our neighbours' enjoyment of their land and property – a situation commonly known as the 'law of give and take'

■ an employer's right to receive work from his or her workforce is balanced by the duty to pay for the employees' labour

■ the state's right to punish is balanced by its duty to provide a fair and impartial trial.

The task of the court is to balance out these competing interests, ensuring that all sides have an opportunity to air their case and that issues are handled without bias towards the needs of either party.

Police powers and procedure

It is also necessary to ensure that there is a balance between preventing crime and apprehending those involved with protecting liberty. The police need substantial powers to fulfil their responsibilities to maintain

Activity

Using the internet to assist you, find out about the PACE Act and the ways in which the state tries to protect people suspected of crime from abuses of power by the police.

law and order in the community, but if those powers are exercised indiscriminately or excessively then individual rights can suffer. Likewise, when suspects are interviewed or detained, they need to have their rights observed, for instance to see a solicitor and not to be detained for longer than the law allows.

The judicial process

The judiciary is the branch of government responsible for the adjudication of law and the arbitration between parties in any legal dispute. The term includes those individuals and bodies (primarily judges and the courts) involved in administering and interpreting the meaning of laws. In democratic countries, it is expected that the judicial system will be able to function freely without any interference from the government of the day.

The independence of the judiciary and how it is secured

In many states, the constitution provides for an independent judiciary. Its existence is a fundamental characteristic of liberal democracies. Judicial independence implies that there should be a strict separation between the judiciary and other branches of government. It is expected that the judicial system will be able to function freely and without any interference from the government of the day.

Key terms

Supreme Court: the body recently created to act as the final court of appeal in all matters under English, Welsh and Northern Irish law, from 2009. In effect, it takes over the judicial functions of the House of Lords, currently handled by the law lords.

Law lords: members of the House of Lords by virtue of their high judicial positions. They retain their seats for life, so that there are always more law lords than necessary to enable the House of Lords to fulfil its judicial functions.

Further information

Judicial independence

For the first time in almost 900 years, judicial independence is now officially enshrined in law. The Constitutional Reform Act (2005) provides for the separation of the judiciary (legal system) from the legislature (Parliament) and the executive (government). The key constitutional changes include:

- reforming the office of the Lord Chancellor, transferring his judicial functions to the Lord Chief Justice
- the establishment of a new **Supreme Court** separate from the House of Lords and the removal of the **law lords** from the legislature
- the new independent Judicial Appointments Commission.

The independence of the British judiciary is supposed to be protected in three main ways:

- the way in which judges are selected
- their security of tenure
- their political neutrality.

The selection of judges

In Britain, judges have traditionally been appointed by the government of the day. The most senior ones were appointed by the prime minister following consultation with the Lord Chancellor. However, new arrangements were announced by the Lord Chancellor in mid-2003 and subsequently included within the framework of the Constitutional Reform Act 2005. A new Judicial Appointments Commission (JAC) now examines the way in which judicial appointments are made. It puts forward nominations, and there are clear restrictions on the ability of the Lord Chancellor to reject them. For appointments to the new Supreme Court, the minister should receive only one name from the JAC.

The security of tenure of judges

Once installed in office, judges normally retain their position, subject to their good conduct. They should not be liable to removal on the whim of particular governments or individuals. In Britain, the Act of Settlement 1701 established that judges be appointed for life. They are very hard to remove and serve until the time of their retirement. Today, those who function in superior courts are only liable to dismissal on grounds of misbehaviour. This can be done only after a vote of both Houses of Parliament and has not actually happened in the 20th or 21st centuries. Lower judges are not normally dismissed either. Dismissal only applies in cases of dishonesty, incompetence or misbehaviour. In 1983, one judge was dismissed for whisky smuggling!

Judicial neutrality

By convention, judges are above and beyond politics, apolitical beings who interpret but do not make the law. As such, their discretion is limited. They are expected to refrain from partisan activity. The 1955 **Kilmuir Guidelines** urged them to silence since 'every utterance which he [a judge] makes in public, except in the actual performance of his judicial duties, must necessarily bring him within the focus of criticism'. The reason why they should remain politically neutral is clear. If they make a partisan utterance, it is felt that this would undermine public confidence in their impartiality. They need to be beyond party politics, committed to the pursuit of justice.

> ### ▪ Key terms
>
> **Kilmuir Guidelines:** principles set out by the then Lord Chancellor in 1955 that restricted the freedom of judges to speak out on matters of public policy.

Yet in the UK the separation of judges from the political process is not quite as clear-cut as the concept of an independent judiciary might suggest. Some holders of judicial office also have a political role, among them the Lord Chancellor, the attorney-general and the solicitor-general. Although they are supposed to act in a non-partisan manner in their judicial capacity, at times this can be difficult. The legal advice given to the Blair government by the solicitor-general over the legality of the decision to send troops into Iraq was especially controversial. Critics allege that he did everything he could to support the ministerial case for intervention.

Judges may find themselves caught up in political controversy in other ways too. They may be asked by the prime minister to chair important inquiries and make recommendations for future action. Lord Hutton was asked to enquire into the death of Dr David Kelly, the former weapons inspector who committed suicide in 2003 after suggestions that the case for military action against Iraq had been 'sexed up'. Sometimes, the findings of such enquiries are contentious and inspire criticism of the judge involved. Hutton was accused of producing a report that 'whitewashed' the Blair administration while heaping blame upon the BBC, which had carried the 'sexing-up' allegation.

Furthermore, in a greater spirit of openness, senior judges have been willing to express their views on public policy, although this is not to ally themselves with backing for one party. As some leading judges have publicly acknowledged, today they are not simply administering the law in a passive way. There is much potential for them to make law as they interpret it, a process often known as judicial activism.

The administration of justice

For many years, some commentators have argued the case for having a Ministry of Justice. They pointed to inadequacies in the judicial system and difficulties in obtaining information in the House of Commons because of the division of legal functions between the Lord Chancellor

■ **Further information**

The Lord Chancellor and Lord Chief Justice

The terms of the Constitutional Reform Act 2005 include the following:

- The Lord Chief Justice has become the overall head of the judiciary.

- Previously he was second to the Lord Chancellor, but that office lost most of its judicial functions. The Lord Chancellor has now become the Secretary of State for Justice and Lord Chancellor.

- The Lord Chancellor is no longer a judge, but still exercises disciplinary authority over the judges, jointly with the Lord Chief Justice. He also has a role in appointing judges.

- The Lord Chancellor no longer participates in the judicial business of the House of Lords.

Fig. 8.1 *Lord Phillips, Lord Chief Justice*

and home secretary. They wanted to see a single 'minister of justice' at the head of a department with undivided responsibility for the administrative aspects of the judicial system.

Under the new arrangements that operate from 2007:

- The *Ministry of Justice* has responsibility for sentencing policy, probation, prisons and prevention of re-offending in England and Wales. It is responsible for dealing with all suspected offenders from the time they are arrested, through until convicted offenders are released from prison.

- At its head is the Lord Chancellor who retains the roles and responsibilities given to him under the Constitutional Reform Act 2005 (CRA) and is now known as the *Secretary of State for Justice and Lord Chancellor* (the Lord Chief Justice has responsibility for the system of courts and judges).

- The *home secretary* retains responsibility for the police and the security service, as well as oversight of crime reduction, counter-terrorism and other crime-related areas.

■ The powers of the courts

There are several different kinds of courts and several categories of judges in the United Kingdom.

The Court Structure of Her Majesty's Courts Service (HMCS)

Her Majesty's Courts Service carries out administrative and support work for the Court of Appeal, the High Court, the Crown Court, the magistrates' courts, the county courts and the Probate Service.

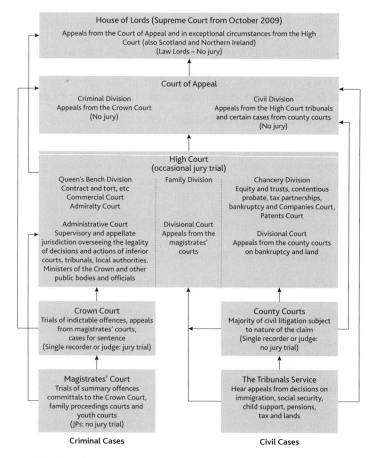

Fig. 8.2 *The UK court structure*

Criminal courts

Magistrates' courts

Magistrates' courts hear more than 95 per cent of all criminal cases in England and Wales. The magistrates receive training to give them sufficient knowledge of the law and of the nature and purpose of sentencing. A court clerk advises them on law and procedure. In some circumstances, district judges preside over magistrates' courts instead of JPs. Legally qualified and salaried, they tend to deal with longer and more complex cases and also have jurisdiction to hear cases involving extradition. (See pages 129–30 for more information on magistrates.)

Fig. 8.3 *Bedford magistrates' court*

Table 8.1 *The courts in which particular categories of offences are tried*

Category of offence	Example	Type of trial
Summary offences	Minor offences such as minor criminal damage, the majority of motoring offences, non-payment of council tax, failure to pay TV licence etc.	Magistrates' court
Indictable offences	More serious offences, such as rape and manslaughter	Referred from the magistrates' court to the Crown Court for trial by judge and jury
Offences triable either way	Offences that can be minor or serious, depending on what is actually done in a particular case, e.g. theft or assault	Magistrates' or Crown Court, depending on what the accused has opted for. Even if he or she chooses a magistrates' court, the case can still be referred to the Crown Court for the sentencing stage

Magistrates' courts are of great importance in the legal system. There is a magistrates' court in every county and in the majority of boroughs. They are busy courts, for all criminal cases start in them. They:

- handle the first hearing of all criminal cases
- try summary cases
- try those cases that are triable either way, where it has been decided to use the magistrates' court.

In summary cases, magistrates cannot normally order sentences of imprisonment that exceed 6 months (or 12 months for consecutive sentences), or fines exceeding £5,000. In cases triable either way, the offender may be committed by the magistrates to the Crown Court for sentencing if a more severe sentence is thought necessary.

Case study

The closure of magistrates' courts

In recent decades, many magistrates' courts have been closed down. The current closure rate runs at about 5 per cent a year. Today, there are just under 360.

Key terms

Summary offences: relatively minor criminal cases that are always tried by magistrates.

Indictable offences: serious criminal offences that must always be tried by a Crown Court, before a judge and jury.

Offences triable either way: offences that can be serious or relatively minor, depending on how they are committed, such as theft. They can be tried in a magistrates' or a Crown Court.

Activity

Make a list of well-known criminal offences, using reports in local newspapers to assist you. Divide them into the more and less serious. Look up on the net to see if you have correctly allocated them as indictable or summary offences.

Hint

Examiners like to see the use of up-to-date examples, so read the newspapers and make a note of any cases mentioned. List the offence and the sentence given.

We must hold on to local justice

Many of the 30,500 lay, unpaid justices of the peace feel so undervalued that demoralisation is rife. There are record resignations and a shortage of quality replacements. The imposition of the extra burdens of the Human Rights Act, personal assessments and, of course, imposed court closures are at the root of the malaise. JPs feel simultaneously the Cinderellas of the judicial system and its packhorse, handling more than 90% of all criminal cases plus many civil ones ...

Among the facilities which a market town of 10,000-25,000 requires is a magistrates' court. Yet the vast majority are now without one. Take the recent shutting down of the court in the Suffolk town of Haverhill, with a population of around 25,000. The closure report quanitified potential annual savings of £11,160 without, bizarrely, taking any account of consequential costs 'that may be placed upon other organisations and individuals'. So witnesses, families, police and JPs must now travel 15 miles to Bury St Edmunds or Sudbury.

Among the reasons for discontinuing Haverhill was that 'the women's toilet was observed to be in an untidy state with the paper-towel dispenser being too small for the towels so that it could not be closed properly'.

Too often, the quality of such reports is poor, being biased towards the closure which bureaucrats so assiduously promote on the narrowest of 'value for money' criteria. Shiny new court complexes are the rage. A court will be closed for (inter alia) inadequate disabled access, regardless of the same disabled people then having to travel many miles extra (as many as 50 in parts of Wales).

Source: A. Phillips, The Observer, *2 December 2001*

Magistrates who have undergone appropriate training can also sit as a youth court, where they deal with young offenders and exercise special powers of sentencing. Youth courts sit at a different time or place from the full magistrates' courts, in order to protect the young people involved from contact with adult offenders who may be involved in more serious cases. Press reporting is restricted in cases involving young people who are again staffed by a panel of three magistrates, there always being a man and women on the panel. In youth courts, magistrates can impose a sentence of youth detention, via a detention and training order (DTO) of up to two years in custody.

Magistrates' courts have some civil jurisdiction. They handle cases such as:

■ recovery of civil debts, such as income tax or electricity/gas payments
■ family and matrimonial matters, such as applications for separation and custody of a child, maintenance orders etc.
■ granting licences for showing films or for the sale of alcohol or gambling.

Crown courts

Crown courts operate on a circuit system, with judges travelling around the courts in one of the six circuits in England and Wales to hear cases. They try more serious cases. Crown courts hear indictable cases and offences triable either way, where the accused selects trial by jury. They also handle sentencing, in cases where magistrates have referred this to them having tried the case in their own courts.

Indictable offences can be classified into four categories:

- Class 1 offences include murder and treason
- Class 2 offences are very serious, such as manslaughter
- Class 3 offences are indictable ones not in Classes 1, 2 or 4
- Class 4 offences are the least serious, such as those triable either way, causing death by dangerous driving and causing actual bodily harm.

Whereas Class 1 offences can only be tried by a High Court judge operating in a first tier Crown Court, Class 2 offences are heard by a circuit judge in a second tier court and offences in category 4 may be tried by a circuit judge or recorder in a third tier court. Broadly, the higher the tier, the higher the judge and the higher the category of offence.

Crown courts also have a civil caseload, as in cases of appeal over licensing matters.

There is an appeals process, by which cases from the Crown Court may be appealed to the Court of Appeal (criminal division) and ultimately to the House of Lords, the highest court of appeal until 2009 when the new supreme court is due to assume that role.

Civil courts

Some courts handle civil and criminal cases, so that rather than refer to civil courts it is more appropriate to speak of those with civil jurisdiction. As seen above, some civil cases are heard in the magistrates' courts. Apart from licensing and debt issues, the bulk of this work is matrimonial. They can grant a separation but not a divorce. They can deal with payment orders, but not the actual property settlement.

County courts handle a range of business, including contractual issues, probate, landlord–tenant disputes, uncontested divorces and associated family matters relating to children and property. Almost any civil case other than defamation can begin its hearings in a county court. Any claim worth less than £15,000 or personal injuries or contract claim under £50,000 must use this route. Generally, matters between £25,000 and £50,000 may be heard in a county court or the High Court.

Again, there is an appeal process, via which cases may end up in the Court of Appeal.

The role of judges

Judges perform several specific functions:

- They preside over criminal trials for serious offences, being responsible for all matters of criminal law (determining what it means and how it applies in changing circumstances) and making sure that all of the rules of procedure are properly applied.
- They deliver what they believe to be appropriate sentences – maybe imprisonment or, in cases where the guilty person presents no obvious danger, a community punishment.
- They peacefully resolve civil disputes between individuals, adjudicating (giving a decision) in controversies within the limits of the civil law and awarding compensation or making a legally binding order for the parties to behave in a particular way.

Activity

List any reasons why an accused person might choose to be tried at the Crown Court, in cases triable either way. What disadvantages might there be in so doing?

Summary questions

1 To what extent is there a balance between the powers of the police to investigate crime and the rights and liberties of those suspected of committing it?

2 What is meant by the term judicial independence? How is it secured in the UK?

3 Are judges neutral? If so, in what sense(s)?

4 Magistrates' courts are cheap, but it is wrong that matters of vital concern should be decided by amateurs. Do you agree?

5 What are the possible advantages of trial in a magistrates' court?

6 What is the difference in work performed by magistrates' and Crown Courts, in criminal and civil matters?

7 According to Her Majesty's Court Service, their primary goal is that: 'All citizens according to their differing needs are entitled to access to justice, whether as victims of crime, defendants accused of crimes, consumers in debt, children in need of care, or business people in commercial disputes. Our aim is to ensure that access is provided as quickly as possible and at the lowest cost consistent with open justice and that citizens have greater confidence in, and respect for the system of justice.' Is this goal to a large extent achieved?

Further information

Early appointments of the Judicial Appointments Commission (JAC)

- It was intended that by its appointments the JAC would break the stranglehold of privately educated white male barristers over the High Court Bench.

- The first appointments of the JAC have not done anything at all to create a more diverse judiciary. No women or members of ethnic minorities have yet been appointed. All 10 are white male former barristers and six of the nine educated in Britain went to leading independent schools.

- Of the current 108 high court judges, only 10 are women, one is from an ethnic minority and one is a former solicitor.

- Of the next 11 awaiting appointment as suitable vacancies arise, three are women. None of the three ethnic minority candidates were successful, neither were any of the seven solicitors.

Source: The Guardian, 28 January 2008

- They uphold the will of the legislature, acting as guardians of the law, taking responsibility for applying its rules without fear or favour, as well as securing the liberties of the person and ensuring that governments and people comply with the spirit of the constitution.

- Particularly in states with a codified constitution, they have responsibility for judicial review (see pages 151–7) of particular laws and administrative actions.

- Senior judges may be asked to chair inquiries, such as the **Hutton Inquiry** (see also pages 141 and 199) in the aftermath of the invasion of Iraq.

- Law lords sit in Parliament, contributing to its debates on public policy and sharing in the various tasks performed by the House of Lords. From 2009, they will instead operate in the new Supreme Court.

What sorts of people are appointed as judges?

The social background of judges has changed less than that of senior civil servants or even diplomats. Overwhelmingly, they are white, male, upper middle aged and upper middle class. At the turn of the 21st century all of the law lords were men, educated at Oxford or Cambridge universities; half of them were from three colleges that have a traditional reputation as 'nurseries for lawyers'. Their average age in mid-2003 was 68.5 years.

Critics of judges have sometimes complained that they are unable to understand the habits and terminology of everyday life, reflecting instead the social thinking of 30 or 40 years ago. In particular, critics have doubted the ability of such people to preside over cases involving highly politicised argument on issues of human rights and civil liberties. Of course, recruitment patterns are not necessarily a guide to judicial opinions. It does not follow that people from a privileged background necessarily hold socially conservative views.

Table 8.2 *Women and ethnic minorities on The Bench as at 1 April 2007*

Rank	No. of women	No. of ethnic minorities
Lords of Appeal in Ordinary (12)	1	0
Heads of Division (5)	0	0
Lord Justices of Appeal (37)	3	0
High Court judges (108)	10	1
Circuit judges (639)	73	9
Recorders (1201)	179	53
Recorders in training (5)	3	0
District judges (450)	101	14
Deputy district judges (780)	219	30
District judges in magistrates' court (139)	33	7
Deputy district judges in magistrates' court (169)	42	9
Overall total (3,545)	664	123

N.B. *Figures in brackets represent the total number of each category*

Source: figures adapted from those provided by the Department for Constitutional Affairs

Activities

1 Check the current figures of female and ethnic minority representation on The Bench. Consult the Ministry of Justice website to get your information.

2 Suggest reasons why it might be considered desirable to have more women and members of ethnic minorities on The Bench.

3 Look up the differences in the work done by the various categories of judge, as listed in Table 8.2.

4 Find out more about the age, education, ethnicity, gender and legal backgrounds of the current law lords.

Summary questions

1 Can we respect judges?

2 How representative of society are our judges?

3 Are judges out of touch with attitudes and behaviour in modern society? If they are, would that situation be changed if there were more women and members of ethnic minorities on The Bench?

4 How might you defend judges from some of the criticisms made about them?

The courts and the Human Rights Act

Since the passage of the Civil Procedure Act (1997), civil cases that go before the courts are allocated to the small claims track, the fast-track procedure or the multi-track procedure. The allocation depends on the complexity of the issues raised and the amount of the claim involved. A case manager (usually the judge) has responsibility for ensuring that the case proceeds as quickly and simply as possible.

The first stage of the civil process involves claimant (or the 'plaintiff') issuing a claim, which is served upon the defendant. The defendant can admit liability and settle; deny liability; accept some liability but dispute the amount of the claim; or make a counter-claim. In a contentious case, the case manager will send a questionnaire to those involved and then list the case under one of the three categories. The parties will provide relevant documents and agree witness statements and evidence in advance, so that by the time of the trial only the disputed areas will be covered. In many cases, before the case goes to trial, the matter will be 'settled at the door of the court'.

Remedies for breach of rights protected by the European Convention on Human Rights

As we have seen, the European Convention on Human Rights (ECHR) covers a wide area of rights, from the right to life to freedom from torture, inhuman or degrading treatment, from the right to a fair trial to respect for a person's private and family life, home and correspondence. Although states can derogate from most of their obligations in time of war or emergency, this does not cover freedom from torture, inhuman or degrading treatment. The ECHR does not cover the whole field of human rights, notably omitting general economic and social rights such as the right to housing, a minimum income and free healthcare.

Further information

For more information on the remedies available under civil law (e.g. damages, injunctions and specific performance orders), see pages 117–20.

Prior to the entry into force of Protocol 11 of the European Convention on Human Rights (1998), individuals did not have direct access to the court at Strasbourg. They had to apply to the European Commission on Human Rights, which if it found the case to be well-founded would launch a case in the court at Strasbourg on the individual's behalf.

Prior to incorporation of the European Convention via the Human Rights Act, the record of British governments in Strasbourg was poor for many years. They lost many cases, judgments often coming down on the side of the aggrieved individual. The following resulted:

- prisoners won the right to consult a lawyer or write to an MP (this was the first case brought under the Convention, in 1975)
- corporal punishment in schools was ruled out of order, if parental views had not been taken into consideration
- birching was ended in the Isle of Man
- the armed forces were criticised for acting illegally by banning gays and lesbians from serving
- it was said that the child killers of James Bulger did not receive a fair trial as they could not have understood the proceedings and that it was wrong for the Home Secretary to determine what was meant by a life sentence. The decision led to a change in the law via the Criminal Justice Act (2003), which removed much of the power of home secretaries to set sentences.

The role of the UK Supreme Court

The Constitutional Reform Act 2005 made provision for the creation of a new Supreme Court for the United Kingdom. There had, in recent years, been mounting calls for the creation of a new free-standing Supreme Court separate from the highest appeal court (the House of Lords) and for transferring the current Lords of Appeal in Ordinary (law lords) from the chamber to the new creation.

Fig. 8.4 *The Middlesex Guildhall, the location of the new Supreme Court*

At present, there are 12 Lords of Appeal. They can currently take part in the proceedings of the House of Lords, but when they sit in the new body from October 2009 they will be entirely separate from the parliamentary process.

The Supreme Court will become the highest court in the land, the supreme court of appeal. It will act as the final arbiter on points of law for the whole of the United Kingdom in civil cases and for England, Wales and Northern Ireland in criminal cases. Its decisions bind all courts below it in the structure illustrated on page 142.

The Supreme Court will be a United Kingdom body legally separate from the England and Wales courts since it will also be the Supreme Court of both Scotland and Northern Ireland. As such it falls outside of the remit of the Lord Chief Justice of England and Wales in his role as head of the judiciary of England and Wales.

The role of the European Court of Human Rights (ECHR)

The European Court of Human Rights, which was set up in 1959 in the French city of Strasbourg, considers cases brought by individuals, organisations and states against the countries that are bound by the ECHR – in effect, all European nations except Belarus. The Court aims to apply and to protect the civil and political rights of the continent's citizens.

Fig. 8.5 *The Court of Human Rights in Strasbourg*

- The cases brought before the Court take many forms. They include allegations of human rights abuses, discrimination, the improper conduct of trials and the mistreatment of prisoners. Countries must comply with the Court's verdicts, although it cannot directly enforce this. (It is the role of the Committee of Ministers of the Council of Europe to supervise the execution of Court judgments, though it has no formal means of ordering compliance. However, the ultimate sanction of non-compliance is expulsion from the Council of Europe and thus becoming a 'pariah' state within Europe. Moreover, as the European Union takes a keen interest in the Convention and Court, any country that does not comply is likely to be viewed badly.)

- The Court will only hear a case when all domestic legal avenues have been exhausted. Also, plaintiffs must show that they have been a direct victim of an alleged violation and that they cannot bring cases against individuals or private bodies.

 Activity

Using the internet, look up details of some recent cases handled by the European Court of Human Rights, particularly any involving the UK. Make a list of the range of topics covered in judgements of the ECHR.

Membership

The European Court of Human Rights comprises as many judges as there are members of the Council of Europe (47 in March 2009). The current British representative is Nicolas Bratza, a member of the Court since 1998, who has become one of its most senior figures.

No two judges may be nationals of the same country. A country can nominate a representative of a non-European state, as did Liechtenstein in 1990 when it selected a Canadian as a choice. Those appointed to office are expected to be persons of a 'high moral character who have the necessary qualifications to serve in high judicial office'. They tend to be experts in national or international law. They serve for renewable six-year periods. Their terms of office expire when they reach the age of 70, although they do continue to deal with cases already under their consideration.

The organisation and workings of the Court

As presently constituted, the Court was brought into being by Protocol 11 (November 1998). This amendment made the Convention process wholly judicial, whereas previously a Commission had exercised a 'screening' function to sift applications and reduce the workload of the Court. In 1998, this task was entrusted to the Court itself. The workings of the Court were accordingly reorganised:

- Every judge is assigned to one of the five Sections, whose composition is geographically and gender balanced and takes account of the different legal systems of the member states. The composition of the Sections changes every three years.

- The great majority of the judgments of the Court are given by Chambers. These comprise seven judges and are constituted within each Section. The Section president and the judge elected in respect of the state concerned sit in each case. Where the latter is not a member of the Section, he or she sits as an *ex officio* member of the Chamber.

- Committees of three judges are set up within each Section for 12-month periods. Their function is to dispose of applications that are clearly inadmissible.

■ The Grand Chamber of the Court, comprising 17 judges, deals with cases that raise a serious question of interpretation or application of the Convention, or a serious issue of general importance.

The caseload of the Court

The Court has seen its case-load grow rapidly, from just under 6,000 cases in 1998 to almost 14,000 by 2001. In 2006 it received more than 50,000 new requests to judge cases.

Much of this increase has come from the newer democracies of Central and Eastern Europe, where there is less trust in local judicial systems. Russia is currently the biggest single source of cases.

Because of the number of cases brought to the Court, it can take years for the judges to reach a final verdict. A backlog of cases – running to 90,000 in early 2007 – has prompted calls for more judges to be appointed and for the Court's functions to be streamlined for handling minor cases. It has become a victim of its own success.

Cases affecting the UK

Since the passage of the Human Rights Act, most cases under the European Convention are resolved in UK courts, with the highest court of appeal being the House of Lords sitting in its judicial capacity. Cases can however still reach Strasbourg, although this is usually only as a last resort if all else fails. An interesting case occurred in February 2002, when the European judges had an opportunity to say whether British judges had correctly heard a case that was based on the provisions of the Convention. Mrs Diane Pretty (who was suffering from motor neurone disease) was given 'fast track' access to the European Court to determine whether or not her husband was to be allowed to help her to kill herself. Two months later, it ruled that the original decision in the High Court had been correct and dismissed her appeal. For some other cases handled by the Court, look at the case studies below and on page 155, and the Belmarsh judgment on page 103–4.

Activity

Make a list of the sorts of cases that can be handled by the European Court of Human Rights and those that cannot.

■ **Case study**

The European Court of Human Rights at work (as resolved in February 2007)

M v the United Kingdom, concerning a psychiatric patient's inability to change her 'nearest relative'

The person appointed as the nearest relative of the applicant was her adoptive father, whom M claimed had sexually abused her when she was a child. She successfully applied to the High Court for a declaration that the relevant legislation was incompatible with her right under Article 8 of the Convention to respect for her private life, in that she had no choice in the matter, nor any legal means of changing the appointment.

In her complaint, M alleged, *inter alia*, that the government had failed to change the law in relation to nearest relatives along the lines that had been agreed in a friendly settlement of the earlier *JT v the United Kingdom* case. In her own case, a friendly (out-of-court) settlement was reached by which the government agreed to rectify the incompatibility and to pay the complainant damages, costs and expenses.

MacDonald v *the United Kingdom*, concerning the applicant's rejection of a government offer to pay compensation for compulsory resignation from the military on grounds of homosexuality

The applicant joined the RAF and applied for a compassionate posting as his mother was ill. For the posting, he required developed vetting (DV) security clearance. He expected to be asked about his homosexuality in the course of the vetting procedure. He confirmed his leanings and was denied the job. Moreover, it was decided by the RAF to re-interview him about his homosexual activities, to establish the extent of those activities, with whom he had been involved and whether other service personnel were involved. As a result he surrendered even the basic level of security clearance required of all members of the Force. He was asked to resign, but – upon legal advice – did not agree to do so voluntarily. He was then dismissed.

He submitted a claim to an employment tribunal, stating unlawful discrimination on grounds of sex and that the circumstances of his dismissal amounted to harassment. He lost this appeal, for the tribunal considered that the relevant Act covered gender, rather than sexual orientation. The employment appeal tribunal, however, disagreed with the tribunal and found that the use of the word 'sex' in the Act was ambiguous and should be interpreted as including orientation.

The claimant's case eventually reached the House of Lords, where it was rejected. The case came before the European Court of Human Rights, before which the government offered to make an *ex gratia* payment of £115,000. This was rejected by the aggrieved individual. However, the Court found that given the government's admissions and the level of compensation proposed, there was no longer any justification for further examination of the application.

Doyle v *the United Kingdom*, concerning an overseas resident denied the vote in national elections in the UK, after having lived abroad for 15 years

The applicant, a British national, had moved from the UK to Belgium in 1983 where he has resided ever since. In 2006, he enquired about registering on the UK electoral roll. The Department for Constitutional Affairs claimed that only nationals resident overseas for less than 15 years could so register. He could be reinstated if he returned to live in the UK and could in any case vote in European elections.

The case of the complainant, made under Article 3 of Protocol 1, was declared inadmissible by the Court. It found that the time-limit of the original Act had been the subject of great parliamentary scrutiny and that the imposition did not appear to be either disproportionate or irreconcilable with the underlying purpose of the Protocol. There was 'no effective disfranchisement or impairment of the very essence of the right to vote'. Hence, the complaint was 'manifestly ill-founded'.

Judicial review

Judicial review is the process that enables judges to override the decisions and laws of democratically elected governments. Specifically, it covers three main areas:

Activity

Note the outcomes of the three case studies. Do you think that, in each case, the finding of the Court was an appropriate one? On the basis of these cases and others mentioned in this section, how well do you think the Court protects the human rights of European citizens?

Key terms

Judicial review: the power of the courts to overturn executive or legislative actions they hold to be illegal or unconstitutional. The UK has a weak form of judicial review. The courts cannot strike down an Act of Parliament, but they can review executive actions, deciding whether the executive has acted *ultra vires* (beyond its powers), unfairly or without reference to relevant and material facts.

■ rulings on whether specific laws are constitutional

■ resolving conflicts between the state and the citizen over civil liberties

■ resolving conflicts between different institutions or levels of government.

Judicial review gives judges a unique position, both in and above politics. In the US, judges have strong powers of judicial review, enabling them to strike down laws as unconstitutional. In Britain, interest in the process of judicial review has developed relatively recently and operates in a weaker form. It enables the courts to monitor the way in which public officials carry out their duties and it empowers the courts to nullify (cancel out) those actions that are considered illegal and unconstitutional, where there is an abuse of legal power and in which a decision is irrational or unreasonable, or unfairly reached.

The system of judicial review is a system by which the High Court reviews the decisions of government and other officials, inferior courts, public bodies, local councils and other bodies whose decisions affect the individual. Certain public bodies are exempt from the possibility of review. For example, it was ruled in a 1998 case that decisions of the Parliamentary Commissioner for Standards could not be subject to review. His decisions operated as part of the proceedings of Parliament and were non-justiciable (not appropriate for judicial consideration or resolution).

Applications for review are made to the High Court. Hearings are usually held before a single judge of the Queen's Bench Division. Statistics indicate that there has been an increasing resort to the process in recent years. The number of annual applications for permission to seek judicial review increased rapidly from the 1980s onwards, rising from around 500 in the early 1980s to more than 4,000 by the late 1990s. (Many more applications for judicial review are initiated, but difficulties in obtaining financial aid and the High Court's refusal to grant leave for review, rule them out of consideration). About a third of these cases refer to actions taken by local authorities; around a quarter by government departments. Many of those involving a department fail, perhaps some 10 for every one that is successful. Those that succeed are high-profile cases of political significance, which therefore get the headlines.

The development of the practice of judicial review by the higher courts since the late 1960s has become a recognised feature of our constitutional arrangements. The effect of the passage of the Human Rights Act was to systematise the process and to elevate the law lords in particular into a form of constitutional court, charged with deciding whether particular legislative acts or executive actions were consistent with the obligations under the Convention that the Act codified.

Judicial review and natural justice

Natural justice is a legal philosophy used to determine whether legal proceedings are just and fair. Underlying it is the idea that certain basic legal standards are required by nature, for they are so obvious that they should be applied universally without needing to be enacted into law.

The rules of natural justice stress the importance of procedural fairness. The guidelines of any system based upon them include the the 'rule against bias' (for instance, people making decisions should declare any personal interest they may have in the proceedings) and the 'right to a fair hearing' in which the views of all relevant parties are aired. Decision-makers should take into account any relevant considerations and extenuating circumstances. All parties to proceedings are entitled to ask questions and contradict the evidence of the opposing party. Irrationality challenges have become increasingly harder to make in recent years.

The courts do not consider the merits of decisions and cannot reverse them merely because they consider them wrong. They can only be wrong if they are so unreasonable that no responsible official would have made them. This is sometimes referred to as 'Wednesbury unreasonableness', following the case of *Associated Provincial Picture Houses Ltd v Wednesbury Corporation* (1948).

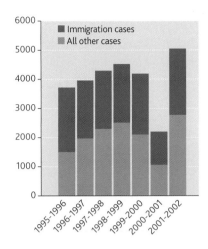

Fig. 8.1 *Applications for judicial review*

Source: adapted figures from G. Peele, Governing the UK, Blackwell, 2004

Case study

The case of *Associated Provincial Picture Houses Ltd* v *Wednesbury Corporation* (1948)

Associated Provincial Picture Houses (APPH) were granted a licence by the defendant Wednesbury local authority to operate their cinema on condition that no children under 15 were admitted to the cinema on Sundays. They said this was unacceptable and beyond the power of the Wednesbury Corporation to impose. However, the court held that it could not intervene to overturn the decision, simply because it disagreed with it. To be able to so do, it would have to form the conclusion that:

- in making its decision, the Corporation took into account factors that ought not to have been taken into account or
- the Corporation omitted to take account of factors that ought to have been considered or
- the decision was so unreasonable that no reasonable authority would ever consider imposing it.

As the situation in Wednesbury did not fit into any of these categories, the claim of APPH failed and the decision of the Wednesbury Corporation was upheld.

Remedies available through judicial review

The civil law offers a range of remedies (forms of redress) that may be available in any case of judicial review:

- Declarations are statements of the legal position which declares the rights of parties – e.g. 'X is entitled to a tax repayment'. Declarations are not enforceable, but public bodies do not usually disobey them.
- Damages involve payment of money by way of compensation. They may be general or specific.
- Injunctions are court orders given to defendants. They can be prohibitory, requiring the defendant not to do something or mandatory, ordering him or her to do something.

In addition to any civil law remedies, the High Court can order a series of remedies that come under the heading of prerogative orders. These are discretionary, so that even if an applicant for review proves that the public body acted illegally the court can still refuse a remedy.

The following remedies are available:

- *Certiori:* This is an order that quashes an *ultra vires* decision. If, for example, a local authority did not award a mandatory student grant, then such an order is likely to be sufficient.

■ *Mandamus:* This is an order to a public body such as a court or local authority to fulfil its duty. For instance, it could be employed to force a local council to produce its accounts for inspection by a local resident or to compel a tribunal to hear a previously refused appeal. An applicant is likely to seek a certiori and a mandamus order, thereby ensuring that the decision is quashed and that the public body decides the case on the basis of its legal powers.

■ *Prohibition:* This can order a body not to act unlawfully in the future. A certiori order quashes a decision that has been made, whereas a prohibition prevents a decision from being taken that – if it is made – will be subject to a certiori order.

Criticisms of the judicial review process

Under the Conservatives (1979–97), ministers were overtly critical of judges and complained about judicial activism, while some judges felt there was a campaign to discredit them. The tabloid press joined in the so-called 'judge bashing', complaining of the 'galloping arrogance' of the judiciary.

Under the Labour government there have been several cases in which the verdict of a judicial review has gone against the minister. Often, they have involved issues of immigration and the rights of asylum seekers. Some ministers have publicly expressed their concern about the activities of the courts in scrutinising government actions and striking them down with the regularity with which they do. Ex-minister Paul Boateng pointed out that 'the judges' job is to judge, the government's job is to govern'. At various times, the-then Home Secretary David Blunkett accused judges of routinely rewriting the laws that Parliament had passed and bluntly made it clear that he did not agree with their findings. As he put it after the judges had declared that parts of the Nationality, Immigration and Asylum Act 2002 were in breach of the Human Rights Act 1998:

> Frankly, I'm fed up with having to deal with a situation where Parliament debates issues and the judges then overturn them ... Parliament did debate this, we were aware of the circumstances, we did mean what we said and, on behalf of the British people, we are going to implement it.

The legislation introduced by Labour in response to the perceived terrorist threat has fallen foul of the judges. In a review of the Anti-Terrorism Crime and Security Act 2001, they found the detention of foreign terror suspects without trial and then the introduction of 'control orders' unlawful. Human rights groups argued that these were incompatible with both Article 5 (the right to liberty) and Article 6 (the right to a fair trial), a position upheld by the courts. The law lords also ruled against the government on its immigration control policies re Roma migrants, Czech citizens of Romany origin.

We have already noted the concerns of government ministers about the increasing use of judicial review, via which their decisions are being challenged in the courts. The two case studies on pages 155–6 illustrate the difficulties that governments can face when dealing with high-profile issues such as security and immigration. Ministers feel irritated by the way in which their attempted actions are being thwarted.

Many politicians and some academics regret the trend towards politicisation of the judiciary, meaning that they feel unelected judges are taking a more active political role and becoming increasingly significant actors on the political scene. They stress that under British constitutional arrangements, Parliament is the main protector of our liberties. It is a sovereign body and its members alone should make decisions. Because they are elected, politicians need to remain sensitive to the wishes of the voters, whereas unelected judges lack accountability and are seen as a group remote from present-day reality.

In other words, according to this view, the solution to any inappropriate behaviour by the government of the day should be in the polling booth rather than in the courtroom. Politicians should not rely on judges to make difficult decisions. In any case, they are inappropriate persons to do so, given their narrow backgrounds and preference towards defending established interests in society.

Case study

Two high-profile cases of judicial review

The detention of terrorist suspects

Britain, alone in Europe, has withdrawn or derogated from Article 5 of the Convention. This guarantees the right to a fair trial and allows only limited circumstances under which a person may be deprived of liberty. Under Part 4 of the Anti-Terrorism Crime and Security Act (2001), ministers were empowered to detain those considered a security threat, without trial. As a result, foreign nationals were held for three years in Britain's highest security prisons, Belmarsh (see Further Information on pages 103–4 and page 150) and Woodhill.

In December 2004, the law lords decided that the detention of foreign terror suspects without trial was unlawful. There was no legal obligation for ministers to abide by the opinion of the senior judges, but the fact that they sat as a panel of nine rather than five was an indication of how seriously they viewed the threat to British liberties. In the words of Lord Scott: 'Indefinite imprisonment … on grounds not disclosed is the stuff of nightmares'. The punishment was considered disproportionate to the threat posed and discriminatory in that it applied only to foreign nationals.

Charles Clarke, the home secretary who had to deal with the ruling, accepted that there was a breach of human rights law. He acted to allay the concerns by proposing a new control order that would involve release of the detainees who would be placed under conditions of strict surveillance, including a ban on use of the internet or mobile phones and possibly house arrest. He also removed the discriminatory aspect of the 2001 Act, by allowing British – as well as foreign – suspects to be treated in the same way. This too was successfully challenged in the courts by critics who saw it as detention by another name. Article 5 allows only limited circumstances under which a person may be deprived of liberty. When a member of the Italian mafia was required to live on a tiny island for 18 months while awaiting trial, the European Court in Strasbourg held that he had been denied his human rights.

The development of human rights law is becoming a feature of the work of all the higher courts, not merely the law lords. Around the same time as the Belmarsh judgment above, the High Court ruled that human rights law applied to the actions of British troops in Iraq, and the law lords ruled against the government on its Roma immigration control policies. Both cases involved human rights principles.

Activity

Using the net to assist you, see if you can find out any recent cases of judicial review, whether high-profile cases or ones that do not make the headlines.

The Prague Airport case: judicial review in operation

In December 2004, the House of Lords ruled that the UK government had discriminated on racial grounds against Roma people by preventing them from travelling to the UK in order to stop them from claiming asylum upon arrival. In 2001, the Czech Republic agreed that the UK could station immigration officers at Prague Airport to screen all passengers travelling to the UK. The overwhelming number of passengers who were refused permission to enter the UK under this operation were Roma. Statistics showed that Roma were 400 times more likely to be refused entry to the UK than non-Roma. The practice was described by the Lords as 'inherently and systematically discriminatory' against Roma, and contrary to Article 3 of the 1951 Refugee Convention. The decision was highly significant in its condemnation of racial discrimination in the area of border regulation.

From the alternative point of view of those seeking review, there are various things that cause difficulty. Those taking judicial review proceedings are often poor and disadvantaged through no fault of their own. The decision made about their cases may determine whether they will have carers to assist them or whether a criminal prosecution should go ahead because their son was killed by others. They may encounter problems along the following lines:

1 *The broad discretionary powers of public bodies:* The Housing Act (1980) gave the secretary of state the power to 'do all such things as appear to him necessary or expedient' to enable council tenants to buy their own council houses. Two years later, a different secretary of state decided that this allowed him to remove the sale of public housing from the hands of local authorities who were not acting as quickly as he believed they should be doing. When challenged in court (*Regina v Secretary of State for the Environment*, 1982), the ruling was in favour of the minister, because it was recognised that ministerial powers were so widely drawn that little could be considered to be *ultra vires*.

2 *The strictness of the unreasonableness test:* In the case of *Regina v Ministry of Defence, ex parte Smith* (1995), the applicants had been dismissed from the armed forces on account of their homosexuality. They wanted a review of the Ministry's ban on homosexuals, but the court found in its favour on the grounds that the ban was legal because it was not unreasonable. It was acknowledged that the decision might not be irrational, even if the case did not appear to be convincing.

3 *The restrictions on applications:* Restrictions on applications to the High Court apply, such as imposing a three-month time period for taking action. Also, the complainant has to prove to a judge that he or she has an arguable case. These restrictions are designed to limit applications that are needlessly distracting, time-consuming and unlikely to succeed. This ensures that many worthwhile cases can proceed and that relatively speedy justice can be obtained. Yet such limitations might mean that ordinary people could be reluctant to take action, believing that conditions make it too difficult for them to win.

4 *National security:* Sometimes, considerations of national security prevent a review from taking place. The fear is that the courts are reluctant to assess the evidence seriously when ministers argue national security concerns. For instance, in the case of the *Council of Civil Service Unions v Minister for the Civil Service* (1985), the civil service union challenged a ban on employees at GCHQ, the government

Summary questions

1 In what sorts of cases has judicial review caused problems for British governments?

2 Is judicial review a key element in British democracy?

3 Does judicial review bring judges too much into the political arena?

intelligence centre in Cheltenham, belonging to trade unions. At the appeal stage, ministers argued that their ban was necessary on national security grounds, as was illustrated by industrial action at GCHQ some years earlier. This claim had not been advanced when the ban was introduced and in the mean time the union had been willing to consider the insertion of a no-strike clause in their contract. But the ban was upheld. (**NB** Recent home secretaries might be surprised to learn that the courts were too concerned about national security at the expense of the individual – see the case study on page 155.)

AQA Examination-style questions

Note that the syllabus content and marking schemes have been revised since these papers were sat, although the subject matter used here remains relevant to the current specification.

1   Read the source below and answer parts (a) to (c) which follow.

> The Race Relations Act 2000 is concerned with people's actions and the effect of those actions on others. You do not have to show that the other person had racist attitudes, only that you were treated less favourably as a result of their actions. The law gives people protection from racial discrimination which may be direct, indirect, victimisation or harassment. The Act also protects people from racial discrimination in most, but not all, situations. One exception is an owner-occupier selling or letting their property if they do not advertise or use an estate agent. Another exception is clubs and associations set up especially for people of a particular ethnic or national group (unless the discrimination is on the basis of colour).

Your answers should refer to the source as appropriate, but you should also include other relevant information.

(a)   Using the source to help you, explain what is meant by 'discrimination' and show how it differs from prejudice.   *(4 marks)*

(b)   Briefly examine in what ways and why some minority ethnic groups experience poorer life chances than the general population.   *(10 marks)*

(c)   Assess the ways in which governments can attempt to reduce discrimination based on race and ethnicity.   *(16 marks)*

Adapted from question 1 AQA Unit 3 January 2007

2   (a)   Briefly examine the ways in which *one* of the following may be the basis for discrimination:

(i) disability; (ii) social class; (ii) sexuality.   *(10 marks)*

(b)   Assess how far government policies aimed at reducing poverty have been effective.   *(20 marks)*

AQA Unit 3 June 2007

3   Read the source below and answer parts (a) to (c) which follow.

> The Human Rights Act 1998 incorporated the European Convention on Human Rights into UK law. The effect of this is to strengthen the protection of individual rights by UK courts and to provide improved remedies where these rights are violated. The Convention is now applicable directly in the UK courts. It is no longer necessary to go all the way to the European Court of Human Rights in Strasbourg to enforce Convention rights.
>
> Under the Human Rights Act 1998, UK courts are required to interpret all legislation in a way that is compatible with Convention rights 'so far as it is possible to do so'. However, if it is not possible to do this, legislation which is incompatible with the Convention is still valid – the judges cannot strike it out. In these circumstances, judges can make 'a declaration of incompatibility'. The government may then amend the legislation to bring it in line with the Convention.
>
> It is unlawful for public authorities to act in a way which is incompatible with Convention rights. A public authority includes central and local government, the police and the NHS.
>
> There has been some debate as to whether the Act allows individual citizens to enforce Convention rights against other individual citizens. The courts appear to have accepted that the Human Rights Act allows this, at least to a limited extent.

Source: adapted from C. Elliott and F. Quinn, English Legal System (6th edition), Pearson Education, 2005

Your answers should refer to the source as appropriate, but you should also refer to other relevant information.

(a)   Using the source, outline what is meant by 'the Human Rights Act 1998 incorporated the European Convention on Human Rights into UK law'.   *(4 marks)*

(b)   Briefly explain, using examples, two ways in which the Human Rights Act 1998 can be said to strengthen the protection of the rights of individual citizens.   *(10 marks)*

(c)   'Citizens are unable to fully exercise their human rights because the Freedom of Information Act 2000 does not actually give them sufficient access to information.'

Assess this claim.   *(16 marks)*

AQA Unit I January 2007

4   (a)   Briefly explain *two* ways in which a citizen, without the means to pay for them, can obtain advice and representation in a dispute with a neighbour.   *(10 marks)*

(b)   'Cases in the magistrates' court should be tried solely by a district judge and not by a bench of lay magistrates'. Assess this view.   *(20 marks)*

AQA Unit 1 June 2007 and Unit 1 January 2007, respectively

Learning objectives:

- to be able to define the concepts of power, authority, influence, democracy and mandate

- to understand the relationship between power and the state and the nature of political power within the UK

- to know who holds political power in the UK

- to be able to define the concepts of economic power and control

- to understand the role of the government and the financial sector

- to understand the economic power of the state, of companies and of the citizen sector

- to have knowledge of the different media and how they are owned and controlled

- to understand how public opinion is created and the role of political 'spin'

- to understand how government and the media are linked

- to know how the media are regulated by statutory bodies.

Key terms

Key terms for this page appear on page 160.

The concept and nature of power

In any society, there has to be a system of law and order so that people can live peacefully with each other. Relationships between people have to be regulated and organised. They have different views about what goals should be pursued and about the best means of achieving those goals. Whenever they are engaged in making decisions, conflict is inevitable. It may be mild verbal disagreement or it may be more dramatic physical confrontation. The process of resolving conflicts and the priorities for policy action that are established is a political process. Politics is, then, about the peaceful resolution of disputes and the allocation of resources. As an American writer entitled his book back in 1936, *Politics: Who Gets What, When and How?*

Governments are responsible for maintaining law and order. Those in government who have responsibility for organising society and making decisions exercise power over us. They have the ability to **influence** the way our community is run and the way in which we live our lives. They have power over us. The concept of power is central to any study of politics, which is why some people would define politics as 'the struggle for power and influence' or as 'the authority to govern'.

What is politics?

Politics is about the theory and practice of **government**. It concerns the ways in which decisions are made about government, state and public affairs; where power lies; how governments and states work; and different theories and practices such as **democracy**, **equality**, **tyranny** and violence.

The importance of power in politics

The notion of power is central to politics. It enables the collective decisions of government ministers to be made and enforced. As Hague and Harrop (2004) put it: 'Without power, a government would be as useless as a car without an engine. Power is the tool that enables rulers both to serve and to exploit their subjects.' Politics is concerned with the distribution, exercise and consequences of power.

Power takes several forms. We are primarily concerned in this chapter with political, economic and military power. But in addition to these, it can be argued that other institutions and systems can from time to time exert influence, on occasion some degree of power:

- *Organised religion has influence* over the lives of those who attend some places of worship and over some of those who stay at home. It may have a profound influence on their thinking and outlook. In the past, some Protestants and Roman Catholics in Northern Ireland have waged their sectarian struggle in the name of their religion. More recently, some young radical Muslims on the mainland of the UK have been influenced by the teachings of 'extremist' **mullahs** in their mosques.

Key terms

Influence: the persuasive effect of one person or body on the actions and ideas of another. This influence or sway may result from factors such as ability, position or wealth.

Politics: the struggle for governmental power and influence between competing individuals and groups in society.

Government: the exercise of political authority over the actions and affairs of a political unit. The government is the policy-making branch of the state (see page 169), enforcing its rulings and acting under its authority.

Democracy: people power, in Abraham Lincoln's phrase 'government of, by and for the people'

Equality: the belief that people should be treated equally and given equal opportunities, as long as there are not grounds for treating them differently.

Tyranny: oppressive and unjust government by a tyrant or despot.

Mullahs: Muslim religious leaders or scholars.

Mass media: the collective name for the organisations involved in publishing, broadcasting or other forms of political communication that channel information to individuals. Forms of the media include newspapers, periodicals, magazines, posters, the cinema, radio, television and video, as well as e-mail and the internet. All are concerned with the transmission of ideas and information in one way or another.

Persuasion: the act of convincing or of trying to convince another.

- *Schools exercise power*, not just in the classroom situation of teachers seeking to maintain control over their pupils. The education system controls the flow of ideas and information we all receive, via the national curriculum. In Citizenship lessons, there is a deliberate attempt to develop democratic values. In the words of the influential Crick Report, political education should 'include the nature and practices of participation in democracy'.

- *The **mass media** also exercise power,* having the ability via newspaper headlines and television news bulletins to set the agenda for what we think and what we think about. In this way, they help to shape opinion. In the case of 20th-century dictatorships such as Hitler's Germany, government propaganda was spread via film and in various art forms.

Most of us as individuals actually possess very limited power. Power tends to be concentrated in relatively few hands and at national level. Those who exert the various forms of power have an impact upon our political life in some way or another. It is important in any democracy that they should be held accountable for the way they carry out their responsibilities. As a former Labour MP and minister, Tony Benn, habitually asked on meeting persons in high office: 'What power have you got? Where did you get it from? In whose interests do you exercise it? To whom are you accountable? How do we get rid of you?'

The difference between power and authority

There is a difference between power and authority:

- *Power* is the ability to get things done, if necessary involving making others do what they would not do by free choice. Other means of **persuasion** may be deployed, but underlying their use is the ability to reward or punish. It is a key ingredient of politics, enabling collective decisions to be made and enforced; the tool that enables rulers to serve or manipulate the people over whom they rule.

- *Authority* is the ability of governments and individuals to direct others and achieve their goals because the mass of people accept that it is their right to tell them what to do, rather than because of the power or force they have at their disposal. It is a broader concept than power, being power cloaked in rightfulness. Usually, the exercise of authority implies that others will obey without force having to be used. It is legitimate power, based on respect and recognition that the person exercising it is justified in so doing.

In any organisation where people exercise power, be they running a football team, a school or a government, questions like these are often asked:

- Who gave you the right to order us about?
- Are you going to make me do it?
- What authority do you have for saying that?

Such questions help us explain what we mean when we speak of power and authority. Power is the ability both to demand that people do something and to say how it should be done or organised. Dictators and unpopular governments can maintain themselves in power by the use of force if required, but in democracies the power of governments is justified by being granted through consent, which means that people have given their agreement to what is being done. Where power is granted by consent, the term 'authority' is used.

The difference between the two concepts can be seen in two examples. A blackmailer has power, but lacks authority, whereas a police officer has both attributes. A medieval king had the power to increase the tax on beer. After an election victory, a prime minister has the authority to ask for an increase in taxation. What justifies his or her authority is **legitimacy**. The freely elected government of a country is often known as the legitimate government, for it is rightfully in office.

Influence

Slightly different from power and authority is influence. Influence is the persuasive effect of other people's ideas or behaviour, whether or not it is consciously intended. It is based on agreement or respect, making it more similar to authority than to power. News and current affairs broadcasting on the BBC might be said to be influential. However, the BBC does not have power over us. Its views may be respected because it is widely accepted that its editors and journalists are people who possess an authoritative knowledge and understanding of the subjects with which they deal and seek to convey information in an impartial manner. We can have faith in and respect for what they are telling us.

Democracy

Power can depend on naked force or coercion. It is used in many **authoritarian regimes** to maintain leaders in office, the rule of dictators often ultimately relying on intimidation, physical threat and terror. By contrast, in a democracy, those who govern have the authority to do so. They derive their legitimate authority from the consent of those over whom they govern, as determined in periodic, free and meaningful elections. In a democracy, there is free competition between parties and **participation** by the mass of voters in elections.

Mandate

The party that wins an election has a **mandate** to govern. It will have outlined its ideas and policies in an election manifesto. If sufficient numbers of the voting population liked the programme enough to elect that party into government, then those who lead it can be said to have the right to pass the proposals into law. They have been granted authority and therefore have a licence to do what they want to do.

Summary questions

1. Why might it matter if some people exercise more power than others?
2. Is there any way that someone sleeping rough on the streets at night can exercise power, authority or influence?

Power and the state

When discussing the nature of politics, the terms state and government are frequently used. It is important to distinguish between the two:

- *The UK is a state:* A state is an independent entity whose main institutions include the **executive**, the **legislature**, the **judiciary** and the bodies enforcing the law such as the police, the courts, the security services and the armed forces. It exercises **sovereign power** and authority over all individuals and groups within a defined territory. It is an abstract and permanent body, which does not

Key terms

Legitimacy: implies some justification for the exercise of ruling power. Claims to legitimacy may be based on personal popularity, tradition or – in a democracy – on success in the most recent election. A legitimate system of government is one in which the authority of the government is widely accepted by those who are subject to it. We speak of the authority of an official, but of the legitimacy of a regime.

Authoritarian regimes: non-democratic countries in which there is very strong central direction and control. There may be elections, but the range of candidates is usually strictly limited or the campaigning made very difficult for those who take an alternative view to those already in power.

Participation: the engagement of the population in forms of political action.

Mandate: the authority of the government (as granted by the voters) to carry out its programme according to the promises it advanced in its election manifesto (see opposite).

Executive: the branch of government responsible for directing the nation's affairs and the initiation and execution of laws and policies – e.g. the UK government.

Legislature: a type of representative assembly with the power to make or adopt laws.

Judiciary: the branch of government responsible for interpreting and applying the laws in particular cases, e.g. the British judges.

Sovereign power: full legal power.

Activity

Write a paragraph or two explaining – in your own words – the difference between power and authority. Think of examples that illustrate the distinction.

Key terms

Consensus: implies a wide measure of agreement. In political life, it refers to a circumstance where a large proportion of the population and of the political community are broadly agreed upon certain values, even if there is some disagreement on matters of emphasis or detail.

Coercion: compelling by force.

The Crown: a term used to separate the government authority and property of the government from the personal influence and private assets held by the current monarch of a kingdom. The Crown is regarded as an impersonal, legal concept representing the total of all powers exercised by the executive, that is, by ministers and their departments.

Parliament: the highest law-making body in Britain. It comprises the House of Commons, which exercises effective power and the upper chamber, the House of Lords.

Civil service: comprises the non-elected professional and permanent paid officials who conduct the detailed business of public administration. Many of these are clerical or managerial staff, distributed in government offices up and down the country. Those in senior positions exercise significantly more power, advising ministers and applying ministerial decisions.

Manifesto: a document produced early in an election campaign, which sets out the ideas, policy proposals and legislative intentions of a political party, intended to form the basis of their programme should they win sufficient electoral support to form a government.

Ministers: politicians who hold significant public office in a national or regional government. In the UK, ministers in charge of important government departments are usually in the Cabinet. They are known as the secretary of state for the department they run, although in some cases they may have a special title, as in the case of the Chancellor of the Exchequer.

change when a new government is elected or when political leaders are replaced. It has the power to use **consensus** or – if necessary – **coercion** to effect its policies. Institutions in the UK that may be included when referring to the state are the **Crown**, **Parliament**, the **civil service**, government itself and the bodies administering the law, such as the police, the courts and the armed services.

■ *The state is more than its government:* Government refers to the group that has the authority to run the state. Its core legislative functions are to make law (legislation), to implement law (execution) and to interpret law (adjudication). It also enforces the rulings of the state and acts under its authority. Unlike the state, the government is transient, representing – in a democracy such as Britain – a temporary majority derived from a Parliament chosen by the voters at the most recent election. It has a mandate to administer or change the laws, according to what it promised in its **manifesto**.

Further information

Key elements of the state – a summary

■ Territory – clear and recognised boundaries

■ Sovereignty – ultimate legal power over the citizens within its territory

■ Legitimacy – decisions are binding on all citizens, as state represents the interests of society

■ Citizens – members of the population born in a country or who have acquired citizenship

■ Institutions – power is delegated to institutions such as Parliament and the police

■ Constitution – every state has a written or unwritten one, setting out the powers and composition of state institutions, their relationship to one another and to the citizens

■ Nation – a body of people identified by common background, culture, language or traditions

■ Civil society – the arena of social life between the state and the family (e.g. voluntary organisations) which operates under the authority of the state.

The mechanisms of state power

In a democracy, the state has a monopoly of the use of authorised force. It claims not just the capacity but also the right to use it.

Law enforcement and punishment of offenders are among the traditional tasks of the state. Protecting the state and its citizens from internal threats and external aggression is the most traditional role of any government. Most citizens expect their life and liberty to be safeguarded and that those who transgress and threaten their safety and property will be punished and brought to justice.

Many disputes between countries can be resolved without resorting to actual military hostilities. Diplomatic pressure, economic sanctions and the threat of using violence may be sufficient to settle disputes, but the threat of military action may at some point and on rare occasions be backed up by the use of armed force. At home, defending law and order has been the traditional priority of any government. **Ministers** are responsible for maintaining internal security from those who threaten the fabric of the state.

In any state, it is expected that people will abide by its rules. Transgression of them is likely to lead to some sanction or punishment.

Catching and bringing to justice those who break the law is a responsibility of the police, but government is ultimately responsible for ensuring that suitable procedures and funding are in place. Government also develops policies to punish those who break the law, the motivation for punishment being fourfold. (See page 120 on the purposes of punishment.)

The police, the security services and the armed forces

The police maintain civil order within the community and investigate breaches of the law. This involves being pro-active to prevent crime from taking place and – when criminal acts are committed – catching offenders so that they can be brought to court for trial.

In addition to the police, most countries have national organisations created to deal with special criminal activities and intelligence, such as the Federal Bureau of Investigation (FBI) in the United States. Internal security and counter-intelligence is the province of the Security Service (MI5), while espionage against overseas targets is undertaken by MI6, the Secret Intelligence Service. In recent years MI5 has sought to expand its role to include areas traditionally dealt with by the police, while MI6 has seen its activities reduced with the ending of the Cold War and good relations established with the new democracies of Eastern Europe.

MI5, MI6 and **GCHQ** are parts of the intelligence machinery that come under the direction of the **Joint Intelligence Committee**. The broad remit of the security services is the protection of British parliamentary democracy and economic interests, fighting serious crime, espionage and **terrorism** within the UK.

Finally, the armed forces in any country possess enormous physical power, having the technology (in particular, the weaponry) and expertise to intervene in political life and ultimately to seize control of the state. The downfall and replacement of some civilian regimes around the world has been brought about as a result of the intervention of the army. In a number of countries, rule by the military is not uncommon. In others, military personnel have often been called upon to restore law and order.

In general, the stability of political life within Britain means that there has been no need for direct military involvement. This leaves the troops available to perform their more traditional purpose of defending the national interests against other countries, responding to some perceived threat or actual military attacks.

The limitations of state security

Governments devote much time and money to protecting the state and those who live within it. But their powers to do so are limited:

- No government can guarantee a risk-free society, just as no government can eliminate crime.
- Developments in the modern world make the problem of maintaining order more difficult than ever before. The growing interdependence and interconnectedness of peoples across the world means that national borders are now less effective in preserving a state's control over what happens within its own territory. Two particular challenges to security are provided by international crime and terrorism.

Terrorism

Terrorism assumes both domestic and global forms. It has existed for a very long time, but in recent years events have concentrated the

Key terms

GCHQ: the government communications headquarters, the centre for Her Majesty's Government's Signal Intelligence (SIGINT) activities.

Joint Intelligence Committee (JIC): part of the Cabinet Office and is responsible for providing ministers and senior officials with coordinated interdepartmental intelligence assessments on a range of issues of immediate and long-term importance to national interests, primarily in the fields of security, defence and foreign affairs.

Terrorism: the use of forms of violence such as bombing, hijacking, kidnapping, murder and torture to spread fear and horror within a population for the pursuit of political goals. Some might view it as a kind of 'freedom fighting', which is justifiable or necessary in particular circumstances.

minds of many national leaders as well as populations upon it. Most terrorist groups take action against states or governments of which they disapprove, although innocent third parties can get caught up in the struggle. **Basque nationalists**, members of the **Irish Republican Army (IRA)**, Palestinian bombers and **Al Qaeda** are examples of groups that have been prepared to resort to terrorism, usually briefly defined as the use of violence to achieve political aims.

■ Further information

The Prevention of Terrorism Act 2005

Passed in the light of the London bombings in 2005, in its final form the Act allowed:

■ the police to detain terror suspects for a maximum of 28 days

■ the creation of an offence of 'glorifying terrorism' in the UK or abroad

■ new ground rules for banning certain extreme organisations

■ and powers of closure over places of worship used to incite extremism.

Many critics portrayed some clauses of the resulting Act as an unwarranted inroad into long-established civil liberties. Ministers countered that it was a necessary response to an unparalleled terrorist threat. On becoming prime minister, Gordon Brown set out to persuade the House of Commons to support an increase in the time limit for detention to 42 days.

The British and other governments have assumed new powers in tough anti-terrorist legislation. The Prevention of Terrorism Act (2005) contained proposals designed to ensure that the police, intelligence agencies and the courts have the tools they require to tackle terrorism and bring those who use it to justice.

■ **Summary questions**

1. To what extent do the problems of global terrorism necessitate an increase in the powers of states?

2. Can you think of any evidence to show that in recent years government ministers have got the balance between maintaining order and protecting individual liberty wrong? (You might refer back to pages 97–100.)

3. Can terrorism ever be justified in the pursuit of a political goal? (See the Further information features in the margin alongside).

■ The nature of political power

Political power is concerned with the ability to make decisions that affect the way society is organised and the goals it chooses to pursue. However, it is no longer possible to speak of political power purely in isolation from other types of power. Economic power, military power and the power of the media all impact upon the way in which the political system and those who lead it operate and how effective they can be in particular circumstances. So too do changing circumstances. Power can be influenced by the sort of problems that suddenly erupt onto the political scene and cause huge headaches for government ministers. A crisis abroad, an outbreak of foot-and-mouth disease in farm animals or the problems of a bank in difficulty (e.g. Northern Rock in 2007) are all examples of the sorts of issues that can seemingly arise out of nowhere. They have the capacity suddenly to throw a government 'off course' and make it seem as though ministers are no longer in control, in office but not in power.

The distribution of political power

The political executive

In Britain today, there is a case for saying that political power rests with the executive, in particular the political executive, better known as the elected government. Members of the government (in particular, the **prime minister** and his or her **Cabinet**) develop policies on a range of areas and put forward bills to Parliament, which will in most cases become laws binding on the whole community. A government with a reasonable majority in the **House of Commons** can normally get its proposals passed into law. Governments therefore have the power to change the way we live, determining issues as far apart as whether we can use mobile phones when driving, the licensing hours of pubs and the right to have an abortion.

The official executive

Some would say that the official executive, the civil service, is the seat of power. It is responsible for administering the laws that Parliament has passed. The 750 to 800 senior officials, based in the large Whitehall departments and a range of executive agencies, carry out a number of key functions, among them advising ministers, preparing and drafting discussion documents and legislation, and implementing government decisions. Increasingly over recent decades these higher civil servants have not only offered the advice on which ministers make decisions but found themselves actually making some decisions themselves. Because of their abilities, experience, expertise and permanence, they can exert a powerful influence over what happens in a department, hence the talk of '**mandarin power**'.

The legislature

A case can be made for saying that power resides with the legislature, Parliament, comprising the more powerful House of Commons and the less powerful House of Lords. The doctrine of parliamentary sovereignty gives Parliament supreme and unique legislative authority, with the power to make, amend or unmake laws. In reality, Parliament debates and votes upon bills, most of which originate with the government but a few of which are introduced by individual members of the House of Commons (MPs) or House of Lords (peers). As such, it tends to pass laws rather than actually to make them. Nonetheless, particularly when there is a government with only a small majority and/or in political difficulties, Parliament can exert its influence. A **minority** [Labour] **government** lost power in 1979, because of its inability to muster enough support among MPs to win a 'vote of confidence'. In this case, Conservative, Liberal and nationalist members came out in opposition to its continuation in office.

Most academics and commentators on British politics would say that as a general trend over many decades, power has passed from Parliament to the executive, which dominates the House of Commons, controlling its timetable and agenda. Many would go much further and say that in recent years there has been a centralisation of power in Number 10 Downing Street, with strong prime ministers being able to dominate the administrations they lead even to the extent of keeping some members of the cabinet in the dark about their plans.

Key terms

Basque nationalists: support independence for the Basque country of north-eastern Spain.

Irish Republican Army (IRA): the main republican paramilitary organisation in Northern Ireland. For several decades, it operated beyond the mainstream of the political process. In recent years, its political wing, Sinn Fein, has been a player in the peace process in the province and is now in government.

Al Qaeda: an international network of Islamic militant terrorist organisation, agents of which have been responsible for attacking civilian and military targets in various countries, most notably the World Trade Center in New York (9/11).

Prime minister: the most powerful politician in the country, the chairperson of the Cabinet. At the beginning of the 20th century, the prime minister was thought to be 'primus inter pares', first among equals, but today most prime ministers are significantly more powerful than they were then, hence talk of 'prime ministerial government'.

The Cabinet: comprising some 20–24 senior members of the government, it has traditionally been the key formal decision making body within the executive, directing the work of government and coordinating the activities of individual departments. Today, it has a reduced role as a decision-making body.

House of Commons: the elected, lower chamber of the legislature (Parliament) in Britain.

Mandarin power: refers to the power and influence of those senior civil servants who belong to the top administrative grades. They are often referred to as 'mandarins' or, collectively, as 'the higher civil service'.

Minority government: a government made up of a party (or parties) that has the highest number of seats but does not command a majority of seats in Parliament.

Fig. 9.1 *10 Downing Street: some say that power is increasingly centralised in the hands of the PM. Here, Gordon Brown greets Angela Merkel, the German Chancellor*

■ Key terms

Referendums: votes of the people held on a single issue of public policy, e.g. on some proposed law or policy, perhaps to amend the constitution.

City of London: London's financial and commercial district, which occupies a square mile or so of the old City of London. It includes the Bank of England, the stock market and the head offices of leading UK financial institutions, such as banks, investment houses and insurance companies.

Bank of England: (sometimes known as the 'Old Lady' of Threadneedle Street) the central bank of the United Kingdom. Founded in 1694, it was nationalised in 1946 and gained independence in 1997. It stands at the centre of the UK's financial system. It is committed to promoting and maintaining monetary and financial stability.

Trades unions: organisations that represent groups of workers in order to defend their interests, by working for better pay and conditions.

The judiciary

A further case could be made for saying that power resides with the judiciary. The political role of unelected judges has been much increased throughout the Western world over recent decades. They have been far more willing to enter into political arenas that would in the past have been the preserve of politicians and national parliament. In Britain, judicial intervention in public policy has become apparent in several ways. They are much more willing to review the legality of governmental action than in the past, as part of the process known as 'judicial review' (see page 158–63); they have been involved in many 'rights' issues brought under the European Convention on Human Rights or – more recently – the Human Rights Act; and they are more willing to speak out publicly to air their disapproval of government policies.

'People power'

An alternative viewpoint would be to argue that in a democracy power must ultimately reside with the people, hence the common translation of the term as 'people power'. But the majority of people are only called on to make a decision at general election time once every four years. As we have had very few national or local **referendums**, the voters have little opportunity to decide on individual issues, particularly those that arise during the lifetime of a government and on which they therefore have had no chance to express their verdict in an election. In normal circumstances, therefore, it is difficult to argue that the individual is armed with much actual power. Indeed, some commentators would see the individual voter as largely powerless, unable to influence the course of events.

As we have seen, as a result of the changes introduced since the 1970s, two new foci of power are important:

1 The European Union, membership of which means that many important decisions are no longer made in London, but in Brussels.

2 As part of its package of constitutional changes, the Labour government after 1997 introduced a policy of devolution. The devolved machinery in Scotland means that several issues are now decided by the Edinburgh Parliament.

Where does political power lie?

Does political power rest in London, with elected politicians (perhaps the prime minister or with the parties and their members in Parliament)? Or has it passed upwards to the European Union and downwards to the devolved bodies? Or does it reside with the unelected judges or with the public? Or – in the case of many important financial decisions – does it rest with the financiers in the **City of London** or the **Bank of England**, which determines interest rates and thereby affects our mortgage payments or savings? Or is it with the editors or journalists of the media who decide on any day what stories to focus upon in their news bulletins/headlines and have an influence over the issues we discuss. Or is it with the employers who, by the decisions they make on investment and pricing, have a key role in determining levels of national prosperity? Or is it with the **trades unions** who have the power to back up their demands for wage increase by going on strike? Or is it with the international organisations that cut across national boundaries, such as **NATO**, the European Union or the European Court of Human Rights? Or **multinational companies (MNCs)**, which – because of their size – can have a significant impact on government policy? (MNCs are also known as transnational companies/TNCs.) (See pages 185–6 for further information on MNCs.)

▪ Further information

The significance of MNCs

- ▪ The development of MNCs/TNCs has impacted on the power of states such as the UK.
- ▪ Very large MNCs have budgets that exceed those of many small countries, so that the role and importance of business in politics are growing.
- ▪ Such is their economic power and so great are their resources that MNCs can have a powerful influence not only in their national economies but more widely in international relations.
- ▪ Brecher (2000) illustrated this most vividly in his finding that of the 100 largest economies in the world, 51 were corporations rather than countries.

Modern government has become highly complex. The age of centralised decision-making in London has passed and political power is diffused in our **pluralist democracy**, divided among many institutions and groups. Their relative importance is liable to change, with some losing power and others acquiring more of it.

Within government, the relative power of prime ministers in relation to their cabinets fluctuates. A highly dominant premier such as Margaret Thatcher was followed by **John Major** who by contrast was widely portrayed as 'weak' and 'indecisive'. By 1997, the country seemed to be ready for a display of strong leadership again and for several years Tony Blair exploited the potential power of his office. Like Margaret Thatcher, on occasion he tended to inform his Cabinet colleagues of what he and others had already decided elsewhere, in small committees, with his advisers or in bilateral conversations with the appropriate government minister.

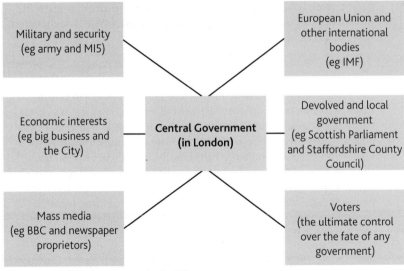

Fig. 9.2 *The diffusion of power in the UK*

▪ Key terms

NATO (North Atlantic Treaty Organization): an alliance of 26 countries from North America and Europe committed to fulfilling the goals of the North Atlantic Treaty (1949). It was formed to establish a system of collective defence, in which member states agreed that an attack upon any one of them was to be regarded as an attack upon them all.

Multinational companies (MNCs): business corporations with manufacturing, sales or service subsidiaries in one or more foreign countries. Typically, they develop new products in their native country and manufacture them abroad, often in developing nations, enabling them to benefit from trade advantages and economies of labour and materials. Most are American, Japanese or West European.

Pluralist democracy: refers to a society in which there are diverse and competing centres of power (pluralism literally means 'rule by the many').

John Major (1943–): a Conservative MP from 1979 to 2001 and prime minister between 1990 and 1997.

▪ Case study

One writer's view of the search for power in the UK

In 1962, the journalist Anthony Sampson wrote his first edition of *The Anatomy of Britain*. Having updated the original on four occasions, he finally wrote *Who Runs This Place?*, published shortly before his death in 2004. Taken together, they thoroughly chart many of the changes in British society in the post-1945 years. The

▪ Hint

MNCs are in the specifications for this section. See pages 185–6 for more information on the power MNCs wield over national economies.

■ Hint

We have now distinguished between power and authority and referred to different types of power, economic (see also, pages 183–98), military and political. Ensure that you have a clear understanding of each concept and the institutions and other bodies that exercise it. It is worth writing a few sentences on each one for reference, for, after all, the distribution and exercise of power is the theme of this Unit.

■ Key terms

HM Treasury: the UK's economics and finance ministry. It is responsible for formulating and implementing governmental financial and economic policy.

Establishment: a generally pejorative term to refer to the traditional conservative ruling class elite and the institutions that they control.

■ Activities

1 List the possible locations of political power mentioned in this section. Note down any others you can think of. For each one, write a sentence or two to state how it exercises power.

2 Read through the Sampson passage from the *Anatomy of Britain* and then write a few lines to explain his 1971 and 2004 conclusions. Do you recognise the picture of power in Britain conveyed in the last paragraph?

books were intended as a guided tour of the political and economic power structure in Britain.

In 1971, Sampson concluded that:

Any quest for the sources of power must be a frustrating journey; the politician, the journalist or the ordinary citizen who sets out to discover the caves of decision-making finds himself led through a maze which turns out to have no centre, which leads in the end back to where it began – to the ordinary people, the workers, the voters, the consumers.

The ambitious member of parliament, climbing up the rungs of government to the Cabinet, still finds that decisions are taken mysteriously somewhere else; 'Power?, it's like a dead sea fruit,' said Harold Macmillan when he was [Conservative] prime minister [1957–63]; when you achieve it, there's nothing there': and Harold Wilson's premierships [Labour PM, 1964–70, 1974–6] are a sad testimony to how much he felt himself in the control of others – whether fellow-politicians, bankers, **HM Treasury** officials, or foreign speculators …

In any working democracy, the notion of a centre of power – except in wartime – is a contradictory one: the sovereignty of the people by definition excludes a concentration of power. Power in Britain today depends on a confederation of interests, which rarely work together … the different spheres of institutions and interest groups [pressure groups] connect up with each other and sometimes overlap, but they have no decisive centre …

In the meantime, from inside the institutions and companies, the authority of those at the top is increasingly questioned. 'Democracy is breaking out all over', not only in trade unions, but in universities, in communications, among scientists, backbenchers and even civil servants.

Source: Sampson, The New Anatomy of Britain *1971*

In 2004, Sampson again looked at the whole panoply of power, from Number 10 to the murky world of intelligence spooks, from corporate boardrooms to banks and pension funds. He noted how power in the UK has become much more centralised than in the post-1945 decades and rests largely at Number 10. He also argued that the lure of money now plays a much more important role in the **establishment** than in previous years with many talented young people being drawn into the corporate, banking, legal or accountancy professions, rather than choosing politics, the civil service, trade unionism or academia.

■ The tiers of UK government

Even the most authoritarian government would find it difficult to take all decisions at the centre. Many people would consider it desirable to decentralise decision-making for the reason once given by the 19th-century Liberal Prime Minister William Gladstone: 'making power local makes it more congenial'. But in any case, it would be impractical for any set of ministers to understand the needs of every area and to involve themselves in the minutiae of detail concerning their public administration. Governments recognise the need to allow some scope for regional or local initiative.

The United Kingdom has a **unitary system** of government. Parliament at Westminster makes laws for all parts of the UK. Some areas of the UK have powers devolved to them, Scotland and Wales since 1999 and Northern Ireland (after early attempts that had been suspended) since 2007. There is also a long-established system of local government. Nonetheless, all parts of the UK and all sub-national administrations are subject to the legislative supremacy of Parliament. The doctrine of parliamentary sovereignty means that Parliament has absolute and unlimited authority to make, repeal or amend any laws.

There is nothing new in having different levels of government in the UK. There has always been a distinction between central and local government. In addition, between 1922 and 1972, Northern Ireland experienced 50 years of **devolved government**, for the province had powers over issues such as education, housing, policing and welfare. But in the UK today, we have **multi-level government** or **multi-level governance**, which is novel in scale. Whereas in the past, we had a basically centralised system, with all significant power based in London and the other tiers operating at the margins, today these other tiers have assumed new importance. The 'new tiers' of our multi-levelled system are a defining feature of how policy is made and carried out.

We must now think of British politics as a system involving four main tiers, ranging from the **European Union** above and beyond the UK to the most local of political systems in our neighbourhoods. There are distinctive systems of government in the four home countries of England, Scotland, Wales and Northern Ireland.

Power is distributed in a complicated way across many levels:

- The British government shares authority over several important policy areas with the institutions of the *European Union* – e.g. agricultural, environmental and regional policy.
- National government located in London (and based on *Whitehall and Westminster*) exercises key powers in areas such as the British economy, immigration, welfare, defence and foreign affairs.
- There are three directly elected popular *devolved assemblies*, in Scotland (the Scottish Parliament), Wales (the Welsh National Assembly) and Northern Ireland (the Northern Irish Assembly), which exercise varying degrees of power (see pages 211 and 221–7), including in Scotland and Northern Ireland to make their own laws in a number of policy areas such as economic development, education, health and tourism.
- *Elected mayors* in cities such as London are a growing source of power, for they have authority over a range of issues concerning the capital. Elsewhere around the country, a system of *local councils* is responsible for making decisions and carrying out policy in their areas, ranging from planning and road maintenance to paving and lighting.

Who exercises social and political power?

It has often been pointed out that those who have influential positions in British public life tend to share a similar background and sometimes attitudes as well. Many – but not all – leading figures of our main political parties have had a privileged upbringing, often involving attendance at public school and **Oxbridge**. So too many of our MPs were brought up in comfortably off, middle-class homes and went to the best schools and

Key terms

Unitary system of government: one in which all legitimate power is concentrated in the hands of central government. Devolved governments exist only with the consent of the national legislature, Parliament in London.

Devolved government: refers to a situation in which power is granted from central government in London to a regional or local level, enabling the sub-national government to assume responsibility over several policy areas.

Multi-level government: the multiple layering of government and a description of the way in which the British political system operates today. It is no longer the Westminster system of the past, with institutions and powers concentrated in London. There are various tiers of government, with the EU at the top, then the UK government, the devolved bodies and local administration.

Multi-level governance: a wider term than the above. Whereas government refers to institutions, governance covers the processes of government in which businesses, voluntary organisations and community groups may be involved. It also includes a number of unelected bodies (quangos) that exercise considerable power.

European Union (EU): an organisation of 27 states with both economic and political aims. It was previously known as the European Community (see page 245) and was established in 1957 by the signing of the Treaty of Rome.

Oxbridge: a collective term used in reference to two ancient, highly prestigious academic institutions, Oxford and Cambridge universities. Critics suggest that they are bastions of privilege and superiority whose graduates exercise undue influence in British society.

Fig. 9.3 *José Barroso: the most powerful person in the UK?*

Fig. 9.4 *Shami Chakrabarti: one of the most powerful people in the UK?*

Activities

1 Ensure that you know what each of the top 10 persons or institutions in the BBC poll does. Write a couple of sentences on each of them, to show whether or not they merit their inclusion.

2 Make a list of 10 people who you think exercise significant power in modern Britain. Write a couple of sentences to justify each of your choices. For each of them, bear in mind how they use the power they have and consider whether or not they are accountable.

Key terms

Political parties: organisations of broadly like-minded men and women that seek to win elections in order that they can then assume responsibility for controlling the apparatus of government with a view to implementing their policies.

universities. The same could be said of top business people, bishops, judges, senior civil servants, media editors and journalists, military leaders and other figures who possess influence or exert power. Shared backgrounds may be reflected in shared social values, ideas of what really matters in life. In their approach to issues, they may tend to view the world in a similar way and seek similar solutions to problems that arise.

Case study

Popular opinions about who runs Britain

In a *Who Runs Britain?* poll published by BBC Radio (2 January 2006), listeners were asked to vote for Britain's most powerful person. Some opted for an institution or collective entity, rather than a single man or woman. The findings were that more people felt Rupert Murdoch of News International had greater power than Parliament or Tony Blair, who as prime minister was on a par with the chief executive of Tesco and received less backing than the Cabinet secretary and chief civil servant, Sir Gus O'Donnell. First place went to the president of the European Commission.

The top ten names were:

1 Jose Manuel Barroso, 22%   **6** Terry Leahy, 7%
2 Rupert Murdoch, 15%   **7** Tony Blair, 7%
3 Parliament, 14%   **8** Google, 6%
4 the British People, 12%   **9** Gordon Brown, 4%
5 Gus O'Donnell, 10%   **10** Shami Chakrabarti, 4%

Summary questions

1 Where does power lie in modern Britain?

2 Conservative Prime Minister Harold Macmillan once said that there were three bodies no sensible man should directly challenge: the Roman Catholic Church, the Brigade of Guards and the National Union of Mineworkers. To what extent do any of these exercise significant power today?

3 Is there still an Establishment that controls the main seats of power in Britain today?

4 Has the Establishment been weakened, or has power been concentrated in even fewer hands?

■ The role of political parties and their members

Western liberal democracy is unthinkable without competition between **political parties**. They bring together a variety of different interests in society. Via the electoral process, they determine the shape of governments. European, US and other democracies are party democracies.

The United Kingdom has a system of party government. The party that wins the majority of seats in the House of Commons in a general election assumes office, its leader becoming prime minister. Parties have played a significant role in British politics for more than 200 years. They influence all aspects of government and politics. Their primary purpose is to win elections. This is the main feature that distinguishes them from pressure groups, which may try to influence elections but do not usually put up candidates for office.

The functions of political parties

Parties are central to British democracy. They fulfil several functions:

- *They sift ideas and organise opinion:* They take on board the ideas of individuals and groups and aggregate (put together) and simplify them into a package of policies. In this way, they clarify the political process for the voter who is confronted with a choice of alternative proposals, programmes and leaders. The voter is then able to choose the party that most resembles his or her own policy preferences.

- *They are a source of political knowledge:* Even for voters who lack any strong party ties, their ideas and outlook are likely to be influenced by the information that parties offer and by their perception of what the parties support.

- *They act as a link between the individual and the political system:* Most people rely on various political interests to represent their concerns and demands. Parties formulate, aggregate and communicate a package of such demands, and if they win power they attempt to implement them. In this way, parties act as bridge organisations, mediators between the conflicting interests of government and the electorate.

- *They mobilise and recruit activists:* Parties offer a structure into which individuals can channel their interests. They provide contact with other individuals and groups and an opportunity to become political foot soldiers or local or national politicians. In many democracies including Britain, the recruitment, selection and training of parliamentary candidates is a key task. Parties offer candidates support during election campaigns and are responsible for local and national campaigning.

- *They provide an organisational structure via which to coordinate the actions of government*, encouraging those who belong to them to work towards shared objectives. Leaders and their colleagues (including **party whips**) seek to persuade members of the legislature to vote for their policies. Where necessary they do coalition deals to secure a majority for particular programmes.

- *They serve as a source of opposition:* The parties not in government provide explicit, organised opposition. In Britain there is a fully institutionalised party known as Her Majesty's Loyal Opposition, with its own shadow ministerial team.

The individual and the political parties

Few people join political parties, far fewer than in the early years after 1945. Party membership has been declining in most of Europe over the last few decades, but as the figures overleaf indicate, they are particularly low in the UK.

Key terms

Party whips: the officials who manage the supporters of their party in the House of Commons and are responsible for maintaining discipline and unity. In British politics, the chief whip is assisted by between eight and 10 assistant whips, all members of Parliament.

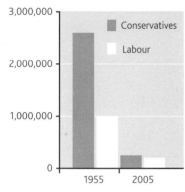

Fig. 9.5 *Party membership 1955–2005: declining fortunes*

Table 9.1 *Party membership figures*

1990–2000: membership as percentage of electorate, European countries	Party membership in Britain, December 2006	
Austria: 18	Conservatives:	250,000
Finland: 10	Labour:	200,000
Norway: 7	Lib Dems:	73,000
Germany: 3	SNP:	12,000
UK: 2	Plaid Cymru:	8,000

Further information

Getting involved in the Conservative Party

- Join the party
- Donate
- Join a donor club
- Contact headquarters with your views
- Do paid work for the party
- Involve yourself in social action
- Show your support on the internet, via web sites and discussion chat-lines and forums
- Keep informed about party policy
- Help the local constituency association, especially at election time
- Register to vote

Source: www.conservatives.com

Activity

Using the internet to help you, try and find out any benefits of membership of:

- the Conservative Party
- the Labour Party.

N.B. Full membership of the Conservative Party costs £25 per year. Membership of the Labour Party costs £36 per year.

How party members influence party policy

Those who join parties join their local **constituency** associations, many of which were created when the right to vote was extended to many working class male voters in the late 19th century. The pattern in both main parties of the time (the Conservatives and the Liberal Party) was that authority flowed downwards from the top rather than upwards from the bottom. Decisions were taken at and policy statements issued from the centre in London and handed down to the local branches. The active members did useful work in canvassing the electorate, trying to persuade voters to choose their party on polling day. They were usually prepared to accept their limited role and leave decisions to the leadership, for they were keen to see the party prosper in and between elections.

Today, in many European parties the leaders – who are the face of the party most well known to the public – still have a key role in determining the direction of party policies and strategies. In the UK too, the pattern of top-down decision-making continued until recent years. Over the last two decades, there has been more emphasis on giving members a greater say in how their party functions, while at the same time ensuring that the leadership retains key powers – for instance, to keep out dissidents who might bring discredit upon the organisation and undermine its chances of election victory. The Green Party has been particularly interested in democratic consultation with its membership.

In the two main parties, opportunities for active involvement include:

1 *having a say in the choice of candidate* in local council, European or general elections (for a very few there is the chance to become the candidate)

2 *having a say in the choice of party leader:* both parties allow party members to have a voice in the final choice

3 *attending the annual party conference*, an opportunity to meet up with members from other constituencies and speak on key issues of party policy (the conferences tend to be stage-managed for media effect and the expression of dissident views is discouraged)

4 *[very occasionally] taking part in occasional votes of the mass membership* on policy issues or matters of party strategy

5 *participating in party policy forums* in which ordinary members can be consulted about policy.

Both parties, for all of the talk about recruiting a mass membership and involving and empowering members, remain highly centralised. The leadership of the Conservative and Labour Parties wishes to take the important decisions on policy and strategy. In this way, they can be sure that they convey an appealing and united image to the electorate.

The exercise of power in Britain's two-party system

In the same way that in international football the World Cup requires teams representing many countries, a **party system** usually requires the interaction of several parties. The term refers to the network of relationships between parties that determines how the political system functions.

The most usual means of distinguishing between different types of party system is by reference to the number of parties involved. Britain has a **two-party system** in which each of the two main parties has a strong chance of obtaining a majority of seats in the legislature and winning political power. There are other parties – some sizeable – but they have not competed for office in recent elections with any realistic hope of winning. Supporters of two-party systems say that they promote effective, stable and strong government. The party in power is clearly accountable to the electorate for what it has done and left undone. By contrast, in the coalition governments that are common on the European continent, two or more parties share power and responsibility is less clear-cut.

The two-party system since the 1970s

Britain has had a two-party system for most of the last 200 years, Labour and the Conservatives being the dominant parties since the 1930s. Only once since 1945 has one of the major parties failed to win an outright majority in the House of Commons. The peak of the two-party system was in 1951 when between them Labour and the Conservatives won 98.6 per cent of the votes and 96.8 per cent of the seats. Since then, the two-party system has generally been resilient, although the rise in **third** and **minor party** support since the mid-1970s has made the picture more confused. The two main parties have lost electoral support and their overwhelming dominance in parliamentary seats.

The election of 2005 provided confusing evidence as to whether we still have a two-party system. The two main parties won just over two-thirds of the popular vote, yet between them gained 554 seats at Westminster. Their joint share of the parliamentary seats was the lowest in any post-1945 election (85.6 per cent), with the Liberal Democrats winning 62 seats (the strongest performance by a third party since 1923). In view of the strength of this third party, some commentators would refer to the UK as having a two-and-a-half party system, or a two-party system and three-party politics.

In fact, the situation is more complex than this. In 2005, no fewer than six parties (and two independents) won seats in Great Britain and another four parties won seats in Northern Ireland. Moreover, in recent elections, there have been national and regional variations that make the two-party system primarily an English phenomenon. Leaving aside Northern Ireland, which has a distinctive political system, Scotland and Wales both have a strong nationalist party. In general elections, Labour is the largest of the four parties in both countries, so that in effect there is one-party dominance but four-party politics.

Key terms

Party system: the more or less stable pattern of political parties that normally compete in national elections and the way in which they interact with one another.

Two-party system: a party system in which two parties compete for political power with a reasonable prospect of success. Third and minor parties may exist, but do not have a meaningful chance of winning.

Third party: one that is capable of gathering a sizeable percentage of popular support and regularly gains seats in the legislature, e.g. the British Liberal Democrat Party. On occasion, it may win – or threaten to win – sufficient support to influence the outcome of an election.

Minor party: one that gains only a tiny percentage of popular support and almost never gains representation in the legislature, e.g. the British National Party.

Table 9.2 *The outcome of the 2005 general election*

Party	Votes won (%)	Number and % of seats won
Labour	35.2	356 (55.1)
Conservative	32.3	197 (30.5)
Liberal Democrat	22.0	62 (9.6)
Other	12.5	30 (4.8)

Key terms

FPTP (first past the post): an electoral system that operates in single member constituencies. The candidate with the most votes is elected; even though it may be that he or she receives less than half of the votes cast. Supporters feel that it is easily understood, provides strong government and a close relationship between an MP and the constituency. Opponents lament its 'unfairness' and lack of proportionality. It is harsh on third parties, which sometimes accumulate a considerable number of votes nationally but win no/few seats.

Ideologues: people strongly committed to one body of ideas.

Political spectrum: a convenient means of visualising different political positions, stretching from the far left parties that want radical or even revolutionary change, through more moderate groups of left, centre and right, to far right extremists such as neo (born-again) fascists and neo-Nazis.

Fascism: the political creed and movement associated with the regime of Benito Mussolini in Italy between the two world wars. It is usually regarded as authoritarian, militaristic and in practice extremely right wing.

Activity

These factors may help to explain why third and minor parties have made little headway in post-1945 elections:

- Few influential financial backers.
- No reliable body of support within the electorate.
- No distinctive identity.
- Voters' fear of wasting their vote.
- Few opportunities to get message across.
- Voters' fear of wasting their vote under the **FPTP** electoral system

For any three of the third and minor parties that fought the 2005 election, see if you can find out about the importance of each of these six factors. You might answer in list form.

Party ideologies: Left and Right

Parties are created around broad principles. Although most of their members are not strict **ideologues**, these broad ideologies provide recognition and mean something to many people. Budge *et al* (1998) describe ideology as 'a theory about the world and about society, and of the place of you and your group within it'. These ideologies are important 'not only in telling leaders what to do but in telling their supporters who they are and thus making them receptive to leaders' diagnoses of the political situation'.

The terms 'Left–Right politics' or the 'Left–Right **political spectrum**' are commonly used as a means of classifying political ideologies and political positions. Broadly, those on the Left – traditionally identified with the interests of the masses – support an increase in governmental activity. They want to create a more just society in which economic and social problems can be addressed. Accordingly, they favour political, economic and social change, and want to promote greater equality. Those on the Right – traditionally identified with preservation of the interests of the established, propertied classes – broadly oppose the type of change favoured by the Left. They are more wary of state intervention and seek to limit the scope of government as much as possible. They place more emphasis on personal responsibility and individual enterprise.

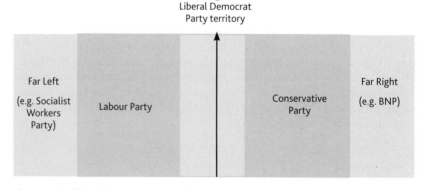

Fig. 9.6 *Traditional party positions in the UK. New Labour in the 1990s and first years of the 21st century had a broad appeal, extending into the middle ground and making inroads on the moderate Right at a time when the Conservatives were faring badly. The Liberal Democrats have on some issues been to the left of Labour*

A linear spectrum of Left–Right ideas looks like this:

LEFT Communism < Socialism < Liberalism > Conservatism > Fascism RIGHT

Parties and their leading members in Britain are often described as left wing or right wing, although these labels can be misleading and confusing. People who seem left wing on one issue may adopt a right-wing stance on another. Nonetheless, the terms remain as a convenient shorthand by which to summarise different attitudes on important political, economic and social questions.

The appeal of the two main British parties

In Britain as in other parts of democratic Europe, the essential Left–Right battle over ideas and policies has been between socialism and **conservatism**. But in recent years, this broad ideological divide has become less clear-cut. New Labour under Tony Blair increasingly employed terminology and adopted approaches traditionally associated with the British Conservative Party. The party appeared to shed its nominal socialism and positioned itself firmly in the political centre, seeking to maximise its appeal to moderates of the Left and Right as part of a '**big tent**' approach. As the Liberal Democrats inhabit similar territory, it means that the middle ground is very crowded.

The party leaderships are aware of the need to attract and maintain support from a wide variety of interests and from people with a wide range of political beliefs. To some extent, as is common in most two-party systems, Labour and the Conservatives are **catch-all parties**, in both cases having their own left and right wing whose members advance a range of views on the issues of the day.

Activity

Make a list of all of the political parties represented in the present House of Commons. See if you can label them as left- or right-wing parties. Use the internet to help you if necessary.

Key terms

Conservatism: a creed that generally opposes innovation and change, and advocates preserving the best of the established order in society.

Big tent: refers to a governing approach that attempts to attract people with diverse viewpoints and does not require belief in some ideology as a criterion for membership. In Britain, it is a bid to cater for the right of the left, the middle and the left of the right in the large moderate centre ground.

Catch-all parties: umbrella or 'broker' parties that seek to maximise their voter appeal by reaching out to as many groups as possible, rather than representing specific class, regional or partisan interests.

Summary questions

1. Are political parties essential in a democracy? If so, why?

2. Why do you think party membership in the UK is in decline?

3. What is the difference between the approach of a person on the political Left and one on the political Right?

Economic power and control

Economic power can be defined broadly as the capacity to influence other states through economic means. It comprises a country's industrial base, natural resources, capital, technology, geographical position, health system and education system. Throughout human history, military power has always been seen as more significant than economic power. But in today's world, Japan, China and even the United States have used their economic prosperity to finance formidable military forces. Conversely, Iraq and North Korea have relied on their military to build economic power with little or limited success.

The concept of economic power is vaguer than that of military power. The ultimate test of military power –war – is the classic zero-sum game. If Country A has a more powerful military than Country B, then Country A is likely to win in a war between the two. And in the lead-up to war, Country B is more likely to back down. So having military superiority is clearly a good thing. There is no parallel in economics because economic competition is not a zero-sum game. On the economic battlefield, the success of one country does not imply the defeat of another. Country A

Nationalisation: the transfer of industries and utilities from private into public ownership.

Privatisation: the transfer of ownership of industries and utilities from the public sector to the private sector.

International Monetary Fund: an international organisation of 185 countries that oversees the global financial situation. It was established to promote international monetary cooperation, exchange stability and orderly exchange arrangements; to encourage economic growth and high levels of employment; and to provide temporary financial assistance to countries to help ease balance of payments adjustment.

Organisation of Petroleum Exporting Countries (OPEC): a permanent inter-governmental organisation of 12 oil-exporting nations that coordinates and unifies the petroleum policies of its member countries.

Eurozone: the area covered by the 16 states with a population of just over 325 million people that have adopted the euro as their single currency system.

may be richer than Country B, but both will be better off through trade if the other grows richer.

However, the concept of economic power is far from meaningless. For the citizens of most countries today, the success of their economy in the harsh world of global competition is of crucial importance. Governments must be concerned with the levers that they have to wield economic power and to protect themselves against the economic threats posed by others. The prosperity of any country depends on the extent to which it can produce goods and services efficiently and the way that those who wield economic power can advance or frustrate such production.

Who has economic power in the UK?

In the 20th and 21st centuries, governments have become increasingly involved in regulating economic forces by a variety of means. At times, this has involved the introduction of price controls and import restrictions, legislation on trades unions and the **nationalisation** of large sectors of manufacturing and service industry, including coal, iron and steel, and the railways. Indeed, prior to the move towards **privatisation** of state-controlled industries and utilities that began in the late 1970s but got swiftly under way in the following decade, the government had become a major employer of many workers in manufacturing industry.

Other than government, three main sources of economic power are:

■ multinational companies, large industrial combines such as Ford and Sony

■ trades unions, such as the Associated Society of Locomotive Engineers and Firemen (ASLEF)

■ financial institutions, such as the Bank of England.

However, there are various organisations beyond UK national boundaries that either continuously or periodically exert economic pressure on British governments. These external bodies include the **International Monetary Fund** (IMF), the **Organisation of Petroleum Exporting Countries** (OPEC) and, most importantly, the European Union (EU). In addition, overseas ownership of many businesses and industries in the UK and its dependence on the health of the US economy also serve to undermine its ability to pursue its economic policy in splendid isolation.

The impact of EU membership on the British economy is now very significant. Britain is not part of the **eurozone**, the surrender of economic sovereignty being a problem for many opponents of a single currency. However, in other ways the EU can influence the nature and character of economic activity. Its decisions on issues ranging from competition to harmonisation policy, from the environment to regional aid all help to shape the character of the national economy.

The economy of an advanced industrial society gives individuals and groups great power. However, this power does not rest exclusively with any one group at any time. Each group has some power and at different times the balance of power may tilt in one direction or another. The trades unions or employers may at a particular time be powerful, but governments act as an umpire between rival interests. They 'hold the ring', their duty being to ensure that they govern in the national interest, rather than according to the dictates of any one element within the economy.

The importance of economic policy

Economic policy lies at the heart of British politics. The most important issues dividing parties and groups in society are economic. Leading individuals and institutions in government spend the largest part of their time struggling with economic problems. And the range of institutions that can affect economic policy goes well beyond bodies like HM Treasury. It extends to the outer reaches of the government and beyond into the private sector. In the wider society, decisions about economics, about how to manage the economy, and about how to distribute the results of economic production provide the basis for some of the most important arguments in British politics.

Economic prosperity has become the most important expectation that we have of our politicians and consequently it has become the holy grail of modern governments. They know that an expanding economy will enhance international influence and help them retain power at election time, while evidence of economic slowdown or decline will highlight inequalities, generate disillusioned bitterness and lead to electoral defeat. For any modern Cabinet, therefore, the search for a combination of economic growth, low inflation and unemployment, and stability in the financial markets must be a high priority. As a combination, it has often proved elusive in the post-1945 era.

The evolution of economic policy since the 19th century

In the middle of the 19th century, economic policy was not viewed as an important area of governmental activity. Governments did not claim to understand how to regulate unemployment or control prices, nor did they see it as their role. They believed in the *laissez-faire* approach first advocated in France one hundred years or so before. Its supporters opposed any government interference with trade, the term later becoming associated with the application of strict free market economics. They claimed that private initiative and production should be given free rein. They disliked economic interventionism by the state beyond that which was necessary to maintain individual liberty, peace, security and property rights.

By the end of the 19th century, some politicians and thinkers were beginning to doubt the value of laissez-faire policy and urging an alternative approach. They felt that the problems of poverty and unemployment needed governmental attention. Socialist critics of **capitalism** noted the cycles of boom and slump in the economy. They began to speak of such policies as land nationalisation and a redistribution of wealth from rich to poor.

The end of laissez-faire and the growth in economic management by government cannot be precisely dated, but such developments were greatly accelerated by the First World War. Between 1914 and 1918, the government was compelled by force of circumstances to exercise unprecedentedly stringent controls over the national economy. Many of these were dismantled after 1918, but interventionism continued. This was not a matter of political choice. It was made necessary by the continuing crises of the British economy.

Techniques of interventionism improved following the work of **John Maynard Keynes** who saw **monetary** and **fiscal policies** as a way of smoothing out the trade cycle, minimising unemployment and stimulating economic activity. Before the full impact of Keynesian thinking could be felt, however, the Second World War had broken out. Again, the government exercised comprehensive control over economic

■ **Key terms**

Laissez-faire: means 'leave to do'. In economics, it refers to the belief in the merits of allowing individuals to pursue their business and trading interests with minimal governmental interference.

Capitalism: refers to private ownership and/or control of the means of production, distribution and exchange.

John Maynard Keynes (1883–1946): a leading British economist who favoured government intervention (e.g. by use of the tax system) to tackle the problems of unemployment and recession, as part of a bid to make capitalism work more efficiently and fairly.

Monetary policy: a form of economic policy that stresses minimal governmental involvement in economic matters, except for controlling the money supply as a means of holding down inflation.

Fiscal policy: a form of economic policy that uses adjustments to taxation and public expenditure levels to manage the economy.

Inflation: a continued rise in the prices of goods and services, in conjunction with a related drop in purchasing power. It occurs when too many people chasing too few goods.

New Right: a strand of Conservative thinking in the 1980s that was supportive of the Thatcher leadership. It blended some traditional conservative elements (e.g. strong government, family values and patriotism) with some neo-liberal attitudes (e.g. support for free markets, privatisation and minimal state intervention).

Free market: operates when business is governed by the laws of supply and demand, and not subjected to governmental interference or regulation. The New Right sees the free market as the cornerstone of economic and political freedom.

Recession: a significant decline in general economic activity extending over a period of time, technically over at least three successive quarters of the year.

Thatcherism: the set of beliefs associated with Margaret Thatcher, involving a market-based economic system, and emphasising competition, free enterprise, lower taxes and curbs on trade union power. She was a strong believer in family values and the 'Victorian virtues' of hard work, thrift and self-help.

Chancellor of the Exchequer: the British Cabinet minister who heads the Treasury and is therefore responsible for all economic and financial matters.

Deregulation: involves the reduction of worker protection legislation in a particular industry, usually introduced to create more competition and potentially more employment opportunities. The aim is to establish a business environment in which competitors are controlled by market forces, rather than by government regulation.

activity. It had to manage the economy for a single purpose, winning the war with Germany.

The remarkable success achieved by the managed economy in wartime naturally strengthened the view that was particularly attractive to socialists, namely that there should be a similar sense of direction and purpose in peacetime. Having won the war, they wanted to see the state use its new-found powers to strengthen the British economy and support a rising standard of living. Economic planning had become a central issue.

In the 1970s, there was a combination of high **inflation**, poor levels of economic growth and rising unemployment. Britain needed to seek support from the IMF in 1976, an indication of the gravity of Britain's economic problems. Members of the Conservative **New Right** began to reassess economic and social policy, many of its members never having really approved of growing state intervention in and regulation of the economy. They opposed interference with the **free market**, as well as the style of decision-making between key figures in government and the major economic interests, business and labour. They soon counted Margaret Thatcher (elected as Conservative leader in 1975) as one of their supporters. They offered a different vision from that of previous recent governments, Conservative or Labour.

Thatcherism

As prime minister after 1979, Margaret Thatcher saw it as her mission to reverse what she saw as a long-standing era of economic decline. She was not deflected by the unpopularity created as a result of sharply increased unemployment in the **recession** of the early 1980s. During her administrations, the policy of privatisation of industries and utilities was introduced and became increasingly popular.

The Thatcher administration was keen to reinvigorate British industry, by a combination of cuts in direct taxation, encouraging profitability and enterprise, and curbing strike action in key industries. By the end of the Thatcher era, there was some evidence that the medicine she prescribed was working and that the market philosophy was 'delivering the goods'. Many people saw a considerable improvement in their living standards. Indeed, by the early 1990s, **Thatcherism** had become a highly influential creed, for it was accepted by all the main British political parties that a market economy was inevitable and appropriate for Britain.

Labour in office

With the exception of a period of recession in the late 1980s/early 1990s, the British economy generally fared well in the Conservative years. These improved fortunes continued throughout the Blair years, when Gordon Brown was **Chancellor of the Exchequer**. The Labour government disappointed some of the party's traditional Labour supporters who wanted to see a reversal of the policy of privatisation. Indeed, some were angered by its enthusiasm for 'public–private' financing or Private Finance Initiative (PFI), whereby the private sector builds roads, transport systems, prisons and increasingly hospitals, which are then leased back to the state. Many other people suggest that in the modern world it is not actual ownership of such industries, utilities and other facilities that matters. Rather, it is important that they are subject to public control.

Some traditional New Labour backers were also troubled by the failure of their party in office to reverse the earlier Conservative policy of **deregulation** of labour markets. Labour has gone further than many of its centre-left counterparts on the Continent in embracing deregulation and done its best to ensure that European interference in such matters is limited to a 'light touch'.

Recession: the end of sustained economic growth

In 2007–8, events suggested a 'slowing down' of the good times, with the prospect of recession a real possibility. In such circumstances – and particularly in the light of the **Northern Rock** experience (see pages 180–2) – banks began tightening their credit regime and became less willing to embark on risky initiatives.

The imprudent sale of mortgages to Americans on the sub-prime market (see page 188) triggered pain on both sides of the Atlantic. By autumn 2008 there was alarm about the financial stability of leading US and European investment banks and insurance firms. The failure of Lehman Brothers in the States and the difficulties of Northern Rock, HBOS and Bradford and Bingley in the UK (all of which had made very risky investments) were but part of a wider banking collapse, which rapidly descended into a global credit crisis.

Faced by a tightening **credit crunch**, in which mortgages and other sources of credit were drying up, housing sales collapsing, shops and companies going into receivership and unemployment mounting, the British government responded with a massive **bail-out** of the banks and a **fiscal stimulus** to encourage people to spend and hopefully thereby boost demand for goods and keep businesses afloat. Whereas ministers turned to Keynesian policies of spending in a period of recession and drew upon the **New Deal** for their inspiration, the Conservatives were alarmed by massive increase in government borrowing, which they saw as a burden for future administrations.

Summary questions

1. Why did the governments of the 20th century see a need to 'manage the economy'?

2. In what ways did Thatcherism seek to transform the traditional post-1945 approach to government and the running of the economy?

3. What have been the main features of the recent recession?

The role of the financial sector

In any country with a substantial industrial base and trading interests much power resides with those institutions that control the flow of funds and credit. In Britain, the 'City' plays a large part in determining the level of business confidence and the prospects for the success of any enterprise.

The City is a key seat of economic, political and social power, a centre that has developed over centuries. In its own terms, it is a very successful financial base, for it has retained a leading position in international markets. The size of its assets is breathtaking. It remains significant in spite of Britain's relative economic decline as a leading economic power in the world.

The City is not a single, organised interest. It includes institutions such as the **Stock Exchange**, the Bank of England, the **clearing banks**, the **merchant banks**, large insurance houses and other financial organisations involved in investment and other financial dealings. Its leading organisations belong to the **Confederation of British Industry**, despite the bias of the umbrella organisation towards manufacturing over finance.

Key terms

Northern Rock Bank: formed in 1997, when the former building society of that name floated on the London Stock Exchange.

Credit crunch (or squeeze): a situation in which there is a dramatic reduction in the availability of loans and other types of credit which banks and capital markets can lend to businesses and consumers.

Bail-out: refers to a situation in that a government develops a rescue package via which it offers money to a failing business or businesses, in order to prevent the consequences that would arise from its failure (e.g. Labour's October 2008 £37 billion package, designed to prop up the banking system from near collapse).

Fiscal stimulus: a tax cut and/or increase in government spending designed to inject money into the economy and thereby increase the level of economic activity.

New Deal: an ambitious programme introduced by American president Franklin Roosevelt in the 1930s designed to combat the depressed condition of the US, by introducing measures to bring about relief, recovery and long-term reform. It included a massive increase in public spending to 'prime the pump' and create an upward spiral of economic activity.

Stock Exchange: the physical location where bonds or other securities are bought and sold. It acts as an organised marketplace in which brokers and dealers execute orders from investors.

Clearing banks: commercial banks that are members of the London Bankers Clearing House (a cheque-clearing system). Clearing enables a customer of one bank to write out a cheque to a customer of another bank. The clearing system then works so that when the cheque is deposited in the system, money is transferred from one bank to the other. Clearing can also be carried out electronically.

The City has a major influence on the fortunes of the British economy and therefore of the national government. Firstly, its institutions own much of British business, via their shareholdings. Secondly, manufacturing industry borrows from them to finance production and expansion. Bank decisions as to whether to make loans and how much to charge for them affect the activity of the whole economy. So also decisions taken on the level of investment, the rationalisation of public utilities and interest rates can affect a government's popularity.

The influence of the City is both direct and indirect. On the one hand, the Bank of England sets interest rates (an early decision of the Blair government was to hand over this power to the Bank, rather than for rates to be set after meetings between the Governor of the Bank of England and the Chancellor); the Governor meets senior ministers; and representatives of large financial companies may also be in contact with the Treasury team to advance their ideas. On the other, there are important indirect connections. Through MPs – and especially Conservative ones – many companies have a voice in the House of Commons. There are many informal links between people in the City and those who inhabit the world of Whitehall and Westminster, often of a social kind.

Case study

Northern Rock and its troubles

Northern Rock is a British bank based in the North of England. Originally a building society, it floated on the Stock Exchange in 1997. At the time, it distributed shares to its members, as a reward for their having savings accounts and mortgages with them. Although it had long been anticipated that it would be taken over by one of its larger rivals, it remained independent.

On 13 September 2007, Northern Rock requested and was granted a liquidity support facility from the Bank of England following problems it was experiencing in the credit markets that were created by a financial crisis in the **sub-prime mortgage market** in the United States. A liquidity support facility refers to money made available to ease cash flow, as a means of coping with short-term difficulties. The bank was having difficulty in raising funds in the money market to replace maturing money market borrowings, even though its assets were strong enough to cover its liabilities. Institutional lenders had become nervous about lending to mortgage banks in the light of what was happening in the US.

The support given by the Bank of England was made known publicly in what was meant to be an act of reassurance, in the light of rumours about Northern Rock's viability. Government ministers emphasised that investors and those with mortgages with the bank had no cause for alarm. On television there were scenes of people queuing in a desperate bid to ensure that they were able to retrieve their savings, accompanied by a dramatic collapse in its share price.

After some £2 billion had been withdrawn within the first three days of the story breaking, Chancellor of the Exchequer Alistair Darling announced on 17 September that the British government and the Bank of England would guarantee all deposits held at the Northern Rock. In the following weeks, as the share price continued to dwindle, interest was expressed by various companies in taking over the troubled bank whose brand name had been irretrievably damaged. Alistair Darling made it clear that the government would have to approve or veto any sale, in the interests of taxpayers, depositors and wider financial stability. Further financial support was provided by the Bank of England.

With the failure of any proposal to be turned into a concrete bid, there was speculation that ministers might decide to nationalise the company as a short-term expedient. In December ministers prepared emergency legislation to nationalise the bank, in the event that the rival takeover bids should fail. Nationalisation took place in February 2008 for 'a temporary period'. This was seen as the best means of protecting public financial support for Northern Rock, after two bids to take over the bank proved unsuccessful, neither being able to fully commit to repayment of taxpayers' money. It subsequently became known that the best part of Northern Rock's mortgage business, comprising mortgages worth some 40 per cent (£47 billion) of the company's assets had been transferred to a Channel Islands-based company, Granite. The taxpayer was therefore left with the more risky mortgages on its books.

The players involved in resolving the crisis: who had the power to act?

Northern Rock was the only British bank to receive emergency financial support from the Tripartite Authority (the Bank of England, the **Financial Services Authority/FSA** and HM Treasury). There was a widespread feeling among commentators that the regime of divided financial regulation between the three organisations had too many in-built conflicts and was ill-equipped to tackle a fast-moving crisis.

- The problems at Northern Rock proved a profound shock to the City's reputation and had serious political ramifications. It put in doubt the future of the governor of the Bank of England, Mervyn King, after his hard-line approach to the crisis left him at odds with some leading figures in the City. Criticism centred on his initial refusal to pump money into the debt markets that had ground to a halt, in the way that other central banks had done.

- It raised questions about the judgement of the chancellor, Alistair Darling, who waited three days before announcing an improvement to the investors' protection scheme, in particular the initial guarantee of depositors and borrowers. The FSA and the bank had sought the change months earlier.

- It raised doubts about the FSA's competence as a light-touch regulator after it had failed to spot that Northern Rock was an accident waiting to happen.

- For the average consumer the crisis at Northern Rock meant that they would find loans and especially mortgages harder and more expensive to come by. As well as higher costs, they faced stricter credit checks when applying for loans. The first to be affected were those in the low-income bracket, the self-employed and those with a poor credit rating.

- More generally, the failure of the bank created a climate of uncertainty and much turbulence in the financial markets of the UK, itself a reflection of a wider global uncertainty.

■ Further information

'The run on the Rock'

The House of Commons Treasury Select Committee report (January 2008) criticised:

- ■ [strongly] the *bank's* reckless business model: its failure to ensure that it remained 'liquid, as well as solvent' and to provide against the risks being undertaken

- ■ [strongly] the *FSA* for 'a substantial failure of regulation' in not providing adequate supervision of the bank and its business model: neither did it allocate sufficient staffing and resources to its supervisory role. Above all, it did not fulfil its duty to ensure that Northern Rock did not endanger the banking system in general and thereby the public purse

- ■ [only very lightly] the *Bank of England* for being insufficiently pro-active at a time of lack of confidence in the money markets

- ■ [fairly lightly] the *government/ Chancellor* for not setting up a stronger regulatory regime and for initial slowness in its response to the problems of Northern Rock and in announcing its guarantee of support.

Fig. 9.7 *Queues outside a branch of Northern Rock*

The role of government and the Bank of England

Since 1945, voters have had a firmly entrenched expectation that central government should be responsible for the management and performance of key areas of the economy. Four main objectives have dominated policy in recent decades:

- ■ a high and stable level of employment
- ■ reasonable stability of prices – i.e. low inflation
- ■ steady economic growth and improvements in the standard of living
- ■ the achievement of a balance of payments surplus.

■ Further information

The balance of payments

- ■ The balance of payments (BOP) measures the payments that flow between an individual country and all other countries. It summarises all international economic transactions for that country over a specific time period, usually a year.

- ■ The BOP is determined by the country's imports and exports of goods, services and financial capital.

- ■ It reflects all payments and obligations to foreigners and all payments and obligations received from foreigners.

- ■ The balance of payments is one of the major indicators of a country's status in international trade.

- ■ Governments have a keen interest in overseas trade. They seek to achieve a balance of payments surplus, sometimes by directly controlling imports but especially by promoting exports.

Some of these aims have at times proved to be incompatible. To get ministers out of one difficulty, perhaps a balance of payments crisis or runaway inflation, restrictions on earnings or public spending may have to be imposed. Short-term measures to achieve one aim often prevent the achievement of another. For example, tax increases designed to reduce spending power in order to keep down imports may cause prices to rise and by reducing the number of goods sold might lead to unemployment.

Members of the political Left might add another aim, the achievement of greater equality in terms of money income and wealth, as part of a move towards a wider social equality. This involves an attempt to redistribute wealth in favour of the lower income groups. On the other hand, a Conservative-led administration might well be in favour of cutting taxes for the high income earners, in order to restore incentives. Those of Green inclination will also wish to consider the impact of economic growth on the quality of life. They would doubt whether the endless pursuit of material prosperity is desirable. They would urge that **sustainable development** and quality of life considerations must be recognised.

Fiscal and monetary policy

There are three main instruments of government control over the economy, the first of which is really a wartime or emergency expedient, namely direct control and intervention; fiscal policy; and monetary policy.

Direct control and intervention

In 1939–45, the government intervened to control virtually every aspect of production and employment. In peacetime, most of these controls were dismantled, but on occasion governments still employ direct measures – if necessary backed by law – to deal with particular problems. For example, prices and incomes policies in the 1960s and 1970s sometimes involved a statutory freeze. Also, subsidies to economically disadvantaged regions have been given in order to promote geographically better-balanced growth.

Fiscal policy

The government can seek to control its own income and expenditure, which can have repercussions for the whole of the economy. This is fiscal policy, aimed at controlling the level of supply and demand. The chancellor can reduce demand by increasing taxes (such as income tax and **VAT**) or increase it by lowering them. This control is normally exercised only once or twice a year, most notably in the budget. It may be that there are also mini-budgets of the type used by the Labour chancellor in the mid to late 1970s, to provide extra 'fine-tuning' of the economy.

Chancellors must be careful not to allow demand to rise too quickly, for if this happens the economy may not be able to meet it and imports will be 'sucked in'. If imports exceed exports by too much or too regularly, an undesirable balance of payments situation is likely to result. This can have several unfortunate effects, the most obvious of which is that the rate at which other countries are prepared to exchange their own currency – the foreign exchange rate – begins to decline, making imports more expensive and nudging inflation upwards.

Government spending is very relevant to fiscal policy. By allowing it to rise (e.g. by embarking on costly capital projects, such as a major road-building programme), this can stimulate demand in the economy, creating employment. More goods have to be produced to match the increased demand, thereby promoting an upward spiral of economic activity.

> ## Key terms
>
> **Sustainable development:** development capable of being maintained at a steady level without exhausting natural resources or causing severe ecological damage. A sustainable society is one that meets present needs without compromising the prospects for future generations.
>
> **VAT (value added tax):** an indirect tax (expressed as a percentage) applied to the selling price of most goods and services. At each stage of the commercial chain, the seller charges VAT on sales but owes the government this amount of tax minus the VAT paid on purchases made in the course of business. VAT has been levied at 17½ per cent, but in the recession was reduced to 15 per cent in order to stimulate spending.

Fig. 9.8 *Alistair Darling (1953–), Cabinet member since 1997 and the first chancellor during the Brown administration*

Using the internet to assist you, list and briefly explain the economic and political arguments for a) governments raising the rate at which income tax is levied and b) lowering it.

■ Further information

Income tax

■ Income tax is a tax on income.

■ It is progressive on successive slices of income, so that the more you earn the higher the incremental rates of tax you pay.

■ Not all income is taxable. Everyone who is resident in the UK for tax purposes has a 'personal allowance', the amount of taxable income you are allowed to earn or receive each year tax-free. You are only taxed on 'taxable income' above that level.

■ After your tax-free allowance (£5,435 in 2008–9) and any deductible allowances and reliefs have been taken into account, the amount of tax you pay is calculated using a series of tax bands.

■ The bands for 2008–9 are:
20 per cent on taxable income £1–£36,000
40 per cent on taxable income £36,000 upwards.

Monetary Policy Committee: the committee of the Bank of England that decides on the official interest rate in the UK. It comprises nine members who each have one vote of equal weight. They include the governor of the Bank of England and his two deputies, two other members of the Bank and four external members appointed by the Chancellor of the Exchequer for a three-year term.

1 What should be the main aims of government economic policy?

2 Which do you think is the fairer form of taxation, income tax or VAT?

Monetary policy

The supply of money (and money that can be borrowed, credit) present in the economy will influence the level of economic activity. The more money available, the greater the capacity of people to buy things (demand), hence the need for production of goods, which in turn creates employment. The government can generally influence the amount of cash available through the nationally owned Bank of England, but credit available from many sources such as banks, building societies and various finance houses is harder to control.

A main instrument of the government until 1997 was the control over interest rates at which loans can be made. The higher the interest rate, the more expensive repayments become and the less attractive it is to borrow. The lower the rate, the easier it is to borrow money. Interest rates are raised when it is desirable to reduce the money supply to keep inflation under control. They are lowered when the amount of money in circulation needs to be increased. Labour gave away this power almost as soon as it came to office. Responsibility for setting interest rates was handed to the **Monetary Policy Committee** of the Bank of England. This was a willing surrender of a key economic power at the government's disposal.

The role of the Bank of England

Standing at the centre of the UK's financial system, the Bank of England carries out all of the functions of a central bank. Two particular goals are the maintenance of *monetary stability* (which involves keeping inflation down and prices stable) and of *financial stability* (which involves vigilance to secure the stability of the banking system). In performing these functions and contributing to the health of the national economy, the Bank works with the Treasury, the Financial Services Authority (FSA) and other central banks and international organisations to safeguard the international financial system. Since its formation, the Bank has always been the government's banker and for more than 200 years it has been banker to the banking system more generally, so that it acts as the bankers' bank. As well as providing banking services to its customers, the Bank of England manages the UK's foreign exchange and gold reserves.

The Bank is most visible to the general public through its issue of banknotes and, more recently, its interest rate decisions made via the Monetary Policy Committee (MPC). Apart from establishing the current arrangements for the Bank's monetary policy responsibilities, the Bank of England Act (1998) handed much of its supervisory work to the newly-formed FSA.

The Monetary Policy Committee (MPC)

Before 1997, the Treasury determined the level of interest rates.

In May 1997, the new Labour administration handed over operational responsibility to the MPC, which meets every month to decide the official UK interest rate. The MPC comprises the governor of the Bank of England, the two deputy governors, the Bank's chief economist, the executive director for market operations and four external members, appointed by the chancellor. Each member has one vote of equal weight.

Decisions are made with a primary aim of achieving price stability, as defined by the government's annual inflation target (2 per cent since January 2004). A secondary aim is to promote the government's economic policies, e.g. its targets for growth and employment

The Bank's governor must write an open letter of explanation to the chancellor if inflation exceeds the target by more than one percentage point in either direction (as happened in April 2007, when inflation had reached 3.1 per cent, and again for a longer period beginning in mid-2008).

The economic power of companies

Businesses are legally recognised organisational entities existing within an economically free country designed to sell goods and/or services to consumers or other businesses, usually in an effort to generate profit. In predominantly capitalist economies, most businesses are privately owned. They are formed to make a good financial return and increase the personal wealth and power of their owners, in exchange for their enterprise, investment and acceptance of what can be a high degree of risk.

Local, national and multinational companies

There is a vast number of business organisations, some 275,000 according to the Annual Reports of the Certification Officer. (Many more may choose to be 'unlisted'.) They include many well-known names, as well as a host of smaller companies and family firms, ranging from home decorators and plumbers to computer service providers and small manufacturing concerns.

Giant firms dominate the British economy, as you will all know from your daily lives. Nearly three-quarters of all groceries bought in Britain are purchased in one of four supermarket stores: Tesco, Sainsbury, Asda and Morrisons. The giant firm is a characteristically dominant form in the economies of most advanced capitalist societies. Such firms have huge resources and have the power to make decisions that are vital to the interests of government because they affect so many people. A decision by a major firm to make an investment or to close an industrial site can create or destroy thousands of jobs.

Many of these giant firms are multinationals, which organise their functions, research, production and marketing across many different countries. The largest among them, such as automobile firms or oil conglomerates, in effect treat the whole globe as their sphere of operations. Such enterprises are common across the globe, but have a special significance in Britain because of its membership of the European Union. Since Britain joined the European Community in 1973, it has been the most important location for investment by non-European multinationals in the EU. In addition the City of London is by far the most important location in the EU for the activities of multinational financial services firms trading in world financial markets.

Activities

1 Choose any one well-known multinational company such as Ford or Sony and write a brief profile of its business activities in the UK and worldwide.

2 Find out about how some leading MNCs have fared in the recession. In particular, note the problems of MNCs operating in the car industry, such as Ford.

Case study

Toyota, a leading multinational company

The Toyota Motor Corporation is a multinational corporation headquartered in Aichi, Nagoya and Tokyo, in Japan. It is currently the world's largest vehicle manufacturer. It also has a financial services division and creates robots. In total, Toyota amounts to one of the largest conglomerates in the world. It is at the heart of global manufacturing, a company that has grown within 70 years to become the world's largest vehicle manufacturer. It sells the world's best-selling model, the Corolla.

Toyota is a multinational business, building vehicles in factories on six continents around the world and directly employing more than a quarter of a million people. It manufactures or assembles vehicles for local markets in countries as diverse and far apart as Australia, Canada, India, Indonesia, Poland, South Africa, the US and the UK. Its products are sold in 160 markets worldwide.

The UK is a key market for Toyota both in terms of sales and manufacturing. As part of its wider European strategy, the company has established two production centres here: a vehicle plant at Burnaston, near Derby; and an engine factory at Deeside, in North Wales.

Burnaston is the sole production centre for the New Toyota Avensis, launched in the spring of 2003. It also builds three- and five-door versions of the Toyota Auris.

Fig. 9.9 *Well-known multinational brands*

The impact of business on government and society

Businesses are of strategic importance in the economy, and governmental interests and their own often tend to coincide. They are usually well organised and financed.

Business is therefore a major influence on government. Its importance was clearly highlighted in two developments over the last couple of decades:

■ In 1988, Edwina Currie was sacked as health minister under the Thatcher government following pressure from outraged producer and retailer interests, after she had declared that most egg production was infected by salmonella poisoning.

- In 2001, following the collapse of Railtrack, it looked as though shareholders would receive little or no compensation. However, pressure from business and financial interests led to a reversal of policy, not least when it became apparent that government would find it more difficult to raise private finance for other pubic investment if compensation was refused.

The social consequences of the concentration of economic power in the hands of those persons controlling 'Big Business' have been a constant concern both of economists and politicians for more than 100 years. Various attempts have been made to investigate the effects of 'bigness' upon labour, consumers and investors, as well as upon prices and competition. Big Business has been accused of a wide variety of misdeeds that range from the exploitation of the working class to the corruption of politicians and the fomenting of war.

Summary questions

1. What do you understand by 'the City'?

2. Who should be blamed for the failures surrounding Northern Rock?

3. What do you think some right-wing enthusiasts mean when they say they favour 'less government in business and more business in government'? Do you think that such a view has any merit?

4. In what ways do multinational companies exercise significant power? How has this been affected by global recession?

5. Why is business important in determining the fortunes of governments?

Economic power and the citizen

We are all parts of the economic system, not separate from it. We all have a number of roles and the decisions that we and those who represent us make as economic actors have an impact on the way the system functions. We are:

- consumers (all of us)
- employers (in some cases)
- employees (in most cases)
- welfare recipients (in some cases)
- investors (in some cases)
- savers and borrowers (in most cases).

Citizens as employers

An employer is a person or institution that hires employees to whom they pay wages or a salary, in exchange for the labour provided. Employers are engaged in a vast range of activities. We normally think of large-scale concerns, which may employ hundreds or even thousands of workers; in the UK, as in most other countries, governments are the largest single employers. But the vast majority of the workforce is employed in small and medium-sized businesses within the private sector. At the very bottom end, employers include those who hire the services of a nanny or cleaner.

Devedon Unitary Council

We have vacancies for advisors to work with teachers in our primary and secondary schools in the areas of:

- English
- History
- Mathematics

These are new posts, salaries on the approved scale, depending on age and experience.

Devedon is an equal opportunities employer and encourages trade union membership. We are a caring authority and provide the best possible conditions for all staff.

Fig. 9.10 *A typical local authority advert for school posiions*

Activities

1. In the above job advert, what do you think Devedon meant by saying that it is an 'equal opportunities employer'?

2. Why might a large council like to see its staff belong to a union?

3. What sort of things might be included in 'the best possible conditions'?

Activity

In recent years, the Labour–union tie has been loosened. Using information from the internet or other sources, list a few points you might make in answer to the two questions:

- Does Labour really need the unions?
- Do the unions really need Labour?

Employers have duties in regard to those who work for them. For example, they:

- must pay employees the agreed amount if the employee arrives for work and is able to work (and not less than the minimum wage)
- recognise employment rights such as those regarding the number of hours worked, the right to join a trade union and various rights under the Employment Protection Act (see page 77)
- must give employees correct information about rights under their contract
- must provide employees with a reasonable opportunity to have their complaints looked at
- must make sure any reference is completed with reasonable skill and care and is true, accurate and fair
- have a duty – along with their employees – of mutual trust
- must observe Health and Safety Regulations.

In the important area of health and safety, among other things employers have a duty to:

1 protect the health and safety of employees and other people who might be affected by what they do

2 consult employees (through safety representatives, if the organisation has any).

Citizens as employees: the role of the trades unions

The British labour force is currently larger than ever before, at more than 31 million people. The majority work in services (almost 81 per cent), the rest in industry (18 per cent) and agriculture (just over 1 per cent). Some 28 per cent of UK workers belong to trade unions.

Further information

Union–Labour financial ties

- Fifteen trade unions are affiliated to the Labour Party, for they see the industrial and political wing of the Labour movement as having a shared desire to promote the interests of working people.

- Members of affiliated unions pay a 'political levy' into the union political fund, unless they opt out.

- Affiliated unions pay all or most of the money in this fund to the Labour Party, to boost its annual income. As an election nears, they may pay extra money to party headquarters.

- Union funding of the party had dropped significantly, as the Blairite party became more reliant on business donations. However, in the last year or so, as the party has run up debts, it has been getting more than half of its money from unions.

A trade union is an organised group of workers. Its main goal is to protect and advance the interests of its members by obtaining for them the best possible living standards and working conditions.

The role of trade unions has been a central issue in British politics in recent years for two reasons:

1 The role of unions within the Labour Party has raised questions about their economic and political power. Many people believe that by the 1970s the unions – particularly, but not exclusively under Labour governments – had acquired too much power and that their influence needed to be curtailed.

2 Trade union power and organisation was one of the major targets of the Thatcher government in the 1980s. There was an extensive programme of 'trade union reform', much of which has been accepted by New Labour, in office. This acceptance has led to disillusionment on the part of many trade unionists with the Blair/Brown administrations.

■ **Further information**

Thatcherite 'anti-union' legislation

Six substantive Acts were introduced by the Conservatives between 1979 and 1997. Among other things:

- ■ new closed shops arrangements meant that no employee could be forced to join a union (so either they could choose not to join or if there were difficulties with this they were eligible for compensation)
- ■ trade union leaders were to be periodically elected
- ■ limits were applied to secondary picketing, a form of protest in which people who do not work in a factory, shop or workplace congregate outside (e.g. picketing a retail store that sells products made by a company against which industrial action is being taken)
- ■ strikes were only lawful if they were preceded by a secret ballot of all employees concerned.

Citizens as consumers

Consumers are individuals or households that use goods and services generated within the economy. In free market or capitalist economies, consumers have ultimate control over the type and quality of products, as well as some influence over how goods and services are produced. While it is true that a single individual has relatively little leverage, consumers collectively have power in the market because producers depend upon their goodwill for their income and profit.

Consumption of individuals of goods and services is linked to the level of available disposable income. The more money people have to spend, the more they can exercise their freedom to make purchases. This in turn benefits those who produce and sell them. Consumers are therefore generally considered to be at the centre of economic activity.

Consumer protection

Consumer protection refers to governmental regulation that protects the interests of consumers. It is linked to the idea that citizens have rights as consumers (see page 117) and to the formation of consumer organisations (e.g. the Consumers' Association or more specific bodies that deal with one sector, such as the British Campaign for Real Ale, CAMRA) that help consumers make better choices in the marketplace.

In the UK, consumer protection issues are dealt with by the **Office of Fair Trading (OFT)**, which investigates, can impose an injunction or ultimately take the matter to court. It also acts as the UK's official consumer and competition **watchdog**, with a remit to make markets work well for consumers. At the local level, protection is afforded via the **trading standards departments**.

Consumer rights

Much of the protection available to British consumers derives from five fundamental rights:

■ **Key terms**

Office of Fair Trading (OFT): enforces consumer protection law and competition law, reviews proposed mergers and conducts market studies.

Watchdog: a body established by government to act in the public interest as a vigilant guard against inefficient, illegal or wasteful practices – e.g. a consumer protection organisation.

Trading standards departments: local council departments responsible for enforcing consumer legislation. Among other things, they check garages to ensure that – in accordance with the Weights and Measures Act (1963) – the right amount of petrol is pumped; any premises preparing food only serve what is fit for human consumption; and enforce the Trade Descriptions Act (1968).

The EU and consumer protection

The EU's first consumer programme was issued in 1975. Since then, there have been directives requiring national action to protect consumer rights in areas such as:

- the safety of cosmetic products
- the labelling of foodstuffs
- advertising aimed at children
- the selling of financial services
- guarantees and after-sales service
- the safety of toys
- the safety of building and gas-burning services.

■ **Activity**

What rights do individuals have as e-consumers? Look up www.internetrights.org.uk/factsheets and list any protection available. What protection is available under the UK Consumer Protection (Distance Selling) Regulations (2000)?

■ **Summary questions**

1. Why has trade union membership declined over the last 30 years or so?

2. Do unions still have a valid role in modern Britain?

3. How easy is it for consumers to complain if goods purchased are sub-standard? Does it make a difference if purchases are made via the internet?

4. Are consumers 'fair game'? Do they deserve to be 'ripped off' if the seller can get away with it?

5. Is it true that it is consumers rather than producers who have real market power in today's society?

- *The protection of health and safety*, involving banning the sale of products that may jeopardise them.

- *Protecting the consumer's economic interests*, involving regulation of misleading advertising, unfair contractual agreements and unethical sales techniques such as those used in selling time-shares.

- *Granting the right to full information about goods and services offered*, including the labelling of foodstuffs, medicines and textiles.

- *The right to redress*, involving the rapid and affordable settlement of complaints by consumers who feel they have been injured or damaged by using certain goods or services.

- *Consumer representation in the governmental decision-making process* in Whitehall (via consumer associations such as Which?) on issues such as the case for new legislation to improve levels of public protection.

Much legislation on consumer affairs is the responsibility of the British government. However, some of the protection derives from membership of the European Union, although the guideline for EU legislation in this area is 'as little regulation as possible, but as much as is necessary to protect consumers'. EU legislation either fills in gaps left by national laws or covers areas where the consumer in one member state has a complaint concerning another member state, as when a British consumer is the victim of dubious time-share sales in Spain.

Consumer responsibilities

Apart from an entitlement to claim their rights, consumers also have responsibilities. They can be expected to make an effort to meet financial obligations for items purchased and to treat them with reasonable care and in appropriate conditions. They should make only a just claim upon those who provide goods and services. This might involve seeking a replacement or refund for goods that are faulty and not fit for purpose. It does not involve compensation for purchases that are subsequently regretted or which were bought from a different store to the one being asked for restitution.

Responsibility also means reporting faulty workmanship, fraud, scams and other forms of wrongdoing to relevant agencies, in order that they might investigate, if necessary expose and prevent others from falling victim to the same mistreatment. Depending on the issue, this might involve contacting the following:

- *Rip-off tip-off*, the body set up by local trading standards to encourage members of the public to report traders who may be running a scam (e.g. cowboy builders, doorstep traders, counterfeit product sellers, loan sharks, bogus home-working schemes and bogus competitions).

- *Trading Standards*, when faults or problems with goods are identified or illegal street trading is taking place.

■ What is the influence of the media?

The term 'mass media' is a catch-all phrase, which includes all popular means of communication such as newspapers, periodicals, magazines, posters, the cinema, radio, television and video, as well as more recent innovations such as e-mail and the internet. All of these are concerned with the transmission of ideas and information in one way or another. Since the 1950s, the press and broadcasting have been the dominant forms. But the media are constantly changing, with new developments constantly taking place. When considering the political and social role of the media today, the internet, **blogging** and **YouTube** cannot be ignored.

The mass media certainly are massive, for the following reasons:

1 In many homes, a newspaper is taken or people have access to one. On an average day, nearly 60 per cent of people over the age of 15 read a morning paper. Depending on the newspaper, there is usually coverage of political events and issues in the news, rather less in the popular **tabloids**, more (though a declining amount) in the quality **broadsheets**.

2 Most homes (over 97 per cent) have a television, some two or even three or more. Even though many programmes are for entertainment only, nonetheless current affairs, documentaries and news bulletins all regularly deal with political stories and developments.

3 Internet access in UK homes has grown at an astonishing rate. Some 50 per cent of UK homes now have access to the internet (this is strongly linked to income and education).

4 With more than 77 million subscribers, the mobile phone **penetration rate** has achieved an astonishing 127.6 per cent of the whole population. Mobiles have evolved from being simply a voice communicator to a hub for a range of additional services, such as text messaging, email and MMS. The small screen on your phone has taken its place alongside the personal computer and television as an important way for people to connect with one another.

Table 9.3 *Daily newspaper sales*

Newspaper		Average circulation December 2006	Average circulation December 2008
Popular	Daily Mirror	1,624,490	1,346,916
	Daily Star	795,451	725,671
	Sun	3,164,150	2,899,310
Middle market	Daily Mail	2,362,162	2,139,178
	Daily Express	816,046	728,296
Qualities	Financial Times	431,242	435,319
	Daily Telegraph	899,923	824,244
	Guardian	378,378	343,010
	Independent	253,878	200,242
	Times	665,764	600,292

Source: ABC

Readership figures for any given newspaper are generally around three times higher than the circulation figures.

Developments in the media

Whereas quality papers such as *The Observer* and *The Times* have existed since the late 1700s, the popular press began publication around the turn of the 20th century. Today, newspaper readership in Britain is high by international standards, but it has been in long-term decline. Sales peaked in the early post-1945 era, records having been established in the

Key terms

Blogging: refers to the practice of producing a blog (weblog), a personal online journal that is frequently updated and intended for general public consumption. Blogs represent the personal musings of the author, with commentary on internet and other political/social issues and links to other sites.

YouTube: a popular free video website, which allows users to upload, view and share video clips. It allows unregistered users to view most videos on the site, whilst registered users can upload any number of videos.

Tabloids: also known as red-tops, small-format newspapers such as the Sun that convey information in a sensational style, with bold or even lurid headlines. Stories are presented in a salacious manner and may be shamelessly biased. The style has appeal to readers whose attention span and/or available time is limited.

Broadsheets: traditionally large, quality newspapers that presented news and information in greater depth and with greater analysis than tabloids. Now that some long-standing broadsheets (e.g. The Times) publish in tabloid size, the term 'compact' is often used to describe their present form.

Penetration rate: the extent to which a company manages to increase its market share among the population.

Activities

Calculate the percentage decline in readership over the two years between December 2006 and December 2008.

1 How did the quality sector fare, in comparison with the populars and mid-markets?

2 Suggest reasons for the decline in newspaper sales in the period covered.

1940s and 1950s. The number of national dailies in England was 21 in 1900: today, there are 10. Overall circulation figures are approximately 12 million for daily papers and 13 million for those published on Sundays.

Of the choice of papers currently available, the tabloids have a far greater circulation than the qualities. To a greater extent than in most other European countries, the tabloids are heavily focused on entertainment. Their political content is thin and few people buy such papers for political reasons. Quality newspapers present news and information in greater depth and with greater analysis, although the amount of political coverage has arguably declined in recent years.

The arrival of television

Broadcasting has replaced newspapers as the most popular means of mass communication. Radio was popular between the two world wars and on BBC channels 4 and 5 Live there is still regular and often detailed reporting and discussion of news and current affairs. Television first appeared in the 1930s, but became more widespread from the 1950s onwards. It is now the main source of political information for most voters (see Further Information: sources of political knowledge). For years, it has informed people about events, issues and personalities. Television, being less overtly opinionated, has been a counter to the obvious partiality of much of the press.

Political exposure on television comes via several outlets. Politicians appear on a range of programmes from news bulletins to current affairs episodes, from the broadcasting of political events to special election features. There are also newer types of coverage. Americans speak of 'infotainment', programmes that employ the techniques of entertainment to present more serious issues. Among them are chat shows that have a markedly reduced political agenda but which still provide an opportunity to project personality and get the message across in a less demanding atmosphere. Chat shows have become popular outlets with politicians who like the less intense atmosphere than they experience in a grilling by a journalist such as Jeremy Paxman on *Newsnight*.

Key terms

Deregulation of the media: refers to the process by which governments in the 1980s and subsequently have removed, reduced or simplified restrictions on media ownership and content, with the intention of encouraging the efficient operation of markets.

Television was a monopoly of the BBC from 1922–54, before the introduction of commercial television. Then the duopoly of BBC and ITV had a long run, without any competition. Each station had two channels by the 1980s. Since then, Channel Five has been added, and **deregulation of the media** and technological developments have made possible a massive expansion of consumer choice. Satellite and cable became available in the 1980s. Since 1998 (when BSkyB began to offer its satellite customers the choice of digital or analogue satellite dishes), digital television has opened up the possibility of more channels for viewers who do not have access to them.

New technologies

Enthusiasts often claim that eventually the internet will become a key source of political information, as voters seek out news and comment on personalities and issues. Candidates and parties have responded to the challenge it presents, spending vast sums on creating web sites and e-mail address lists. Others have used it to build up support for their campaigns, as with the efforts of musicians such as Billy Bragg to encourage tactical voting in recent elections. The impact of such activity is as yet hard to assess. Of those with regular access to the net, the number using it for political purposes is growing rapidly, although they are more concentrated among younger and more educated voters. There is little indication that it has as yet had much impact on undecided voters. The Kavanagh and Butler study of the 2005 election concluded that 'the internet again proved to be a marginal battleground for the parties and of interest to a minority of the UK public … it did not shift votes or alter the results to any noticeable extent'.

What creates public opinion?

Public opinion is a frequently used but vague term. It is used as if its source was capable of positive identification, but it is really an abstraction referring to a collection of individual opinions, varying in detail, intensity and permanence. In the 19th century, it was used to refer to the views of the informed majority. Today, it is usually employed to refer to the majority opinions of the mass of people.

Public opinion may be created in different ways:

- Public opinion depends on the freedom to air and exchange ideas and information. As such, it is more easily expressed in those societies where communications are largely free from restraint.

- In countries with free institutions, people are encouraged to express and exchange ideas about public affairs. Where debate is restricted, they lack the opportunity to do so.

- It may be that a minority of people who are interested in politics spread ideas among their acquaintances. Discussions in the school, home, workplace or pub may help clarify thoughts. It is unlikely that the opinions of the interested have much impact on the apathetic or uninterested.

- The media almost certainly have an influence, though arguments vary about the impact of television and newspapers.

- In the long run, people are influenced by a multitude of factors that make up their experience of life, on the basis of which they form judgements and acquire preferences.

Media ownership and control

In most Western countries, ownership of newspapers tends to be concentrated in the hands of a small number of rich and right-wing proprietors. In the UK today, several national dailies and Sundays, as well as much of the regional and evening press, are owned by a few large organisations. These companies exist to make a profit and any newspaper titles that fail to flourish do not often survive. *Today* and *The Sunday Correspondent* were unprofitable and disappeared in the 1990s. News International, the empire owned by Rupert Murdoch, is responsible for about a third of the newspapers sold in Britain.

Because they are commercial organisations run on the basis of private enterprise, newspapers are free to print what they like as long as they do not break the law. Each paper has its own identity, but overall for many years the bulk of the British press was pro-Conservative. An anti-Labour, anti-union bias was evident in tabloids such as the *Sun*. In the 1980s and 1990s, its editors often gave Labour a hard time, being especially harsh on Neil Kinnock, its leader after 1983. He suffered rough headlines, such as this one in 1992: 'If Kinnock wins today, will the last person to leave Britain please turn out the lights.'

In 1997, after very careful wooing by Tony Blair, the *Sun* supported Labour, which also had a remarkably favourable treatment from several other papers. Even the pro-Conservative *Daily Mail* ran several damaging stories about divisions among Conservatives on Europe. In 1997, 2001 and 2005 the majority of the newspaper readership supported Labour, as Table 9.4 indicates.

Further information

Sources of political knowledge in the 2001 election campaign

- 89 per cent television
- 89 per cent direct mail
- 77 per cent opinion polls
- 75 per cent friends and family
- 74 per cent newspapers
- 61 per cent billboards
- 55 per cent party election broadcasts
- 39 per cent radio
- 19 per cent direct contact with candidates/MP
- 7 per cent internet

Source: MORI survey for Electoral Commission, June 2001

As the political climate became increasingly difficult for Labour towards the end of the Blair era, so it lost press support. The process was accelerated in late 2007 as a number of problems beset the Brown administration. With the Conservatives climbing in the polls, traditional Conservative newspapers such as the *Daily Mail* and *Daily Telegraph* regularly featured headlines that were damaging to Labour. Even the Sun, which had been very sympathetic to the Blair leadership, was losing its enthusiasm for the party, not least over the issue of new constitutional arrangements for the European Union.

Table 9.4 *UK daily national newspapers: ownership and political leanings*

Newspaper		Owned by	Party supported 2005
Popular	Daily Mirror	Trinity Mirror	Labour
	Daily Star	Northern and Shell	No preference declared
	Sun	News International	Labour
Middle market	Daily Mail	Daily Mail and General Trust	Not a Labour victory
	Daily Express	Northern and Shell	Conservative
Qualities	Financial Times	Pearson	Labour
	Daily Telegraph	Telegraph Group	Conservative
	Guardian	Guardian Media Group	Labour
	Independent	Independent Newspapers	Inclined to Liberal Democrats
	Times	News International	Labour

The ownership of television

The British Broadcasting Corporation (BBC) was actually established as a **public corporation** in 1927. By its charter, it was made responsible for **public service broadcasting** in the UK, its task being to provide high-quality programmes of broad appeal. The BBC is financed by the **television licence fee** that is levied on all who own at least one television.

Commercial television was established by the Television Act (1954). Ownership of the regional television companies was to be in private hands, but it was to be subject to public regulation and strict guidelines. Although there were significant differences in the ethos and funding of the two stations ITV was to some extent fashioned in the BBC's image. It was expected to follow a commitment to public service broadcasting. As Wedell (1968) has observed, both companies shared a belief in the importance of news and current affairs programming, and recognised the importance of informing the nation. They became two halves of the same system, 'derived from a single root and ... these branches, instead of diverging over the years ... stabilised their concentration more or less in parallel. There was a circumscribed [limited] form of competition as BBC and ITV producers vied for their reputations, critical renown and audience approval.'

Activity

On any one day, take a tabloid and a broadsheet paper. Compare the front page news stories, the headlines and the style of coverage. Record your thoughts on any similarities and differences that you observe.

Key terms

Public corporation: an organisation created to perform a governmental function or to operate under a loose form of government control – e.g. the BBC. Many of the well-known public corporations of the post-1945 era were established to run the amenities and industries nationalised by the post-1945 Attlee government.

Public service broadcasting: refers to a regulated broadcasting whose primary aim is to provide a public service. It aims to inform and educate, as well as catering for minority tastes. It has objectives other than entertaining viewers and ensuring profitability.

Television licence fee: refers to the charge levied for using any television receiving equipment such as a TV set, set-top box, video or DVD recorder, computer or mobile phone to watch or record TV programmes as they are being shown on TV.

These features underpinned the duopoly of British broadcasting. The domination of the two companies, BBC and ITV, remained unchallenged until the 1980s, when Channel 4 was launched. It had a distinctive brief, to be innovative and experimental, producing programmes that were educational, informative and catered for minority subjects. Like ITV, it was to be financed by advertising. As a result of the passage of the Broadcasting Act (1990) at the end of the Thatcher era, it too is now run as a public corporation. The same Act provided for the introduction of a fifth channel – now known as Five – under the ownership of Channel 5 Broadcasting Ltd.

> ■ Further information
>
> **The television licence fee**
>
> ■ Currently, a colour TV licence costs £135.50; a black-and-white one £45.50.
>
> ■ The fee finances the BBC, allowing it to run a wide range of services for everyone, free of adverts and independent of advertisers, shareholders or political interests.
>
> ■ In 2006/7 every month 92.5 per cent of the UK population used the BBC.
>
> ■ Critics point out that the BBC no longer dominates viewing habits, as it did when the fee was introduced: the trend is for its market viewing share to diminish.
>
> ■ Its defenders say that it ensures the BBC can provide a range of programmes of a traditionally high standard, including catering for minority interests. This is the essence of public service broadcasting (see page 203).
>
> ■ The fee is effectively a tax. Just as non-motorists pay for the road network, so non-BBC viewers are asked to pay for funding the Corporation.

In 1989, direct broadcasting by satellite began. Provision soon fell into the ownership of Margaret Thatcher's favourite media mogul, Rupert Murdoch whose trans-global company owned BSkyB. Her attention was then directed to the established players, the BBC and ITV. ITV was subject to fundamental surgery in the 1990 Act. There was to be an auction of franchises for the 15 regional licences. Following the first auctions, mergers of regional companies occurred, eventually leading to the key one in 2004 between Carlton and Granada, which meant that only one player remained, which is now simply known as ITV plc and runs independent television.

Is television biased?

As we have seen, the press is privately owned. There are no charters or licences that enable ministers to maintain close control over the operation of newspapers. Their owners are free to take any political line that they wish to take, the main constraints being that they need to ensure that it does not offend their readership and therefore jeopardise sales. Newspapers – in particular, the tabloids – tend to be biased and partisan.

In contrast, the charters of the BBC and ITV require that they are impartial in their political coverage: both aim for fairness and objectivity. The commitment to impartiality means that neither channel is supposed to be supportive of one particular party or standpoint. It also means that in the coverage of events, the media are supposed to report in a neutral fashion, presenting a balanced picture that covers all sides of an argument.

From time to time, both channels have been criticised for alleged unfairness to one party or the other. The BBC had problems during the Thatcher/Major years, when it was referred to as the Bolshevik (or later

> ■ Hint
>
> Particularly in the run-up to a general election, political party managers are concerned to monitor television for any signs of media bias. Be aware of the different forms that overt and hidden bias may take. As you view the news on television or hear it on radio, look out for examples that you might record to keep your fund of examples up-to-date. Pay particular attention to the political commentators that newscasters turn to for elaboration in news bulletins.
>
> Decide whether you think that each of the main parties gets a fair deal.

■ Key terms

Glasgow University Media Group (GUMG): a research-based grouping of academics within the sociology department of Glasgow University. Their purpose is to promote the development of new methodologies and substantive research in the area of media and communications.

■ Activity

On any one evening, listen to three or four main news bulletins (e.g. BBC, ITV, Channel 4, Five or Sky). Make a list of the five main stories in each case and for those that overlap compare the treatment and priority they receive. Record what differences you detect. Is there evidence of overt or indirect bias?

■ Further information

The Pearson Group

The Group's wide-ranging worldwide media interests include:

Press

- ■ *Financial Times*
- ■ *The Economist*
- ■ Westminster Press
- ■ More than 100 local titles
- ■ Papers in Canada, France and Spain

TV

- ■ Thames TV
- ■ Grundy in Australia
- ■ Sky

Books

- ■ Addison-Wesley Longman
- ■ Penguin
- ■ Simon & Schuster
- ■ Future Publishing

Blair) Broadcasting Corporation. Norman Tebbit, a minister and party chairman in the Tory years after 1979, was harsh on the BBC, accusing it of 'insufferable, smug, sanctimonious, naïve, guilt-ridden, wet, pink orthodoxy'. He and others constantly complained of programmes in which the behaviour and views of Conservative ministers were questioned, sometimes very sharply. Labour ministers have also had a hard time at the hands of tough and skilful interrogators on *Newsnight* and the *Today* programme on the radio. The party has always been concerned to ensure that it gets a fair deal on airtime, being conscious of its traditionally unfavourable treatment in the commercial press (see also page 198–9 for more on Labour and the media, in office).

Even the Liberal Democrats have been known to complain about their treatment. They have suffered not so much from the content of programmes as from neglect. As a third party, they find it hard to get media exposure in between elections. Like the other parties, they carefully monitor media coverage of elections, to check that they get a fair share of airtime and that references to them are free of partisanship.

Overt bias in television coverage of news and current affairs is rare, but the **Glasgow University Media Group** (GUMG) has researched 'hidden bias'. It claims that the intonation or emphasis of the newsreader, interviewer or commentator can be important. The GUMG has in the past documented examples of reporting in industrial relations issues in which management representatives were often interviewed calmly seated at their desks, whilst union leaders were seen haranguing their audience in militant language, which whipped up support for strike action. Some critics claim that television bias does not result from any deliberate manipulation of the news. It arises from the background of those who work in the media. Many journalists – especially those at or near the top – are 'white, male and middle class'. They have 'moderate', broadly safe/conservative views, which are said to incline them to prefer middle-of-the-road politics and make them suspicious of minorities, such as ethnic groups, gay people and republicans.

The debate about media ownership

In Britain, the rest of Europe and America there has been a trend towards concentration of ownership and similar concerns have been voiced about whether this is harmful to democracy. Powerful tycoons head vast corporations often owned and dominated by a few individuals and families, many of whom also have extensive publishing and broadcasting empires including television and the wider entertainment industry. These moguls find that ownership of the media can be a very lucrative business. Beyond making money, however, they wish to influence public opinion and the political arena.

By their own testimony, the multi-millionaires who can afford to own newspapers are not just in the business of making a fast profit. Indeed, in the case of *The Times*, Rupert Murdoch has been content to suffer a loss for much of its existence. His purpose, and that of some other corporate giants, is to shape the political environment in which they operate. In the longer term, the rewards of Kerry Packer in Australia, Silvio Berlusconi and the Agnelli family in Italy and the Murdoch family in Britain, are considerable. They can propagate their views and hope to influence decision-making in areas that matter to them, such as the future of their business empires.

Private ownership of newspapers, rather than any form of state control or interference, is widely seen as a guarantee of freedom of choice and a bulwark against state tyranny. But some commentators wonder if it is healthy if a few proprietors can dominate the dissemination of ideas. After all, moguls of the past have been open about their motives. Many years ago, Lord Beaverbrook made it clear that he ran the *Daily Express* 'for the purpose of propaganda, and with no other motive'. Lord Northcliffe referred to his wish to be able to tell the people 'whom to love, whom to hate, and what to think'.

Cross-media ownership

As the potential profitability of television became apparent, news and radio proprietors have been keen to buy into television so that a pattern of cross-media ownership was established (see the example of the Pearson Group on page 205). In the eyes of their critics, such combines can have very detrimental effects:

- They determine entry into the media market, promoting their own interests by eliminating the prospect of rivalry.
- They erode diversity of choice, resulting in a more homogeneous presentation of issues so that the public has less varied information.
- They reduce the availability of countervailing power-centres to governmental policy. (If the powerful proprietors are sympathetic to those in office, then there is less likely to be any serious dissent or critical analysis, and there may be 'no-go' areas for investigative reporting – in the way that Rupert Murdoch is sometimes alleged to be reluctant to criticise the Chinese Communist regime for fear of jeopardising his prospects of developing his company's foothold in that country, via Star television.)
- They use their outlets to act as a megaphone for the proprietors' own social and political ambitions.

The media sector is a fast-changing one. It is difficult to establish a regulatory framework that can keep up with technological advances, cross-media alliances and global networks. Both Britain and America have tried to limit cross-media ownership, prohibiting newspaper owners from dominating the television industry as well. But they have recognised that the issue is complex and controversial. It seems self-evident that the existence of a diversity of media organisations must be to the benefit of the public, as this should ensure that the opinions and perspective of different groups within society get a hearing. Yet to impose strict curbs on ownership might be to affect adversely the economic prosperity of the media sector, one of the fastest growing sectors of the modern economy.

Globalisation of the media

Globalisation of the media has provided improved access to overseas events and made it possible for viewers to see immediate coverage of what is happening around the world. In the global village that has come about, British and American viewers could see the bombing and invasion of Iraq as it happened, whereas in the past there was a significant time-lag before news of fighting overseas reached the home country. Today, the ability to receive and transmit programmes has become available in those less developed parts of the world that were previously beyond the reach of television.

Since the 1980s, there have been two other themes in the development of the media in addition to globalisation: **commercialisation** and **fragmentation**. The old duopoly of the BBC and ITV has been broken down, with cable and satellite players providing subscribers with a greater range of programming from within the UK and overseas. In addition,

Key terms

Commercialisation: refers to the increase in for-profit broadcasting in recent years. It allows new media moguls to build transnational broadcasting networks that operate on a global scale. In the UK and some other parts Europe, the first television station (the BBC) was publicly funded, not commercial.

Fragmentation: refers to the vast range of channels now on offer, as well as to the availability of programmes on demand – e.g. via video.

new commercial channels have been created to widen choice still further, with unlicensed pirate channels further complicating the picture. The combined impact of these developments has been to splinter the audience, so that traditional providers such as ITV now struggle to retain a strong market share.

The overall effects of the three themes is to reduce national political control over broadcasting; to allow listeners and viewers greater choice and escape from news and current affairs altogether, if they wish to do so; and finally to encourage the growth of open and informed societies. Governments can no longer easily isolate their populations from stories and developments from Britain and overseas that they would prefer to keep 'in the dark'.

Government and the media

Relations between government ministers and journalists are often noted for mutual wariness and suspicion. They need each other, but frequently come into conflict. Politicians take the view that they are the elected representatives of the people and dislike the way that highly paid journalists who do not represent anyone can put them on the spot and ask questions that are difficult or inconvenient to answer. These journalists and interrogators often misrepresent their ideas and cut them off during interviews, rarely allowing them to develop their viewpoint as they would wish. Yet the media are useful to ministers, enabling them to get their views across to a vast audience and 'leak' selected information as they find convenient.

Journalists need the information that those in government can supply. Their stories and the follow-up to them often depend upon getting ministerial comment. But, in their search for truth, they have an interest in being confrontational with politicians, for this can make good listening and viewing. They ask difficult questions and demand answers. They often find politicians evasive and unwilling to offer the sort of straight yes/no response that they prefer. Unsurprisingly, the relationship between the two groups is liable to go wrong and from time to time all governments have difficulty in '**managing the media**'.

The relationship can be the more difficult when a government has been in power for a long time. Invariably, there are problems that have not been solved by ministers and new ones for which they do not have a ready solution. Ministers cannot easily blame their predecessors for unsuccessful policies and problems in society left neglected. It is easy for journalists to expose failings and scandals that tend to beset governments long in office. The Conservative governments between 1979 and 1997 and Labour since then have run into increasing difficulty with journalists of the press and in broadcasting.

Ministers of both governments have often felt unfairly treated. They feel vulnerable to adverse publicity and criticism, finding that in an age of 24-hour news it can be difficult to have a chance to develop policies. They point out that it is easier to find what has not been done than to defend the status quo. They claim that their policies are misinterpreted, their achievements ignored and their deficiencies emphasised. Any reasonable and inevitable differences of opinion between them are magnified out of all proportion and used to create an impression of serious disunity.

Case study

The war of words between the BBC and ministers, 2002–3

In 2002–3 the BBC and the Labour government were involved in a furious public battle over the content of an issue of the *Today* programme. The story concerned Andrew Gilligan, a *Daily Mail* columnist not much liked by New Labour **media minders**. On the programme, he stated that ministers actually knew that the claim in the so-called September dossier that Saddam Hussein could launch a missile attack in 45 seconds was wrong, yet still went ahead and published it. This led to a massive confrontation between ministers and the BBC.

The BBC felt that in essence its story was true, although some details of the Gilligan claim may have been incorrect. In the unfolding of the story and its aftermath, the BBC suffered much abuse and pressure from Alistair Campbell, the immensely powerful ex-journalist who handled communications issues for Downing Street. Ministers claimed that the Gilligan story was seriously damaging to the reputation of Tony Blair and his colleagues, amounting to a charge of deliberately lying. It wanted a retraction, but instead the BBC management seemed to rally in support of Gilligan. In the Hutton Inquiry (see pages 141 and 146), the performance of the BBC was seriously criticised, whereas Downing Street escaped lightly. This further embittered the tensions between the two sides, the BBC feeling that they lost a director general and chairman of governors over the conflict whereas there were no ministerial resignations.

Fig. 9.11 *Alistair Campbell, New Labour's highly influential director of communications and strategy for much of the Blair premiership*

How governments seek to control the media

Direct ministerial control

The home secretary has direct powers under the terms of the BBC's Charter and the legislation concerning ITV. The minister can lay down the hours of operation and veto the broadcasting of any particular topic or type of topic. However, these are reserve powers and their use in normal circumstances is almost inconceivable.

In times of war, such as in the **Falklands dispute** (1982) different rules might prevail and some form of ministerial intervention is possible. But it is highly unlikely that the government would actually stop the expression of opinion through direct censorship. In 1982, tight guidelines were issued, the Ministry of Defence preventing the BBC and ITV from broadcasting combat film for 24 hours. In today's globalised media, with so many sources of information available, any such control is unlikely to be effective. Indirectly, of course, a minister can threaten to use the power of direction or – in the case of the BBC – to be unsympathetic when the licence fee needs to be fixed for future years. Such methods are a rarity. So too is the use of DA-Notices, as issued by the Defence, Press and Broadcasting Committee (DPBC), which comprises press and government nominees. Originally set up in 1906 as an alternative system to direct press censorship, the role of the DPBC is to 'advise' newspapers on matters relating to the publication of sensitive information.

Beyond statutory restrictions and ministerial recommendations, the supply of information can be limited by the tradition of secrecy in British government. A culture of secrecy has existed in Whitehall over many

Activity

- Find out more about the row between ministers and the BBC over the Gilligan broadcast. Decide whether you think the government got off lightly in the Hutton Report.

- List any reasons why governments that have been in office for several years might run into conflict with the broadcasting authorities. You may be able to think of some of your own.

Key terms

Falklands dispute (1982): the conflict between Argentina and the UK over the ownership of the Falklands Islands, South Georgia and the South Sandwich Islands. War was triggered by the occupation of South Georgia by Argentina in March 1982, followed by the occupation of the Falklands. It ended when Argentina surrendered in June 1982.

decades. Journalists find it hard to ferret out the truth, faced as they can be with official reluctance to disclose information. Government has been opened up to some extent in recent years by the passage of the Freedom of Information Act (2000), but we still operate under the restrictive Official Secrets Act (1989).

Other methods of conveying the governmental case include the following.

- *Use of the Central Office of Information:* This is meant to inform the electorate on issues of public interest in a non-partisan manner, but has sometimes been used for overtly political purposes
- *Use of governmental advertising:* This can be on such issues as the dangers of AIDS, driving without due care or under the influence of drink.

Indirect management of the news

All governments are anxious to ensure that they receive the best publicity possible and to limit the damage that may be caused by adverse stories appearing in the press, on radio and on television. The management of information is something to which they devote considerable attention. They wish to see that the government gets its case across clearly and effectively.

Several players are involved in the process of managing the news. They tend to specialise in different areas of responsibility:

- *The press secretary* has traditionally served as the spokesperson for the prime minister and on occasion the government as a whole. He or she also acts as an adviser on the presentation of ministerial policy and coordinates and conducts the government's communications orchestra. Notable examples have been Sir Bernard Ingham under Margaret Thatcher and Alistair Campbell under Tony Blair. Both were high-profile figures, the targets of much publicity and criticism. The press secretary (operating as 'sources close to the prime minister') may brief journalists with 'black propaganda', damaging information about ministers whose fortunes are on the way down. This can be done via the **parliamentary lobby system.**
- *Various minders and speechwriters or* '**wordsmiths**' advise ministers on how to convey their case to the media and the public. Some offer advice on how to present themselves and improve their image, to ensure that ministers look good. Others provide script, insert **soundbites** and advise on the presentation of speeches, in order to make the best impression. Media advisers know how to make the headlines, who to approach and how to present information in a media-friendly way. They are adept at 'putting a spin' on a story.

The importance of the media in a democracy

Democracy implies the existence of certain basic freedoms, among which the rights to express and listen to opinions are fundamental. Traditional liberal democracies are associated with the idea of a free press and with broadcasting services that operate in a climate in which editors and journalists are able to gather and use information as seems appropriate for their programming.

The media are today central to our democracy. They feature strongly in many of our lives. Increasing standards of living have made many of their offerings widely available. The quality of their output must be of concern to all who respect democratic values.

Are the media good for democracy?

Arguments in favour

- *The media are today's means of educating the people:* We rely upon them as a means of conducting our political communication. In Ancient Greece, politicians could address the relatively small number of citizens directly. In the vast democracies of the present day, it is unrealistic for politicians to be able to address many of the voters directly. The media – and television in particular – enables them to reach numbers never previously possible.

- *The media allow the public to become better informed about political issues:* They spread ideas and information, organise debate and take up matters of public concern and importance. Moreover, in as much as they convey such material in an interesting and palatable manner, this benefits democracy in that they are enhancing public understanding of the body politic.

- *They investigate major controversies of the day and seek to expose facts and problems that may be of interest to their audience:* Much of this is material government ministers would prefer to keep to themselves for it can prove politically embarrassing. Journalists performed a public service in throwing the light of publicity on the unsafe conviction of the **Birmingham Six**, as they have more recently in alerting the public to the scandals surrounding Labour Party finances.

- *They help to widen public debate:* This ensures that discussion of traditional issues such as immigration and asylum seeking is brought up-to-date as new information comes to light and 'new' issues such as the environment and global warming are addressed by the government.

Arguments against

- *There are problems surrounding the ownership of the media:* The trend towards monopoly in Britain and elsewhere is damaging in a democracy, in that it threatens the availability of a diverse array of viewpoints. The development of cross-media ownership in global media empires is a particular cause for concern.

- *The demands of 24-hour news* in an era of rolling news bulletins on Sky, BBC 24 and Five Live places relentless pressure on politicians whose every action comes under such scrutiny that there is not a rational atmosphere in which issues can be debated and decided. The pressure to be available to answer questions at moments when silence and careful consideration are required makes it increasingly difficult for politicians to act in a way that is uninfluenced by popular clamour for action. Issues can be trivialised or over-simplified in the rush to make quick responses.

- *Too often, readers of popular newspapers and viewers of some television programmes do not receive serious and balanced coverage of issues:* In the press, the treatment can be shamelessly biased. On television, interviewers often seek to dramatise situations, going for lively confrontation and personalising issues between rival sides in an argument.

- *Reporting can easily become sensational in the cause of stoking up interest:* In particular, the tabloid press is notably prone to scandal-mongering. This may be in the public interest if dubious financial dealings are brought to the reader's attention, but in other cases stories are purely salacious in intent. Investigations into the lives of well-known figures often have little to do with the ways in which they conduct their public roles. It is more often a question of pandering to

> ### Key terms
>
> **Birmingham Six:** six men who received life sentences for their role in the Birmingham pub bombings (1974), widely alleged at the time to have been carried out by members of the Irish Republican Army. Their convictions were declared unsafe and quashed by the Court of Appeal (1991).

what interests the public, than emphasising what the public have a right to know.

■ *The media are infatuated with personalities, particularly at election time:* It is easier to tell stories in personal terms, rather than to do justice to the issues. Election campaigns pay undue attention to party leaders, their ability to perform well on television being a criterion of how effective they are in carrying out their roles.

Case study

Tony Blair's views of the media

At the Labour Party conference (2006), Tony Blair spoke of 'the harsh climate of the 24/7 media, in which gossip and controversy are so much more newsworthy than real news'. He elaborated on his criticisms of the media shortly before he left office:

The ... media ... increasingly and to a dangerous degree is driven by 'impact'. Impact is what matters. It is all that can distinguish, can rise above the clamour, can get noticed. Impact gives competitive edge. Of course the accuracy of a story counts. But it is secondary to impact. It is this necessary devotion to impact that is unravelling standards, driving them down, making the diversity of the media not the strength it should be but an impulsion towards sensation above all else.

Broadsheets today face the same pressures as tabloids; broadcasters increasingly the same pressures as broadsheets. The audience needs to be arrested, held and their emotions engaged. Something that is interesting is less powerful than something that makes you angry or shocked.

The consequences of this are acute:

First, scandal or controversy beats ordinary reporting hands down. News is rarely news unless it generates heat as much as or more than light.

Second, attacking motive is far more potent than attacking judgement. It is not enough for someone to make an error. It has to be venal (capable of being influenced by promises of money or material gain) ... What creates cynicism is not mistakes; it is allegations of misconduct. But misconduct is what has impact.

Third, the fear of missing out means today's media, more than ever before, hunts in a pack. In these modes it is like a feral beast, just tearing people and reputations to bits. But no-one dares miss out.

Fourth, rather than just report news, even if sensational or controversial, the new technique is commentary on the news being as, if not more, important than the news itself. So – for example – there will often be as much interpretation of what a politician is saying as there is coverage of them actually saying it ...

In turn, this leads to a fifth point: the confusion of news and commentary. Comment is a perfectly respectable part of journalism. But it is supposed to be separate. Opinion and fact should be clearly divisible. The truth is a large part of the media today not merely elides the two but does so now as a matter of course.

The final consequence of all of this is that it is rare today to find balance in the media. Things, people, issues, stories, are all black and white. Life's usual grey is almost entirely absent ... It's a triumph or a disaster. A problem is 'a crisis'. A setback is a policy 'in tatters'. A criticism, 'a savage attack'.

Source: Speech by Tony Blair, June 2007

I found the media's [generally critical] response – and particularly the response of the television industry – to the Blair challenge pretty depressing. Hardly anyone engaged with the substance of the criticisms – of our triviality, our short-sightedness, our preoccupation with conflict.

Jeremy Paxman, Edinburgh Festival, August 2007

Activity

Explain in a couple of sentences what you think Tony Blair was referring to when he spoke of the 24/7 media. In what way is this a relatively new phenomenon? Is it a good thing?

Summary questions

1 Are television interviewers and presenters often unfair on politicians? If so, in what respects?

2 Some media commentators and interviewers seem to see themselves as 'tribunes of the people'. Are they appropriately qualified to act in this way?

3 Do you think that on balance the media serve our democracy well?

4 How much truth do you recognise in the package of criticisms of the media advanced by Tony Blair? Can you rebut them point by point?

Regulation of the media

There are two broad approaches to organising the media in a democracy, the Public Service model and the Market model.

The Public Service model

The Public Service model emphasises regulation of the media in the public interest. The justification for regulation is that if the news coverage is left in the hands of media moguls or multinationals, there is a danger of bias. Regulation is therefore necessary to ensure accuracy, balance and impartiality in the reporting of news and current affairs.

The Public Service model of broadcasting operated in the UK from the 1920s to the 1980s. As there were only a few radio and television stations – and those owned by the BBC were paid for by the licence fee – regulation was feasible and some would say desirable. It was recognised that there were dangers in direct state control of the media, so the procedure of supervision was handed over to agencies that were not controlled by government, known as **quangos**. The BBC was an obvious example of a supervisory board that operated under a degree of public control and adopted a public service ethos.

In this period, of course, the press was in a different position. They operated in a market situation and their fate was determined in the marketplace. They needed to sell as many papers as possible. As commercial organisations, their output was not impartial. The only controls that operated over newspapers were the laws that governed blasphemy, obscenity, sedition and race relations – and, more recently, the protection of privacy.

Key terms

Quangos: publicly funded bodies that operate at arm's length from a government department and carry out executive and advisory functions. Their members are not elected and therefore are not accountable to the voters.

The Market model

Deregulation has been a dominant theme of the media market since the 1980s, when the Market model was introduced in the United Kingdom and most European countries. Its supporters often argue that the previous Public Service model stifled innovation and was patronising. It was more concerned with what people should want, rather than what they actually did want. Also, they saw regulation as a means of allowing the government to interfere in broadcasting by the 'back door', for the BBC in particular was beholden to ministers for its funding. They determined the level of the licence fee.

Enthusiasts for the Market model prefer to allow the commercial forces of the market to operate. They accept that there may need to be some market regulation to ensure that there is genuine competition and that no one mogul ends up controlling all media outlets. But beyond that they dislike the idea of regulation. In an age when there is a vast range of options available to the listener and viewer, they feel that there should be minimal regulation of broadcasting, just as there is with newspapers. They believe that the battle for audiences between providers will ensure that a range of views are aired on radio and television and that there is free competition of ideas. In addition, they wish to see regulation of content kept to a minimum, for content regulation is viewed as being inconsistent with free speech.

Content regulation

Supporters of deregulated broadcasting do not wish to see regulations about how much news or political coverage should be provided on each channel. Nor do they wish to be expected to show **Party Political and Party Election Broadcasts**. They want a free hand to provide the programmes that they feel will win audience approval, even if this drives down standards and results in a general 'dumbing down' to the lowest common denominator of public tastes. They accept that there must be some content regulation of the media in the public interest. This means that there are controls over such things as the amount, content and distribution of advertising and especially over cigarette advertising. In addition, there are controls over pornography.

Today, some public service channels are still required to observe strict rules of political fairness and balance, with equal time being allocated to the parties at election time. Some commercial channels (e.g. ITV) have to follow the same rules.

Who does the regulation?

The press

There is no state control or censorship of the British press. It is subject to the laws on publication (see page 93). In addition, the *Press Complaints Commission (PCC)* was set up by the industry in 1991 as a means of self-regulation. Owners of newspapers and magazines were concerned that failure to regulate themselves might lead to statutory regulation. The PCC is, then, a voluntary, non-statutory body, funded by the industry through the Press Standards Board of Finance.

The aims of the PCC are:

■ to consider, adjudicate, conciliate and resolve complaints of unfair treatment by the press; and

■ to ensure that the press maintains the highest professional standards and shows respect for generally recognised freedoms, including freedom of expression, the public's right to know and the right of the press to operate free from improper pressure.

It judges newspaper and magazine conduct according to a code of practice drafted by editors, agreed by the industry and ratified by the Commission itself. Six of its members are editors of national, regional and local publications and 10, including the chair, are drawn from other fields.

Recent anxieties raised to the PCC have included a case involving illegal access by journalists to voicemail messages, the trade in personal data identified by the Information Commissioner and the treatment of public figures by photographers working on behalf of the press (for instance, a royal girlfriend being pursued by **paparazzi**). The *News of the World* has often had to defend itself from complaints about some of its news-gathering techniques such as **entrapment** and contentious campaigns such as that to name and shame alleged pedophiles in 2000, following the abduction and murder of a young girl, Sarah Payne.

There are concerns about the effectiveness of the action that the PCC takes, for it is said by its critics to 'lack teeth'. It has a reputation for being lenient to editors and journalists who transgress its code. When an apology is required, editors tend to give it low prominence and relegate it to some obscure section of their paper.

Broadcasting

Until 2003 broadcasting was regulated by the Broadcasting Standards Commission (BSC), which regulated taste, decency and fair treatment on television and radio. It is now regulated by *Ofcom*, which was established as a statutory body by the Office of Communications Act (2002) to regulate the UK communications industries, with responsibilities across television, radio, telecommunications and wireless communications services. The Ofcom Board of up to 10 members provides strategic direction for Ofcom. It has a chairperson appointed by the secretary of state. Its executive is the senior management team responsible for day-to-day running of the organisation.

Ofcom's duties include:

- ensuring a wide range of TV and radio services of high quality and wide appeal
- maintaining plurality in the provision of broadcasting
- applying adequate protection for audiences against offensive or harmful material
- applying adequate protection for audiences against unfairness or the infringement of privacy.

Ofcom handles all media issues about content except those concerning impartiality, inaccuracy and some commercial issues relating to the BBC. These remain the responsibility of the *BBC Trust*. Established by charter, the purpose of the Trust is to establish the strategic direction of the BBC, exercise supervision of how it spends its money, work on behalf of licence fee payers (ensuring the BBC provides high quality output and good value for all UK citizens) and protect the independence of the BBC.

Advertising on television is regulated by the **Advertising Standards Agency**.

The internet

New developments and inventions open up new possibilities, both in the present, the near future and into the far distance. As with all other forms of the media, there is a need to watch developments on the internet

Activity

Use the internet to help you find out examples of advertisements that have fallen foul of the ASA and had to be withdrawn.

closely and see what regulation becomes desirable and necessary. The question of ownership by powerful media multinationals arises, as does the opportunity for the network to be used to spread racist propaganda or pornographic material. The difficulty is that with the internationalisation of the media, it is more difficult to achieve effective control.

Fig. 9.12 *Jo Moore, whose e-mail sent on 9/11 provoked a political furore …*

Summary questions

1. What advantages might television have over newspapers and vice versa in the area of political coverage?

2. Has deregulation of broadcasting in the UK provided viewers with improved choice and a better chance of acquiring knowledge and understanding of current affairs? Give examples to illustrate your response.

3. What do you understand by the term 'public service broadcasting'? Is it well protected by the BBC today?

4. Does the concentration of media ownership really matter?

5. What are the dangers inherent in the trend towards cross-media ownership?

6. Is television coverage on the BBC and ITV biased in any way?

7. Is there still a place for party political and election broadcasts on television? Explain your response.

8. Do we need more controls over what is shown on television?

9. Should (could) there be control over the political content of information carried over the internet?

Political 'spin'

Spin has become an accepted feature of news management. The term derives from the spin given to a ball in various sports, to make it go in a direction that confuses the opponent. Politicians are often accused of spin by their political enemies. It is a usually critical term, signifying a heavily biased portrayal in one's own favour of an event or situation. It often, though not always, implies less-than-frank, deceptive and/or highly manipulative tactics.

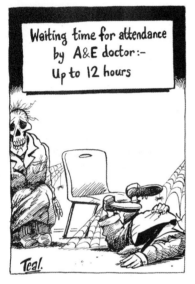

The techniques of spin include selectively presenting facts and quotes that support one's position (cherry-picking), phrasing in a way that assumes unproven truths, the use of euphemisms to disguise or promote one's agenda and the 'burying' of stories by releasing information at times when more important events dominate the news

Another spin technique involves careful choice of timing in the release of certain news so it can take advantage of prominent events in the news. A famous reference to this practice occurred in 2001 when government press officer Jo Moore used the phrase 'It's now a very good day to get out anything we want to bury' in an e-mail sent on 9/11. The furore caused when this e-mail was reported in the press eventually led to her resignation.

Spin-doctors are part of the media team, their task being to change the way the public perceive some happening, or to alter their expectations of what might occur. They try to put a favourable gloss on information and events.

Fig. 9.13 *… and earned a place in the 'Breaking bad news' section on CartoonStock.com*

Labour's concern with public relations became counter-productive in the Blair years. Instead of being about the way a story was presented, it became the story itself. Ministers' alleged economy with the truth was said to encourage people to disbelieve what governmental spokespersons are saying. Some critics were scathing about an alleged Blairite preoccupation with presentation, ensuring that stories were managed to minimise damage to the government's reputation.

Summary questions

1 Is it inevitable that any government long in power will find its relationships with journalists increasingly strained?

2 Does the present government get a rough ride from some radio and television interviewers (e.g. Jeremy Paxman on *Newsnight*)?

3 Is spin a skilful political technique or a scourge upon our political system?

The influence of the media on the political attitudes of citizens

For many people, it seems to be evident that because television is so widely viewed, then it must be a powerful force in shaping our attitudes and behaviour. But it is much more difficult to pinpoint what its effects might be. Of course, they are likely to be very different on different people. If there is bias in the media, then this could be damaging to the parties and personalities that are the victims of it. In any case, we cannot assume that biased articles or programmes produce an indoctrinated electorate.

In the 1970s the Glasgow University Media Group (GUMG) began to stress the importance of **agenda-setting** by television and newspapers. This suggests that the media influence the electorate by more subtle means, by determining what is seen and heard. The media may not determine what people think, but they do determine what they think about. GUMG went further and argued that hidden bias, resulting from the background and outlook of those who work as television journalists, does tend to make us adopt more pro-moderate, pro-consensual views and be critical of those who challenge society's prevailing ideas. These include strikers, protesters and others portrayed as extremists or militants.

Many writers now support the Independent Effects theory. Television is watched for so long and by so many people that common sense suggests that it must influence us. Saturation coverage of politics at election time means that we cannot escape the barrage of news and views. This must have some effect, even if we cannot be sure what it is. At the very least, television especially expands our knowledge: we should know more than our parents and grandparents could ever find out. Over a long period, it probably has some imprecise influence over our thinking. The effects may be different on different people, some being passive spectators who take little notice of what they see, others being much more involved and open to persuasion. If the effects of media influence are not immediately apparent in the short term, it is likely that over a longer period cumulative exposure may make a more lasting impression.

Summary questions

1 Which is the most important source of information from which you derive your information on news and current affairs?

2 How useful do you find a) the tabloid press and b) the broadsheets as sources of information?

Activities

1 Find out more about the Jo Moore episode, as a good example of spin in operation.

2 List any examples of situations where the Brown government has resorted to careful management of the news or spin in getting its message across. Did they work?

Key terms

Agenda-setting: the theory that the mass media may not exercise much influence over what we think, but can significantly influence what we think about. By focusing on some issues and not others, the media can highlight the importance of some issues in the public mind.

10

Government and the citizen

Learning objectives:

- to be able to define the role of government, its functions and responsibilities; and the interrelationship between the different levels of government within the UK

- to understand how government and its actions impact on the lives of citizens

- to understand the structure of government within the UK

- to understand the relationship between the centre and the locality

- to examine citizen participation within local government including the role of the elected representative

- to understand the impact of the European Union on the daily lives of citizens in the UK – looking at the social, political and legal impact

- to understand the relationship of the UK to Europe from the founding of the EEC

- to be able to compare and contrast the working of the 'government' of the UK and the EU.

Governments make decisions concerning the running of public affairs. They resolve outstanding doubts and problems about what is to be done. They also work out how those decisions are to be put into effect. Wars must be fought as well as declared, taxes raised as well as established and a whole range of other policies, once agreed, have to be implemented by turning them into laws (Acts of Parliament). Citizens have to abide by these laws. The government has the ability to lay down punishments for those who commit crime, and so if you break the laws, you may end up in prison.

The key functions of government are therefore to make law (legislation), to implement law (execution) and to interpret law (adjudication). There is no escape from government. Even if you leave the country and go elsewhere, you will live under another government. Life without government is not an option, but the nature of the governing regime varies across the world.

The role of government

The government is the Executive agent of the state. It enforces the laws of the state (see page 224) and acts under its authority. In other words, it runs the country. Whereas the state is said to be a permanent, abstract entity, the actual institutions can change and evolve and people involved in their running may come and go. Look again at page 160–3 to be sure that you are clear about the distinction between the state and the government.

In a narrow sense, 'the government of the UK' refers just to the highest tier of political appointments, in the British case the prime minister and Cabinet. In a wider sense, government refers to all bodies concerned with making and implementing decisions on behalf of the community. By this definition, civil servants, judges and the police all form part of the government, although none of these groups is elected. In this wider sense, government provides the landscape of institutions within which we experience public authority.

Forms of government

There are various types of government. Democracy became an increasingly popular form of government in the closing decades of the 20th century. However, until then, most of the global population lived in authoritarian states of one type or another. This has been the norm throughout human history, whether they were ruled by the chiefdoms, absolute monarchies and empires of the distant past or the dictatorships of the last century. Since the 1920s, there have been several brutal dictatorial regimes, ranging from Mussolini's Italy, Hitler's Germany. Stalin's Russia and Mao's China to Pol Pot's Cambodia.

Authoritarian regimes are non-democratic regimes in which those in power wield great power and enforce their will upon those over whom they have power. They include forms of military rule where the head or heads of the armed forces rule personally or as a **junta**. However, many of the authoritarian regimes are also **totalitarian regimes**. Several of the 20th-century dictatorships were of this type. Communist and fascist rulers believed in a creed that they sought to impose upon their country. They wished to transform society and were brutal to those who in any way opposed their vision. In totalitarian regimes, the state influenced every aspect of everyday life, national and local. **Theocracies** are a further – and much less common – form of authoritarian rule. In Iran, religious leaders (ayatollahs and mullahs) play a leading role.

The role of government

The distribution of power

Under any political system, it would be impractical for any set of ministers to understand the needs of every area and to involve themselves in the minutiae of detail concerning their public administration. Governments recognise the need to allow some scope for regional or local initiative.

There are two basic solutions to the territorial organisation of power, unitary government and **federal government**. Most states are unitary, meaning that within them legal sovereignty lies entirely at the centre. **Sub-national administrations**, devolved or local, may exist and be responsible for making as well as implementing policy, but they do so only as long as the central government permits them so to do. However, the trend in recent years has been for unitary states to devolve power. France, Italy and Spain have all introduced elected regional governments.

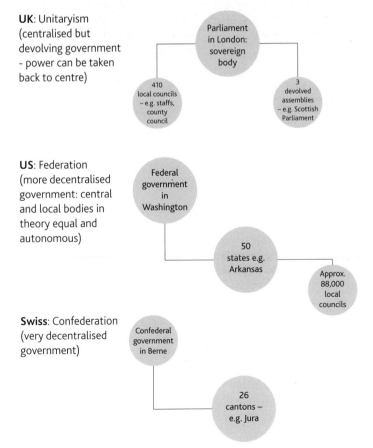

Fig. 10.1 *Unitary, federal and confederal government*

Key terms

Junta: a group of military officers holding the reins of power in a country, especially after a sudden violent or illegal seizure of power.

Totalitarian regimes: non-democratic countries in which there is very strong central direction and control. They are a form of authoritarian regime in which those who rule aim for the total penetration of society in an attempt to transform it. They seek to dominate not only political life, but also social and economic life – as did the Nazis in Germany in the 1930s and 1940s.

Theocracies: governments led by religious leaders, such as the regime established after the overthrow of the Shah in Iran (1979) and which continues today. Literally, a theocracy means 'rule by God', so that in theocracies religious authority prevails over political authority.

Federal government: exists where power is shared between a central authority and subordinate units such as states.

Sub-national administrations: levels of government below the national level.

Table 10.1 *Unitary and federal systems: strengths and weaknesses*

	Advantages	Disadvantages
Unitary	Clear ranking of authority: centre supreme and few tensions between centre and regions	Excessive concentration of power at the centre
	Clear focus of loyalty for citizens who identify with country as whole	Inadequate representation of regional diversity
Federal	Check on central power, states preventing undue concentration of power at the centre	Some overlap of powers: possible conflict between centre and states – gridlock or stalemate
	National unity in large countries, yet catering for diversity and regional/local responsibility: acceptable compromise between need for effective government and strong regional/local recognition	Broad tendency for power increasingly to be exercised at centre, especially on key economic issues. Trend towards central control over much of US history, up until the 1980s
	States useful as 'laboratories for democracy', where policy experimentation can proceed and politicians be groomed for national stage	Sluggishness – difficulty in getting things done quickly, as over the US government's effort to enforce civil rights legislation in 1960s

The United Kingdom has a unitary system. Parliament at Westminster makes laws for all parts of the UK. Some areas of the UK have powers devolved to them; Scotland and Wales since 1999 and Northern Ireland (after early attempts that had been suspended) since 2007. There is also a long-established system of local government. Nonetheless, all parts of the UK and all sub-national administrations are subject to the legislative supremacy of Parliament.

By contrast, in a federal system such as that of the United States, legal sovereignty is shared between central and state or provincial governments. Neither level can abolish the other, so that the position of the 50 states such as Arkansas and Wyoming is protected.

What is happening in the UK?

The United Kingdom remains a unitary state, but the important changes of recent years seem to indicate a move towards a kind of federalism. Devolution has been the British route to **decentralisation** (see pages 231–8). Ultimate power remains in Westminster's hands, although it is hard to imagine that it would be politically acceptable in Scotland, Wales or Northern Ireland if any government in London tried to regain control over areas of policy that have been delegated to Edinburgh, Cardiff or Belfast.

We now have a Parliament for Scotland, a National Assembly for Wales, an Assembly for Northern Ireland, along with appointed Regional Development Agencies (RDAs) and indirectly-elected Regional Chambers around England. Each of these authorities has a different degree of power, even those of similar names. Another development has been the introduction of an elected mayor and assembly for London, followed by the creation of the office of elected mayor in several other towns and cities.

Because we are moving in a decentralist direction, with power devolved to the component parts of the UK, some writers talk of 'creeping federalism'. Bogdanor (2003) uses the phrase 'federal devolution' to

Key terms

Decentralisation: the process of transferring responsibilities and powers from national bodies to more local ones.

describe the present British situation. As in Spain, it is not an even spread of power around the country. We have **asymmetric devolution**, with different parts enjoying different degrees of autonomy. The country is a devolving unitary state that lacks a uniform pattern of devolution.

The UK's multi-layered government

In all but the smallest countries, government is organised like a set of Russian dolls, with one unit tucked inside another. The smallest unit is often a community or neighbourhood council, which fits into the system of local government, which itself may be part of a system of devolved government. Local or devolved government is itself part of the national system of government. The national government is a member of various organisations of national government. Layers of government below the national level are collectively known as sub-national or non-central government. Those above may be termed international organisations or in the case of the European Union as a **supranational** organisation.

UK government today no longer follows the straightforward pattern of the past, when all political roads led to London and all major decisions were made in **Whitehall**. We live in an age of multi-layered government, in which there are several locations of power that have authority over us, ranging from Brussels to the most local tiers of parish and town councils. Accordingly, in the rest of this chapter, we will examine national government, devolved government, local government and the European dimension that comes about via our membership of the European Union. But before we do so, it is useful to be aware of the range of services provided at each level.

Table 10.2 *The services provided by the different tiers of UK government*

Level of government	Examples of the range of services provided
European Union	Agriculture, fisheries, trade and the environment to a great extent; growing involvement in areas such as drug-trafficking and foreign affairs and security
National government	Economic policy, education, health, justice, immigration, welfare and foreign affairs and security
Devolved government (as in Scotland, Wales and Northern Ireland)	Agriculture, economic development, education and training, health, housing, local government services, sport and transport
Local government	Cemeteries, education, environmental health, highways, libraries, social services and waste collection and disposal

N.B. There is some variation between the powers of the devolved bodies in the three countries and in the level at which some functions are exercised by local government.

Summary questions

1 Why do we need government?

2 Distinguish between democracies and authoritarian states and between authoritarian and totalitarian states.

3 What do we mean by referring to the UK's multi-layered system of government?

Activity

List any points that you would make to answer the following question: 'Is the United Kingdom worth preserving?' Refer back to the discussion on the social diversity of the UK in Chapter 2.

Key terms

Asymmetric devolution: transfer of powers to a devolved body on a piecemeal or evolutionary basis, in which different regions are granted different levels of autonomy.

Supranational: in a supranational organisation decisions are made by processes or institutions that are largely independent of national governments. Supranationalists are supporters of the idea that decision-making should be carried out by institutions that are 'above nations or states'.

Whitehall: the road that runs from Trafalgar Square to the Houses of Parliament and is the location of several government departments. Hence, we refer to decisions made 'in Whitehall'.

Above	Global	United Nations and its institutions (e.g. International Monetary Fund)
	Trans Atlantic	North Atlantic Treaty Organisation
	European	European Union Council of Europe/ Court of Human Rights
	The Centre Whitehall Westminster	
Below	Devolved	Scottish, Welsh and Northern Irish devolved bodies
	Regional	Regional Development Agencies, Regional Chambers
	Local	410 councils, below which are parish/ community councils

Fig. 10.2 *The tiers of government impacting upon the UK*

■ How do the actions of government affect our lives as citizens?

For much of the 19th century the role of the government was strictly limited. Government was concerned with conducting foreign policy, securing our national defences and maintaining law and order. By the turn of the century, there was a growing recognition that governments needed to assume more responsibilities for public welfare. By the 1920s and 1930s they began to play a more interventionist role in the economic and social life of the nation. However, it was after 1945 that there was a new emphasis upon collectivism, the idea that all of us are 'our brother's keeper', in other words that we all have a responsibility for each other. This involved higher social spending to support those in various forms of need. State welfare was to be a new priority. The state also took over the running of key industries and utilities such as coal, electricity, gas and the railways.

The phrase 'Welfare State' was first used in the 1930s, but it only came into common use after 1945 at a time when the Labour Government (1945–51) was introducing measures to maintain high levels of employment, provide security and a better life for all. Decent living standards began to be thought of as an entitlement, rather than as a cause of gratitude. Today, most of us have come to assume that the state has a responsibility for our welfare and we have come to expect comprehensive protection against sickness, poverty, unemployment, ignorance and squalor, the five 'giant evils' recognised in the Beveridge Report (1942). Beveridge spoke of care 'from cradle to grave'; others use the phrase 'from womb to tomb'.

Fig. 10.3 *A warm reception to the publication of the Beveridge Report, 1942*

How government impacts upon our lives today

Most of us experience governmental provision at various points throughout our lives. We may be born in an NHS hospital or with the service of an NHS midwife. We may attend state-funded nursery facilities. We go through compulsory state education from five to 16. We then are either subsidised to go to university, or go to work and pay taxes determined by the government or receive benefits from it should we be unemployed or incapacitated. We receive a retirement pension at 60 (women) or 65 (men). We are buried in a local authority cemetery or incinerated in a local authority crematorium.

During these various phases, if we fall ill we have the care provided by the National Health Service. We are entitled to a range of benefits for other situations, such as maternity grants for pregnant women and welfare benefits to those at work or in retirement whose income does not reach a certain threshold. Should we be the victims of a criminal attack, we may be the beneficiary of victim support compensation. Should we end up in court, we may be able to receive some form of legal aid. Should we purchase inferior goods, we have forms of consumer protection. Government matters to us all. Indeed, if anything goes wrong in society it is a common reaction to say: 'Why doesn't the government do something about it?'

Case study

Services provided by the Department of Work and Pensions (DWP)

The DWP provides benefits and services for a wide range of people. All of us will come into contact with it at various points in our lives. Its focus is on the following 'customer groups':

- children
- people of working age
- pensioners
- disabled people and their carers.

The main businesses of the DWP are as follows:

- *Jobcentre Plus*, which provides an integrated service to people of working age. It offers help to people looking to move into work and support for people who can't. Jobcentre Plus also provides a range of services to help employers fill their vacancies quickly.
- *The Pension Service*, which is a dedicated service for current and future pensioners. It provides state financial support to over 11 million pensioners delivered at a national and local level and in partnership with other organisations. It also helps people to plan and provide for retirement.
- *The Child Support Agency*, which is responsible for running the child support system. It assesses, collects and pays child support maintenance, ensuring that children whose parents do not live together are financially supported.
- *The Disability and Carers Service*, which supports disabled people and their carers, whether or not they work. It is responsible for delivering attendance allowance, disability living allowance and carer's allowance.
- *The Health and Safety Executive*, which protects people's health and safety by ensuring risks at work are properly controlled.
- *The Rent Service*, which provides a rental valuation service for housing benefit purposes, fair rent valuation for landlords and tenants, and advice to customers within the public and private sectors on these issues.

The DWP has a range of sponsored public bodies to help it to achieve its objectives. These include Executive, advisory and tribunal non-departmental public bodies (NDPBs), public corporations and other arms-length and short-term bodies. Among the NDPBs are such bodies as the Disability Employment Advisory Committee, the Industrial Injuries Advisory Council, the National Employment Panel and the Pensions Ombudsman.

Activities

1. Make a list of the public services that may be provided for children and young people from birth to adulthood (18). By the side of each, say which agency or level of government provides them.

2. Make a list of the ways in which the lives of yourself and close members of your family have been affected in some way by the DWP or its predecessor bodies.

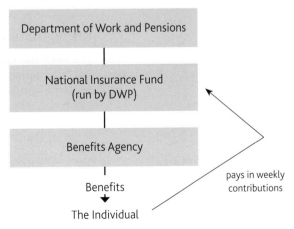

Fig. 10.4 *The Department of Work and Pensions and the benefits claimant*

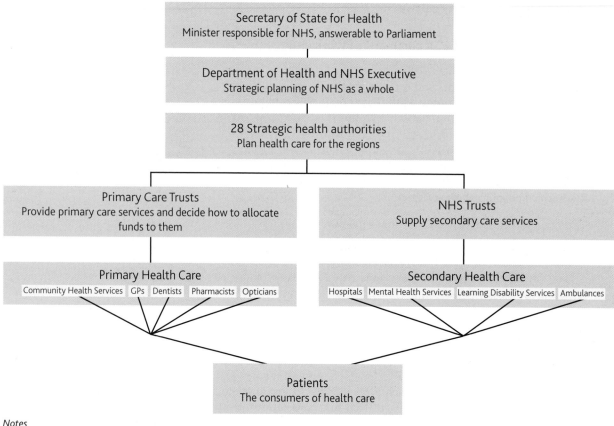

Notes
1. The GP is normally the first 'port of call', able to refer us as necessary to more specialist services.
2. Primary services are provided near to where people live, perhaps on a main street.
3. We use secondary services less often, for they are more specialised.

Fig. 10.5 How the NHS impacts on those who use it

■ The structure of national government in the UK

As with any political system, there are three branches of government in the United Kingdom, the legislature (which passes laws), the executive (which creates and implements the laws and policies) and the judiciary (which interprets and enforces the laws).

The legislature

The word roots of the word 'legislature' are the Latin terms *legis* (law) and *latio* (bringing, carrying or proposing). Legislatures are the branch of government empowered to make the law. They are the structures in which policy issues are discussed and assessed. The roots of the name of the first modern legislature, the British Parliament, suggest this crucial function, '*parler*', to talk.

Most large countries have **bicameral legislatures**. The British Parliament comprises the lower chamber, the elected House of Commons and the upper chamber, the appointed House of Lords.

The House of Commons

There are 646 Members of Parliament (MPs) in the House of Commons. Individually, they have responsibility to their parties and for their constituencies.

Key terms

Bicameral legislatures: legislatures that have two chambers, e.g. Australia and the UK.

Case study

MPs and the help they give to constituents

Alan Meale, Labour (Mansfield)

As your Member of Parliament I am not in Parliament to deal with all the problems that you might have. For instance I am not there to help you in private disputes as they may be with others of my constituents. I am not there to interfere with decisions made by the court, except when a clear case of innocence or wrongful verdict is apparent. I am, however, there to help with matters for which Parliament or Central Government is responsible. So, if your complaint is about local authority services like dustbins, housing repairs or playing fields, you should contact your local councillor.

Only if help cannot be gained from this quarter should I then be contacted on such matters. As your MP I am normally very generous about giving advice on all sorts of things, but as I have in excess of 100,000 constituents to look after, it is important that I do not have to spend time diverting queries which should have been taken elsewhere.

The sort of things I as your MP can help with mainly relate to work carried out by Central Government. These include:

■ Tax problems involving the Inland Revenue and Customs and Excise Departments of Central Government (but not Council Tax paid to the local authority)

■ Problems with the Department of Health – hospitals, the national Health Service

■ The Department of Social Security: Pensions and National Insurance

■ Immigration, which is dealt with by the Home Office, and

■ Matters like school closures and grants, which are administered by the Department of Education Science.

Sian James, Labour (Swansea East)

I regularly hold surgeries in Swansea East , so that you are able to come and see me about any problem or concern; e.g. problems with benefits, pensions, asylum & immigration, or other Central Government matters.

If your concern does not relate to Central Government in London, i.e. it relates to the National Assembly for Wales or City & County of Swansea Council, I will make sure your concerns are passed to the appropriate person.

There is no need to make an appointment to attend my surgery, just attend during the time shown below, it is on a first come, first served basis.

If you are unable to attend surgery on the following dates, there are other ways of getting in touch with me. You may write, email or telephone.

Sources: the respective websites of the MPs

Prime minister's questions (PMQs): held for half-an-hour on a Wednesday (12.00–12.30). The session provides MPs with the chance to question the prime minister. In terms of drama, PMQs is usually the high point of the parliamentary week, particularly the regular joust between the party leaders.

Leader of HM opposition: the leader of Her Majesty's opposition, which is the second largest party in the House of Commons.

Chief whip: in either party responsible for maintaining discipline and unity among MPs, trying to ensure that they stay loyal in parliamentary votes.

Life peers: those members of the House of Lords created under the terms of the Life Peerages Act (1958). This permitted men and women to be created as peers for the duration of their lives. The purpose was to diversify membership of the chamber by bringing in people from various walks of life (without excluding their heirs from membership of the Commons).

'Elected hereditaries': those hereditary peers allowed to remain in the House following the passage of the 1999 Act, which removed the right of most of them to sit in the chamber.

Hereditary peerages: peerages that came about as a result of a title inherited within the family. The Act allowed 92 to remain. They were to be elected by and from among their fellow peers – not by the whole population.

Collectively, the House of Commons has three main roles:

1 *Law-making:* Most public bills come from the government of the day, although some are introduced by backbench MPs. In Parliament, bills pass through 11 stages, five of which are in the lower house.

2 *Raising and spending public money:* Parliament's permission is needed for both aspects of financial control, but it has difficulty in exercising stringent control over the ways and efficiency with which money is spent.

3 *Acting as a watchdog over government:* Probably the most important feature of the contemporary House of Commons is scrutinising and influencing the government. Scrutiny is carried out in several ways, via questions (e.g. **prime minister's questions**), debates, committees and by the opposition parties. The **leader of HM opposition** and opposition **chief whip** are salaried posts.

The House of Lords

The House of Lords has a fluctuating membership of usually around 730 members. This includes predominantly **life peers**, archbishops and senior bishops, law lords and '**elected' hereditaries**. It was reformed by the Blair government in 1998 to eliminate its many **hereditary peers**, but further change in the character of the upper House has been under consideration over the last decade. There is difficulty in reaching agreement between the main political parties over the future composition of the Lords. Some want it fully elected, some partially elected, some indirectly elected and some fully appointed (without the 92 elected hereditaries).

The second chamber spends around 60 per cent of its time examining legislation and 35 per cent or so on scrutinising the work of government. Its specific roles are as follows:

■ *To act as a revising body, considering and amending bills that have been passed through the House of Commons* as they go through five more stages in the upper house. (Once approved by both chambers, bills are sent to the Queen to receive the Royal Assent.)

■ *The initiation of some non-controversial bills:* About a quarter of bills begin their parliamentary life in the House of Lords, ones on which there is unlikely to be strong party disagreement.

■ *To exercise – where necessary – a power of delay over bills from the House of Commons where peers are unhappy with the legislation brought forward:* Under the Parliament Act (1949), they have a power of delay, which provides an opportunity for further consideration and reflection.

■ *To hold general debates:* Peers have a less crowded timetable than MPs and more opportunities to hold general debates on important themes such as climate change and leisure opportunities.

The executive

We can distinguish between the political executive (the elected politicians who are part of the government of the day) and the official executive (the bureaucracy of officials whose task is to administer the policies that ministers have laid down). We are primarily concerned with the elected politicians who are ultimately accountable to us and over whom we exercise some control by the use of our votes on election day.

The government comprises some 125 paid and unpaid members. The junior ranks include ministers of state and parliamentary under-secretaries who work in departments of state such as the Treasury and Home Office. We are more concerned with the 20 or more ministers who head their departments and serve in the Cabinet. Of these, the prime minister is the leading figure.

The Cabinet

The Cabinet is the central committee that directs the work of government and coordinates the activities of individual departments. It has been described as 'the core of the British constitutional system'. Its members assume responsibility for all decisions on behalf of the government. It was common to describe the British political system until the mid-20th century as one of 'cabinet government'. Today, it is rather more common to hear references to 'the passing of cabinet government' or to 'prime ministerial dictatorship'.

Fig 10.6 *The first Brown Cabinet in jovial discussion, June 2007*

There is a pecking order within the Cabinet. In Cabinet meetings, the attitudes and preferences of more senior ministers normally carry more weight than those of others present. The prime minister is at the helm, followed by the Chancellor of the Exchequer, foreign secretary and home secretary. The relationship between prime minister and Chancellor is crucial. If they are united in their stance on a particular issue, other ministers will find it hard to achieve any contrary objectives. Throughout the Blair administrations, there was regular tension between the Prime Minister Blair and Gordon Brown.

The prime minister: prime ministerial government

The prime minister (PM) is head of the executive branch. The prime ministerial role includes:

- leadership of the party in the country and in Parliament
- responsibility for the appointment and dismissal of members of the Cabinet, acting as its chairperson; appointment of other members of the government
- leadership of the government at home and abroad
- responsibility for a wide range of appointments, exercising a considerable power of patronage
- determination of the date of the next general election within the five-year parliamentary term.

The PM has several other responsibilities, ranging from overseeing the security services to liaising with the monarch in a weekly meeting, keeping

Further information

Membership of the House of Lords (March 2009)

- 742 peers in total (of whom 148 were female)
- 601 life peers
- 92 elected hereditaries
- 23 law lords
- 26 bishops.

Activity

Go to the Parliament website (www.publications.parliament.uk/pa/pabills) and find examples to illustrate the recent legislative work of the House of Lords. List any that you think are particularly beneficial or harmful to the citizen.

her informed of what the government is doing and advising on matters such as the constitutional implications of a royal marriage or divorce.

Some of the central elements of prime ministerial power are:

■ electoral success

■ the power of appointment and dismissal of Cabinet and other ministerial offices

■ power over the structure and membership of **Cabinet committees**, any of which the PM may chair

■ the central, overseeing non-departmental nature of the office

■ leadership of the party

■ the distribution of patronage

■ [for some] wartime leadership

■ use of the media, in particular television

■ a high degree of public visibility.

These features operated for much of the 20th century, but since the 1980s prime ministers have been more high-profile than ever previously. They are regularly seen on television as a result of international summitry, gatherings of the United Nations, NATO, **G8** and the European Union or bilateral meetings with the American president.

Summary questions

1 What is the role of Parliament in the system of government?

2 Why do some commentators say that we now have 'government by prime minister'?

3 Does your experience of life under the Brown government confirm the thesis that prime ministers dominate their cabinets?

The judiciary

The term 'judiciary' includes those individuals and bodies (primarily judges and the courts) involved in administering and interpreting the meaning of laws. For further elaboration of the character, role and personnel of the judiciary, see Chapter 7 The Legal Framework.

The role of judges in the political life of Britain and several other democracies has been expanded in recent years, particularly since the 1980s. Senior judges have been more vocal in venting their views on issues of public policy and more willing to challenge governmental decisions.

■ Local government and why it matters

By local government, we mean the government traditionally provided by elected local authorities, usually known as councils. These councils originally provided many of the local public services, but they do not do so today.

Local government is part of the framework of multi-level governance in the UK, with its European, national and devolved dimensions. Many people agree that it is a good idea to have a tier of administration close to them, but they generally show little interest in or enthusiasm for the actual work of their councils.

The case for local government is based on two interrelated themes – policy effectiveness and democracy. Local government is based on the principle that public policy decisions should be made as close to the people as possible. The reason for this is that centrally imposed solutions may prove inappropriate in many areas. Local councils can provide the most appropriate local response to a particular situation, based on their local knowledge, matching services to particular needs. Councils are also more accessible to local people who can more easily seek redress for any problems they face. Finally, individual councils can be used to experiment with new ideas and policy innovations. Overall, local government allows for diversity and flexibility.

In addition, because local government is closer to the people than central government, it is therefore more accountable. Elected local councils help to strengthen the democratic process, encouraging as they do the participation of citizens, by voting or standing for office. Moreover, the network of councils means that there are multiple centres of power, acting therefore as an important safeguard against an over-powerful national government, a bulwark against excessively centralised control.

Should we care about local government?

- *It plays an important part in our lives:* Although it has lost functions and powers in recent decades, the Local Government Association calculates that it still provides around 700 different functions. Local authorities educate our children, provide social services for people who are vulnerable or need support, safeguard and protect the environment, and provide libraries, cultural and leisure facilities. They are at the very heart of our daily lives. Some 2.1 million staff work in local government, which is responsible for about 25 per cent of all public expenditure.

- *The principle of **local democracy** is an important one:* Whether or not people turn out and vote in council elections, local government still matters precisely because it is local government. People who know the area are more likely to be sensitive to local needs and be better able to respond when action is needed than someone who operates from Whitehall. It also provides scope for community government and local participation. Most residents who show any interest will be content to be voters, but a few may choose to stand for office. Either way, the chance for participation is provided and via local involvement some people will go on to engage in national politics. Such involvement means that government has local support. This helps to strengthen democratic values.

There are several grounds for anxiety about the health of local democracy. These include:

- the loss of powers to unelected alternatives
- poor turnouts
- the tendency for voters to cast their vote on national grounds
- the use of the FPTP (first-past-the-post) electoral system
- low levels of interest and participation in local government
- widespread ignorance of what it actually does.

Add in the criticism of the quality of many local councils and councillors, and the number of scandals that have seriously undermined public confidence, and the picture of local democracy in action may seem a dispiriting one.

Key terms

Local democracy: a principle that embodies both the idea of local autonomy (self-government) and popular responsiveness. In action, it implies the active interest and participation of an informed citizenry in elected local government and all that it represents.

Key terms

Unitary councils: all-purpose councils that provide the whole range of local government services.

Directly elected mayor [of London]: the spokesperson for the capital; establishes strategies on transport, spatial development, economic development and the environment; and sets budgets for the GLA, Transport for London, the London Development Agency, the Metropolitan Police and London's fire services. The Greater London Assembly scrutinises the mayor's activities, questioning the incumbent about his or her actions and decisions.

Corporation of the City of London: provides local government services for the 'Square Mile' of the City of London. It combines its ancient traditions and ceremonial functions with the role of a modern and efficient local authority, looking after the needs of its residents, businesses and over 320,000 people who come to work in the 'Square Mile' every day. The City is the oldest local authority in the country. It operates on a non-party political basis.

The structure of local government

(NB In this section, the emphasis is on local government in England and Wales. Scotland has distinctive arrangements. For instance, the Scottish government is contemplating the end of the council tax and replacing it with a local tax on incomes.)

Local government has been frequently reorganised in a series of Acts passed by central government in recent decades. As a result, there is now a patchwork system, in which some areas have one tier and others two tiers of authorities to provide their services.

The one tier or **unitary councils** include 36 large metropolitan areas (e.g. Birmingham, Coventry and Walsall) and a further 46 in the rest of England (e.g. Bristol, Milton Keynes and Reading). Scotland and Wales both have a system of unitary authorities. Unitary authorities are said by their admirers to have certain advantages. Notably, they:

- promote local democracy by placing responsibility on one authority for the whole range of local services
- reduce administrative costs
- improve the quality of local services.

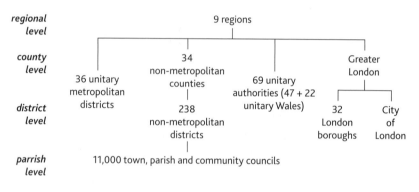

Fig. 10.7 *The structure of local government in England and Wales*

In other parts of England, there is a two-tier structure of 34 county councils, below which are 238 district councils. In a shire county such as Staffordshire, there is a county council and below it a series of district councils (e.g. Cannock Chase DC and Lichfield DC).

The two-tier system has been strengthened by the Labour proposal, backed in a capital-wide referendum in 1998, to recreate an all-London assembly led by a **directly elected mayor** responsible for overall strategy in Greater London. The new system of London government began to operate in 2000. London retains its 32 borough councils (which have a status similar to the metropolitan district councils in shire England) and the **Corporation of the City of London**.

The councils referred to above are sometimes designated as 'principal authorities'. In addition, an historic and diverse tier of around 10,000 sub-principal authorities also exists in the form of community, parish and town councils, made up of nearly 100,000 councillors. These first-tier councils cover very small areas and do not possess much formal political power. They have influence at the very local level, deriving primarily from their ability to respond to the needs of the local community. Many are involved in tasks such as providing and managing facilities such as cemeteries and churchyards, community centres and parking places, as well as having responsibilities for licensing, planning and promoting tourism.

The difficulty in any of the attempts to reform the structure of local government in recent decades has been to achieve a balance between promoting efficiency and maintaining a sense of community. Units need to be large enough to be viable and able to operate and sustain a broad range of services. But they also need to match the local communities with which people easily identify.

Further information

Large and small local authorities

The general assumption is that the larger the organisation, the more efficient it can be. Large local authorities have the merits of:

- being able to go in for bulk purchasing of resources
- using manpower more efficiently
- being in a position to raise substantial funds for large-scale local projects
- being able to cope with large tasks such as economic development, road building and transport.

However, changes in local government have helped smaller authorities, in that:

- It is now easier for local authorities to cooperate to organise large-scale services. This enables authorities to remain small, yet share in the control of major responsibilities.
- The trend to 'buy in' rather than provide local services means that they can negotiate to obtain services at the best price available from private companies and voluntary organisations.

What local authorities do?

- District councils are responsible for environmental health, housing (including the provision of social housing and housing benefit), leisure, refuse collection, revenue collection and local roads.

- Counties are responsible for more strategic services such as education, fire and ambulances, libraries, main roads, refuse disposal, social services, trading standards and transport.

- Unitary authorities exercise all of these functions.

Local authorities sometimes provide services on a joint basis with other authorities through bodies known as joint boards. Joint boards are not directly elected but are made up of councillors appointed from the authorities covered by the service. Typically joint boards are created to avoid splitting up certain services when new unitary authorities are created or a county or regional council is abolished. In other cases, they are established if several authorities are considered too small in terms of geographic size or population to run a service effectively by themselves. Typical services run by joint boards include fire services, public transport and sometimes waste-disposal authorities.

Devolved government

Before 1999, there was, in Scotland and Wales, a system of **administrative devolution**. But decisions were still made in Westminster and implemented in Edinburgh and in Cardiff, where the Scottish and Welsh Offices were respectively located. From the late 1960s onwards, there was a growth in Scottish and Welsh **nationalism**. Many people in Scotland and Wales were dissatisfied with the way in which they were governed for the following reasons:

Activities

1. List any arguments in favour and against the idea that local authorities should be as small as possible.

2. The election of the mayor of London, Boris Johnson, in 2008 placed media spotlight on the office. Find out more about the powers the mayor exercises and the budget he controls.

Key terms

Administrative devolution: the transfer of administrative offices and responsibilities from central government in Whitehall to outlets around the country. It represents a decentralisation of the government machine.

Nationalism: the desire of a nation to be recognised as a state and run their own government.

Activity

Find out more about the 'oil issue' in Scotland. Why do many Scots think that the oil in the North Sea is Scotland's oil and why does it matter to them?

■ *Economic discontent:* Many Scots and to a lesser extent Welsh felt that their area suffered from unfair burdens, perhaps bearing the worst impact of economic recession, industrial decline, higher unemployment, poor housing or an **infrastructure** in need of regeneration.

■ *Remoteness from London:* There was a developing feeling that those who made the decisions knew or cared little about those who would be affected by them.

■ [In Scotland] *The 'oil issue':* For the Scots, there was in the early 1970s a new argument, the discovery of oil in the North Sea. To Scottish **nationalists**, 'Scotland's Oil' made the idea of a self-governing Scotland more viable.

■ [In Wales] *The 'cultural issue':* Welsh nationalism had been traditionally concerned with preserving the Welsh culture and language, rather than the pursuit of some form of home rule. Welsh nationalists were keen to see Welsh names used on road signs and more recognition of Welsh identity in the media.

The demand for devolution in Scotland and Wales

In Scotland in particular, there was an increased sense of national pride, a feeling that Scotland was a nation capable of governing itself. It had done so before it joined with England in the Act of Union (1707), which is why it still has distinctive features in the UK (e.g. its own currency and legal system). For many Scots, it was time to regain control of their national destiny.

The growing nationalist feeling in Scotland was expressed in support for the Scottish National Party (SNP), in Wales for Plaid Cymru (now simply known as Plaid). Many of the Scots who voted for the SNP probably wanted to vote for a party that more obviously put Scottish interests first, just as voting for Plaid Cymru was another way of expressing 'Welshness'. Many of them did not necessarily want national independence, complete separation from the rest of the UK, which was the stated policy goal of the two nationalist parties.

Pro-devolutionists wanted to see a transfer of decision-making to Scotland and Wales, so that decisions would be made by a Scottish Parliament subject to democratic control. They wanted **legislative devolution**, the power to make laws.

When New Labour was elected in May 1997, it carried out its promise to put the issue to the voters in Scotland and Wales. In referendums held in September 1997, the Scots overwhelmingly supported the creation of a Scottish Parliament with tax-raising powers. In Wales, the pro-devolutionists won by a very narrow margin. The Conservative Party (which won no seats in either country in the election) was opposed to devolution and campaigned against it in the referendum campaigns.

The passage of the Scotland Act and the Wales Act in 1998 gave expression to the wishes of the Scottish and Welsh voters.

Devolution in Scotland

Under the Scotland Act (1998), Scotland has a Parliament of 129 members (MSPs). The leader of the largest party in the chamber becomes first minister, the equivalent position of prime minister. He or she chooses an executive (since the 2007 elections, more often referred to as the Scottish government) that acts as a cabinet and is responsible to Parliament. The powers granted to the new devolved machinery cover broadly the same areas as those provided by the old Scottish Office, ranging from criminal law to education and policing to local government. '**Reserved powers**' remain with Westminster.

Fig. 10.8 *Inside the Scottish Parliament building at Holyrood*

The Scottish Parliament's power to make and amend laws means that it can shape a nation that is very different from England. Moreover, its tax-varying power gives the Scots flexibility in planning their social provision and the chance to offer more generous help to various groups than exists south of the border. The executive manages an annual budget, which in 2007–8 was more than £30 billion.

The Scottish Office continues to exist, but as much of its work has been taken over by the Parliament it operates on a much reduced scale and fulfils a different role. Headed by the secretary of state for Scotland, it is now part of the Ministry of Justice, based in Whitehall, London. Its role is generally to represent Scotland's interests at Westminster and to ensure that the devolution arrangements work as was intended.

Between 1999 and 2007, Labour controlled the executive in coalition with the Liberal Democrats. Since 2007, Alex Salmond has been first minister of an SNP minority government, backed by the Greens on a 'policy-by-policy' basis.

Strengths and weaknesses of Scottish devolution in practice

Labour justified its devolution proposals on two grounds. They would:

- strengthen democratic control; and
- make government more accountable.

In pre-devolution literature, there was discussion of 'a new style of government'. The suggestion was made that too often in the past those who made decisions on Scotland's behalf were out of touch with the prevailing views of the Scottish people. The new Scottish Parliament would differ from Westminster in that it would be responsive to the wishes and values of the Scottish people.

The number of Scottish decisions on Scottish issues has significantly increased since 1999, as the Scottish Parliament and executive have assumed responsibility for matters previously carried out by UK institutions. Several of the policies introduced by the coalitions have been

Key terms

'**Reserved powers**': powers reserved to Westminster, in other words still dealt with by the UK Parliament in London and not devolved to the Scottish government. These include matters concerning the constitution, foreign policy and defence, the exploitation of North Sea oil and abortion.

Activity

Find out how the graduate tax operates in Scotland. How does it differ from the English system of loans to finance higher education in England?

Fig. 10.9 *Alex Salmond (1954–), SNP politician elected as first minister of the Scottish Parliament in May 2007*

distinctive from those pursued in England and Wales. Under the Labour-led coalition:

- student tuition fees were abolished in Scotland, a graduate tax operating instead. An early move of the Salmond government was to end all fees paid by Scottish students studying at Scottish universities

- Clause 28 (on the teaching of homosexuality in schools) was abolished before other parts of the UK followed suit

- elderly people were given entirely free care in nursing and residential homes

- fox-hunting was abolished

- there was a gradual cull of the number of unelected quangos.

After more than eight years, it is possible to offer some initial assessment of the case for devolution and how it is working in practice.

In favour

1 *Devolution is widely seen as democratic:* It allows people to express their distinctive identity and have a say in the development of the life of their own particular regions. The new system has 'strengthened democratic control' and 'made government more accountable'. Such control of decision-makers and their accountability to an elected body are key criteria in any democratic system. Moreover, because the electoral system includes a strong element of proportionality, the executive can claim 'legitimacy' for its actions.

2 *Devolution provides a socially representative chamber:* The **list system** of proportional representation that elects 56 MSPs enables the voters to opt in greater numbers for minority parties and groups such as women and ethnic minorities who otherwise might fare badly under FPTP (first-past-the-post). The social composition of the Scottish Parliament has an impressive gender balance relative to that at Westminster. In 2007, 43 women (33.3 per cent) were returned, as was the Parliament's first ethnic minority member (a retired India-born businessman, who was brought up in Pakistan, became an SNP representative).

3 *Devolution preserves the UK as a political entity:* If it works, it could be the saviour of the UK, granting just enough power to satisfy legitimate national aspirations. Many people believe that the four nations count for more in the world by being part of the UK than they would individually. Also, they claim that interdependence is both inevitable and desirable in an island the size of mainland Britain.

4 *Devolution has resulted in distinctively Scottish policies:* The Labour-dominated executive, influenced by its coalition partners, introduced a range of measures that differed from those introduced by ministers at Westminster. In many respects, they have involved more generous treatment of particular groups in the population, such as students and the elderly.

Against

1 *Devolution got off to a poor start:* Disputes over the leadership of the executive and the soaring costs of the Parliament building served to discredit the cause in the short term.

2 *Devolution could lead to the break-up of the United Kingdom:* With different parts of the UK enjoying a degree of self-government, this is now a possibility. There is likely to be greater friction between London and Edinburgh now that the two centres of power are each controlled by different parties. The SNP will not be satisfied with devolution, a

---

Key terms

List system: the proportional voting system used in Scottish devolved elections, known as the additional member system.

Further information

The case for an independent Scotland

Estonia became independent in 1991 and since then has been building with innovation and originality to create an open, accessible and successful country … Visiting Estonia filled me with sadness on one hand and hope on the other. The most successful countries in Europe, both socially and economically, are the small to medium sized independent ones and Scotland has the potential and the resources to be immensely successful, but instead we are held back by a government centred on policies that are aimed at the South of England but which are irrelevant to Scotland. And we have to contend with a Scottish executive which takes its policy and its motivation from London. Jack McConnell and his Cabinet are not paperless; they are pointless.

Alex Salmond, 2005

halfway house between unity and independence. It views with envy the experiences of the Baltic States that have in recent years gained their independence and argues that – given its resources – Scotland also has the potential to exist as a viable state. It has an interest in creating conflict with London, to show that devolution cannot work in the long term. With the Scottish Nationalist Party heading the current administration, this is likely.

3 *Devolution has created a constitutional anomaly, the **West Lothian Question (WLQ)**:* The WLQ poses the issue of whether it is just or fair that members of the UK Parliament elected from Scotland can vote on issues only affecting England, whereas English MPs cannot vote on these same aspects in relation to Scotland. Moreover, it raises the issue of how it can be right that MPs elected to Westminster from Scottish constituencies can vote on educational policy for England, but not on educational policy affecting their own constituencies (a devolved matter handled by the Scottish Parliament).

The WLQ is a consequential feature of devolution, of treating parts of the UK differently from the whole. There is no easy answer to the situation, but a consequence of Conservative campaigning on the issue has been to make some English people feel that they are being treated less well. After all, Scotland has a Parliament (unlike England), plus a secretary of state in the Cabinet, over-generous representation at Westminster (more MPs than it was entitled to) until 2005 and a subsidy from the Exchequer.

Devolution in Wales

Under the terms of the Wales Act (1998), Wales was granted a 60-strong National Assembly rather than a Parliament. Elections are held under the same electoral system as in Scotland. Again, there is a first minister and executive, since 2001 more usually known as the Welsh Assembly Government.

The National Assembly is a less powerful body than the Scottish Parliament, as its name implies. It was not granted primary law-making powers, although in 18 areas it was given responsibility for secondary legislation and empowered to flesh out bills already passed at Westminster. It was also envisaged that it might act as a pressure group on the London government for greater consideration of Welsh interests.

Fig 10.10 *The Welsh National Assembly building, in Cardiff*

Welsh devolution in practice

Since devolution, Wales has experienced both minority and coalition governments. Labour has been in office, the executive currently being led by First Minister Rhodri Morgan. Critics have dismissed the devolved machinery as a 'talking shop', pointing to its lack of effective power. It is true that the powers are limited, but this has not stopped Wales from embarking on some policy initiatives that distinguish Welsh arrangements from those in England. SATs tests for seven-year-olds and prescription charges for under-25s have been abolished, and the first Children's Commissioner has been established in the UK. In addition, the **quangocracy** in Wales (much disliked by many Welsh people) has been tackled. Even before the new machinery was established, the Wales Act (1998) had provided for the removal of nine quangos and more were due to be abolished at a later date.

Having had experience of limited devolution in practice, many Welsh politicians have argued that the Welsh National Assembly needs more power. The former Labour Secretary of State for Wales Ron Davies always claimed that devolution 'was a process, not an event'. In other words, it would be possible to build upon the existing arrangements. In the White Paper, 'Better Government for Wales', published in mid-2005, the UK government proposed a halfway house between the status quo and giving the National Assembly full Scottish Parliament-style legislative powers. The resulting Government of Wales Act (2006) reformed the National Assembly for Wales and allowed further powers to be granted to it more easily. It created a system more akin to that of Westminster. Some of its provisions were:

- to make the executive body – the Welsh Assembly Government – separate from the legislative body, the National Assembly for Wales (previously, it was in effect a committee of the Assembly)
- to grant the Assembly a greater legislative role, more similar to that in other devolved legislatures. In particular, it provided a mechanism for **Orders in Council** to delegate power from the Westminster Parliament to the Assembly, giving it more power to make 'measures', although Order-in-Council requests were made subject to the veto of Westminster.

After the 2007 elections First Minister Rhodri Morgan, in the third Assembly term, led a Labour–Plaid coalition administration, the first Welsh Assembly government to be in a position to utilise the increased powers.

Devolution in Northern Ireland

The politics of Northern Ireland have been complicated and often bedevilled by the weight of past history. It is the least integrated part of the UK, often viewed as 'a place apart'. It has a distinctive history and political culture, and poses a unique constitutional problem. The Protestant majority prefer the province to be governed as part of the UK, whilst many members of the large, predominantly Catholic minority would prefer to see the island united as one Irish republic. Reaching any accommodation between two groups that adopt a very different outlook has been extremely difficult despite the efforts in recent years of the British and Irish governments to bring about a resolution of the problems.

The Major government took steps to bring about a peace process in Northern Ireland. For the first time, **Sinn Fein** had the chance to become involved in the negotiations about its future. After 1997, the Blair government gave the process a new momentum that culminated in the publication of the **Good Friday Agreement** (1998). Under its terms an

---

Key terms

Quangocracy: the collective name for the many unelected quangos that make up what some see as a quango state.

Orders in Council: a type of legislation formally made in the name of the Queen by the Privy Council.

Sinn Fein ('We ourselves'): a political party that supports the idea of a united Ireland and wishes ultimately to sever the link between Northern Ireland and the British Crown.

Good Friday Agreement: signed in April 1998 by the British and Irish governments and the parties in Northern Ireland. It created the machinery for devolved government and a mechanism for resolving the troubles that had long beset the province.

Assembly and executive were established, although they were suspended on four occasions. However, in May 2007 the machinery was re-activated and is now up-and-running. The power-sharing executive is controlled by an unlikely coalition of the two traditionally hard-line groups within the political community, the **Democratic Unionists** and Sinn Fein.

Table 10.3 *The differing powers of UK devolved bodies: a summary*

Type of devolution	Scottish Parliament	Welsh National Assembly	Northern Ireland Assembly
Administrative devolution: Execute services Allocate funds Organise administration	Yes	Yes	Yes
Legislative devolution: Make, repeal and amend laws	Yes	No law-making powers, but can now 'make measures'	Yes
Financial devolution: Ability to raise taxes Vary taxation independently	Yes	No	No

Regional government in England

There are many different interpretations of the term 'regionalism'. In some minds, the term is used to refer to the presence of offices of central government located in the regions that have responsibility for particular aspects of administration. At the other end of the spectrum, it implies a more radical change to the constitutional structure, the creation of elected regional assemblies. England has no tier of elected regional government, although it does have a long tradition of administrative regionalism.

The case for elected regional government has at times been advocated by some academics and Labour politicians, as well as by the Liberal and then Liberal Democrat Party. It rests on a number of arguments, well summarised by Stoker (1996):

1 The *political case* stresses the way in which a system of regional government could serve to revitalise British democracy. It emphasises the centralised nature of British government that fails to cater adequately for the differing interests, needs and values of the various regions. It wishes to draw power down from the centre, restoring faith in politics by bringing it close to the people.

2 The *economic development case* is based on the need for effective governmental capacity at the regional level in order to produce coherent strategies for economic growth in all regions. This would draw on local capacities, skills and resources and plan a coordinated approach to investment, training and transportation for each region.

3 The *European case* is based on the idea that a 'Europe of the Regions' has been a developing theme within the EU. In several countries, there has been a recognition that the best way of maximising influence in Brussels and ensuring a flow of EU aid is for regions to make their own bids for economic assistance.

4 The *technocratic case* is based on the complexity of problems in today's society. Ecological, economic and social problems are complex and require tailor-made and appropriate solutions, rather than top-

Key terms

Democratic Unionists: a hard-line Unionist political party in Northern Ireland, currently the leading party in the Northern Ireland executive.

Activity

List any reasons why Northern Ireland was granted a more powerful form of devolution than that given to Wales.

down ones imposed by central government, which lacks the time and expertise for strategic and policy planning.

Labour's initiatives post-1997

When Labour came to office there was no strong tradition of regional government in England and a complete absence of elected representative regional institutions. The party was sympathetic to regional development, but settled in the short term for the following:

■ Eight Regional Development Agencies (RDAs) plus a later one in London, from 2000. RDAs are appointed by and directly accountable to ministers in Whitehall. Their task is to further economic development and the regeneration of the regions, as well as promote a regional strategy.

■ Indirectly elected Regional Chambers (usually called assemblies) in each of the RDA regions, to provide a modicum of democratic oversight and accountability. From 2003, each region could establish an elected assembly, if approved by the voters in a referendum. In 2004, the North-East voted overwhelmingly against such an assembly. Other referendums planned for North-West England, Yorkshire and the Humber were either postponed or abandoned.

Rising English national feeling

The early policies of the devolved government in Scotland (e.g. its more generous treatment of students and the elderly) encouraged some people in England to think that the Scots are favourably treated and that England is the loser under devolution. There has been a rising tide of English nationalism. It has its roots in a perception among many people in England that they are English, rather than British. However, it can best be seen as a reaction to the establishment of devolved administrations in Scotland, Wales, Northern Ireland and in other historic European nations such as Catalonia and Flanders. Of particular importance to the rise of English nationalism has been the publicity surrounding the West Lothian Question (see page 234), which is widely seen as being hard to justify on a logical basis.

Activities

1 Find out more about the referendum in the North-East (2004), in which the voters rejected the idea of an elected regional government for the area. Were the voters unwise to reject the chance to have an elected assembly?

2 Is there a case for having such an elected regional tier of government? What problems might the introduction of such a scheme encounter? To help you in your response, try thinking of how you would divide England into eight to 10 regions.

Campaign for an English Parliament

The future of England

An open one-day conference on the future of England post-devolution

SPEAKERS INCLUDE

Frank Field MP
Birkenhead

Canon Kenyon Wright CBE
Executive Chair,
Scottish Constitutional Convention

Simon Lee
Department of Politics & International
Studies, Hull University

Bob Peedle MBE
Royal Society of St George

Saturday 26 April 2008

Conway Hall, 25 Red Lion Square
Holborn, London WC1R 4RL

10.30 am – 4.30 pm

Fig 10.11 *Poster issued by the Campaign for an English Parliament, which advocates 'a devolved parliament with all the powers of the Scottish Parliament, maintaining the unity and the identity of England as a distinct nation with her people receiving the same advantageous and generous financial deal as Scotland and Wales receive'*

■ Further information

England's disadvantage?

'The real loser from Labour's chaotic approach to the constitution is England. The people of England now find themselves governed by political institutions that are manifestly unfair to them. First, the English are under-represented in Parliament … second, the English do not have an exclusive say over English laws.'

William Hague, Conservative MP and former party leader

Some Conservatives believe that at Westminster only English MPs should be able to vote on English legislation. The proposal would make defeat of a Labour government more likely on contentious legislation, for most Labour governments of recent years have been reliant on their electoral success in Scotland and Wales to provide them with a parliamentary majority. The government responds by questioning the existence of purely English legislation.

Summary questions

1 Has devolution been good for Scotland and Wales? Has it been good for the United Kingdom as a whole?

2 Could devolution eventually lead to the break-up of the UK? How might this come about?

3 Has England got a 'raw deal' under devolution?

4 How decentralised is British government today?

Activity

Is there a case for an English Parliament? You might consult the website of the Campaign for an English Parliament (www.thecep.org.uk) to help you make up your mind.

The powers of local government

Local government in Britain has no constitutionally secured powers, as the UK lacks a written constitution. All local authorities have been created by Acts of Parliament and Parliament is free to remove functions from local councils as it wishes. Local government can only act in those areas specifically laid down by Parliament.

In spite of these controls, the system of local government was for many years an active and vibrant one. It reached its heyday in the period after 1945, in what now seems to have been in some respects a golden period for local government. The growth in local spending coincided with the creation and expansion of the welfare state. Councils assumed additional responsibilities particularly in areas such as social services, spending a growing share of the national income, employing more people and enjoying a considerable degree of freedom to determine local policy responses. The boundaries of policy were laid down in London, but local government was responsible for the direct delivery of the majority of public services that directly impacted upon people's lives, notably in education and housing. There was ample scope for authorities to adapt the specifics of national policy to local conditions according to the mandate they received from their local electorate.

Local government since the 1970s

The situation began to alter in the mid- to late1970s, when the expansion of provision came to an end. Most noticeably, it was the impact of Thatcherism that began to change the political agenda as far as local councils were concerned. Conservative ministers of the 1980s–90s wanted a greater role for the private sector in the delivery of local services, stressing the enabling rather than the direct service provision role of local government. In the field of public housing, in addition to the policy of selling council houses, active encouragement was given to the involvement of non-governmental agencies such as housing associations. In education, previously an area of relative local **autonomy**, central control was increased in several ways, most obviously by the introduction of the national curriculum. The government placed the emphasis on consistency and efficiency rather than diversity and choice.

As a result of the changes made, many commentators felt that after 1979 there was increased central control over local councils, involving a reduction in the degree of local autonomy. In 1997, the new Blair government was committed to giving councils a higher profile and restoring life and vigour into the way they functioned. Prime Minister Blair was keen to revive this failing area of British democracy. It would be 'modernised … re-invigorated … reborn and energised' under Labour rule. New Labour's plans for reviving of local democracy included:

Key terms

Autonomy: self-government, in effect allowing greater freedom to subordinate authorities to shape the character of their communities.

Key terms

Compulsory competitive tendering (CCT): compelling local authorities or other bodies to ensure that specified services are opened up to private tender when new contracts are being awarded. It was introduced by the Conservative government in the 1980s, in an attempt to bring cost-cutting and greater efficiency.

Best Value: contracts are awarded on the basis of evaluation of cost and non-cost factors, which is intended to ensure that services meet the needs of local people in terms of quality and efficiency.

Progressive: in terms of taxation means that those who earn more in income pay proportionately more in taxation. It therefore helps the lower paid, who pay a more modest amount.

Capital value: the amount that a house is worth on the open market – i.e. the amount for which it might be sold. The council tax at present is based on 1992 values and is therefore very out-of-date.

Activity

List the reasons why local government was in an expansionary phase for some 30 years after 1945 and the steps taken by central government that began to undermine it thereafter.

- the proposal for an elected mayor of London and a new assembly
- allowing councils throughout England the chance to consult the people in their vicinity about how they would operate in future
- replacing **compulsory competitive tendering (CCT)** with **Best Value** in 1998, retaining the principle of competition, but allowing contracts to be awarded on the basis of other factors as well as price.

Given the arrival of new players on the service provision scene (housing action trusts, registered social landlords (housing associations) and private companies etc.), councils have increasingly become enablers rather than providers, in the words of Osborne and Gaebler (1992) 'steering rather than rowing'.

Finance

The subject of local government finance is an important one because local councils are responsible for approximately a quarter of all public spending. National government, wishing to monitor the overall level of public expenditure, seeks control over the volume of local spending. It is also interested in the ways by which local authorities are financed. These methods may prove harmful to a significant element among the supporters of the party in power at Westminster. Voters might blame national government when they are asked to pay more in local taxation.

Since the 1970s there have been many suggestions about the most desirable way by which people should pay for the local services they use. On paper, any proposed system may seem preferable to the existing one, but in time they all founder on the fact that some group in the community seems particularly burdened by them. All have their winners and losers. In time, the losers begin to complain loudly about the unfairness they endure.

The trends in financing revenue expenditure over recent years have been that central government grants have significantly increased in importance (thereby reducing the financial independence of local authorities) and that the impact of locally raised resources has diminished. The most well-known form of local taxation is the controversial council tax, which was introduced by the Conservatives, via the Local Government Finance Act (1992).

The council tax

The council tax is a banded property tax. It is **progressive** in as much as it is broadly related to the wealth of the person who lives in it, as judged by the value of the house. (Better-off people tend to live in more expensive houses.) It is calculated on the basis of two adults living in the accommodation. There are rebates for the disadvantaged, including the least well-off and those who live alone.

In order to calculate the level of tax payable, property is rated according to its **capital value** in eight bands, A–H. These were laid down in the 1992 Act. The intention was that the banding of each house should be reassessed every 10 years, but as yet no revaluation has taken place.

At first, the council tax seemed to work fairly well and there were no serious problems in collecting it. Its basis was generally accepted as fairer than its predecessor. However, more recently, the tax has become highly unpopular and there have been calls for its replacement. Those who dislike it talk of its 'unfairness', wondering why we cannot have a system more geared to people's ability to pay. In particular, many older voters have felt unduly penalised.

Further information

Sources of revenue for local authorities

Councils have four main ways of financing their current (revenue) expenditure, which is used for spending on pay and the day-to-day costs of running services such as education:

- the council tax
- income from fees and charges for services (e.g. swimming pools and parking meters)
- grants from central government (or the devolved administrations in Scotland, Wales and Northern Ireland). These are in the form of the revenue support grant (RSG), the main block grant to local authorities, and special or specific grants, money allocated for a particular purpose such as policing
- income redistributed from central government, deriving from the uniform business rate (the property tax levied on businesses and other non-domestic properties) for the area; the rate is determined by central government.

Council tax banding, as determined by the capital value of domestic properties

Present bands

- Band A = up to £40,000
- Band B = £40,000–£52,000
- Band C = £52,000–£68,000
- Band D = £68,000–£88,000
- Band E = £88,000–£120,000
- Band F = £120,000–£160,000
- Band G = £160,000–£320,000
- Band H = £320,000 upwards

Activities

1 Try and find out what band your house is placed in, if it is a privately owned property. Also try and find out how much council tax is paid by your family per annum. Do you think that as a family you get value for money for the amount of council tax you pay?

2 See if you can find out any information about the Lyons Inquiry (2007), which examined the financing of local authorities. In particular, see what it had to say about two possible alternatives to the council tax: local sales tax and the local income tax.

Citizen participation within local government

Councils consist of local people, chosen by voters at regular and regulated elections to represent the communities in which they themselves live and work. These councillors or elected members are our representatives, our local government: elected by, accountable to and ultimately dismissible by us.

Many people know little and care less about what councils do. They seem to regard local government as hardly worth their attention, let alone their voting participation. Turnouts are traditionally low, lower than in many other Western democracies. As a broad trend, they have been falling in the post-1945 era. Today, only rarely does more than a third of the electorate bother to vote.

In 1999, average turnout in local council elections was 29 per cent – around 12 per cent in certain inner wards in Hull, Manchester, Sunderland and Wigan. In 2000, in one ward only 16 turned up at the polling booth (1.6 per cent). Since then, the average figure has hovered just under 30 per cent. In 2004 it was higher because polling was held on the same day as the Euro-elections. It was unusually high again in 2005, because election day was the same for the local and general elections. In 2007, it was 37 per cent.

Other than by voting, in what other ways can people convey their views to their councillors?

- By sending letters, e-mails and faxes, and via phone calls.
- By attending **surgeries**, which many councillors hold on a regular basis to discuss community issues.
- By attending council meetings, some of which are open to the public and where there may be a chance to speak.
- By attending any public question-time sessions that are held in several areas every few months.
- By responding to public consultation exercises on matters of community importance, such as development plans.

Key terms

Surgeries: held by councillors in local government as a means of meeting the people whom they represent on the local authority on which they serve. They are usually held at regular intervals, perhaps fortnightly. In the same way, MPs hold surgeries to meet their constituents.

Service as a councillor

The most active means of involvement is to stand for election to the council. Becoming a councillor is a rewarding form of public service that puts people in a privileged position where they can make a difference to the quality of other people's daily lives. However, being an effective councillor requires hard work. Every day, councillors have to balance the needs and interests of their residents, voters, political parties and the council. All of these groups will make legitimate demands on the councillor's time on top of their personal responsibilities to family, workplace and friends.

The work done by councillors

The councillor's role includes representing his or her ward and its residents, decision-making, policy and strategy review and development, overview and scrutiny, regulatory duties, and community leadership and engagement. However, the primary role of a councillor is to represent their ward and the people who live in it and to communicate council policy and decisions to them. Councillors representing political parties (as the overwhelming majority do) may find that their party offers advice and guidance on doing this.

Councillors cannot do the work of the council themselves and so are responsible for the appointment and oversight of officers, who are delegated to perform most tasks. Local authorities nowadays have to appoint a chief executive officer, with overall responsibility for council employees, and who operates in conjunction with department heads.

Councillors are not paid for their duties. However, regulations issued in 2004 allow authorities to provide basic, special responsibility and childcare and dependants' carers' allowances. The amounts payable are a matter for local determination. In this way, councils can take full account of their particular circumstances. The lack of payment discourages less well-off individuals in the community from coming forward, ensuring that many councillors tend to be self-employed or retired people who can make time available for council work.

Activity

Using the local newspaper to assist you, find out about the sorts of issues that councillors take up.

Case study

The role of councillors on Scarborough Borough Council

Why are Councillors important?

The position of councilors is vital in the local community because:

- they are a voice of the community
- they are champions of the users of local services
- local people know what is best for local communities
- they are critical to the effective functioning of democracy
- they play a very important role in helping to shape future services for the benefit of the local people.

What do Councillors do?

Councillors or Members are elected by local people to plan, run, monitor and develop Council business.

This includes taking part in partnerships with others to do this. Councillors work to improve the quality of life for people within the Borough and make decisions about local issues. Councillors are essential in deciding what is in the public interest amidst a range of conflicting issues and views.

Councillors usually represent a political party or they can be independent. All councillors represent all the citizens of the Borough.

The role of a councillor can be very varied and it is up to each individual councillor how they work. However, the three main areas of responsibility are:

1 Representing the people in their area (ward) and becoming a representative of the Borough

2 Community leadership

3 Helping to formulate Council policy.

A councillor's role ..... as a representative

Many councillors see their first and foremost role as representing their ward and the people who live there. To do this they can:

■ Hold 'drop-in surgeries', usually in community buildings such as a local community centre

■ Deal with constituent's enquiries about aspects of Council business e.g. claiming a discount for Council Tax

■ Undertake case work such as making representations on behalf of an individual or a family

■ Explain Council policy and ensure that the policy is carried out fairly

■ Support local community partnerships and organisations

■ Campaign on local issues, championing the causes, which further the interests, quality of life and development of the community

■ Help to bid for resources for their ward

■ Encourage community participation and citizen involvement in decision making

■ Listen to the needs of local people and take their views into account when considering policy proposals and in decision making.

They also need to ensure local people are informed about services in the area, decisions that affect them and the reasons why decisions are taken by the Council.

A councillor's role ..... as a Community leader

Community leadership is central to the Government's thinking about modern local government. It involves partnership with other organisations ...

A councillor's role ..... as a policy maker

All councilors are involved in decision making. Councillors as members of full Council, meet with councillor colleagues from all political and other groups, to debate and approve Council business in a formal setting.

How much time would I have to commit?

It is for you to decide the level of commitment you are able to give to being a councillor and it also depends on your role within the Council and the number of commitments you take on. Most Councillors work between 10 and 30 hours per week, which includes attending Council meetings.

> **Activity**
>
> List the ways in which a councillor can help his or her community. Write a few sentences to say why people might wish to become a councillor.

Source: Extracts from A Councillor? Who .... me?, *produced with the kind permission of Scarborough Borough Council, www.scarborough.gov.uk*

The backgrounds of councillors

Table 10.4 *Backgrounds of councillors*

Characteristic	Conservative	Labour
Male (49)	74	74
Female (51)	26	26
Ethnic minority (6)	0.9	5.5
Managerial (17)	53	23
Professional (27) (technical)	26	28
Academic teacher/lecturer (4)	4	16
Administrative/clerical/sales (22)	11	14
Manual/craft (30)	7	19

Source: adapted from D. Wilson and C. Game, Local Government in the UK, *Palgrave, 2002*

N.B. The percentages for the whole adult population at the time of the survey are given in brackets after each group.

Why does local government not arouse more enthusiasm?

Several explanations have been offered:

■ *Local government lacks glamour.* Many people feel that all of the interesting and important things are decided nationally. In contrast, local councils can do so little that their work hardly inspires any effort to vote. Their powers have been curtailed by central government, successive pieces of legislation having severely restricted the functions and powers of local authorities.

■ *Some voters might think that voting is not worth while because in their area control never changes.* For several decades after 1945, Labour dominated in places such as Doncaster, Manchester, Sheffield and Stoke. If people feel that there is a chance that they might be represented by a candidate standing for their own party, there might seem more point in turning out.

■ *Local government has a poor image.* Often because of one-party dominance, there have been many stories in recent years of **cronyism**, **sleaze**, contentious land deals and wasteful 'junkets' (trips made at public expense) by councillors. The media has often focused on such 'negative' stories, partly because they are good items for local news bulletins and partly because local authorities do little that seems interesting or exciting.

How could people be made to care more about local government?

■ Create smaller authorities to encourage local democracy – but turnout is not always related to size and in any case this might not allow for the efficient provision of services.

■ Use a proportional voting system that is arguably more fair – but this is unlikely to improve turnout very much.

■ Encourage local authorities to create small area committees – but such community councils do little to arouse enthusiasm.

■ Grant local government more powers, so that voters know that key decisions are made locally.

Create a local supremo to get things done, as some authorities have by choosing to have an elected mayor for their region.

Summary questions

1 Does local government make any difference?

2 What are the benefits of the UK's unitary system of government?

3 Is council tax fair?

4 Do the views of citizens get sufficiently taken into account by local councils and councillors?

5 Does the individual citizen have a genuine voice in local government?

The impact of the European Union on life in the UK

The European Union (EU) today is a supranational and **intergovernmental union** of 27 European states. Established in 1993 by the implementation of the Maastricht Treaty, it is one of the largest economic and political entities in the world, having a total population of 494 million. Since its formation, new accessions have increased its membership and its competences (areas of policy responsibility) have greatly expanded.

The EU is difficult to characterise. It is neither a state nor just another international organisation, but it has elements of both. EU members have transferred considerable sovereignty to it, more than to any other non-sovereign regional organisation. But in legal terms, the states remain the masters, because the Union does not have the power to transfer additional powers from states to itself without their agreement expressed via further international treaties. Indeed in some key areas, member states have given up little national sovereignty, particularly in the matters of foreign relations and defence.

How the EU evolved

In the mid-1950s, representatives of six Western European countries met at Messina to discuss the steps they might take along the road to closer cooperation. In March 1957, they signed the *Treaty of Rome*, which established the *European Economic Community* (EEC). The Treaty still forms the basis of the European Union today. Its immediate goal was the creation of a customs union in which all internal barriers to trade would be removed, thus creating a tariff-free market. Beyond this, the countries aimed for 'a harmonious development of economic activities, a continuous and balanced expansion, an increased stability, an accelerated raising of the standard of living, and closer relations between its member states' (Article 2). The Common Market (as the EEC was widely known) was a means to an end, not the end in itself. The member states had in mind a greater goal – political union.

In 1986, all members of what was by then simply known as the European Community signed the *Single European Act* (SEA). According to the terms of the SEA, the remaining and more recently constructed trade barriers and customs duties between members of the by-then enlarged Community were removed, thereby creating a single market. In addition, agreement was reached that:

- there would be 'free movement of goods, persons, services and capital'
- the powers of the European Parliament would be increased

Key terms

Intergovernmental union: a union in which decisions are reached by cooperation between or among governments, by bargaining and often on the basis of consensus. It is often contrasted with supranationalism, which involves the transfer of some national sovereignty to a supranational organisation, that in turn acts on behalf of all the countries involved e.g. the transfer of powers from the UK to the EU.

■ Key terms

Qualified majority voting (QMV):
the method of voting within the Council of Ministers. Large states have more votes than small ones and specified numbers of votes constitute 'qualified majorities'. For instance, France, Germany, Italy and the UK all have 29 votes, Romania 14, Cyprus four and Malta three.

Social Chapter: was a protocol of the Maastricht Treaty committing member states to a range of measures concerned with the social protection of employees. It was subsequently incorporated into the Treaty of Rome at the Amsterdam summit (1997). Britain originally had an opt-out, but the Blair government soon signed the Chapter, under which rights such as paternity leave and the 48-hour week were granted.

■ the principle of qualified majority voting (**QMV**) would be introduced in EC decision-making.

The 12 states that signed the Single European Act agreed in its preamble that it marked another step towards 'ever-closer-union' of the European peoples. In 1992, member states went further and signed the Maastricht Treaty, which created the European Union (EU), as we know it today. They planned for the creation of a single currency (what was to become today's eurozone); promised social legislation via a new **Social Chapter**; extended cooperation into the areas of justice and internal security, and defence and foreign affairs; and introduced the concept of citizenship of the EU. All of us are citizens of the European Union.

Since then, the EU has continued to develop and expand. Further treaties signed at Amsterdam (1997) and Nice (2000) developed the Union by, among other things:

■ extending the powers of the Parliament and the use of QMV
■ introducing new and more transparent decision-making procedures
■ planning for enlargement
■ assuming greater powers over a number of policy areas such as justice and home affairs and the environment.

The relationship of the UK to Europe since the founding of the EEC

Table 10.5 *The enlargement of the EU*

Enlargement	Countries joining (size of EU)
1957, the starting point	France, Germany, Italy, Belgium, Luxembourg and the Netherlands (6)
First (1973)	Britain, Denmark and Ireland (9)
Second (1981)	Greece (10)
Third (1986)	Portugal, Spain (12)
Fourth (1995)	Austria, Finland, Sweden (15)
Fifth: part one (2004)	Cyprus, Czech Republic, Estonia, Hungary, Latvia, Lithuania, Malta, Poland, Slovakia, Slovenia (25)
Fifth: part two (2007)	Bulgaria, Romania (27)

In Britain, from the earliest days of post-1945 cooperation on the continent, there were doubts about the wisdom or desirability of the closer union that some European statesmen favoured. British ministers of either main party preferred the idea of cooperation in appropriate areas, where nations found working together to be to their mutual benefit.

However, by the early 1960s a growing number of British politicians began to reconsider Britain's aloof position, seeing dangers in isolating Britain from events on the European mainland. They came to believe that there were good economic reasons for Britain to seek membership of the EC. Many of them also concluded that Britain would have more chance of influencing world events from inside the Community.

■ Key terms

General de Gaulle (1890–1970):
a French general and statesman, who became the first president of the Fifth French Republic in 1958.

Edward Heath (1916–2005):
Conservative Party leader in 1965 and prime minister in 1970, he took the UK into the European Community in 1973. Later, he became a critic of Thatcherism and of Margaret Thatcher for her attitude to the EC.

Britain within the Community/Union

After **General de Gaulle** had twice blocked British moves to join the EC (1961 and 1967), the government of **Edward Heath** made a successful bid for entry. Britain joined in 1973. In a referendum held to confirm British membership in 1975, there was a majority of two to one in favour of continued membership on renegotiated terms. Many people believed that Britain would have a better future inside the Community than outside. However, there was little evidence of widespread popular enthusiasm for working in partnership with other member states.

The broad sympathy for British involvement began to change in the Thatcher years of the 1980s. But after the signing of the Maastricht Treaty, there was a developing and widespread popular feeling that membership was bringing difficulties rather than benefits. Moreover, as the tabloid press frequently pointed out, Brussels seemed to be too fond of interfering in our national life.

In office (and subsequently), Margaret Thatcher was a strong supporter of **intergovernmentalism**. She disliked the integrationist tendencies within the EC. Her preference was for an enlarged Community, one that was broader and looser. She always remained a firm **Atlanticist**, seeing merit in the '**special relationship**' that her government developed with US President Ronald Reagan during the 1980s. Subsequent Conservative leaders have shared her broad outlook. Her views were set out clearly in a speech at Bruges, in 1988 (see Further Information).

In opposition and office, New Labour has been broadly supportive of the EU. As prime minister, Tony Blair employed pro-European rhetoric and argued for 'constructive engagement' in the Union. His approach was at first well received by continental leaders. Yet the language used in the 1997 election was not markedly different from that of the Conservatives. It spoke of 'an alliance of independent nations choosing to co-operate to achieve the goals they cannot achieve alone'. Within a few years, several issues arose on which he found himself firmly defending national interests and in opposition to our European partners. The prime minister recognised that he was operating in a country where enthusiasm for the Union was limited and sometimes reluctant, in which membership was often seen as a necessity rather than a cause for celebration.

Further information

The Thatcher (Bruges) and Howard speeches
In a famous speech in Bruges (1988), Margaret Thatcher:

- rejected any form of **European super-state**
- made it clear that it was neither possible nor desirable to 'suppress nationhood and concentrate power at the centre of a European conglomerate'
- supported 'willing and active cooperation between independent states', rather than movement to ever-closer-union.

In Berlin (2004) then-Conservative leader Michael Howard expressed similar sentiments:

- Like some other British politicians, he was willing to strike a markedly more positive pro-European tone when addressing a continental audience.
- Yet, having stressed his wish for Britain to 'remain a positive and influential member of the European Union', he explained his wish to see a flexible EU. He also said that the Union must primarily serve the national interests of its members.

The UK and recent developments: enlargement and the Reform Treaty

The British have long been supporters of enlargement. Under the Thatcher and Major governments, they liked the idea of extending deregulated trading areas and welcomed the fact that the **new democracies** of Central and Eastern Europe saw free market solutions as being British driven. The Blair governments continued with the same policy. Above all, perhaps, the British have been attracted to the idea of enlargement towards the East because ministers have felt that it might help to slow down the pace of **integration** in the West. Being more committed to closer economic rather than political union, enlargement makes sense. It caters for the first, while making the second less certain

The enlargements of the Union to date have tended to take place in 'waves' of multiple entrants all joining at once, apart from in 1981.

Key terms

Intergovernmentalism: the process whereby decisions are reached by cooperation between or among governments. The usual method of decision-making involves a search for consensus. National sovereignty is not undermined by any surrender of the right to make decisions in the national interest.

Atlanticist: someone who is sympathetic to the US and favours a strong and positive relationship with it.

Special relationship: describes the warm political and diplomatic relations between the US and some Western nations, particularly Great Britain. The relationship has been the centrepiece of British foreign policy in the post-1945 era

European super-state: the idea of a centralised European state that is considerably more powerful than individual nation states. It represents the fear of those who detect the creation of what Churchill called 'a United States of Europe', which some see as the inevitable outcome of the trends of recent years, e.g. the creation of a single currency.

New democracies: those countries that formerly were controlled by the Soviet Union. After the fall of the Berlin Wall, almost without exception they became democracies and in several cases were keen to join the EU and benefit from its large market. Examples include Hungary and Poland, both now member states.

Integration: the process whereby independent states relinquish or 'pool' national sovereignty to maximise their collective power and interests. There has long been an integrationist thrust within the EU – led by France and Germany – as several member states have tried to strengthen the ties between member states by adopting common policies such as use of the euro.

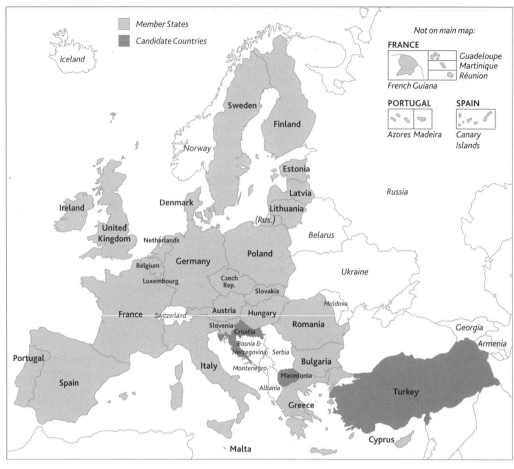

Fig. 10.12 *The 27 member states of the EU*

However, a more individual approach is likely to be adopted in future, although the entry of pairs or small groups of countries may yet coincide:

- Croatia may be expected to join at an early date (possibly around 2010).
- Albania, Bosnia and Herzegovina, the Republic of Macedonia, Montenegro, Serbia and Turkey are all likely future members.

Turkey's membership is contentious. It is regarded as a European state, but there are concerns over its record on human rights, its continued occupation of Northern Cyprus and its strong leanings towards **Islamicism**. Some commentators – including EU governments such as that of Austria – regard Turkey as too big, too poor (rapidly growing population and low average income) and too culturally different from the other member states to be an appropriate member.

Agreement on the Reform Treaty

In December 2007, Prime Minister Brown signed the Reform (Lisbon) Treaty, which was designed to streamline the workings of what had become a much-enlarged Union. It passed through and was ratified by the British Parliament early in 2008. However, all member countries have to ratify it before it can come into force. Its rejection by the Irish electorate has created uncertainty about how the EU can and should move forward.

The impact of the EU on government and politics in the UK

Membership of the EU has had an important impact on the British Constitution and on political life since the UK joined in 1973. With the passing of the SEA (Single European Act) and the signing of subsequent treaties, the trend towards more decision-making in Brussels has accelerated. In the process, many of our constitutional and political arrangements have been modified. Some of the most important effects have been those concerning the constitution and Parliament.

The impact on the constitution

Membership has had an important impact on the British Constitution and on British law. By joining the European Community, the UK agreed to accept a body of constitutional law that had already been passed since the creation of the EC. It continues to be bound by European law. This includes primary legislation (as found in the Treaty of Rome and the other treaties) and secondary law (as found in EU **regulations** and **directives**). European law takes precedence over UK law, is binding on the UK and applicable by UK courts. In several areas of policy, pieces of European economic and social legislation have conferred important rights on British workers, as in the area of equal pay.

On joining, the UK accepted 43 volumes of existing legislation that had never been passed by the House of Commons. Since then, most obviously in the *Factortame* case, several judgments have illustrated how the courts can overrule parliamentary legislation that conflicts with Community law. European law trumps national law. Such rulings have undermined the doctrine of parliamentary sovereignty. A sovereign Parliament acknowledges no restraint on its powers and can pass legislation without fear of being overridden. British law can now be changed by EU regulations and directives, even though the British government might oppose them. This is because the use of QMV in many areas of policy means that British ministers have no **veto** over what is decided in Brussels.

Fig. 10.13 *UKIP expresses its disapproval of the Reform Treaty, blaming commission president José Barroso for its return to the political agenda*

Further information

The *Factortame* case

- Came to prominence when a Spanish fishing company appealed in the UK courts against restrictions imposed on them by the Merchant Shipping Act (MSA) (1988).
- The company claimed that their trawlers were entitled to fish in UK waters under EC law.
- The High Court granted an order to disapply the relevant part of the MSA.
- The Court of Appeal and House of Lords took the view that under the British constitution the British courts did not have the power to suspend Acts of Parliament.
- The European Court of Justice ruled that national courts could disapply legislation that conflicted with EC law.
- Consequently, the Lords ruled in favour of the company, Factortame.

Key terms

Regulations: a kind of secondary legislation that is binding on all states, in the form that it is introduced (i.e. without any need for national legislation).

Directives: a kind of secondary legislation that is binding as to the result to be achieved, but can be implemented in a way suitable to each individual country (i.e. it passes its own national legislation to carry out the general intention).

Factortame: a landmark constitutional case (involving a fishing dispute) in the UK, which confirmed the primacy of EU law over UK law.

Veto: the right of any country to block a proposed initiative or law in the Council of Ministers. (It has been undermined by the extension of QMV in several policy areas.)

The impact on the executive and legislature

At the highest level, the PM and members of the Cabinet regularly have dealings with the EU. Some government departments are particularly involved in EU policy, so that the relevant secretaries of state will from time to time attend or even chair meetings of the Council of Ministers. The PM has a key role in the European Council. At home, in Cabinet and

■ Further information

A pro-European case

'It is patriotism, it is national self-interest, to argue for Britain's full engagement as a leading partner in Europe. It is a betrayal of our nation and our future constantly to obstruct every fresh opportunity for cooperation.'

'Britain must be at the centre of Europe ... it [is] almost the largest market in the world. It [is] the most integrated political union between nations ... To separate ourselves from it would be madness. If we are in, we should be in wholeheartedly ... For fifty years we have hesitated over Europe. It has never profited us ... ... We can indeed help to be a bridge between the US and Europe and such understanding is always needed. Europe should partner the US and not be its rival.'

Source: Tony Blair, speeches in 2000 and 2003

■ Key terms

Eurosceptics: people who are wary of the actions, institutions and policies of the European Union

Europhobes: people who dislike intensely any actions, institutions and policies that derive from the EU. Some would press their opposition to the point of withdrawal.

Cabinet committee meetings, European developments and issues often require discussion. Officials working in government departments are also much involved in European work. Within departments ranging from the Treasury to the Department of the Environment, Farming and Rural Affairs, there are European sections.

The workload of both chambers of Parliament has also been greatly affected by our European involvement. They tackle European issues in debates and at PM's Question Time and try to scrutinise the proposals initiated by the European Commission. The House of Lords has a highly-rated Select Committee on the European Communities whose 24 members consider all Union proposals and report to the House on those that raise important questions of principle or policy. Reports of the Select Committee are detailed and thorough, around 20 being issued each year. In the House of Commons, the Select Committee on European Legislation similarly acts as a filter for the Commission's proposals. The government of the day makes time available to consider reports of the Select Committee, though there have been criticisms that debates often get a low priority in the timetable and are relegated to late evening when the House may be poorly attended. In Parliament as in other legislatures of member states, the task of coping with the immense volume of European business poses serious problems. MPs often complain about the inadequate opportunities to examine European legislation.

The impact on the four 'Ps': parties, politicians, pressure groups and the public

The issue of European membership and more recently of the extent of British involvement in and commitment to the European Union has been a difficult one for the two main parties. Labour suffered internal divisions over its attitude to the European Community in the 1960s–70s. The Conservatives found the issue highly divisive in the late 1980s–90s. More recently, Labour has found the issue of the Reform Treaty a cause of schism. At times, the division has been between the Conservative and Labour parties. Sometimes, the intensity of the splits within the parties has been remarkable.

European issues have also influenced the fate of individual politicians. They caused enormous difficulties for John Major as prime minister, for he led a Conservative Party in which there were a few committed pro-Europeans, several strong **eurosceptics** or even **europhobes** and many more MPs in between who disliked the trend of events within the Union and the way in which their party was being damaged by the divisions they aroused. Major found himself trying to strike a middle way between two irreconcilable sides. His task was the more difficult because his predecessor – by then Lady Thatcher – on occasion used the European issue to undermine his leadership.

Whether or not they are pro-European in their approaches, individuals and groups have had to adjust to a world in which many of the policies that concern them are decided not in Whitehall/Westminster, but in Brussels. Most pressure groups have long recognised that in order to influence policy on issues such as agricultural and the environment, there is now more point in lobbying the Commission or MEPs, rather than British ministers or MPs. You will find more about this on pages 284–7.

The public has often seemed ill-informed and confused about the European Union. Its views have been sensitive to the attitudes adopted by political leaders and the media. When the voters were directly consulted on continued membership of the EC in the 1975 referendum, they gave an overwhelming (2:1) response in favour. On that occasion – and rarely since – the case for Europe was set out clearly by pro-European politicians. Since the late 1980s, at a time when there has been a developing momentum within the Union to drive the process of integration forward, the mood has changed. The position revealed in several polls has been that the majority of people broadly support staying in the EU, but lack any enthusiasm for closer integration and are sceptical about the attitudes and motives of continental leaders within the organisation. Most voters still do not feel truly European, in the way that some continentals do. Many French people feel both French and European; as the Dutch feel Dutch and European. This is not true of the British population.

The balance sheet of British membership

The UK has been in the EU since 1973. It has affected many aspects of our national life. It has not been an easy ride for governments or peoples. Those who support active involvement in Union affairs argue the following:

■ *The political case for membership:* The Union has been successful in reconciling two long-standing enemies (France and Germany) and has brought peace and stability to the continent. It has helped to create the growth and prosperity that ensures support for democratic values and institutions. Moreover, the movement towards closer economic and political cooperation has made Europe a respected force in the world, giving our country far more influence than it could exert if it left the EU. If we were to leave, it would be 'cold outside', for we would surrender our ability to influence what happens on the European continent and our voice in the world would count for little.

■ *The economic case:* The case for originally joining the EU was that Britain wanted to benefit from the large market that the original six had created. That market is now much larger and covers nearly 500 million people, providing British businesses with an outlet for their goods. Many businesses have been geared to continued membership, putting in a lot of effort into building up sales on the continent. To leave would cause them considerable disruption. Many British jobs now depend on trade with the EU. Similarly, the flow of inward investment has to some extent come about because Britain is a gateway to Europe, with easy access to its markets.

■ *The economic and social benefits of membership to UK citizens:*

1 The UK has received funding covering those employed in agriculture and those who have lost their jobs in manufacturing industry and benefited from aid from the social and regional development funds.

2 European money has been used on a range of projects around Britain, rebuilding city centres, renovating well-known buildings and landmarks, improving transport and establishing new industries and craft centres, among many other facilities that we all visit or use from time to time.

3 Improvements in environmental standards, such as cleaner beaches and better drinking water that derive from EU policies and court rulings.

4 There is the opportunity to work in the Union, a more realistic possibility since the passage of the SEA (Single European Act) and the harmonisation of qualifications.

Further information

Popular attitudes to the EU in the UK

Eurobarometer 70 (Dec. 2008) found that in the UK:

■ 32% supported membership of the EU (EU ave. 53%)

■ 39% saw clear benefits for the UK of membership (56%)

■ 26% had a positive image of the EU (45%)

■ 48% supported enlargement (48%)

BBC poll (Jan. 2009) found that 23% favoured joining the euro, 71% did not.

Activity

■ Why do you think that British people are more sceptical of the benefits of the EU than its inhabitants on the continent? Why might they be relatively sympathetic to enlargement? (See pages 236–8).

■ Write two paragraphs summarising the case that membership of the EU is good for the UK and a further two to argue the opposite case.

■ Does the European Union interfere too much in British life? List any examples of unwelcome interference. Does it matter?

A case against membership

The UK Independence Party is committed to withdrawing Britain from the European Union. As the debate on the new Constitution has now made clear, the EU agenda is complete political union with all the main functions of national government taken over by the bureaucratic institutions of Brussels.

'UKIP believes that this is not only bad for Britain's economy and prosperity, but it is an alien system of government that will ultimately prove to be totally unacceptable to the British people. UKIP would replace Britain's membership of the European Union with the kind of agreements on free trade and co-operation that we thought we had signed up to when we first joined what was then called the European Economic Community.'

Source: UKIP mission statement

The EU interferes too much

In an episode of the television comedy *Yes Prime Minister*, Jim Hacker won much approval for his lament about the threat to our national way of life:

'The Europeans have gone too far. They are now threatening the British sausage. They want to standardise it – by which they mean they'll force the British people to eat salami and bratwurst and other garlic-ridden greasy foods that are totally alien to the British way of life. They've turned our pints into litres and our yards into metres, we gave up the tanner and the threepenny bit. But they cannot and will not destroy the British sausage!'

European Economic Area: an organisation that enables three of the four members of the European Free Trade Association (Iceland, Liechtenstein and Norway) to benefit from the single market created by the EU, without actually being members of the Union.

5 New social benefits: some additional rights were acquired under the Social Chapter (see page 99), including the compulsory establishment of works councils, rights for part-time workers, parental leave and the 48-hour week. Another gain has been the provision of increased rights for women, particularly relating to equal pay, maternity benefits and compensation to pregnant women for unjust dismissal. Of course, EU involvement in policy areas such as education, health, housing and welfare is minimal, for these matters are primarily the preserve of national governments.

Fig. 10.14 *EU investment in the UK. Since Britain joined the European Community, many millions of pounds have been channelled into projects in the UK. Birmingham has made extensive use of EU funding to improve its facilities*

Those who doubt the benefits of membership make the following points:

1 *There are problems re budgetary contributions:* As a net contributor, we still hand over too much British money into the EU budget. We pay in far more than we get back via the various Union funds.

2 *Countries can flourish outside the EU, as does Norway:* As a member of the **European Economic Area** (as the UK would be), it gets the benefits of membership without any of the anxieties about the moves to integration.

3 *We have lost our ability to determine our own destiny and freedom of manoeuvre:* Too much policy is dictated from Brussels. Community laws and taxes cannot be changed by the British people.

4 *Some individual policies have been disadvantageous to the UK:* We do not benefit from the Common Agricultural Policy in the way that France does. The Common Fisheries Policy is much disliked by British trawler-men, many of whom find it hard to make a worthwhile living. Since enlargement, we have been open to extensive EU immigration from the new democracies of Central and Eastern Europe.

5 *There is a democratic deficit in the government of the EU:* We are subject to laws and taxes that MPs do not enact or even have the chance to scrutinise closely. They derive from the Council and Commission, which we do not elect and cannot therefore dismiss through the ballot box.

6 *The EU has evolved in a way that was never envisaged when Britain joined in 1973:* We thought we were joining an economic community, but its core members have increasingly tried to move the EU towards closer political cooperation. In the process, they are creating a giant super-state beyond our control.

Ultimately, the UK could withdraw from the European Union. This is the element of parliamentary sovereignty that remains unaffected. If one Parliament cannot bind its successors, then in the future a government could always bring in legislation to take Britain out of the Union. No country has yet left the Union, although in 1982 Greenland (a Danish territory) voted to leave in a referendum. Greenlanders were unhappy about the application of EC fisheries policy and felt remote from the distant Brussels bureaucracy.

Two EU policies and their impact on Britain

The environment: Britain directly involved

Green politics did not get under way until the 1960s, so there was no mention of environmental policy in the Treaty of Rome. However, as concern developed about damage to the atmosphere, fauna, flora, habitats, health and landscape, the Community began to adopt a range of initiatives in the 1970s and 1980s.

Above all, it was the passage of the Single European Act (SEA) in 1986 that marked the new departure in Community policy. The EC obtained formal authority to legislate on the environment in its own right. It laid down minimum standards in a number of areas. Three principles were put forward: prevention, remedying damage at source and the 'polluter pays for damage done'. The Maastricht Treaty added a fourth principle, namely that there should be 'sustainable and non-inflationary growth respecting the environment', as part of an attempt to reconcile economic progress with environmental concern. Sustainability has been defined as 'development that meets the needs of the present without compromising the ability of future generations to meet their own needs'.

In the 1980s and 1990s, Britain fell foul of EU requirements in several areas, most notably those involving water quality. There was a long-standing dispute over the standard of bathing water on British beaches, which in many cases failed to meet strict guidelines on water quality. In 1993, Lancashire County Council actually took the British government to the European Court of Justice for failing to clean up beaches at Blackpool, Morecambe and Southport. By the turn of the 21st century, there were significant improvements in beach quality. Beaches judged to be safe for bathing are entitled to fly the EU Blue Flag.

Most measures of environmental protection now originate in Brussels, so that British environmental policy is to a large extent dictated by EU directives. They have covered issues such as the release of pollutants into the air (1980), lead in exhaust gases (1982), the protection of wildlife, flora and fauna (1992) and various aspects of waste disposal (e.g. 2000 and 2001 – see the Activity on page 254).

The euro: Britain not directly involved

At Maastricht, various **convergence criteria** were agreed. Any would-be member of the single-currency zone would have to meet these before qualifying for entry. Eleven states were deemed to have met the convergence criteria in 1999 and proceeded to adopt the euro as their common currency. From day one the European Central Bank set a single

> **Hint**
>
> Now that you have read about the EU and how it works, consider the impact of the Union on you as an individual. How does it affect your life? You will have read in Chapter 1 that you are a citizen of the European Union. You have – or probably will have – a European passport and a driving licence. There is a European flag and a European anthem. Do these things make you feel European? Do you consider yourself to be British and European?

> **Key terms**
>
> **Convergence criteria:** the principles agreed at Maastricht to determine whether the economic performance of individual member states is sufficiently strong to enable them to qualify for membership of the single currency.

Fig. 10.15 *The euro, Europe's currency*

■ Key terms

National sovereignty: national independence, the idea that individual states have the ability to act as they feel appropriate, without having to pay regard to the decisions of some international agency.

interest rate for the entire eurozone. Four countries did not join: Britain, Denmark, Greece and Sweden. Greece became the 12th country to join and Slovenia was the first of the most recent batch of member states to join in 2007, followed by Cyprus and Malta in 2008 and Slovakia in 2009. Euro banknotes and coins have been in circulation since January 2002 and are now a part of daily life for 325 million Europeans living in the euro area.

Conservative ministers adopted a 'wait and see' approach to membership of the proposed single currency in the early to mid-1990s, some sceptical as to whether it would really happen. After the 1997 election, the Labour government advanced the position to 'prepare and decide'. As Chancellor of the Exchequer, Gordon Brown argued for Britain to wait until it was absolutely clear that Britain had satisfied the five criteria that he and his Treasury team had laid down as conditions for British entry. In October 1997, he told the House that he favoured entry in principle, but when he delivered his verdict in June 2003 he announced that only one of the five tests had been passed. Prime Minister Blair always seemed more enthusiastic about entry, but was aware of the lack of popular support for entry into the eurozone as well as the political opposition the issue aroused. Membership of 'euroland' for Britain seems unlikely in the near future.

Many British people are familiar with the euro. Those who go on holidays to several popular European holiday resorts regularly make use of it. Several High Street giants including British Home Stores, Marks & Spencer, Virgin and W.H. Smith agreed to accept it once it became the exclusive currency in the eurozone. In addition, many of those working in the City have embraced it enthusiastically. A large proportion of London business is devoted to euro products, such as bonds and insurance. London-based investment banks are closely involved in eurozone financing deals.

Table 10.6 *The impact of EU membership (see Activity 1 on page 245)*

Area of national life	Impact
Constitution	
Law	
Parliamentary sovereignty	
Executive	
Legislature	
Parties	
Politicians	
Pressure groups	
Public	
Influence in the world	
Economic and social life	

The contrasting workings of 'government' of the UK and the EU

There are five main institutions in the European Union. Three are supranational, involving a transfer of some **national sovereignty** to an organisation that acts on behalf of all the countries involved. Members are supposed to forget their national allegiances and see issues from a

Summary questions

1 What are the differences between supranationalism and intergovernmentalism?

2 How did the British outlook to Europe change when New Labour came to power?

3 What are the elements of continuity in the British approach to Europe in the post-1945 era?

4 'We have our own dream and our own task. We are linked, but not comprised … we are with Europe, but not of it' (Winston Churchill, 1946). Does the history of the British relationship with Europe support Churchill's portrayal of the situation?

5 Does the EU's democratic deficit matter?

6 Has the impact of the EU on British economic, social and political life been a force for good?

7 Is there an alternative to British membership of the EU? Explain your response.

Activities

1 Look up details of the End-of-Life Vehicle Directive (2000) and the one covering the disposal of refrigerators in 2001. Note a few details. These will enable you to demonstrate how decisions made in Brussels impact upon everyday life for British citizens.

2 You have now read through all the information on the EU. Make a larger copy of Table 6. As a recap, fill in the second column, to show you are aware of the impact of the EU on everyday life in the UK.

Further information

The legislative process within the European Union

When the Union decides to legislate, the procedure is broadly as follows, although there can be significant variations at stages 2 and 3:

1 The Commission proposes new legislation.

2 The Council consults on the proposal with the Parliament, which scrutinises (and may suggest amendments) and with the Economic and Social Committee, which advises.

3 The Council decides whether to go ahead.

4 The Commission implements the proposal.

5 The Court of Justice arbitrates on any infringement of the law and resolves any disputes.

European perspective. The other two are intergovernmental, providing opportunities for national governments to cooperate over a range of issues without surrendering national independence.

The three supranational bodies of the European Union are as follows:

1 *The European Commission is the Executive of the EU.* It not only acts as a civil service carrying out particular policies such as the running of the Common Agricultural Policy, but it also makes some policy decisions. Its political arm is represented by the 27 commissioners who collectively form the College of Commissioners. Each commissioner is nominated by the government of one of the member states (e.g. the UK commissioner in 2008, Peter Mandelson, nominated by the Blair administration, was replaced by Baroness Ashton of Upholland). The president of the Commission, from 2004 José Barroso, is the nearest thing the EU currently has to a head of government, attending European Council meetings and representing the EU at international gatherings.

The Commission remains the starting point of the decision-making process. However, in recent treaties, the powers of the Parliament have been increased. What was a dialogue between two institutions (the Council and Commission) has become more of a partnership between three of them.

The administrative arm is the EU civil service of around 20,000 officials who are based in 26 Directorates-General, each of them dealing with a different area of responsibility.

2 *The European Parliament is the legislative of the EU and meets in Strasbourg.* It receives reports from commissioners and holds debates and a question time. Much of its important work is done in committees that meet in Brussels. Parliament's legislative role was initially only advisory, but in every major EU treaty (e.g. the SEA, Maastricht, Amsterdam and Nice) its powers have been increased. On key areas such as the **Common Agricultural Policy** (CAP) and taxation it only gives an opinion, but under the **co-decision procedure** it can veto Union legislation in some important areas such as the single market and consumer protection. It has the power

Fig. 10.17 *The European Parliament in session: a political grouping expresses approval*

Activity

Find out the name of your local MEP. Using the internet to assist you, find out his or her party label. Look up any information about the sort of issue that he or she takes up in the European Parliament. Do you think that a person can achieve more as an elected representative in the House of Commons or in the Strasbourg body?

to dismiss the entire Commission. It can also accept or reject a new president of the Commission.

Parliament has been directly elected since 1979 in five-yearly terms, 2004, 2009 etc. There are currently 785 members.

Fig. 10.16 *The European Parliament in Strasbourg*

Case study

A day in the life of a Member of the European Parliament – Jean Lambert

A teacher by training, Jean has not found it difficult to adjust to the hectic lifestyle of an MEP since her election in June 1999. However since her re-election in June 2004, it seems that her work has increased significantly. Jean usually arrives in the office around 8 a.m. to address the matters that need her urgent attention.

Today Jean arrives in her Brussels office straight from the Eurostar terminal, collects her weekly agenda and then has a meeting with the shadow-rapporteurs and other MEPs about her Report on Asylum. Jean then speaks at an event organised by her office on the human rights situation in India and chairs the subsequent debate on caste discrimination and what can be done at EU level. Often Jean does not have time for lunch and has to grab a sandwich between meetings. Today she has a working lunch meeting on the Working Time Directive with a group of Trade Union representatives.

After lunch Jean goes to the Employment and Social Affairs Committee, which will last the whole afternoon. These meetings take place in Committee rooms specially equipped with microphones and headsets so that the team of translators who sit in the fish-tank like booths around the side of the main room can simultaneously translate the discussion into the Community languages. It is quite something to behold.

Once the meeting has finished, Jean returns to the office to check if there are any urgent messages or emails. She jots down a few notes for her speech at the seminar she has to attend tomorrow and then runs out again to meet representatives from AGE Concern at a reception for the launch of the Inter-group on Ageing (of which she is co President).

When Jean finally arrives back at her small flat situated close to the European Parliament she retires with a detective novel, her preferred literature, for some well-needed relaxation.

Although this has been a busy day for Jean, it is quite a typical day for her and while going to receptions or dinners may seem glamorous, it is the ideal place to meet NGOs, lobbyists and MEPs from other political groups and to exchange views in a more informal setting.

Jean divides her time between her London Constituency where she frequently attends weekend events, and the Parliament either in Brussels or Strasbourg.

'No politician I know works 9–5, Monday to Friday,' she reflects, '... as an elected person you are a public figure who is always in demand. It's just frustrating that there isn't time to pursue every issue raised by the people who voted you in.' Despite the hectic lifestyle, the constant travelling and the separation from her family, it is clear from Jean's animated enthusiasm that she relishes even the more challenging aspects of the job. 'I can't think of any other occupation with more possibilities for somebody who wants to influence real social and political change.'

Source: extract taken from the website of Jean Lambert, MEP

3 *The Court of Justice is based in Luxembourg.* The 27 judges rule on matters of EU law as it is laid down in the treaties and can arbitrate in disputes between member states and on those between the Commission and member states. It can levy fines on those states found to be in breach of Union law and on those that do not carry out treaty obligations. In 1989, a Court of First Instance was created to deal with the consequences of the Single European Act and specifically in order to protect the interests of individuals or organisations who feel that their national governments are penalising them in breach of Union law. This allows the Court of Justice to concentrate more on its interpretative role.

The two intergovernmental bodies of the European Union are as follows:

1 *The Council of Ministers (officially now the Council of the European Union) makes all policy decisions and issues directives like a government of the EU.* One minister represents each of the 27 countries. Usually this is the foreign minister, although it can be the secretary of state for defence if security affairs are being discussed or the secretary of state for the environment if appropriate.

Preparations for Council meetings are handled by COREPER, the Council of Permanent Representatives of Member States. This is made up of national ambassadors who speak and act on behalf of their member countries on lesser issues. Each member state in turn acts as president of the European Union for six months, January–June and July–December (see Table). In that period, the relevant ministers from that country chair all Council meetings.

2 The European Council meets every six months at 'summit meetings' held in the country holding the presidency at that time. It includes the 27 prime ministers or their equivalents from each country. They discuss broad areas of policy and help move the EU forward by

Further information

EU law

There are two categories of law in the EU:

■ *Primary legislation* is the body of law established by the founding treaties of the EC, together with all later amendments and protocols attached to those treaties.

■ *Secondary legislation* relates to all laws passed by EC/EU institutions. The main forms are regulations and directives.

Activities

1 Find out about the membership and role of five other EU bodies worthy of mention:

■ the Court of Auditors
■ the Economic and Social Committee
■ the Committee of the Regions
■ the Ombudsman
■ the European Central Bank

2 For each of the 10 institutions mentioned in this section, list the number of UK representatives who participate in it.

Table 10.7 *Rotating EU presidency, 2007–12*

Year	January–June	July–December
2007	Germany	Portugal
2008	Slovenia	France
2009	Czech Republic	Sweden
2010	Spain	Belgium
2011	Hungary	Poland
2012	Denmark	Cyprus

resolving disagreements between states and progressing difficult policy matters. (The UK has one representative.)

A democratic deficit?

A democratic deficit is a situation in which there is a deficiency in the democratic process, usually where a governing body is insufficiently accountable to an elected institution. The term is often applied to the lack of accountability in the decision-making processes of the European Union. The result is that there is a developing gap between those who are governed and those who seek to govern them. This is partly a consequence of the way in which the EC/EU evolved.

Particularly since the early 1990s, there has been a growing feeling that the EU has been developing in ways that are out of step with popular opinion and that the Union needs to be representative of the people and their concerns. Three specific issues have been singled out for criticism:

1 *The feeling that Brussels interferes where it should not:* To some extent this has been rectified by invoking the use of the doctrine of **subsidiarity**, which says that the functions of government should be carried out at the lowest appropriate level for efficient administration – i.e. at the closest level possible to the people affected by the decision.

2 *The absence of knowledge about what is going on in the central decision-making bodies:* Simpler legislation, better public information and allowing organisations representing citizens to have a greater say in policy making have gone some way to meeting the issue.

3 *The belief that Brussels lacks sufficient democratic legitimacy.*

This third deficiency is more difficult to address. There are concerns over the way in which institutions operate and the lack of democratic control over those who have the power to make decisions. As the EU has assumed more responsibilities, the power of its decision-making institutions has been increased and there has been a shift away from issues being examined in national parliaments. But the Council of Ministers is not elected, nor is the Commission. The Strasbourg Parliament is elected, but there are problems concerning the elections (see Further Information below) and in any case it has traditionally lacked teeth. The result is that there is still no very credible system of democratic control within the Union. There is no effective accountability of the Council or Commission to either the national parliaments or to the European Parliament.

Key terms

Subsidiarity: the idea that action should be taken at the level of government that is best able to achieve policy goals, but as close to the citizens as possible.

Further information

The European Parliament and its democratic credentials

Until 1979, the European Parliament was not elected.

Since then, there have still been problems concerning its legitimacy, such as:

■ the degree of public ignorance and lack of interest in several member states about the work of MEPs and matters concerning the EU

■ low turnouts in Euro elections

■ the lack of a common voting system

■ the fact that elections tend to be fought on national rather than European issues, so that people are not expressing a verdict on how well Parliament is performing

■ the lack of media interest and 'big political names' on the campaign trail.

Summary questions

1 Compare the membership and operations of the British Parliament and the European Parliament.

2 Why might a politically active person be more interested in becoming a member of the European Parliament than the House of Commons?

3 Should we be worried about any lack of democracy in the EU's governing arrangements?

11

Playing your part: how to get involved and make a difference

Learning objectives:

- ◼ to understand the concept of democracy

- ◼ to develop knowledge of democratic values

- ◼ to be able to analyse the question 'How democratic is the UK?'

- ◼ to understand opportunities and barriers to citizen participation

- ◼ to have knowledge of the electoral process

- ◼ to understand the citizen's role in elections

- ◼ to know about electoral participation, including recent turnout patterns and voter apathy

- ◼ to know about the impact of electoral campaigning on the citizen including the role of the media, opinion polling and focus groups

- ◼ to know about pressure groups

- ◼ to understand the targets and tactics of pressure groups

- ◼ to be able to discuss whether pressure groups weaken or strengthen the ability of citizens to influence political decision-making in a democracy.

Key terms

For Key terms for this page see page 250.

◼ What does 'taking part in the democratic process' mean?

The word 'democracy' derives from two Greek terms, *'demos'* meaning people and *'kratia'*, signifying 'rule of' or 'by'. Many people therefore see democracy as meaning 'people power', with government resting on the consent of the governed. According to Abraham Lincoln, democracy is 'government of the people, by the people and for the people'. The two forms of democratic action may be described as direct and indirect democracy.

Direct democracy

The Ancient Greeks were the first people to develop democratic ideas, democracy in Athens being practised in a small city-state. In ancient Athens, every qualified citizen (this did not include women, slaves and non-Athenians) had the opportunity to gather together in a large public place and vote directly on issues of current interest and concern. At that time, it was realistic for all citizens to meet and make decisions. This was **direct democracy** in action. For more on Athenian democracy, see page 1.

Direct democracy as conducted in Ancient Greece is largely impractical today. Scarcely any modern industrial society can claim to practise it in the original form, though elements of it survive in the **town meetings** held in parts of New England in the north-eastern USA. Referendums and **initiatives** also help to keep the flame of direct popular involvement in decision-making alive. Switzerland provides perhaps the closest approximation to the Greek model. It has a decentralised structure with opportunities for the public to vote regularly on political issues and policies, and exercise 'people power'.

Indirect democracy

In today's large and more industrialised societies, people cannot all get together to discuss and vote on issues. They elect representatives to act on their behalf. This is **indirect or representative democracy**. Key elements of a modern representative democracy include:

- ◼ popular control of policy-makers
- ◼ the existence of opposition
- ◼ political equality ('one person, one vote')
- ◼ political freedoms
- ◼ majority rule.

A democratic political system may then be defined as one in which public policies are made, on a majority basis, by representatives subject to effective popular control at periodic elections, which are conducted on the principle of political equality and under conditions of political freedom.

Elections are central to representative democracy, the people being consigned to the role of 'deciding who will decide'. Whereas in a direct democracy, the people can decide issues for themselves, in a representative democracy a few govern and the mass follow. The electors are vote-casters every few years at election time, but in between they have little say. This is obviously a form of 'people power', but a limited one, for the voters are giving away the right of decision-making to a small number of elected representatives who make decisions on their behalf. In effect, this is **oligarchy** or political **elitism**, the few acting on behalf of the many. Elitist democracy was the dominant academic theory of how democracies functioned during much of the 20th century.

A country is a representative democracy if the people have the means of and opportunities for effectively participating in the way in which it is run. Citizen participation is basic to the democratic system. People may not be able to make decisions directly, but those who do make them are accountable to the **electorate** at election time. All eligible adults have gained the franchise or right to vote, sometimes as a result of prolonged struggle. For many of them, this is the extent of their involvement in the political process.

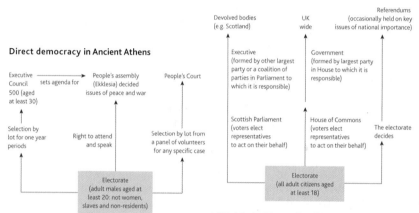

Fig. 11.1 *Direct versus indirect democracy*

Liberal democracy

Britain and other Western democracies are often described as **liberal democracies**. In addition to the features of representative democracy that we have already mentioned (e.g. free elections and the right to oppose), liberal democracies are noted for their commitment to the following ideas:

■ *Pluralism* – the existence of diverse centres of economic and political power, involving a choice of political parties, the existence of many **pressure groups** and freedom of choice.

■ *Limited government* – checks and limitations on the power of government in order to secure essential liberties.

■ *Civil liberties and civil rights* – the existence of essential public freedoms that are often written into law (e.g. freedom of assembly and speech, the right to vote and to a fair trial).

■ *Open government* – non-secretive government that can be seen to be fair and accountable.

■ *An independent judiciary* – a just, impartial and independent legal system based on equal access to the law.

■ *Free and open media* – newspapers and broadcasting being allowed to operate freely without government pressure.

Worldwide recognition of democracy

The contrast between the original Athenian form and democracies of the 21st century is startling. Circumstances have changed dramatically. What we now have is indirect or representative democracy, a situation in which representatives of the people, freely elected, make decisions subject to popular control at election time. Some of these representative democracies will also be liberal democracies, but that is by no means always the case.

Several countries have forms of representative democracy, with regular elections providing for the peaceful transfer of power but also with other, less familiar features. These are sometimes known as 'semi' or 'façade' democracies. They exist in some relatively new countries such as Malaysia and Singapore and in older, established ones such as Russia. Rulers are chosen in elections that can be broadly regarded as free, give or take a few blemishes. But once in office, they govern with little respect for individual rights and may often harass those who express opposition. In addition, journalists may come under heavy pressure to write stories pleasing to the ruling regime and the judiciary may be cowed into subservience.

Since the 1970s, democracy in one form or another has been widely accepted across the world as the most desirable form of government. Whereas at one time it was seen mainly as a Western creed, strong in Western Europe and former colonies such as Australia, New Zealand and North America, that is no longer true today. Democracies are to be found in Southern Europe (Greece and Portugal), most of Eastern Europe (Hungary and Slovenia) and parts of Latin America (Argentina), Africa (South Africa) and Asia (Taiwan). The cause of democracy appears to have triumphed.

Democracy and democratic values

Democracy matters in that without it the wishes of the people can be set aside. We have seen that in a representative democracy we would expect to find:

■ regular and free elections, in which voters do not directly control policy themselves but select representatives to do so on their behalf

■ government that has legitimacy, because those who rule are ultimately accountable to the people and can be removed by them

■ limitations upon the power of government over the lives of individuals and some means of protecting individual rights

■ a commitment to political liberties, such as freedom of speech, to form political parties or associations and freedom to stand in elections.

Other likely characteristics and values associated with democracy and democrats include the following:

■ *Government resting on popular consent, consent that can always be withdrawn:* One of the key differences between totalitarian and democratic government is that in the latter, people can not only criticise ministers without being regarded as enemies of the state, but can also bring about a change of government without recourse to violence.

■ *A belief in peaceful change:* Democratic politics involve patience, a willingness to resolve conflict by negotiation, persuasion and compromise rather than by recourse to violence. The political direction of the country can be changed, sometimes radically, but this is brought about via the ballot box rather than by the bullet. Political rather than military or terrorist means are the order of the day.

■ **Activities**

1 What do you think the dramatist George Bernard Shaw (1856–1950) meant by saying that democracy 'substitutes government by the incompetent majority for government by the privileged few'?

2 Having read about the features of representative and liberal democracy, apply the various characteristics to life in the UK. Make two lists, one to show all the features that qualify Britain as a democracy, the other of points to make you question how good a democracy it really is.

3 Using your own knowledge derived from family experience or travel abroad, or the internet, consider which of these countries meet the criteria for democracy that have been listed: Albania, China, Germany, Greece, India, Iran, Iraq, Pakistan, Russia, United States.

■ Hint

For each of the first ten bullet points on these two pages, look up the relevant section of the book in order that you get a more detailed understanding of why each point may be considered a blemish upon British democracy. Having gained an insight into how our democracy functions, do you consider democracy to be the best form of government? Does it have any disadvantages? Is it the most desirable form of government for any country? Can/should Western-style democracy be transplanted to other countries?

■ *Acceptance of diversity:* In dictatorships, differences between individuals and groups are suppressed, conflict and debate being regarded as at best wasteful and unnecessary, at worst traitorous and detrimental to the ruling regime. In democracies, it is recognised that people have divergent needs and interests and the political approach is to accommodate and reconcile them. They are able to make choices about how they wish to lead their lives, subject to the fact that in the pursuit of their own freedom they do not trample on the liberties of others.

■ *Majority rule, but willing acceptance of minority opinions and rights:* The majority governs, but it has to recognise that there are limits to the restraints it can impose upon the minority. The task of the minority is to make the majority justify its views and policies, in the hope of persuading enough people to support it so that it can one day itself become the majority.

Totalitarian government, on the other hand, is likely to produce people who are already have or find it wise to develop the habit of absolute and implicit obedience, and respect for authority. They will not have or will not express any will of their own; indeed, to hold opinions that might conflict with those of their rulers could land them in prison, or worse. They may be indifferent to public affairs, having never been encouraged to play an active political role unless they are fervent supporters of those in power – apathy that suits the rulers very well.

Part of the case for democracy is that it is more likely to produce people who possess a different set of characteristics. Not all democrats will possess them all; some will possess only a few. But the qualities that might be looked for in democratic citizens include:

■ some degree of interest in and responsibility for the interests of the whole community

■ willingness to become engaged in public affairs and take advantages of any opportunities for popular participation

■ a questioning attitude, rather than being an uncritical, passive recipient of governmental information

■ a belief that people should be encouraged to discuss issues, arrive at their own judgements and exhibit an independence of mind and thought

■ recognition of the same rights for other people, respecting their right to have and express their own opinions and showing tolerance to those with whom they disagree

■ tolerance of not only other opinions, but also of other behaviour, and in particular an acceptance of minority rights, however unusual the views expressed or the lifestyles adopted

■ willingness to compromise and accept that not all individuals and groups in society can have everything they want and that some sacrifices have to be made for the general good

■ commitment to achieving goals by persuasion, not by force. However strong one's personal beliefs, some degree of moderation is thus necessary to democracy. Differences are talked over, not fought over: open debate rather than violence is the means of determining policy.

Britain qualifies as a liberal democracy, but like other democracies there are blemishes within the system. Critics point to the exceptional secrecy of British government, the election of strong governments that lack majority support among the electorate, the relative weakness of Parliament, the lack of opportunities for minorities and independents to gain recognition and failings in the areas of civil liberties.

Activities

1 Contemplate the meaning of the two quotations below and write a paragraph giving your reactions to each of them:

'My people and I have an agreement: they are to say what they like and I am to do what I like.'

'Frederick the Great, 18th-century Prussian 'enlightened despot'

'The ballot is stronger than the bullet.'

President Abraham Lincoln, 19th-century America

2 To what extent do you agree with the sentiments here expressed by Prime Minister Stanley Baldwin in a schools broadcast in March 1934? How fundamental are the requirements he set out?

'Democracy is a most difficult form of government – difficult, because it requires for its perfect functioning the participation of all the people in the country. It cannot function – not function well – unless everyone, men and women alike, feel their responsibility to their State, do their own duty, and try and choose the men who will do theirs. It is not a matter of party: it is common to all of us, because democracy wants constant guarding.'

Stanley Baldwin, broadcast 1934

Here are a few specific points that critics mention:

1 *Many voters are ill-informed* about political issues and there is a significant element that forms an under-class, alienated from the political system. There is widespread scepticism about politicians and what they promise and deliver. Those who are alienated feel that politics has nothing to offer them. It seems irrelevant to their lives.

2 *Turnouts in elections are low:* If democracy thrives on popular involvement and participation, the number of people who are actively involved in the political process is very small (see page 256). We have only occasional referendums, few voters join political parties and even when there is a chance to register a vote an increasing number do not bother. Recent turnouts in local, European and general elections point to significant levels of **apathy**, perhaps linked to feelings of **alienation**.

3 *The first-past-the-post electoral system* may provide strong governments and clear majorities, but some would suggest that the grossly disproportionate power given to the major parties at the expense of small ones is not only unfair but undemocratic. Since the last election, Labour has governed on the basis of 35.2 per cent of the popular vote (21.6 per cent) of the whole electorate. It has introduced highly contentious legislation on the basis of minority support.

4 *The executive has long been criticised as too powerful*, with the allegation that as parliamentary influence has been reduced there has been a concentration of power in 10 Downing Street, with the prime minister becoming a presidential figure who lacks respect for constitutional niceties. The argument recalls the allegation made in the 1970s by Lord Hailsham that Britain had become an 'elective dictatorship'.

5 *The House of Lords remains unelected:* Prime Minister Blair is said to have packed the chamber with 'Tony's cronies', having allegedly gained [for Labour] 'cash for peerages'. As yet, there is no elected element. (Of course, Labour did end the old system of hereditary peerages.)

6 *Local democracy has long been in decline:* Turnouts are exceptionally low in some inner city areas, hardly surprising bearing in mind that many people would say local government has been stripped of so many powers it is no longer worth voting for. There is little public interest in local council activity, the media doing little to focus attention on what happens at this level.

7 *Numerous quangos still exist*, despite the fact that politicians in opposition often criticise their undemocratically chosen membership. They range from NHS trusts to Training and Enterprise Councils. The Tony Benn question (see page 160) about those who exercise power over the rest of us is: 'Can you get rid of them?' We cannot determine the membership of quangos, which are often packed with party appointees.

8 *The media*, which at their best expose wrong-doing and keep us informed about political matters, often fall well below the level we require. We might have a free press, relative to that of former communist countries and present dictatorships. But the trends towards concentration of ownership and the disappearance of some newspaper titles mean that we have less diversity of viewpoint. Some groups cannot easily gain access to television either, such as those who are seen as threatening to the democratic system – students, feminists and militant trade unionists. At worst, television confrontations trivialise political debate, opting for entertaining rather than in-depth discussion; issues often now seem less important

Key terms

Apathy: a lack of interest or enthusiasm, in this case for playing a part in the political system. Others might see it as representing broad satisfaction with things as they are, so that there is no need to exert oneself to register one's own viewpoint or take an active role.

Alienation: generally means a feeling of separateness, of being alone and apart from others. In this sense, it refers to the feeling of being estranged from the rest of the community, society or the world.

Table 11.1 *Further information: the political knowledge of young people (18–24) – overall political quiz performance*

Country	No. of correct quiz answers (max. 56)
Sweden	40
Germany	38
Italy	38
France	34
Japan	31
Great Britain	28
Canada	27
USA	23
Mexico	21

Findings of the National Geographic – Roper 2002 Global Geographic Literacy Survey, based on 3,250 interviews per country

than personalities, and sound-bites are often a substitute for rational argument.

9 *Rights have in recent decades been neglected* in Britain, which lacks a written constitution and formal Bill of Rights. The situation has been partially corrected by the passage of the Human Rights Act, incorporating the European Convention, but we do not have an up-to-date, clear, tailor-made statement of the rights we might claim. The terrorist attacks in London in July 2005 led to efforts to strengthen anti-terrorism legislation, as well as to improve the integration of Britain's Muslims. However, these efforts have given rise to concerns about the erosion of civil liberties. The Blair and Brown governments have often been viewed as illiberal – e.g. over the introduction of ID cards and the attempt to increase the length of time for which suspected terrorists could be detained without trial.

10 *The European Union* increasingly controls key aspects of our lives, as successive treaties have taken us further down the road of closer involvement. Yet the European machinery is noted for its 'democratic deficit'. We might elect our MEPs (on a low turnout), but the unelected European Commission wields considerable power over us.

British democracy might not seem very healthy, after reading this list. There are flaws, although one could argue with a number of the above points. Few countries can claim to have a perfect democracy. Perfection is something to which we can aspire. Meanwhile, democracy should not be taken for granted. At least we have the benefit of living in a country that has evolved by peaceful change, rather than through violent upheaval. We also have a long attachment to freedom. Note the views expressed in the two case studies below.

Case study

Three cheers for British democracy

Fly the flag for good old British values. This month the Union Flag celebrated its 400th anniversary. Here, one of the region's most vocal patriots, the self-styled John Bull, explains why he hopes it's around for another 400 years.

'To me, the Union Flag is a symbol of a country that is the envy of the world.

It is a celebration of our great land of hope and glory, of the freedom, history and great traditions that stem from this great British democracy we enjoy.

A celebration of our nation's multi-culturalism, racial tolerance, steadfastness and defiance that sends the message to never take kindness for weakness for when push comes to shove we will fight them on the beaches.'

Source: The John Bull column, Birmingham Post, 19 April 2006

Case study

Freedom House and British democracy

Freedom House (www.freedomhouse.org) is an independent non-governmental organisation that supports the expansion of freedom in the world. It argues that freedom is possible only in democratic political systems in which the governments are accountable to their own people; the rule of law prevails; and freedoms of expression, association, belief and respect for the rights of minorities and women are guaranteed. Freedom House assesses states to see whether they meet the criteria of being labelled as democracies. It uses this brief definition of democracy: 'A political system whose leaders are elected in competitive multi-party and multi-candidate processes'.

Activities

1 Refer back to pages 169–70 on the exercise of power. Consider whether British democracy is too elitist. Does everyone get to play a part in the democratic process?

2 List five points in favour of the workings of British democracy.

Freedom House scores the UK with the highest grade (1) for the protection of political liberties and civil rights. It is worth remembering this when drawing attention to the features that are often criticised about the state of British democracy.

Activity

List any points that would help you to counter the verdicts on British democracy expressed in the two case studies.

■ The importance of citizen participation

The Report of the Advisory Group on Citizenship (1998) made an interesting contribution to discussion on participation. Known as the Crick Report, the document was influential in paving the way for the introduction of compulsory lessons, in schools, on Citizenship. It observed:

> In the political tradition stemming from the Greek city-states and the Roman Republic, citizenship has meant involvement in public affairs by those who uphold the rights of citizens to take part in public debate and, directly or indirectly, shape the laws and decisions of a state.

For Crick and his team, such participation was both a right and a duty, the foundation of a democratic society and a safeguard for its preservation and protection.

Opportunities for participation

There are many possibilities for individual involvement in the political system, other than voting in elections or referendums. The pensioner who contacts the local authority in order to claim a reduction in the level of council tax; the canvasser at election time who wears a party rosette; the green activist who lies on the planned route of a road in order to prevent construction workers from building a new highway – all are forms of individual participation.

Other than by voting in elections or referendums, it is possible to participate in the following ways:

- *Becoming a member of a political party:* More active membership might involve serving on a committee.
- *Wearing a party badge* at election time or putting up a campaign poster.
- *Seeking election* to the Westminster Parliament, Scottish/Welsh/Northern Irish devolved bodies or to a local council.
- *Membership of one or more pressure groups:* More active membership might involve accepting a key post, for example by becoming a trade union representative rather than just being a passive member.
- *Attending a meeting*, distributing leaflets, canvassing on the doorstep, writing to elected representatives (or ministers, councillors or a newspaper), taking part in a television or radio phone-in programme, participating in an opinion poll or focus group survey, or (more actively) setting up a website.
- *Taking direct action*, ranging from staging or joining in a sit-down protest, taking part in an anti-war march, scribbling political graffiti or painting protest graffiti on a wall, or joining a demonstration in favour of animal rights to going on strike or chaining yourself to the railings of a public building.

Of course political activity can take place within the home or among friends, whether it involves passively watching a current affairs programme; engaging in family discussion about the Iraq War, famine on the African continent or the merits or otherwise of the party leaders; or arguing with or seeking to persuade friends at school or in the pub.

More orthodox forms of participation have declined in recent years. Figures for electoral turnout, party membership and doorstep canvassing for a party are all much lower than a few decades ago. These are signs of public disengagement from the traditional democratic process.

Political violence, ranging from kidnapping a person to hijacking a plane or carrying out bombings, represents the most extreme form of participation. They are generally accepted as being methods that are beyond the boundaries of the democratic political system.

Activity

Study the figures in Table 11.2 and in the information given in the case study on page opposite. Suggest reasons why, on balance, women participate less than men in political activity.

Table 11.2 *Political activism in the UK (%)*

Form of participation	Women	Men
Voting		
Voted in 2001 election	68	66
Campaign-oriented		
Contacted a politician	17	20
Donated money to a party	6	9
Worked for a party	2	4
Had been a party member	2	4
Had worn a campaign badge	10	11
Cause-oriented		
Signed a petition	42	36
Bought a product for political reason	36	29
Boycotted a product	27	25
Demonstrated illegally	5	4
Protested illegally	1	1
Civic-oriented		
Member of a church group	18	10
Member of an environmental group	6	6
Member of a humanitarian group	3	4
Member of an educational group	6	7
Member of a trade union	15	16
Member of a hobby group	14	19
Member of a social club	13	19
Member of a consumer group	28	35
Member of a professional group	9	17
Member of a sports club	20	33

Source: adapted from R. Campbell, P. Norris and J. Lovenduski, 'Gender and political participation', report published by the Electoral Commission, April 2004

Barriers to participation

In most established democracies such as Britain and the US, the level of popular participation falls well below the ideal. Beyond voting, other major forms of participation are sporadic, confined to a small minority even among the more educated and well-off sections of the community.

Many voters are ill informed about political issues or indeed any other issues affecting public affairs. In Britain, surveys have shown a lack of knowledge and understanding in many voters. Large numbers are unable to name their MPs, MEPs and local councillors, and are not very interested in what goes on at Westminster or in the European Parliament. Crewe's survey of young people in Britain and the US (1996) found that 80 per cent of British pupils engaged in very little or no discussion of public affairs at home, even when including local issues of importance to their own communities.

Case study

An Electoral Commission report on encouraging women's participation in public life

… More women representatives may encourage participation among women more generally. Strategies to increase the number of women being selected and standing for election may therefore be necessary to address this issue. Successful measures adopted by some political parties have included equal opportunity strategies and positive action.

In the UK and elsewhere initiatives have also been taken to encourage women as activists and as members of political parties and other organisations. Successful examples include: training, internships, mentoring, women-targeted membership drives and financial incentives to encourage organisational innovation.

- Measures by political parties to modernise the culture and practices of their organisations may also assist the inclusion of more women as members and activists.
- Women's support networks, groups and offices may help overcome the perceived 'male dominated' nature of politics.
- Attention could also be paid to the timing and location of meetings, and the provision of child-care.

Women are more interested in local rather than national politics, so local campaigns may motivate women to become more politically involved generally. The use of innovative communication formats could also be effective. Making voting more accessible – for example through the expansion of all-postal voting, the provision of more conveniently located polling stations and the simplification of the registration process – could also boost participation, particularly among women.

Source: Gender and Political Participation, *The Electoral Commission, April 2004*

Activity

In what sort of political activities do young people most commonly engage? Why do you think that young people are generally reluctant to get involved?

In the US, Milbrath and Goel (1977) used the language of Roman gladiatorial contests to label the population according to their levels of involvement. They distinguished between *gladiators* (the relatively small percentage of activists who are keen participants), *spectators* (the large majority, those who observe the contest but who limit their participation to voting) and *apathetics* (the non-participants who do not even watch the contest and are indifferent to its outcome).

Both in Britain and the US there is a significant element of the

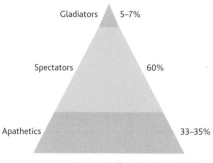

Source: Milbrath and Goel 1977

Fig. 11.2 *Levels of participation in the USA, 1970's*

population that forms an under-class, uninformed about, uninterested in and alienated from the political system. There is widespread scepticism about politicians and what they promise and deliver. Those who are alienated feel that politics has nothing to offer them. It seems irrelevant to their lives. This group is concentrated among the least well-off who feel marginalised from the rest of society.

Table 11.3 *Some factors affecting levels of participation in elections and via other means*

Factor	Impact on participation
Age	Young people (under 35) are less likely to vote and less interested in traditional political outlets, e.g. joining youth wings of main parties. They are more interested in direct action to promote animal rights etc. Middle-aged and older people are more likely to vote and more interested in supporting parties and established pressure groups such as unions.
Ethnic origin	On polling day there is a high turnout of the Jewish population, moderate to high turnout of Asians but low turnout of African-Caribbeans.
Gender	Men are traditionally more likely to vote and join organisations, but in recent years women have become more active. Some argue that in the past male political scientists did not see what was to them 'invisible' female participation via groups such as the Women's Institute.
Location of residence	Participation more likely in urban areas than in rural areas (difficulties of transport may play a part). In inner cities, turnout is often very low.
Socialisation and personality	Those brought up in families that were politically active and in which children were involved in discussion and making decisions are more likely to participate, as are more outgoing personalities. Family background is an important determinant.
Social class	Professional and business people, with a better education and higher income, are much more likely to participate in various ways, especially on polling day. Education is a strong determinant, as much activity involves organising, talking and writing – skills often associated with higher levels of attainment.

Source: adapted from findings of Parry (1992) and Evans (1997)

Activity

Write a couple of paragraphs explaining whether or not you think that people should be more willing to participate in political activity.

Summary questions

1. How does representative democracy in the UK differ from direct democracy as practised in Ancient Greece?

2. Are there any satisfactory alternatives to democracy?

3. Is the UK a democracy?

4. Would it be appropriate to describe the UK as a 'flawed democracy'?

5. Are there any steps that can or should be taken to encourage greater participation in British political life?

6. What are the most effective ways for young people to participate in politics?

Citizens and the electoral process

A country is democratic if the people have the means and opportunity effectively to participate in the way that it is run. Citizen participation is basic to the democratic system. In a representative democracy, people may not be able to make decisions directly, but those who do make them are accountable to the electorate at election time.

Elections are central to democracy. As Farrell (1997) points out, they are 'the cogs which keep the wheels of democracy properly functioning'. The existence of free, competitive elections in which there is a meaningful choice of candidates is an essential criterion for any state claiming to be a democracy. Only a government that is elected has a claim to be a **legitimate system of government**.

In the last quarter of the 20th century, millions of people acquired the right to vote for the first time. On the African continent, elections providing a choice of candidates and **multi-party systems** are now the norm. In the newly-emergent Eastern European democracies, there is free and open competition. Even countries such as communist North Korea allow for a narrow range of candidates, although they belong to the same party.

Elections in established democracies are generally free and fair, in that they enable the will of the majority of voters to be expressed, freely, clearly, knowledgeably and in secret. Today, more countries hold elections that meet these criteria than ever before. Yet even in countries with dubious democratic credentials, elections are still recognised by the ruling authorities as being useful, in that they convey the impression that the government represents the people's wishes.

The value of elections

Elections allow for popular participation. Hence they are not only a means of filling public offices, but they confer legitimacy on those who rule. In Britain, we may only get a vote in a general election every few years, but at least there is a genuine opportunity to express an opinion about those who have presided over our fortunes and to indicate whether we think it is time for a change.

Elections are the principal means by which British citizens participate in the political process. Elections give them a peaceful way to show what they think about the government and the direction of public policy. The voters have a say in determining the policies of the government and the personnel who implement them. In this way, elections ensure that governments are ultimately accountable to the electorate. During the brief period of an election campaign, the voters are the masters, deciding the fate of those who rule over them.

The range of elections in Britain

When considering British elections, many people think of the general elections that are held every four or five years. In addition, there has been an elected system of local government in operation since the 19th century. But the range of British elections has increased in recent years and we now have the following:

- *General elections*, to elect members of the House of Commons. Since 1911, these have been held at least every five years, although the prime minister of the day normally 'goes to the country' after four years. The fate of those who 'hang on' until the last possible moment has not usually been favourable – e.g. in Labour's Jim Callaghan

Key terms

Legitimate system of government: one in which the authority of the government is widely accepted by those who are subject to it. We speak of the authority of an official, but of the legitimacy of a regime.

Multi-party systems: several parties compete for political power, but no single party is likely to emerge with an overall majority of seats in the legislature. Government tends to be based on coalitions of more than one party, maybe three or four. They are the norm in European countries.

in 1979 and the Conservative's John Major in 1992. May has been popular for the choice of elections, although they can be held at any time of the year.

- *Local elections*, to elect members of local councils at various levels (in local elections, voters in London can also vote for a mayor and assembly; some other local authorities also now have an elected mayor). Local councillors are elected in May for a fixed four-year term, although the arrangements for different levels of elections vary according to the types of elections and the area of the country. In the 36 metropolitan councils, one-third of the seats are contested at a time (in other words, there is an election of one councillor for each of the wards in May each year for three years out of four, and no election in the fourth year). County councils are elected in the fourth year. Non-metropolitan district and unitary councils may choose either to vote as do the metropolitan councils, or to vote en bloc every four years.
- *European elections*, to elect members of the European Parliament. They are held in June every five years, 2004, 2009, 2014 etc.
- *Scottish, Welsh and Northern Irish elections*, to elect members of the devolved assemblies in Scotland, Wales and Northern Ireland. These are held every four years, on the same day as the local elections in May.
- *Other elections:* Beyond government, there are now also other opportunities to vote by secret ballot, for example the elections held to choose trade union officials and to decide whether or not to take industrial action.

NB Different types of elections may be held on the same day. In 2004, local and European elections were held in June. In 2005, the general election and local elections were held in May.

In addition, there are occasional by-elections to fill vacancies that may arise when an elected representative dies or resigns during his or her term of elected office. For instance, when an MP dies, loses his or her seat through disqualification or quits while in office, an election will be held in the individual constituency affected. **By-elections** are also held when there are vacancies for elected representatives on local councils and in some circumstances in devolved assemblies or the European Parliament (normally the vacancy is filled by the next person on the party list, but if the list has been exhausted or the person was an Independent an election is necessary).

The citizen and elections: who can vote, who can stand as a candidate

All adults in the United Kingdom have gained the franchise or right to vote, sometimes as a result of prolonged struggle. Elections are the main way in which most people participate. Indeed, for many of them, this is the extent of their involvement in the political process, the only political activity in which they engage. For many of them, this involves voting in a general election, although millions of potential voters are **abstainers**, choosing not to have their say about which party governs. It can also mean voting to choose local councillors; Scottish, Welsh or Northern Irish members of the devolved assemblies; and members of the European Parliament (MEPs).

Worldwide voting ages are not consistent, fluctuating between 15 (until 2007) and 21. Eighteen is by far the most popular choice. In Europe, 18 is a common age (e.g. in Belgium, Denmark, France, Germany, Greece, Italy and Luxembourg, as well as the UK), although in Croatia

---

Key terms

By-elections: contests held between general elections to fill a seat that has become vacant because of the resignation, expulsion or death of an elected representative.

Abstainers: those who do not vote. This may be for involuntary reasons (sickness, not being on the register or the lack of a candidate to represent their particular viewpoint). More often, abstention is a deliberate choice not to vote.

it is 16 (if employed), as it is in the Isle of Man. The voting age in the non-European democracy of Brazil is 16. In some non-democracies, the figures are Cuba 16, Indonesia and North Korea and Sudan 17, and Iran (changed from 15 in 2007), 18. Those under the voting age make up 20–50 per cent of the population in some countries, but they have no political representation.

Further information

The right to vote in Britain

- Some 45 million people are entitled to vote in UK elections.
- Exceptions: those under 18; leading members of the royal family; peers; non-British citizens; some prisoners serving sentences; the mentally ill; and those disqualified because of involvement in past corrupt practices (e.g. bribery).
- The right to vote was limited to a few hundred thousand people in the early 19th century.
- A series of Parliamentary Reform Acts in 1832, 1867 and 1884 (often known as Representation of the People Acts) gradually extended the right to vote to all men.
- 1918: women over 30 were granted the vote.
- 1928: the vote was extended to all women over 21.
- 1969: the vote was extended to 18-year-olds.

The Greens, Liberal Democrats and the Scottish and Welsh Nationalists think the voting age in the UK should be reduced to 16. It has also been contemplated by Gordon Brown. However, campaigners who want 16-year-olds to be able to vote suffered a blow in 2004 from the Electoral Commission, the elections watchdog, which urged that the voting age should stay at 18. (It did recommend reducing the age limit for prospective MPs from 21 to 18 and wanted a further review of the voting age in five to seven years.) Its review was prompted by the 39 per cent turnout among 18- to 21-year-olds at the 2001 general election – the lowest turnout of any age group. Its recommendations were influenced by two considerations:

- Among young people there was not a clear majority in favour of lowering the voting age to 16; while many young people under 18 feel ready to vote, there are just as many who feel that 16 is too young.
- Lowering the voting age could reduce the overall turnout because of young people's disengagement with the political process, as seen in the 2001 contest.

Electoral participation: turnout patterns and voter apathy

Voter turnout refers to the percentage of the qualified voting-age population that actually turns out on polling day. A good turnout of voters is often considered to be a healthy sign in any democracy as it appears to indicate vitality and interest. Many advanced countries have turnouts consistently above 75 per cent, some over 90 per cent, but those with exceptionally high figures (e.g. Australia, Belgium and Italy) have compulsory voting.

Levels of turnout in British elections

Britain has usually had lower turnout figures than those recorded in other established European democracies over the last few decades. Turnout in general elections has varied considerably from one general election to the next. The variation from constituency to constituency is also very large

Further information

Eligibility to stand in UK elections

To be an MP, you must be:

- 18 or over
- British, a citizen of a Commonwealth country or the Republic of Ireland by background or birth.

You must not be:

- in some way employed by the government – e.g. civil servants, judges, police officers and members of the armed forces cannot serve, because they are all working for and paid by the country
- a member of the clergy – e.g. a Church of England vicar
- a peer, because peers already sit in Parliament
- someone who has been in trouble with the law – e.g. bankrupts or those who have in some way cheated in earlier elections
- someone who is seriously mentally sick.

Table 11.4 *Turnout in UK general and European elections, 1979–2005 (%)*

General elections	European elections
1979 76.0	1979 31.6
1983 72.7	1984 32.6
1987 75.3	1989 36.2
1992 77.7	1994 36.5
1997 71.4	1999 23.6
2001 59.4	2004 38.8
2005 61.3	

■ Further information

Turnout in 2005 (%)

Five highest turnouts

- 77.4 Dorset W
- 73.0 Norfolk N
- 72.8 Richmond Park
- 72.5 Mole Valley
- 72.4 Wansdyke

Five lowest turnouts

- 37.3 Staffordshire S
- 41.5 Liverpool Riverside
- 42.4 Salford
- 42.8 Manchester Central
- 43.9 Glasgow Central

Overall turnout in marginal constituencies

- In seats where the lead of the winning party over the second one in 2001 was less than five points, the average turnout in 2005 was 66.7 per cent.
- In safe seats, where the 2001 lead had been more than 20 points, the equivalent figure was 57.4 per cent.
- Overall, turnout was 2.7 per cent higher in marginal constituencies than elsewhere.

(ranging from over 90 per cent to just over 40 per cent). In 2001, 59.4 per cent voted; in 2005, 61.3 per cent. Turnouts in elections for local councils, devolved assemblies and the European Parliament have usually been very low, in the region of 30 to 45 per cent.

The turnout in the 2005 general election was slightly better than in 2001, perhaps because of the prospect of a closer contest. Although the Conservatives lacked popular appeal, there was the opportunity to pass a verdict on the then Prime Minister Tony Blair and give him a 'bloody nose'. There was greater reason for interest than in the previous election in which the result seemed to be a foregone conclusion. Significantly, in those constituencies where there was a genuine prospect of political change, turnout was higher, as the figures in the Further Information section indicate.

■ Activities

1 Look at the figures above for turnouts in marginal constituencies. How do you account for them?

2 If necessary using a map of the UK to assist you, jot down any general thoughts about the location of constituencies with the highest and the lowest turnouts.

3 How do you react to this comment of Professor Jeffery on election turnout in 2001 and 2005?

… the real problem lies not in the voters' sloth but in the failure of politicians to inspire trust, to communicate clear policy platforms and to reach out to habitual non-voters. That failure seems deeply embedded at the UK level but is also present in the devolved nations, despite extravagant claims made in the 1990s about a new politics of better participation for ordinary citizens.

Source: Report of ESRC, Seven Deadly Sins, June 2005

Turnout in Europe and the US

Most democracies have found that the figures for turnout have declined in the last few elections and this has led to alarm about the degree of apathy towards, or even alienation from, the political system that many voters now experience. Many voters across Europe and America seem increasingly disillusioned with the performance of parties in office and with the politicians who represent them. Nowadays, the distinctions between party programmes are often not fundamental ones.

Some writers would suggest that rather than lower turnouts being a sign of apathy and resentment, they may reflect broad contentment. Abstention or non-voting may amount to general satisfaction with the conduct of affairs, so that voters do not feel stirred to express their feelings at the ballot box. Of course, the motives of voters may vary among different groups, some feeling that they do not need to go out and vote because everything seems to be going along satisfactorily, while others – often the young, the poor and members of ethnic minorities – may feel that there is nothing in the choice of party or candidate relevant for them.

Election campaigning and its impact on citizens

Political parties are in one sense always engaged in an **election campaign**, in that they gauge their actions according to the likely impact they will have upon the voters. But during the actual campaign leading up to polling day, their activity becomes more intense and much effort, political skill and professionalism is used to convey the party message.

Although the actual campaign must last at least three weeks it usually goes on for four or more – in 1997 it was 44 days; in 2005 it was 28.

In the 1960s, voting behaviour was habitual and ingrained. Voters tended to have a traditional allegiance and many of them were rarely persuaded to abandon it. They were unlikely to be strongly influenced by the election campaign, unless they were '**floating voters**'. These voters – especially those living in **marginal constituencies** – determined the outcome, and the parties were keen to identify and target them with their message.

The purposes of campaigns

Campaigns may have an impact when the outcome of an election is far from clear. Accordingly, the national campaign is designed to:

- reinforce the views of those who are already committed to the party
- recruit those who are genuinely undecided
- convert waverers in other parties.

The local campaign is still important in marginal constituencies where a small number of votes can change party control. Here, the purpose is to get out the maximum vote, by speech making, visits to places such as hospitals, **canvassing** and organising postal voting.

British electioneering, past and present

Constituency campaigning has been transformed in recent years into something much more sophisticated than it was until the 1980s. Party headquarters now play a significant role in planning and managing local campaigns. Resources are increasingly targeted on marginal constituencies ('target seats') and in particular on categories of voters within them such as 'school gate mums'. The use of computers and telephone banks has enabled party campaigners to develop a profile of individual voters and send them an appropriate message.

Party leaders now engage in frantic tours around those constituencies that may change hands. Their itineraries are planned in great detail, as they are whisked from one end of the country to another in a carefully controlled schedule of meetings and events. They address gatherings in large towns and cities, sometimes attend and make statements at daily morning press conferences, and prepare for their television broadcasts, interviews with established interrogators and appearances before studio audiences.

During the campaign, the amount of political activity intensifies dramatically, and great political expertise and professionalism are employed to get the message across. Today, packaging and presentation have become central to the campaign, leading some to observe that the essence of modern politics is style rather than substance.

The role of the media in forming political opinions

Much of this concern for party image is reflected in the skilful use of television, the main medium of communication today. Bowler and Farrell (1992) refer to the 'increasing importance of television as a tool in election campaigning'. In their survey of marketing and strategies, they note how today electoral contests are 'media-driven', and suggest that 'free elections in a modern democracy would easily collapse if the mass media … were to ignore election campaigning'.

Election campaigns today are made for television. TV dictates the form and style of electioneering. In addition it has a significant influence over

Key terms

Election campaign: the organised effort made by parties and individuals to influence the voters in the period between the declaration of an election and polling day.

Floating voters: members of the electorate who are not strongly affiliated with one party and are liable to switch their vote from one election to another or possibly move from abstention to voting or vice versa. They are obvious target voters for the parties, as their reactions on polling day may swing the outcome.

Marginal constituencies: parliamentary seats where one party has a narrow majority over another. The voting in a relatively small number of marginals usually determines the outcome of the entire election. Currently, the most marginal constituency is Crawley (West Sussex), where Labour won 0.1 per cent more votes than the Conservatives in 2005 and has a 37 majority.

Canvassing: seeking support for a candidate or party, by knocking on doors to meet potential voters.

Activity

Write a couple of sentences to explain why voters in marginal constituencies are important to party campaign managers. List the ways in which they might try to capture their support.

Further information

Negative campaigning

- Negative campaigning involves seeking to gain political advantage by referring to negative aspects of an opponent and their policies (perhaps via a personal attack) rather than the strengths of one's own case, e.g. the Conservatives' 1997 attack on Tony Blair as 'Demon eyes', suggesting that behind his apparent 'niceness', there lurked a dangerous, left-wing fanatic ('New Labour, New Danger').

- Conventional wisdom holds that negative campaign messages are more persuasive than positive messages. Consumers can take in only so much information at any one time. It is easier to implant a negative message than a positive one in a brief broadcast. This is why in the USA political advertisements tend to 'go for the jugular' and expose deficiencies in the moral character of an opponent.

- Critics suggest that such attacks increase voter cynicism about politics.

Key terms

Photo opportunities: occasions/ newsworthy events that lend themselves to (or more usually are deliberately arranged for) taking photographs to provide favourable publicity for those who are photographed. Leading figures are set against a particular background, perhaps to demonstrate concern for the location and those who work there.

the agenda for discussion. Agenda-setting has an important effect on what people learn about the politicians and their beliefs. TV producers have the power to draw attention to issues that they believe to be interesting and/or contentious, and so they help to determine the content of election discussion. By stressing some areas and ignoring others, they can assist in shaping the impression the public acquires of particular parties, leaders and policies.

Television producers like a good story (particularly one with pictures), and party media advisers seek to ensure that they are given a plentiful supply of both. In other words, skilful politicians and their consultants themselves help to determine the agenda, by maintaining a regular flow of material 'ready-made for television'. Most leaders have been willing to take advantage of **photo opportunities**, carefully stage-managed episodes in which the leading figure is set against a particular background perhaps to demonstrate concern for the area or its industry.

In the campaign, leaders visit local party committee rooms, take part in staged events, visiting places where they can be film by TV cameras and doing campaign walkabouts. Just occasionally, for all of the careful pre-planning, something happens to disturb the arrangements. In 2001, an angry Sharron Storer waylaid the prime minister as he entered a Birmingham hospital, protesting at delays in the treatment for her partner, a victim of cancer. The scene was much relayed on screen. So too was the famous (or infamous) Prescott punch when the then Deputy Prime Minister John Prescott landed a punch on an egg-throwing protester in Rhyll in North Wales in 2001.

It is quite possible for a party to run an impressively organised and professional campaign and still lose the election. In 1987 and 1992, Labour was widely credited with winning the campaign but in each case it still lost the election. As Kavanagh (1993) observes: 'Packaging and presentation can only do so much'.

Activities

1. Suggest two reasons why the last two campaigns have failed to ignite voter enthusiasm.

2. Using the net to assist you, find a copy of the 'Demon eyes' poster and record your reactions to it. Did it deserve to be award-winning?

3. A Conservative poster in the 2005 campaign used the issue of Iraq to damage the standing of Tony Blair:

   If He's Prepared to Lie

   To Take Us to War

   He's Prepared to Lie

   To Win an Election.

   Explain your reaction to negative advertising aimed at undermining the reputation of someone on the other side.

Debates between party leaders

In several countries television debates are held between the party leaders during the election campaign. The USA has done so since 1960, Germany since 1969 and Australia since 1984. In these and other democracies, they are now an established part of the political process and attract large audiences. In Britain, they have not been introduced.

Opposition parties tend to argue for them, recognising that they provide a useful opportunity to attack the prime minister. Managers on the government side are wary of allowing their leader to be subjected to them, perhaps because – as with the political interview – once in the studio and under starter's orders, politicians are effectively on their own. As Bruce (1992) explains: 'Any incumbent who accepts the challenge of their opponent in this form needs their head examined. The latter has very little to lose and the former very little to gain.'

The role of opinion polling

Opinion polls have become a familiar feature of election campaigns. In recent elections, random sampling (based on the electoral register) has become the most common means of polling, for within the market research industry it is widely considered to be the most accurate form. Moreover, it is now possible to get high response rates because of the greater use of telephone contact.

In the 1950s and 1960s, pollsters were remarkably successful in pinpointing the actual outcome of elections. Since the 1970s, in an age of greater voter volatility, it has proved less easy to gauge the true intentions of the electorate and to be sure that those who favour one party would actually turn out and vote for it. The performance of the pollsters in 1992 was particularly poor. Most polls predicted a '**hung Parliament**', in which Labour would be the largest party. The error in the predictions of the likely gap between the two parties was greater than it had ever been.

There are still serious doubts about the performance of the opinion polls. In 1997 and 2001, they were accurate in predicting the winning party, although bearing in mind the scale of the Labour victories this success was unsurprising. Throughout the 2005 campaign, the polls generally agreed that Labour seemed destined to win, but with a reduced majority. They differed on how much the majority might fall. Of the final polls, the one taken by National Opinion Poll Research UK was the most accurate, although none of the major polling companies was far out. Collectively, their surveys were the most accurate predictions ever made of the outcome of any British general election. As can be seen from Table 5, every individual estimate was within 2 per cent of the result for each party.

Table 11.5 *Results of final polls during the 2005 campaign (%)*

result	ICM	MORI	NOP	Populus	YouGov	Actual
Labour	38	38	36	38	37	36
Conservatives	32	33	33	32	32	33
Liberal Democrats	22	23	23	21	24	23
Other parties	8	6	9	9	7	8

Source: information based on data provided on the MORI website and covering surveys conducted wholly or partly after Monday, 2 May

Polls are useful to the parties, enabling them to find out which issues are causing the greatest popular concern, which voters they should target, and the strategies they should devise to maximise their appeal.

Prime ministers may find polls helpful in determining when to call an election. Some have been skilful at 'playing the polls', in other words timing the election date to coincide with a period when the polls are showing that their party is 'riding high' in public esteem.

Activity

Use the internet to find out more about the Kennedy v Nixon debates and why Kennedy is widely judged to have fared better. Do you think such debates are a useful idea? Do they have any disadvantages?

Key terms

Hung Parliament: a post-election situation in which no party achieves an overall majority in the House of Commons.

Activity

Using the net to assist you, choose any one polling company and find out about the results of its most recent poll on the state of the parties. See if you can also find out details of the method of sampling it employs and the number of people it interviews.

A few countries ban publication of polls in the build-up to polling day in case they influence the way people vote. Some commentators have suggested that there is a **bandwagon effect** in favour of the party in the lead, while others have mentioned a contradictory **boomerang effect** in favour of the party in second place. There is no consistent evidence one way or the other.

The role of focus groups

Focus groups are another means of assessing what people think about political and social issues. First used in the United States, they are groups of citizens employed by image specialists to test out party approaches and ideas, in order to allow party strategists to tailor and package ideas appropriately. Moderated discussions take place among a small number of respondents who discuss a particular topic. The intention is to find out the thinking and emotions that underlie popular attitudes. Questions are asked in an interactive group setting where participants are free to talk with other group members.

Referendums and voting

A referendum involves a public vote on some single issue of public policy. It is a means of presenting a question of importance for popular consideration and decision. In recent years referendums have been much more widely employed in most parts of the world.

On occasion, British governments have found them helpful in resolving controversial issues that cut across the party divide. They tend to be held because ministers want to get the public to express a view on difficult and contentious matters, rather than make the final decision themselves. Labour is most clearly associated with the use of referendums. It has taken the view that the device is a democratic one in that it gives people a direct voice in decision-making, so that any decision made acquires legitimacy. Three referendums were held in the last period of Labour ascendancy (1974–9).

Since 1997, referendums have been used to resolve the issue of devolution and the future shape of London's government. Also, in votes held on the same day, the voters of the **six counties** of Northern Ireland and of the Irish Republic signified their approval of the **Good Friday Agreement**. In the early Blair years, ministers suggested the possibility of a vote on electoral reform and membership of the single currency if it was decided that Britain would join the eurozone. But neither has materialised, nor do they seem likely to do so in the near future.

There have been local referendums on the future status of schools and the ownership of council estates, as well as in a few cases on the issue of whether to cut the level of council tax or to cut services provided.

In Britain, all national referendums have their use for resolving constitutional issues. None have been used to decide social issues. On matters such as capital punishment, crime and immigration and crime, governments generally consider them unsuitable. Public opinion is liable to bouts of emotion. Penal reform – in particular the abolition of the death penalty – would never have come about if the public had its way. The view is taken that it is up to ministers to lead the public.

Because of the commitment to the idea of parliamentary sovereignty, only the British Parliament can cast a decisive vote on any issue. However,

Table 11.6 *National referendums in the UK, 1973–2008*

Year	Topic	Turnout (%)	Outcome
1973	Border poll in Northern Ireland: electorate asked if they wished to remain a part of the UK or join the Republic of Ireland	61.0	Massive majority to remain in the UK
1975	UK's membership of the EEC: electorate asked if they wished to stay in the Community or withdraw from it	64.0	64% (two-thirds) majority to stay in (43% of the whole electorate)
1979	Devolution to Scotland and Wales: each electorate was asked if it wanted a devolved assembly	62.8 58.3	Scotland: narrow majority in favour Wales: majority against
1997	Devolution to Scotland and Wales: each electorate was asked if it wanted a devolved assembly	60.1 50.1	Scotland: strong majority in favour Wales: very narrow majority in favour
1998	Good Friday Agreement on Northern Ireland: voters north (and south) of the border were asked to endorse the package	81.0	Overwhelming majority in favour

N.B. In the case of the 1979 referendums, there was a requirement that a certain percentage of votes (a threshold) should be reached, before devolution came into effect. Although the majority of Scots wanted a devolved assembly, the 'yes' campaign did not achieve the required backing of at least 40 per cent of the whole electorate.

it is unlikely that a majority of MPs would make a habit of casting their parliamentary vote in defiance of the popular will as expressed in a referendum. British governments have accepted that to consult and then to ignore the verdict is worse than not seeking an opinion. In 1975, Prime Minister Harold Wilson accepted that a majority of even a single vote against so doing would be enough to take Britain out of the European Community. In other words, both governments and MPs accept that they should treat the popular verdict as mandatory in the sense that it is morally and politically binding.

Summary questions

1. Why are elections so important to a democracy?
2. Does it matter if turnout figures in general elections have been low recently?
3. What is the purpose of election campaigning?
4. In what ways has television changed election campaigning?
5. Do campaigns change anything?
6. Could (should) parties do more to arouse popular interest in elections?
7. How accurate and useful are opinion polls?
8. Do polls matter?
9. Consider the arguments for and against holding a referendum on whether:
   - the UK should hold a referendum on whether or not to restore the death penalty
   - the UK should join the eurozone
   - the UK should leave the European Union.
10. In Europe, outside Switzerland and the United States, referendums on moral and social issues such as abortion are uncommon. Why do you think they are rarely used?
11. Bale (2005) argues that 'referendums are not a "silver bullet" that can revive ailing democracies'. Could they do just that?

Do pressure groups improve the democratic process?

Human beings are essentially social creatures and it is natural for people to form groups. But there is also another sound motivation for joining together with other people. On their own, individuals are rarely influential enough to influence policy and decisions that affect their lives. Therefore, they act together to secure the introduction, prevention, continuation or abolition of whatever measures they feel are important to them.

The development of pressure group activity

Pressure groups are organised bodies that seek to influence government and the development of public policy by defending their common interest or promoting a cause. Pressure group activity has a long history, although the increase in the number and range of organisations has been dramatic since the 1960s. There are several reasons for this:

1 *The growth in the extent and scope of governmental activity* in the second half of the 20th century, in the areas of national economic management and social services. Many people want to see more and better facilities and benefits in topics such as education, health and housing.

2 *The growing complexity and specialism of modern life:* People belong to many sub-groups, not least those based on their occupation. For instance, ambulance drivers and paramedics may belong to specialised associations as well as the more general union for health service workers.

3 *The surge of interest in single-issue campaigning,* on subjects from gay rights to the export of live animals to the continent, from gun control to the siting of a motorway or other public amenity.

4 *The development since the middle of the 20th century of a multi-ethnic and multicultural society,* which has encouraged the formation of a variety of groups to represent particular minorities.

5 *The emergence of new issues and the onset of post-materialism:* Many younger, better-educated voters want to express their views about a better environment, the future of nuclear energy and the need for social and political empowerment.

6 *Improvements in communication* have facilitated the trend towards association and organisation and further stimulated group development, as with the use of e-mails and other such innovations by those protesting against globalisation.

There is a vast range of groups in modern society. Some of these groups are long-lived, others are transient; some are national, others local. They range from the well-known ones recognised by their initials such as the BMA and the TUC (the British Medical Association and Trades Union Congress, respectively) to the much less high-profile British Toilet Association and the English Collective of Prostitutes. They cover the whole spectrum of policy issues.

Today, most people belong to at least one voluntary association, be it a church, a social or sports club or an organisation concerned to promote civil liberties or rights. Minorities and women have been active in campaigning for the social and political benefits long denied to them. Women have also spoken out on important issues associated with human reproduction.

Pressure groups and political parties

There is some overlap between political parties and pressure groups. Both are vehicles through which opinions can be expressed and serve as outlets for popular participation. Both have a role in the workings of government, in the case of parties by forming or opposing an administration, in the case of groups by providing information and assisting in governmental enquiries. More specifically:

- there may be a close relationship between pressure groups and particular political parties (e.g. 15 trade unions are actually affiliated to the Labour Party)
- within the parties there are groups that seek to influence party thinking, in effect pressure groups within the party (e.g. the Bruges Group in the Conservative Party)
- some **think tanks** act alongside the political parties, sharing their broad outlook but acting independently and seeking to have an impact on the general thrust of public policy (the Institute for Public Policy Research operates on the moderate Left)
- some groups actually put up candidates in an election, as did the Pro-Life Alliance in 1997 and 2001.

However, pressure groups differ from political parties. They do not seek to win elections to gain political office; rather they wish to influence those in office. Indeed, they do not usually contest elections, and if they do, it is mainly to draw attention to some matter of national concern or to gain publicity. Also, their goals are narrower in that they do not attempt to advance ideas covering the whole range of public policy. Some of their aspirations may be generally non-political, like the local football team that only becomes involved in lobbying when its main amenity – their playing pitch – is under threat.

Types of pressure group

Early studies of pressure groups sometimes distinguished between groups involved in different areas of activity, for instance the 'labour lobby', 'civic' groups, and 'educational, recreational and cultural' ones. However, there are two more usual ways of classifying them. The first describes them according to what and whom they represent, the second in terms of their relationship with government and the way in which they operate.

Protective and promotional groups

The distinction originally made by Stewart (1958) and subsequently employed by many others divided groups into:

- *protective, defensive, interest or sectional groups*, those that seek to cater for the needs and defend the rights of persons or categories of persons in society; and
- *promotional, propaganda, cause or ideas groups*, those that seek to advance particular causes and ideas not of immediate benefit to themselves.

Protective groups are primarily self-interested bodies that seek selective benefits for and offer services to their members. Business interests (e.g. motor manufacturers and shipbuilders) are among the most powerful and well known. Many of them are represented in **peak or umbrella organisations**, which bring together within one organisation a whole range of other bodies and coordinate their activity and speak on their behalf (e.g. the **British Retail Consortium** represents the interests of

11,000 stores). Business groups are usually well organised and financed. However, operating on the other side of industry, the trade unions are probably the best-known protective or interest groups.

Other highly significant protective groups cover the interests of those engaged in the professions, accountants (the Institute of Chartered Accountants), dentists (the British Dental Association), doctors (the British Medical Association), lawyers (the Law Society) and teachers (the National Union of Teachers) among them.

Promotional groups seek to advance ideas and causes, which are not of benefit to their membership other than in a most general sense. They are selfless rather than self-interested in their concerns. They are also open to people from all sections of the community who share the same values, whereas members of interest groups have a shared experience. Again, unlike the many interest groups that have been in existence for several decades, many promotional ones have a short life span, disappearing once their cause has been appropriately tackled.

Promotional groups are defined by the cause or idea they represent. The Royal Society for the Prevention of Cruelty to Animals (RSPCA) is concerned with the welfare of animals, Friends of the Earth (FoE) urges greater environmental awareness and Amnesty International campaigns on behalf of political prisoners. Many cause groups are today **single issue groups**. In Britain, **Snowdrop** had a brief existence. It lobbied effectively for a ban on handguns and when the goal was attained, its *raison d'être* (reason to exist) no longer existed.

Insider v outsider groups

Groups may also be classified by an alternative **typology** developed in the 1980s by Wyn Grant. He finds the protective versus promotional distinction unsatisfactory because along with it there tends to be the assumption that protective groups are more influential than promotional groups because they represent powerful interests. Also, it is easy to assume that promotional groups are of greater benefit to society than protective ones because they are more concerned with the general good rather than personal advantage.

Grant's preferred approach is based on the relationship of groups with the central decision-makers in government. For him, the key issues are whether any particular group wants to gain acceptance by government and – if it does – whether or not it achieves that status. In his words: 'The principle on which such a typology is based is that in order to understand pressure groups, one needs to look not just at the behaviour of the groups but also at the behaviour of government.'

Grant divides groups into:

■ *insider groups* that are regularly consulted by government, having good access to the corridors of power; and

■ *outsider groups* that either do not want such access or are unable to attain recognition.

Many but not all protective groups are insider groups and have consultative status. Similarly, in most cases promotional groups are outsider groups. However, there are significant exceptions, such as the Howard League for Penal Reform and the Royal Society for the Protection of Birds, both of which are promotional groups in frequent touch with representatives of government.

■ **Key terms**

Single issue groups: concentrate their attention on the achievement of one specific objective, such as banning abortions.

Snowdrop: a campaigning group founded after the Dunblane Massacre (March 1996) that urged ministers to ban the private ownership and use of handguns in the UK. In opposition, New Labour took up the theme and legislated for such a ban via the Firearms (Amendment) Act (1997). Snowdrop was then disbanded.

Typology: the study of types or categories.

The Grant typology has itself been criticised with the following points being made:

- *The distinction is not clear-cut*, as some groups pursue insider and outsider strategies at the same time (Friends of the Earth engages in dialogue with government and business, while maintaining direct action activities that attract money and popular support)

- *More groups have insider status than Grant originally suggested:* Some 200 bodies are on the list for consultation on issues relating to motor-cycles, so that consultation is hardly a special privilege reflecting insider status. The influence of some may be marginal.

- *The distinction is less valid today because new forms of politics have arisen in the 1990s and subsequently:* Pressure-group politics has changed, with more middle-class involvement in issues such as animal welfare and anti-roads protests. Also, there are more arenas than before, most obviously the European Union. Some groups concentrate much of the time on Brussels where key decisions are made. Some promotional groups that do not gain much attention in Whitehall may be listened to by EU machinery.

The targets and tactics of pressure groups

In any free society, there are many **access points**, formal parts of the government structure that are accessible to group influence. The most obvious ones are the executive (the ministers and their civil servants) and the legislature (Parliament, its two chambers) although in recent years some groups have made use of the courts to further their cause.

The executive

The most powerful groups, such as the National Farmers Union (NFU), often have direct links with *government and the civil service*. They are insider groups, with access to the Whitehall machine. They value their consultative status in Whitehall and often prefer to operate in a quiet, behind-the-scenes way that avoids too much publicity. Both sides, the government departments and groups, find the dialogue very helpful. Ministers and civil servants can get technical information and advice, and maybe assistance in carrying out a policy. In return, the groups learn the department's current thinking and hope to influence its decisions and get bills drawn up in line with their recommendations. They like the opportunities that **lobbying** at this level provides.

Much of the contact at this level may be formal, involving sitting on committees and discussing draft policies. But some of it is informal, so that there will be frequent phone calls and exchanges of e-mails between leading figures in the organisation and officials in the government department. Sometimes, meetings will be with government ministers as well as or instead of civil servants. Groups like to operate in Whitehall if they can, for they know that this is where key decisions are made.

The legislature

Many groups operate at the *parliamentary level*, especially making contact with the elected members of the House of Commons. This can involve the following:

- *Working through a political party:* Many trade unions are affiliated to the Labour Party, so that there is an industrial and a political wing to the labour movement. Unions have a say in making Labour policy, although they are only one sectional interest and the party has other sources of ideas.

Activities

1. List two examples of each of the following categories:
   - protective groups
   - promotional groups
   - insider groups
   - outsider groups.

2. Look up some well-known pressure groups and find out more about the issues with which they are concerned. Note the size of their membership.

3. Label each of the following groups as protective or promotional, insider or outsider. In some cases, you might need to make an informed guess for the insider/outsider categorisation:
   - NUT
   - BMA
   - RSPB
   - BAAS
   - RSPCA.

Key terms

Access (or pressure) points: those parts of the governmental structure that are accessible to pressure group influence.

Lobbying: the practice of meeting with elected representatives to persuade them of the merits of the case you wish to advance.

Activities

1. List any examples of the mutual benefit and help that the British Medical Association and the Department of Health might obtain from their close links.

2. Look up the CBI website (www.cbi.org.uk) and that of the NFU (www.nfuonline.com). See if you can find examples of any issues on which they are having dealings with government and contributing their expertise.

Key terms

Private Members' Bill: introduced by MPs or peers who are not members of the government. They often deal with socio-moral topics on which there is no strict party view, issues that governments sometimes find difficult to handle – e.g. abortion, divorce and stem cell research. Only a minority ever become law (often because of lack of time) but, by creating publicity around an issue, they may affect legislation indirectly.

Further information

Lobbying of the Lords

Lobbying of the upper chamber has increased over the last two decades, as its contribution to the workings of Parliament has become more highly rated.

Many campaigners recognise the benefits of lobbying the upper chamber. They have been active in contacting peers to strengthen their resolve in thwarting or improving several government proposals. Examples include controversial bills involving civil liberties (e.g. legislation on freedom of information, the detention of alleged terrorists, asylum seekers and ID cards).

The Countryside Alliance (see page 303) made extensive use of contacts in the Lords, as a large number of peers shared its broad approach. They made use of circulars to and meetings with peers of sympathetic persuasion.

- *Lobbying MPs:* Groups regularly circularise MPs, with leaflets, letters and petitions, as well as arranging personal meetings with them. Via these means, they hope to persuade MPs to be sympathetic to their aims.

- *Helping individual MPs:* Cause groups often have a draft bill ready, in the hope that an MP who has the chance to introduce a **Private Member's Bill** might take up their particular campaign – perhaps on abortion or country sports. If they find an MP willing to so do, they will help in promoting the bill.

- *Seeking to influence/monitor governmental legislation*, mobilising opinion on issues such as the campaign for stronger action to improve race relations and the advances in cloning technology.

British groups lobby Parliament because it can influence public policy, although the strong system of party discipline in the House of Commons means that MPs are likely to be less responsive to group persuasion. In Rush's 1990 study, 75 per cent of groups claimed to be in regular or frequent contact with MPs. More than half also maintained contact with the House of Lords.

The judiciary

Since the late 1980s, *the courts* have been used by campaigning groups more than ever before. The legal process is slow, expensive and uncertain, so this tends to be an arena of last resort. But on occasion a body such as the Equal Opportunities Commission or Commission for Racial Equality (now combined as part of the Equality and Human Rights Commission) have brought a test case, in order to establish a principle that can then be applied in other cases. The Countryside Alliance has used the judicial route in its attempts to delay implementation of the ban on foxhunting, as well as in subsequently defending some of those who have fallen foul of the law in this area.

Other outlets for campaigning

Groups also operate at the public level, organising what Samuel Finer (1967) once called fire brigade campaigns (a blitz bombardment until the goal is attained, the Snowdrop approach – see page 270) or background campaigns by which over a period of years there is an attempt to create a favourable climate of public opinion. Direct action (see pages 275–8) is used more than ever before, methods including tunnelling under an airport, damaging property, not paying council taxes and obstructing the highway. In a period when the media assume so much importance, direct action can attract much publicity if the television cameras are around.

There are other things that groups can do, such as getting their spokespersons on television (many groups court publicity with press briefings and staged events), targeting business firms (e.g. the oil company Shell has often been lobbied by environmentalists), lobbying local and devolved authorities, and – very importantly today – lobbying the European Union.

Lobbying at international level: the European Union

Many British groups are involved in lobbying at the international level. In particular, those concerned with trade and overseas development issues may be in contact with the United Nations, UN-related bodies such as the World Bank and the G8, as well as representatives of overseas governments. However, it is the European Union that has become the main target beyond British shores.

Further information

Three avenues are open to groups that wish to engage with the European machinery:

1 *Placing pressure on the national government:* Many groups liaise with national ministers and civil servants in order to influence their government's stance in the Council of Ministers and the implementation of EU decisions.

2 *Operating through eurogroups:* Many groups also exert pressure via a eurogroup, a European-level federation of national groups – e.g. the CBI is a member of UNICE, officially now known as BUSINESSEUROPE (The Confederation of European Business) an association of industries and employers.

3 *Direct lobbying:* Direct contacts with union institutions are widely used by many groups. A few large organisations have established offices in Brussels as a means of closely monitoring European legislation (e.g. the CBI) and also as an outlet that can offer protection for members working in the EU (e.g. the Law Society). More usually, contact takes other forms, such as working via MEPs, approaching a commissioner formally or informally, or writing letters to/phoning union institutions.

From the time the UK joined the European Community in 1973, some larger manufacturing interests and organisations such as the National Farmers' Union quickly saw the need to lobby its institutions. Since then, the number of groups involved in EU affairs has increased dramatically, partly because of the passage of the Single European Act, which paved the way for the creation of a single market.

Today, many decisions affecting key areas of our national life are now made in Brussels. On topics ranging from food hygiene to the movement of live animals, from fishing to the outbreak of **bovine spongiform encephalopathy (BSE)** in the early 1990s, the actions of British governments are much affected by what is laid down by the Commission. Many groups – including bodies such as Friends of the Earth and Greenpeace in the environmental field, and the British Veterinary Association and the RSPCA operating in the area of animal welfare – now recognise that their activities have a European dimension. But the growing importance of EU lobbying is not merely a matter of volume but also of quality, as group activity becomes more professional and sophisticated.

For a long time the European Commission was the key target of lobbyists. A relatively open bureaucracy, it considers the views of various 'interests' in the early stages of draft legislation. However, as the European Parliament has acquired more power, it too has become a popular focus for lobbying. MEPs and their party groupings, and committees of the Strasbourg Parliament, also attract the attention of campaigners. Some groups have made use of the European Court of Justice.

Key terms

Bovine spongiform encephalopathy (BSE): a slow-developing viral disease in cattle. There was an outbreak at the time of the John Major administration. In some cases the virus was passed on to humans in the form of CJD.

Activities

1 List five different methods used by pressure groups to get their ideas across.

2 Suggest which level of government you would lobby if you were seeking to persuade the government to introduce legislation on the following?
- Abortion
- Animal welfare
- Increasing the size of the overseas aid budget.

3 Write a few sentences to explain why many British pressure groups now lobby the European Union.

The RSPCA and its lobbying of the European Union

Since the 1970s, much of the legislation on animal protection in the UK has been enacted by the European Community/Union. Examples cover regulations concerning the transport of wild, farm and laboratory animals. This is a trading activity carried out in several countries and across borders. It involves other industries such as farming, slaughter, scientific research and the sale of animals as pets or public zoo exhibits. As a result of successive EU treaties, the Union's capacity to deal with issues such as these has been increased. Nearly all of the legislation on farm animals derives from the Union. So, too, the Union has tackled issues of the protection of native wild animals and their habitats.

Not surprisingly, the EU is an extremely important part of RSPCA campaigning. On the one hand, it lobbies UK government ministers in Whitehall, for instance as when it campaigned successfully to persuade the relevant minister to take a firm line in meetings of the Council of Ministers over the implementation of the EU Directive on battery rearing of chickens.

The RSPCA also targets EU institutions directly:

■ Council of Ministers
■ Commission
■ Committee of Permanent Representatives (COREPER)
■ Parliament.

In addition, the RSPCA now has an office in Brussels, run by the umbrella Eurogroup for Animal Welfare, a federation of national pressure groups in the field of animal welfare. Via its office and by working with the eurogroup, the pressure group has been particularly active, in seeking to improve, apply and enforce animal welfare standards in the newly-enlarged European Union of 25 countries, aware as it was that standards of care have varied considerably across the more recently admitted member states.

NB The RSPCA is a formidable campaigning organisation that deploys its considerable resources to lobby at a variety of access points. It recognises the importance of multi-level governance and lobbies various institutions within the UK, including the devolved bodies. Here, we are exclusively concerned with the European dimension of its activities.

The lobbying approach of the Royal Society for the Protection of Birds

The Royal Society for the Protection of Birds (RSPB) is an insider promotional group. It has developed into Europe's largest wildlife conservation charity, with more than 1 million members (some 10 times more than in the 1970s) and 175 local groups. Membership is open to anyone with an interest and willing to pay the annual subscription. From its initial stance against the trade in wild birds' plumage, the issues that the RSPB tackles have grown hugely in number and size.

As a bird conservation organisation, the RSPB is concerned about many topical issues such as climate change, agricultural intensification, the expansion of urban areas and transport infrastructure and over-exploitation of our seas, which all pose major threats to birds. On all of these issues it lobbies ministers and officials in Whitehall. It is currently trying to persuade individual MPs to support climate change legislation.

Apart from working with government and Parliament on policy issues within its sector, the RSPB has been an effective campaigning organisation. It has marketed its cause with great skill and success, using methods such as direct mailing and catalogue trading, and taking opportunities to convey its views via press advertising and other media. As part of its mode of operation, it sometimes works in alliance with the RSPCA – as when they cooperated in tackling the problems of the international trade in rare birds. It lobbies the European Union, working directly with the Commission in formulating the directive on the conservation of wild birds. Along with other animal welfare and environmental organisations, the RSPB arouses public sympathy. It deals with an issue about which people feel strongly. Its effectiveness derives from its size, its ample resources and organisational strength, its professional expertise and sophistication, and growing public sympathy in recent years for the type of issues with which it deals.

Activities

1 By referring back to the information on the EU (pages 250 and 255–6) as well as using the Case Study about the RSPCA, explain why much of its EU lobbying is targeted at the Commission and Parliament. See if you can identify three broad approaches in the way in which groups lobby the Union.

2 With reference to the Case Study on these two pages, list a) the range of access points it targets and b) the reasons why you think that the RSPB is a successful pressure group. What amounts to success, as far as groups are concerned?

Table 11.7 *The range of access points available to British groups: a summary*

International level:	European Union level:	UK national government:	Miscellaneous:
United Nations	Council of Ministers	Executive	The public
UN-related bodies such as the World Bank	European Commission	Parliament (both chambers)	Other pressure groups
G8	European Parliament	The courts	Private companies and public corporations
Overseas governments	European Court of Justice	Devolved governments and local authorities	The media

The role of direct action

Direct action is not a new phenomenon. For many centuries marches and demonstrations have been used by those wishing to protest against their living and working conditions. But in the last few decades there has been a remarkable upsurge in the growth of forms of direct action by individuals and groups. Forms range from demonstrations and 'sit-in' protests to squatting and striking, from interrupting televised events and non-payment of taxation to the invasion of institutions in which the activities conducted cause offence. Groups committed to opposing hunting or other forms of alleged mistreatment of animals have often been willing to resort to forms of direct action to voice their protest.

What do we mean by direct action?

By direct action we mean doing for yourself what the government has refused to do. This may mean that homeless people find a home by living in unoccupied property. The term has been used more widely to allude to any attempt to coerce those in authority into changing their viewpoint – for example, homeless people might occupy a council office until they are housed. These activities invariably involve law breaking, which may be passive (e.g. obstruction, trespass) or violent (e.g. if a person is threatened or furniture is broken). Today, the usual meaning of the term direct

Activities

1. Use national or local newspapers to find recent examples of direct action. Note down the methods of direct action that were employed.

2. Look up Friends of the Earth (www.foe.co.uk) or Greenpeace (www.greenpeace.org.uk) to find out about their campaigning methods and any instances of direct action in which they have been involved.

3. Is direct action a legitimate weapon? If so, under what circumstances?

action is 'action taken outside the constitutional and legal framework'. In Baggott's words (1995), it describes a situation when a group 'takes matters into its own hands, rather than relying on established methods of decision making, to resolve a problem'.

Direct action does not have to be violent. It can be **militant** without being violent. If violence is used it may be against property rather than against a person. Non-payment of a portion of taxation by Quakers who disapprove of any governmental defence policy based on the willingness to use force is non-violent but illegal. So was the willingness of those seeking the vote for women at the beginning of the 20th century, who organised themselves into the Tax Resistance League (their cry was 'no taxation without representation').

Campaigns of direct action may start off as peaceful protests but can easily become violent. Many people might choose to engage in an orderly demonstration against some motorway development or the export of live animals to the continent. They might find that as passions become inflamed, so disorder creeps in. Protest marches have often turned out to be occasions when violence erupts, and the demonstrators confront the police who are seeking to maintain law and order. Of course, this does not necessarily happen, and the right to peaceful protest is one that civil libertarians strongly defend.

Operating at the extreme end of the spectrum of forms of direct action, hijackers and terrorists among others have shown the impact that techniques of law-breaking can have. Fortunately, few groups are willing to resort to such tactics in order to obtain their desired goals. Because they operate beyond the realms of democratic politics, many would consider that they cannot be included within the scope of any study of direct action.

The growing popularity of direct action: why has it come about?

Since the 1970s, a number of promotional groups have decided to use direct action as an additional means of persuading the government to follow their ideas. They get publicity as the television cameras are likely to be present at a mass protest or demonstration. Many local action and promotional groups have used direct action as an additional tool. Members of **NIMBY** groups have often used this approach in their bid to block the building of housing estates on **green-belt land**, or to stop the felling of some ancient tree in the name of progress. Local papers regularly reveal the activities of groups who seek to gain publicity by some dramatic gesture.

Fig. 11.3 *Environmental direct action: a Plane Stupid protest against an air show in Fairford, Gloucestershire*

Reasons for the growing popularity of direct action include the following:

■ The growing recognition that protest is an effective means of getting concerns placed on the national agenda.

■ The huge increase in interest and concern for the environment. This has triggered a mass of activity (local, national and international), much of it informal, loosely organised and characterised by willingness to resort to less traditional methods of campaigning. Some environmentalist organisations such as Earth First! have been willing to resort to **ecotage**.

■ Limited opportunities for consultation, with previously powerful groups such as trade unions finding themselves more distanced from government than they were a few decades ago.

■ Developing disillusion on the part of many campaigners with the performance of the last Conservative and present Labour government. Environmentalists and civil libertarians are among the ranks of the disillusioned.

Case study

Plane Stupid

Plane Stupid is a network of groups taking direct action against airport expansion and aviation's climate impact. It is part of the new wave of radical green activism seen in Britain, having been inspired by networks like Earth First! and the mid-90s anti-roads protests. The network, which has no hierarchy or central leadership, comprises small 'affinity groups' who organise themselves. It originally came together in 2005, when a group of activists decided to disrupt an international aviation conference, held in a central London hotel. Despite heavy security, they managed to release helium balloons with rape alarms up to the ceiling, as well as heckling key speakers and during the key note speech by a senior British Airways executive.

Actions carried out by the group include various forms of disruption, ranging from the occupation of offices belonging to airport operators (notably BAA and easyJet) to the grounding of planes through the establishment of a 'climate camp' on an airport taxiway. In September 2007, 'The Camp for Climate Action' at Heathrow Airport was a week of action and education, with workshops on a wide range of environmental and social issues (e.g. how people can reduce their carbon footprint).

Fig. 11.4 *Plane Stupid protestors, Heathrow 2007*

Key terms

Ecotage: direct action in the environmental field, including acts of sabotage on buildings and equipment. It is similar to eco-terrorism, eco-terrorists being extremists who are prepared to carry out terrorist acts against companies, industries and other workplaces and their personnel if they feel that unnecessary damage to the environment is being caused.

Activity

Monitor the protests of Plane Stupid and other campaigning groups against the building of an additional runway at Heathrow.

Fig. 11.5 *Campaigners from Fathers4Justice*

Activities

1. Can you think of any NIMBY groups at work in your neighbourhood or nearest town or city?

2. Look up and list three current campaigns of Earth First! (www.earthfirst.org.uk).

3. Look up and list the latest examples of Plane Stupid's and F4J's direct action.

4. Write a few sentences to say whether it is a legitimate campaigning tactic a) to disrupt air traffic, at a time when people are setting off to or returning from their holidays and b) to enter into the property of Harriet Harman and stage a demonstration. Try to think of some general principles that help you decide whether or not the action taken is a legitimate tactic.

Case study

Fathers4Justice (F4J)

Fathers4Justice is a fathers' rights direct action group, formed in 2002 to campaign on behalf of fathers who claim to have suffered injustice in the quagmire of divorce proceedings and feel that the legal system is stacked against them. It has adopted a twin-track strategy based around publicity and pressure, working through the political system via MPs but also using non-violent protest based on the Greenpeace model, in its view 'with a dash of humour thrown in for good measure'. As such, it has engaged in various high-profile stunts, notably in May 2004 when two members caused a security alarm at Westminster when they hurled purple powder at Tony Blair. Following negative publicity surrounding an alleged plot to kidnap the son of the prime minister, the leadership announced that F4J was disbanding. However, some members continued operations as 'Real F4J'. The original organisation soon reformed and is now functioning as it did before.

F4J Storm Minister's House

Campaigners from Fathers 4 Justice dressed as comic book heroes are believed to have occupied bedrooms and the roof of a house belonging to Harriet Harman, deputy leader of the Labour Party in Herne Hill, South London. The protest started at 8.30 a.m. this morning.

Activists Mark Harris and Jolly Stanesby from Plymouth, Devon who are dressed as 'Captain Conception' and 'Cash Gordon' took part in what Fathers4Justice described as an early 'Fathers Day strike' against the government who it accuses of waging an unprecedented war against fathers and fatherhood. A further two unnamed activists are said to be in the property and have unfurled a giant banner from a bedroom window that reads 'A Father is for life, not just conception.'

The campaigners say they will remain in and on the property until the minister reads Mark Harris's book, *Family Court Hell*. Police have since arrived on the scene. Said F4J founder Matt O'Connor this morning, 'Harriet Harman and the government have refused all dialogue with F4J for the past two years. We are now resuming a full-scale campaign of direct action against the government, its ministers and the Judiciary. F4J is now the last line in the defence of fatherhood.'

Source: extract from F4J website, 10 June 2008

Key factors in successful pressure group campaigning

Different pressure groups experience varying degrees of success. For these purposes, success may be interpreted as gaining access to a centre of decision-making and exerting influence over the development of policy. Three general considerations determine the effectiveness of groups:

- their resources
- their political contacts, including the access campaigners have to those who have the power of decision or who themselves might influence it
- the political circumstances and the climate of the times in which groups operate.

Resources

Political resources are those elements that can influence the decisions and actions of those on whom they seek to have an impact. In many cases, they are largely under the control of the group involved. Levels of resources vary considerably. Key factors are as follows:

■ *Large groups are often more successful than small ones*, although what matters more is the commitment, determination and sense of common purpose of those involved. Large groups tend to be well supported financially and are often more able to mobilise time and energy in the service of an issue and carry out research.

■ *Effective leadership is desirable for any group:* Charisma, creative sense, enterprise, flair and strategic direction are definite assets in a leader, as is an understanding of the value of publicity. Shami Chakrabarti, the director of Liberty since September 2003, is a frequent contributor to television/radio programmes and to various newspapers on the topic of human rights and civil liberties. Personable and articulate, she has been a forthright and persistent opponent of restrictive government legislation.

■ *Esteem is an asset:* Groups enjoying high prestige are more likely to carry weight in negotiations and exercise influence. Professional groups tend to have a high social status, doctors being subject to much less criticism than trade unionists.

■ *The ability to form strategic alliances:* For example, Care for Scotland works with other groups as part of the Scottish Evangelical Alliance in order to fight aspects of the 'permissive society' that they dislike, such as the alleged moral decline associated with gay sex, quickie divorces and cohabiting couples.

Access to and contacts with decision-makers

■ *Many groups have strong connections with the Executive:* Insider groups – business, labour and professions among them – are in a better position than outsider groups to claim decisive or exclusive expertise. Decision-makers and legislators are often reliant on the advice and assistance of well-resourced groups. They may well receive detailed assistance in drafting legislation from a well-informed organisation – for instance, Shelter was actively involved in drawing up the Homelessness Act (2002).

■ *MPs too are receptive to lobbyists' influence:* Many pressure group campaigners in the anti-poverty lobby and civil liberties arena have a close connection with individual Labour or Liberal Democrat MPs. One survey found that three-quarters of groups had regular or frequent contact with MPs of one party or another. Such MPs can be a useful conduit to influence parliamentary opinion more widely.

■ *Good media contacts can also be useful:* Many promotional groups have taken up public campaigns in the knowledge that the media can provide information about and publicity for the cause and help to create a more favourable climate of opinion. Causes that can attract the curiosity of journalists by the inherent interest of their campaign and/or by the vivid images they convey may receive wide coverage.

The political circumstances and climate

■ *The attitude of ministers is crucial to any group:* Some groups have goals that are compatible with the aims and outlook of the ruling party, in the way that Labour administrations used to be sympathetic to union influence and pressure. The free market Institute of

The wrong-headed rush to grow biofuels across the world will have serious impacts on the birds you see on your walk in the countryside … In the urgent desire 'to do something' care must be taken that actions are based on logic and evidence.

Source: RSPB website, www.rspb. org.uk

Consider the case of the RSPB. Make a list of the ingredients of its success as a pressure group.

■ **Key terms**

Miners Strike (1984–5): a major industrial action affecting the British coal industry, involving a confrontation between the Thatcher government-backed National Coal Board and the National Union of Mineworkers (NUM). Defeat of the NUM after a year-long struggle significantly weakened the British trade union movement.

■ **Activities**

1 List reasons why NACRO (representing ex-offenders) and Release (representing drug addicts) might find it hard to win support from the government or the public for their messages.

2 Suggest reasons why the RSPCA might find a more receptive response.

3 Choose a pressure group that you know and write a few sentences to explain its aims, its approach to lobbying, its resources and its effectiveness. Do you think that on balance it operates in a self-interested way, or for the greater good of the whole community?

Directors and the Freedom Association both shared a broad philosophy and approach to policy with the Thatcher Conservative governments.

■ *The governmental response may also be affected by the size of the parliamentary majority:* Governments in the 1970s especially Labour ones from 1974–9, lacked the dominance of subsequent ones and felt the need to gain the approval of relevant groups in order to maintain consent for their policies. By contrast, two out of three of each of the Thatcher and Blair election victories left them in an overwhelmingly dominant position in the House of Commons. Ministers felt less necessity to consult or when they did so could ignore recommendations that were not to their liking.

■ *Timing:* Governments are more willing to take tough decisions and override opposition after an election than before one. Also, some groups that once had a very powerful position in the economy find that the tide has moved against them. The miners were in a strong bargaining position in the 1970s when oil supplies were in short demand, but when the Thatcher government confronted them a decade or so later in the **Miners Strike (1984–5)** it was well prepared to resist industrial action, for stocks were ample. There was less of a *threat to power supplies.*

■ *The use or threatened use of powerful sanctions:* Some groups have the capacity to 'hold the country to ransom' by persisting with their demands. This now happens much less than it did in the pre-Thatcher days. Today, if fire-fighters go on strike, ministers are likely to call in the army to provide emergency cover. Other groups such as nurses are always inhibited from taking industrial action because they know that if they do so, there will be massive disruption that could imperil the well-being or even lives of sick patients.

Are pressure groups good for democracy?

It is now time to consider the role of groups in British democracy, whether they enhance or diminish the quality of our democratic political system. In so doing, we face the difficulty that we are dealing with thousands of organisations whose aims, composition and methods vary significantly. Some may be guilty of the charges often laid against group activity, others are not. Some may serve the public good for much of the time, while others have only a marginal benefit. We can only make generalised comments that do not apply to all groups in all circumstances, but here are some arguments to consider.

In the Thatcher and post-Thatcher years, the tendency of many politicians has been to criticise pressure group activity as damaging to the democratic process. Groups are seen as essentially self-interested and lacking in concern for the needs of the wider public. Yet this is only part of the picture, for they also raise issues of popular concern and provide a useful channel through which preferences may be expressed. Democracy would be unable to function without them, for they are at the heart of the policy-making process. Given such a position the need is to monitor their activities and ensure that they are efficient, open and representative, rather than to imagine that their contribution can be either ignored or removed.

Among the specific arguments advanced in favour of and against their contribution to democracy, the following may be borne in mind:

In favour

- In a pluralist society, pressure groups are seen as being at the heart of the democratic process. In particular, they perform a valuable function within the political system for they allow participation in decision-making by ordinary individuals. Many people otherwise only participate in political life at election time, but they can indirectly do so by joining groups, which can influence the decisions of public bodies.

- Groups provide valuable information to government departments based upon their specialist knowledge of their field. In some cases, this is backed by cooperation in administering a particular policy and monitoring its effectiveness. They are indispensable to governmental decision-making because they are available for regular consultation. Indeed, this may be on a very frequent basis, there being continuing dialogue between a government department and key interest groups. The government knows that a group of this type represents the bulk of people in that particular sector. Most farmers are in the National Farmers Union, and therefore its voice is representative.

- They act as a defence for minority interests, especially those connected with parties not in government.

- They counter the monopoly of the political process by political parties and sometimes they raise items for discussion that fall outside the realm of party ideas and policy, and do not tend to feature in the manifestos. They made the running in the 'green' arena, before the political parties took up ecological issues.

- In a democracy such as ours, they are an inevitable feature. The chance to freely voice a viewpoint is basic to a democratic system. The group system has mushroomed in recent years and this growth is unlikely to be reversed.

Baggott (2000) has summarised the value of pressure groups effectively:

> The views which pressure groups convey are legitimate interests ... Modern democracy would not exist without pressure groups. As a channel of representation, they are as legitimate as the ballot box ... They can mediate between the government and the governed.

Against

- Not all sections of the community are equally capable of exerting influence, though virtually everyone is free to join a group. There is not a level playing field for influence. Some, especially ideas groups, are much less likely to be acknowledged. Campaigners can point to the failure of the Child Poverty Action Group and other welfare groups to prevent Labour from cutting benefits to one-parent families and disabled people. Of the interest groups, the voice less frequently heard is that of consumers who are difficult to organise, other than via the ballot box. By contrast, the producer groups and the unions and, particularly in the Tory years, the industrialists have easier access to Whitehall.

- The leadership of some groups is unrepresentative. This was the case with a number of unions before a change in the law forced them to hold elections for the post of general secretary. It is important that any government knows that people it talks to do genuinely reflect their members' wishes, and that deals made with leaders will stick because they have the backing of group supporters.

- Some people worry about the secrecy under which bargains between interest groups and Whitehall departments are made – hence Finer's (1967) plea for 'Light, More Light'. Also, they fear that too many MPs

Activity

As you read this section, identify what you consider to be the two strongest arguments for and against the proposition that 'pressure groups are a threat to democracy'. Give reasons to justify your choices. In a couple of sentences or so, explain which single argument from either point of view is the most convincing.

are beholden to outside groups and business commitments.

■ A pressure group by definition represents a number of broadly like-minded citizens in society. In other words it is a 'sectional interest', in the way that the NFU represents farmers and the NUM miners. Governments have to govern in the 'national interest', and consider the views/needs of all sections of the community, not the voice of the powerful only. The TUC still represents a substantial proportion of working people, but by no means all workers; the miners' voice on pay may be strong, but consumers may have to finance their pay by spending more for their coal/electricity.

■ Group consultation slows down the process of government and can be a barrier to necessary action. Some recent home secretaries have found the civil liberties lobby a thorn in their flesh, as they have tried to introduce legislation on asylum seekers, identity cards and the prevention of terrorism. In the words of one of them, Conservative Douglas Hurd, they are 'strangling serpents', which slow down and distort the work of government. He – and some of his predecessors and successors – have tended to regard many of their group opponents as being out of touch with the real concerns of the public about the abuses associated with asylum seeking and the dangers to society in a terrorist age. In addition, groups tend to oppose developments such as new roads, industrial installations and power plants, even though these may be in the broader public interest. In relation to anti-GM food campaigners, Tony Blair echoed this theme in his suggestion that 'we should resist the tyranny of pressure groups'.

Summary questions

1 Consider any advantages of pressure groups over political parties as vehicles for dealing with the issues of concern to ordinary people.

2 Which classification of pressure groups (see pages 281–3 for a descriptiondo you find to be the more helpful, and why?

3 Using the BMA, CBI and NFU as examples, how would you describe these groups?
   ■ Exclusively self-interested
   ■ Self-interested but responsible
   ■ Strongly concerned for the public interest most of the time.

4 On balance, do you think that pressure groups enhance our democracy or undermine it?

5 Is direct action a good thing?

6 Can we distinguish between the legitimacy of using peaceful direct action and violent protest? Can the use of physical force to obtain a political objective ever be appropriate?

7 Should a democrat be concerned about the work of lobbyists? Does it make a difference if we are thinking about the following groups?
   ■ A peak group such as the CBI and the TUC
   ■ A promotional group such as the National Trust.

8 Based on your reading of this section, do you think that pressure groups are a good thing? If so, in what ways? If not, why not?

12

Citizenship in action: campaigning

Learning objectives:

- to understand the various methods that campaigns use to bring about change

- to understand e-democracy and the role of new technologies in democratic participation and debates

- to evaluate recent UK-based case studies of campaigns to consolidate learning

- to understand the range of factors required for a campaign to succeed and the impact of different factors on the success of a campaign

- to analyse and evaluate recent and ongoing campaigns and their impact in bringing about change

- to analyse and evaluate the impact of various campaigns on political decision making and political attitudes.

How can citizens bring about change?

Of the many campaigns that are under way every day throughout the United Kingdom, some are concerned with individual action, some with local group action, some with wider community action and some with national action. Chapter 11 covers the different methods used by pressure groups in campaigns to bring about change (see pages 283–290).

Individual action

Individual action might concern anything from a personal statement about a matter of strong personal belief (e.g. boycotting goods from a country where people are treated badly) to campaigning for justice for a member of the family (e.g. a person who has a form of cancer that might be susceptible to treatment, if only the health authority would fund the costs of the necessary drug).

Possible action may range from writing letters and making phone calls to contact with an MP and airing the issue in the media. Local radio stations and some television programmes like taking up cases where an aggrieved individual is fighting for fair treatment. Publicity is usually helpful to the campaign, the purpose of which is to arouse interest and perhaps indignation, in order to bring pressure to bear on the government department or other agency involved.

Local group action

Local group action involves a significant number of individuals joining together to take on the relevant authorities that are proposing some action or initiative, which may be harmful to them or their community. Many local groups are of the NIMBY variety (see page 276), essentially self-interested bodies whose campaigning is targeted at some development that they feel will adversely impact upon their lives, perhaps affecting the value of their properties – e.g. the building of a motorway or prison in the area.

Although some groups develop as a result of people cooperating to defend a common interest, their cause may also be beneficial to the interests of the neighbourhood as a whole. They might not like the idea of having a waste disposal site near to their homes, fearing anything from fumes to subsidence. But their cause has a wider benefit to anyone who lives broadly within or passes through the area, perhaps because of a health hazard or unpleasant smell.

Case study

Airport Watch on resistance to airport expansion

(The information in this case study is based on a report on the Red Pepper website on campaigns against airport expansion, 2008.)

From international hubs to tiny airfields, airports are expanding across the UK. Almost every major hub is pressing for more flights, extra runways and new terminals, while at the other end of the scale even tiny airfields such as Lydd in the Kent marshes have their sights set on growth. But equally remarkable is the scale and variety of protest against these airport expansions. Virtually every project is being opposed, by campaigns both locally and nationally.

Airport Watch, founded in 2000, reflects the scope of opposition arranged against airport expansion. A national umbrella group, it loosely links together major international environmental bodies, such as Friends of the Earth and Greenpeace, with conservation groups like the Campaign to Protect Rural England and the National Trust. Also joining the movement have been wildlife organisations including the Royal Society for the Protection of Birds, local anti-noise campaigns, the World Development Movement and more radical direct action groups like Plane Stupid and Rising Tide, to name a few.

The blending of self-interest and green concerns

Cooperation between groups with very different initial concerns has in many places led to major success, not least because by working together groups can neutralise the most regular criticisms levelled at them. Noise campaigners who have also taken on board messages about the melting ice caps are harder to dismiss as 'NIMBYs', whereas a green group allied to the local parish council is better placed to resist '**tree-hugging' stereotypes**.

> Climate change and noise are the two factors driving the campaigners. What initially gets residents campaigning is the noise, the sheer number of planes going overhead. 'But for most of the large environmental groups climate change is the key factor,' says John Stewart, chair of the Airport Watch. 'Local and national are brought together. Government can't be serious about climate change and continue with an aggressive programme of airport expansion.

Yet there still remains a split between the concerns of residents and those of the environmental groups, and this can allow airports to divide and rule campaigns against them. In 2006, the Duchy of Lancaster proposed a £3 million plan to expand the capacity of Tatenhill, a former Second World War airfield near Burton-on-Trent, to accommodate 20,000 more flights a year on top of the current 30,000. During a planning inquiry in November last year into the development, the local opposition – Tatenhill Action Group – dropped its challenge after the Duchy agreed to noise restrictions, limited operating hours and restrictions on jets. Friends of the Earth was left alone, still opposing the expansion on climate change grounds.

Recent events

In August 2007, the Camp for Climate Action at Heathrow attracted international attention. This was helped by a story in *The Independent* which revealed that BAA were seeking an injunction to not only keep groups like Plane Stupid away from the airport and large parts of the London transport network, but also to restrict members of the National Trust, the RSPB and the Woodland Trust because of their affiliation to Airport Watch. By building such a wide coalition against Heathrow, it has become harder for the airports to portray opposition as a radical fringe.

The composition of anti-expansion groups is complex and changing. So too are their methods. Direct action has proved to be the most successful in attracting media attention, with the Camp for Climate Action making headlines and the blockade of a Manchester airport security check-in by Plane Stupid and Manchester Climate Action in October 2007 also receiving widespread media attention.

■ **Key terms**

'Tree-hugging' stereotypes: refers to a popular view of environmentalists as rather wild and woolly idealists. It takes its name from the activities of a group of peasant women in Northern India who were alarmed at the commercial loggers who felled trees on the mountain slopes. Today, it is a label for anyone who supports the preservation of forested land and the restriction of logging.

Celebrity joins in Stansted Airport debate

While employees at Stansted Airport set up a protest last night saying building a new runway would mean more flights and therefore more jobs, author and TV star Will Self has joined the anti-expansion brigade. He has led campaign group Stop Stansted Expansion (SSE) on a Runway Ramble at Hatfield Forest in Essex in a protest against further air traffic which they say could threaten the 1,000-year-old woodland.

Mr Self commented: 'For me, the right to roam and the responsibility to adopt a more harmonious and sustainable lifestyle are one and the same. That's why I joined the ramble'. Hundreds of campaigners joined Mr Self for the five-mile walk, which has been held six times annually so far.

Source: BBC report, 19 September 2007

Activity

According to Airport Watch, what are the ingredients of a successful campaign against airport expansion? Why was the extra ingredient of the Stansted protest a useful addition to the protesters' cause?

Community action

As we have seen, many schemes involving local community action have at least an element of self-interest about them, such as preventing the building of an additional runway or a major road. Others may seem to be of wider benefit, such as pressure group campaigns to halt the closure of a local facility like a hospital, post office or school. Some are more concerned with community improvement that is for the benefit of everyone (including, of course, many of those who campaign). Such schemes vary from attempts to clean up the local environment to major schemes of regeneration and social renewal of the Get Set type (see Case Study below).

Case study

Community renewal and regeneration in practice

(The information in this Case Study is based on an article by Anne Hazell, the manager of Magpie, in *Citizenship PA*, vol. 1:2, 2003. Anne Hazell, a community worker in Deptford, acted as a hands-on leader of Magpie.)

The Get Set Community Project

Deptford, New Cross and Brockley have received millions of pounds of public regeneration money over the last two decades. However, despite many valuable projects, at the turn of the century the area still remained deprived, with the majority of its citizens disempowered.

The Get Set for Citizenship Single Regeneration Budget (SRB) programme aimed to break the cycle of failed regeneration by focusing on community-led, grassroots level projects. It was the outcome of local people sharing their views with projects such as NX project and Deptford Community Forum on how they thought things should be done. Local people appeared to have grown tired and cynical of external forces that tried to regenerate their community. Their experience had shown that the 'outside-in' method of regeneration did not work. The failure of earlier regeneration programmes could be traced to the lack of pre-bid community involvement.

Magpie was the lead body of the Get Set for Citizenship Single Regeneration Budget (SRB) programme. Its role was to make it possible for local people to find out what had gone before, what was going on at the time and what might be on the cards for the future. From the start, it developed a creative outreach approach, focusing on regular open forum events. Its events were as unlike traditional public meetings as possible. Instead, they held forums, spotlight sessions and market stalls. They even converted an old burger bar into a mobile outreach vehicle 'serving tea and strategy on estates'.

At forum after forum local people identified both priorities and potential solutions for the problems of the area, but one statement came through clearer than the rest: 'we do not want any more money until we can be sure that there will be genuine, on-going community control of local regeneration'. This was a cry for community leadership with a strong sense of realism. People knew the failings of previous regimes. They knew that interventions in social realities on ground were complex, dangerous and unpredictable. They were fully aware of how much needed to change in order to create the conditions for truly 'joined-up' community renewal.

Magpie itself arose from a set of unmet needs around community development, information, influence and capacity to participate and deliver. It was able to achieve a great deal, particularly through the Get Set programme. It worked to ensure that local people had opportunities to participate and through this was able to train and recruit a team of local people who are now working in their local community.

Activity

Identify any reasons given in the Case Study on these two pages for the success of the Get Set regeneration project. What advantage did this project have over earlier attempts to improve the area?

Key terms

New Social Movements: movements that have emerged since the 1960s in order to influence public policy on issues such as the environment, nuclear energy, peace and women's rights. They aim to bring about fundamental change in society.

National action campaigns

National campaigns of action can take many forms. They range from the activities of numerous promotional pressure groups (see Chapter 11) and the populist movements that have been a phenomenon of recent years (e.g. fuel protests) to those that are part of a long traditional of radical, left-wing dissent (e.g. anti-war protests and the activities of **new social movements** (see pages 293–6).

■ Key factors in successful campaigning

It is difficult to measure the impact and/or success of campaigns that are often very different in type. Here, by impact we mean whether or not they made people take notice and aroused a reaction. Success involves achieving the desired goal.

Some generalisations can be offered, but they do not apply in all circumstances. Campaigns on the same issue can be more or less successful at some times than others. For instance, the broad coalition in favour of liberalising the laws on Sunday trading was unsuccessful for many years. Yet in the 1990s, agreement was reached on the present situation that enables large stores and garden centres to open for six hours. The circumstances had changed in several respects. In particular, the religious lobby in favour of traditional Lord's Day Observance had lost much of its impact and public support for shop opening had increased, as the nature of family life had changed. Many people thought it was very inconvenient that stores were not open on the only or most suitable day for them to shop.

The three factors relevant to the success of pressure groups apply also to wider campaigns: their resources, their access to decision-makers and the prevailing political circumstances. But how much they matter in individual cases depends on the nature of the issue involved and whether the campaign is an individual, group or community one. Broadly, the issues are as follows.

Individual campaigning sometimes leads to a positive result, especially if the publicity makes the offending organisation seem harsh, mean or shabby in its attitude. On occasion, it might inspire some affluent listener or viewer to offer personal assistance, perhaps by financing the righting of any wrong.

In the case of group campaigns of the local action type:

- *Some have little impact on local decision-making*, especially if those involved are inexperienced in campaigning. Councillors can be reluctant to respond to groups whose causes and activities they find unhelpful and in conflict with their own ideas on what should be done. However, even if campaigns fail to achieve their objectives, participation may be a useful educative experience for those involved which may help then in any future battles. It also gives them a feeling of empowerment, encouraging them to believe that individual or group action is worth the effort because they do get the chance to have their views acknowledged.

- *Others can be effective*, not least because a growing number of decision-makers welcome advice or at least recognise the entitlement of those involved to express their views on and objections to what is being proposed. A survey by Parry (1992) showed that almost a third of the decision-makers interviewed felt that the activities of organised groups had influenced the outcome of the issue under discussion. In several cases, concessions had been granted or the implementation of some aspect of the scheme delayed until a compromise solution could be found.

Key determinants of success in group campaigns are as follows:

- *Strong organisation*, with regular meetings and good communication between the leaders and the community.
- *The advice of informed experts*, who may either live locally or be willing to lend their support and perhaps address gatherings.
- *Evidence of popular support*, bearing in mind that the people affected are all voters or potential voters.
- *'Big names'*, who are keen for their own reasons to associate themselves with the cause.
- *The support of elected representatives*, such as a councillor or local MP. If the local MP happens to be a leading figure in the party, perhaps a member of the government, his or her ability to persuade relevant colleagues may be of assistance.
- *Direct action*, particularly if it is within the law yet eye-catching enough to arouse media interest.
- *Media coverage*, ensuring that local journalists and programme-makers are kept fully informed about what is being planned.

Large-scale community renewal and national campaigns again vary in their impact. Campaigns to bring about regeneration may succeed if they are well resourced (perhaps utilising private and public resources), and genuinely involve and arouse the support of the people who live in

> ### Hint
>
> Make sure that you are well informed about four or five campaigns, about which you could write in detail. Be clear about their aims and tactics. Get an impression about the degree of success that they have achieved. As the Countryside Alliance, Fathers4Justice and the Stop the War Coalition are mentioned in the AQA specifications, it would be wise to include them on your list.

Campaign for Nuclear Disarmament (CND): has long been at the forefront of the peace movement in the UK and claims to be Europe's largest single-issue peace campaign. It was at its peak in the late 1950s–early 1960s, and was again prominent in the 1980s. In the 21st century, it has changed its single-issue focus on the nuclear issue and become part of the broad campaign against US and British policies on the Middle East.

the area. Via a diverse array of approaches, their aims need to be clearly communicated and the benefits made apparent to all.

The major national protest campaigns of the right or left often make an impact, but do not necessarily gain success. They may be successful in gaining publicity from media attention, but this does not mean that they influence decision-makers. Access to Whitehall is important, particularly if the government in power is of a sympathetic disposition. A movement for unilateral disarmament such as **CND (Campaign for Nuclear Disarmament)** may achieve prominence through television coverage of a mass demonstration, but it is never likely to succeed in its objective because this is at variance with the policies of both main political parties in office. So too, the Stop the War Coalition has been able to arouse and mobilise popular dissenting opinion, including that of many young people, against British policy in Iraq and Afghanistan. But its impact on government policy has been minimal, much to the frustration of those involved in the various protests it organises.

The impact and success of some of the groups covered in the previous section is summarised in the table below:

Table 12.1 *The impact and success of some well-known campaigns*

Campaign	Impact	Success
Make Poverty History	Aroused moral concern and in some cases indignation: widespread public interest and support	Gained ministerial attention and helped influence policy-makers at the G8 summit. Ultimate goal probably unattainable
Countryside Alliance	Mobilised rural communities on a vast scale and illustrated depth of feeling on hunting issue, but the majority of people in urban Britain were unconvinced by the case presented	Failed to stop the hunting ban. Perhaps suffered from diversity of the groups involved, some being self-interested – e.g. the Masters of Basset Hounds – as opposed to those concerned with the threat to the rural way of life
Campaigning to Protect Hunted Animals	Much less prominent than the Countryside Alliance, it did not hold rallies of comparable size or get the same media coverage	On the winning side. Its cause gelled with the broad public view on hunting, arousing moral concern. Politically, the time was right, for ministers were keen to settle the issue and concentrate on an issue that might rally support following the divisions over Iraq
Fuel Protests 2000	Made major headlines as a result of the disruption to fuel supplies and for a while seemed to have public support	Success to a limited extent, for concessions were offered once the immediate threat had been lifted
Snowdrop	Aroused popular sympathy and moral concern. Benefited from popular revulsion against Dunblane and other gun-related crimes	Achieved success, after convincing a major party (in government) of the justice of its cause
Anti-globalisation protest	Made headlines at the time of their individual protests, but not a sustained coverage	Globalisation continues and even the disruption has not diverted policy-makers from the paths they wished to pursue
Stop the War Coalition	In a short time, aroused widespread support via mass rallies	Unable to stop the war, however much it exposed the dangers and the 'wrong' involved

Some popular movements and their characteristics

NB Information about the campaigning activities of some individual pressure groups can be found in Chapter 11 – e.g. Fathers4Justice.

There are many examples of popular protest campaigning that regularly make the headlines. The trend has been towards growing citizen involvement in broad-based populist movements that have benefited from communications technology and careful use of the media. In some cases these movements plan a programme of activities over many months (e.g. Make Poverty History and the Countryside Alliance), but often they erupt onto the political scene as in the case of the fuel protests of 2000 and 2005. In this latter case and many others, a single issue captures the public imagination and galvanises people into action.

Case study

Make Poverty History (MPH)

The Make Poverty History coalition – part of the Global Campaign Against Poverty (GCAP) was created in 2004 to galvanise the Western world into action on the issue of world poverty. It coordinated a series of happenings and marches around the country over several months, culminating in the G8 summit at Gleneagles in Scotland. The timing of the main events was designed to coincide with the British presidency of the G8 and of the European Union, as well as with the 20th anniversary of Live Aid.

Fig. 12.1 *The Make Poverty History campaign in action*

The organisers of Make Poverty History wanted to see urgent action by world leaders, as part of a moral crusade 'to tackle the greatest evil of our times'. They argued that poverty was not caused primarily by nature, but by factors such as global trade, debt and insufficient and inefficient aid, exacerbated by the pursuit by governments of inappropriate economic policies.

Coalition backers included many churches, faith and charitable bodies, ranging from Advantage Africa to Afghan Poverty Relief, from the Movement for the Abolition of War to Tradecraft, and from Time for God to Tzedek (the Jewish Action for a Just World), supported by well-known clergy, entertainers (most prominently, Bob Geldof) and politicians, among many others.

At Gleneagles, the assembled delegates took decisions that went some way towards satisfying the demands of campaign organisers and the many people who supported the cause in Britain and around the world. Debt cancellation worth £25 billion and increases in aid were agreed, deals on trade and curbing the arms trade were referred for further discussion, and on climate change a compromise was reached. Perhaps inevitably, those involved were disappointed that more had not been achieved, but most recognised that real gains had been made.

Activities

1 Look up the Countryside Alliance (www.countryside-alliance.org) and the Campaign to Protect Hunted Animals (in particular the League Against Cruel Sports – www.league.org.uk). Compare and contrast the methods they have employed to get their messages across. Why do you think that the League was on the winning side and the Countryside Alliance was on the losing side of the issue of hunting in England and Wales?

2 With reference to the case studies on this and the following pages onwards, list the ways in which the campaigning of popular movements is different from that of traditional pressure groups.

Case study

The Countryside Alliance

The Countryside Alliance was formed in 1997 by a combination of groups committed to the rural way of life, among them the Association of Masters of Harriers and Beagles, the British Field Sports Society, the Country Land and Business Association, the Masters of Basset Hounds and the Timber Growers' Association. Their primary concern was fox hunting, although many inhabitants of rural areas were troubled by the general decline in farming; grievances ranging from falling farm incomes and the handling of the BSE episode; the particular problems of small-holdings that were finding it difficult to compete in global markets; high petrol prices; the closing of local branches of banks, hospitals, schools and post offices; and the recently-enacted **right to roam legislation**.

The Alliance was strongly critical of London-based politicians, particularly those in New Labour who opposed hunting and whom they accused of failure to understand rural living. It held its first mass rally in 1998, a well-organised protest, which attracted more than a quarter of a million people. Four years later, some 400,000 attended its similar Liberty and Livelihood rally.

Apart from mass gatherings, the Alliance's campaigning techniques involved lobbying Parliament (including the House of Lords whose members might be persuaded to delay the anti-hunting legislation), targeting MPs, appearing on the media and taking legal action in the courts. It challenged the Hunting Act's compatibility with the rights granted by the European Convention under Articles 8 (the right to private life), 11 (the right to freedom of assembly) and 14 (the right not to be discriminated against), as well as Article 1 of the First Protocol (the right to peaceful enjoyment of possession). However, judges in the High Court ruled that the ban was 'rational, necessary and proportionate'. In November 2007, the House of Lords rejected a further attempt to overturn the Hunting Act.

Fig 12.2 *The Countryside Alliance protest against the ban on hunting with dogs*

Case study

The fuel protests of 2000

Prior to every budget, the Treasury is advised by various interest groups to lower or at least not increase fuel duties on petrol and diesel, often without success. After the 2000 budget, small businesses in the road haulage and other industries dependent on using petrol and diesel (such as farmers and fishermen) kept up sustained pressure over the high level of fuel tax. The crisis in 2000 centred on the willingness of these discontented groups to use direct action against the Labour government in order to force the chancellor, Gordon Brown, to lower the price of fuel. The events that followed were more reminiscent of French than of British politics, the past behaviour of French farmers providing the inspiration for some of the tactics involved.

The direct action began on 7 September when a number of protesters started to picket the entrance to an oil refinery in Cheshire. Many of the pickets involved in protesting were from the small business sector. Within a few days, hardly any petrol was being delivered to petrol stations throughout Britain. Motorists engaged in panic buying and shortages of fuel developed. The events highlighted the vulnerability of even an advanced, modern economy to disruptive action.

By 11 September, the problem was escalating as petrol supplies were not getting out of the refineries, either because the petrol tanker drivers would not cross picket lines out of sympathy for the aggrieved protesters or because of fear of intimidation and reprisals.

Who was involved?

On the one side: A coalition of small businesspeople, farmers, fishermen and others whose livelihood was affected by the price of fuel (plus sympathetic motorists and politically motivated antagonists of the government).

On the other side: Ministers of the Labour government elected in 1997 and many anti-private transport campaigners in the environmentalist movement.

Who was caught in the cross-fire?

Oil companies, tanker drivers, the police, trade unions and the public.

The government could not be seen to yield to the threat of force, for to do so would be portrayed as weak and indecisive. Moreover, other groups would see that ministers could be pushed around. On the other hand, not to make any move would be to allow essential groups such as ambulance crews and those working in the blood transfusion service to be deprived of vital fuel, causing havoc in essential services; supermarkets would run out of food (panic buying of food soon became an issue); individuals going to work would be affected; and the public would become increasingly dismayed. Many motorists, long aggrieved by the high costs of fuel, were already becoming sympathetic to those engaged in direct action. There was a case for concessions, but they had to be handled sensitively and without undue haste or panic.

Ministers had backing from the trade union movement, for they saw the protest as being right wing in origin, backed as it was by small businesses and the Countryside Alliance; union leaders allowed tanker drivers to cross picket lines to get supplies of fuel moving. The public mood began to change in favour of ending the blockade, with many people wanting to see a cessation of action, for there were problems in getting to work and the danger that essential services would be endangered.

Later on, in November, the chancellor felt able to make a concession, freezing the fuel duties until the following budget and making other changes that effectively reduced the price of petrol and diesel. Direct action had highlighted the issue of high fuel prices and in a sense had the desired effect. The protesters eventually got some of what they wanted. But on the other hand, the government did not quickly back down. The rise and fall of the issue illustrated the importance of public support, if action is to succeed. At first, there was plenty of popular and media sympathy. It began to melt away, as the consequences of the confrontation became apparent.

Common themes in popular protests

From pro-hunt rallies to fuel blockades, from action on GM crops to anti-Iraq war demonstrations, examples of single issue protest have become a regular feature of British politics. Such actions suggest that far from being apathetic – as figures for electoral turnout in general elections might suggest – many potential voters are willing to involve themselves in political activity. However, they have preoccupations that do not neatly fit into the programmes advanced by mainstream political parties and are seeking some other form of expression.

There are common factors in the outlook and behaviour of some of the popular campaigns:

▓ *They tend to emerge abruptly*, perhaps ignited by a spark such as the rapid increase in petrol prices on garage forecourts or the shootings at Dunblane (the fuel protest and Snowdrop, respectively).

▓ *They are usually based on issues that arouse an emotional response*, perhaps fuelled by extensive coverage.

▓ *They often use direct action* to draw attention to their demands.

▓ *They tend to make use of technological advances:* Technology has assisted protesters and also journalists, who have become ever more alive to the opportunities for identifying themselves with causes, the publicising of which might help to establish their own careers. Modern forms of communication have helped, giving protesters increased mobility and access to the worldwide web, e-mail and mobile phones, all of which have become apparent in many protests of recent years and can be collectively grouped as methods of **e-democracy**. For instance, in the fuel protest, groups of activists were able to move rapidly from one hot spot to another and small bands of truck drivers formed slow- moving convoys to disrupt traffic flows. The use of the internet and mobile phones was the key to their organisation.

▓ *They often get a swift – if carefully managed – governmental response*, to head off the escalating protest. They rely on the implied threat that the government will lose votes in the next election if it does not act quickly.

Activity

In what senses can the campaigning activities of the three movements described (MPH, CA and the fuel protest) be considered successful? To what do you attribute any success they achieved?

Key terms

E-democracy: a combination of the words 'electronic' and 'democracy', refers to the use of electronic communications technologies that have become increasingly significant in enhancing democratic processes in modern representative democracies. (The term can include within its scope types of electronic voting, but usually it has a much wider meaning.)

Campaigns may tap into a vein of moral and/or social concern (Make Poverty History and Snowdrop). Often, rather than relying on persuasion and rational argument, and operating through the conventional pressure groups' methods of lobbying the executive and legislature and participating in inquiries and commissions, popular movements often rely more on the implied threat of a mass revolt at the ballot box (the fuel protests and the Countryside Alliance campaigns).

Such activity does not fall easily into the classic typologies of pressure group activity. Movements cannot easily be described as protective or promotional. They have features of both protective and promotional groups (see pages 281–2), for they represent the private interests of those whose lifestyle or livelihood has been threatened or damaged (rural interests in the case of the Countryside March and parents in the case of Snowdrop). But their campaigning quickly develops into a wider crusade for action supported by many people not immediately involved and with no personal interest at stake. Of the fuel tax protesters, McNaughton (2001) notes how: '[they] managed to tie their case to a general concern with high levels of taxation and the poor state of public transport in general'. Their activity illustrates that outsider groups can achieve success, if they can create a high level of public response.

Opinions vary about the contribution that such popular movements make to democracy. It can be viewed as positive, in that they mobilise the interest and encourage the participation of many people who would otherwise remain uninvolved in the political process. They illustrate that ordinary people can have an impact on government and force those who govern to be responsive to public concerns. But on the other hand, their behaviour is coercive in that there is an implied threat that if their grievances are not addressed there will be serious consequences for those in authority, possibly mass punishment at the ballot box.

Finally, among the campaigners who have from time to time captured the political agenda in the Blair/Brown years, a number are bracketed with the political Reft – as many protesters of the past have often been (see the examples that follow). But with the absence of an effective parliamentary opposition between 1997 and 2005, the right-wing press seized on particular themes as the basis for an attack on ministers. As Kirsty Milne (2005) pointed out, 'what is new is the congruence of protest, a partisan press in search of causes and an electorate whose anxieties are not being represented. The fuel protesters, **section 28** campaigners and Countryside Alliance have all championed causes usually associated with the political Right ... Protest has been reclaimed by anyone who feels their identity under threat, be they fox-hunting polo players or villagers with gypsies on their doorstep'.

Radical protest campaigning

The politics of left-wing protest have a long history in Britain. In the 19th century, members of the anti-slavery movement, the Chartist societies and the Anti-Corn Law League, all used forms of direct action within and beyond the law. In the 20th century, the suffragettes and the **Jarrow marchers** of the hungry unemployed used similar methods. But in the late 20th and early 21st centuries, protest has become markedly more widespread and more people have been willing to take part, whether by signing a petition, forming an action group or attending a demonstration. Some have been willing to use more dramatic methods. Today, activists find that they can attract more media attention than ever before, for editors and journalists are keen to seize on issues and actions that make a good story and provide strong visuals.

Further information

e-democracy

- The use of e-democracy is still in its infancy as a democratic tool and the subject of much debate within government, civic-oriented groups and societies around the world.

- To supporters, they increase citizen participation, help make decision-making processes on public policy more accessible and are a more direct means of influence than the traditional democratic forms. They make government closer to the people and give it legitimacy.

- Detractors sometimes portray e-democracy as a form of populism that verges on demagoguery. They do not wish to see government based on the transient whims of those keen to 'sound off' on various issues. Others point to the lack of access to such methods by a substantial section of the population, who are more likely to be the least well off and least powerful already (although today most young people probably have the means to express their views via blogging and other forms of citizen journalism).

Key terms

Section 28: a notorious clause of the Local Government Act, which forbade the promotion of homosexuality in the classroom. Defended by many on the moral Right, it was strongly opposed by many on the Centre-Left. In Scotland – and then later in England and Wales – it provided the material for a political clash, prior to its removal by legislation.

Jarrow marchers: the people who marched to London in 1936 to protest against massive unemployment in their town in the North-East of England. This was the best known of several marches organised by local town councils troubled by the number out of work in their areas. They were joined by many other marchers on their journeys.

Earth First!: a worldwide movement that believes in biocentrism, the idea that life of the Earth comes first. It has no members, but Earth Firsters use a range of campaigning techniques ranging from grassroots organising and involvement in the legal process to civil disobedience and monkey-wrenching (the waging of economic warfare by sabotage, with the intention of slowing down or halting activities that monkey-wrenchers perceive as destructive).

Fig 12.3 *The Earth First! logo for their Autumn 2008 get together, for which the theme was Ecological Direct Action Without Compromise!*

■ **Activity**

Read through the case study on Earth First! What do you learn about the way in which it operates? What advice does it give to those planning a campaign? How does it see its own role in ecological protest? What benefits might be derived from engaging in such protest?

■ Case study

Earth First! and its campaigning approach

According to its website, the general principles behind **Earth First!** are:

non-hierarchical organisation and the use of direct action to confront, stop and eventually reverse the forces that are responsible for the destruction of the Earth and its inhabitants. EF! is not a cohesive group or campaign, but a convenient banner for people who share similar philosophies to work under ...

If you agree with the above and you are not racist or otherwise discriminatory, if you believe action speaks louder than words, then Earth First! is for you. Whether you think of EF! as a movement, a network, an idea or a thing, get involved – you are Earth First!

Set up a group

Want to set up an ecological direct action group or you are an existing group that wants to be part of our loose community?

Talk to a few people, put up posters, stickers, cards in windows, send out emails or whatever. Pick a group name; best to have a more anonymous contact rather than your name or own e-mail address. It only needs you and a couple of others to form a group – then you can plot and plan actions like the best.

Pick issues and approaches that suit you and where you live – you are an autonomous group, so just figure out the way you want to do it, and do it.

Don't forget to share what you get up to, or put a shout out if you need a hand.

Meet others

EF! has always welcomed diversity, and there are EF! groups all over the world.

EF! is many things to many people. Get started and make it how you want it to be.

Every summer we have the EF! summer gathering – come to get involved in ecological direct action, it's also for those already involved to plan for action & share skills. Sometimes when there's been a need, there has been an EF! winter moot, to spend a few days chatting and strategising.

Anti-globalisation protest

The 1990s saw the emergence of a widespread movement of opposition to globalisation. It is not an easy movement to characterise, but three broad points can be emphasised:

■ *The anti-globalisation movement is diffuse:* There are self-appointed spokespersons such as Ralph Nader, Naomi Klein and the late Anita Roddick rather than accredited leaders and there is little in the way of formal organisation. **Anti-globalisation** is best thought of as an umbrella term covering a wide range of groups, from environmentalists, campaigners for debt relief to human rights activists and so on, with a wide range of beliefs and concerns.

It is economic rather than technological or cultural globalisation that has aroused the deepest feelings of opposition: Opponents of globalisation see American-style capitalism as the root cause of world poverty, the debt crisis and environmental pollution. Anti-globalisation thus to a large extent equates with anti-capitalism. Anti-globalisation activists have made business centres and conferences of global financial institutions the targets of their demonstrations. Although a number of these demonstrations have ended in violence it would be quite wrong to conclude that most anti-globalisation activists support violent protest.

There is a strong thread of anti-Americanism running through the anti-globalisation movement: The USA is seen as the architect of the existing international economic order, as the lair of the most powerful multinationals and as the world's worst polluter. Otherwise disparate groups can make common cause in viewing the USA as the enemy – particularly when its president has been (until January 2009) a right-wing Republican whose administration had close links with leading multi-national corporations.

Case study

The right to engage in anti-globalisation protest under the UNDHR (United Nations Universal Declaration of Human Rights)

By organising mass demonstrations at key international meetings, anti-globalisation activists are taking advantage of the universal right to freedom of association and assembly (Article 10) in an innovative way.

While the majority of protesters are non-violent, there is a small camp of radical protesters who actively incite violence at demonstrations by hurling missiles or destroying property.

During anti-globalisation demonstrations, police in several US and European cities have reacted to the violence of these few protesters by allegedly using excessive force in non-violent situations.

Anti-globalisation protestors tend to fall into one of three camps:

- The first group contains those protesters who are unwilling to break any law. The majority of demonstrators fall into this category.
- The second is made up of those who engage in peaceful civil disobedience in the tradition of Gandhi and Martin Luther King.
- Finally, there is a small camp of radical protesters who actively incite violence by hurling missiles or destroying property such as barricades, news-stands and shop windows.

Many would argue that they have effectively surrendered their right to assembly under the terms of the Universal Declaration, which only protects peaceful assemblies.

Source: 'I have a right …', BBC World Service website

Key terms

Anti-globalisation: the political outlook of those social movements that protest against global trade agreements and the impact they have on the world's poorest people, on the environment and on the prospects for international peace. One such movement is known as the Global Justice Movement.

Table 12.2 *Major anti-globalisation demonstrations*

1999	London	May Day demonstration in the City, London's financial district: extensive damage to property
1999	Seattle	50,000 demonstrators protested at a World Trade Organisation conference: turned into the 'battle of Seattle', with 600 arrests made
2000	Davos	Demonstration at the annual meeting of the World Economic Forum at the Swiss resort of Davos; dozens of injuries and hundreds of arrests
2001	Quebec	30,000 protestors took to the streets at the Summit of the Americas: over 400 people arrested as police clashed with demonstrators
2001	Genoa	100,000 demonstrators took part in protests at the G8 Summit, a conference of leaders of the world's eight most powerful economies: one protestor shot dead, dozens injured.

Activities

1 Write a paragraph to explain the nature of anti-globalisation. Do you believe that protesters have a 'right' to air their views in mass demonstrations? In what respects do protesters vary in their broad approach to demonstrating?

2 Find on the internet details and photos of any recent anti-globalisation protests, for instance that in Heiligendamm, the venue of the 2007 G8 summit. Notice what form the protests take.

3 What are the strengths and weaknesses of the Stop the War Coalition as a campaigning movement? Does it provide an appropriate vehicle for any young person who wishes to protest against government actions in Afghanistan and Iraq?

4 Popular protests often arise out of issues to which parties and ministers have on occasion been slow to respond, with those in government sometimes caught unaware or not comprehending of the scale of public disaffection'. Write a list or a few sentences to say whether this is true of the examples in this chapter.

The Stop the War Coalition

Aims

The Stop the War Coalition was formed on September 21st, 2001 at a public meeting of over 2,000 people in London. The platform statement below was ratified at public meetings held in October 2001 in London:

1 The aim of the Coalition should be very simple: to stop the war currently declared by the United States and its allies against 'terrorism'. We condemn the attacks on New York and we feel the greatest compassion for those who lost their life on 11th September 2001. But any war will simply add to the numbers of innocent dead, cause untold suffering, political and economic instability on a global scale, increase racism and result in attacks on civil liberties. The aims of the campaign would be best expressed in the name Stop the War Coalition.

2 Supporters of the Coalition, whether organisations or individuals, will of course be free to develop their own analyses and organise their own actions. But there will be many important occasions when united initiatives around broad stop the war slogans can mobilise the greatest numbers.

3 The Coalition shall elect a steering committee which reflects the breadth of those involved to carry forward the aims and objectives. Local groups should have regular, open and inclusive meetings.

4 We call on all peace activists and organisations, trade unionists, campaigners and labour movement organisations to join with us in building a mass movement that can stop the drive to war.

5 We are committed to opposing any racist backlash generated by this war. We will fight to stop the erosion of civil rights.

Stop the War – as it is better known – has been the most prominent group in Britain campaigning against the wars in Afghanistan and Iraq. Once plans for the invasion of Iraq were under way, the slogan 'Not in my name' was widely used. The demonstration against the war in February 2003 – organised in association with the Campaign for Nuclear Disarmament (CND) and the Muslim Association of Britain – is claimed by its organisers to be the largest public demonstration in British history. Estimates of attendance vary between 750,000 and 2 million people. Prominent speakers included Tony Benn, Charles Kennedy, Ken Livingstone and the writer Harold Pinter.

Since then, a range of national demonstrations have been staged, as well as a number of actions by local branches around the UK. Many of the meetings have attracted enthusiastic support, including that of many young people. Some critics of the Coalition have declared that the Socialist Workers Party has too much influence within the organisation. Others have commented on its failure to condemn the Iraqi regime of Saddam Hussein and terrorist attacks within post-war Iraq.

AQA Examination-style questions

Note that the syllabus content and marking schemes have been revised since these papers were sat, although the subject, matter used here remains relevant to the current specification.

1 Read the extract below and answer parts (a) and (b) which follow.

This extract represents the views of a pressure group.

The Countryside Alliance works for everyone who loves the countryside and the rural way of life. Through campaigning, lobbying, publicity and education the Alliance influences legislation and public policy that impacts on the countryside, rural people and their activities.

The Alliance campaigns on a wide range of rural issues.

Our campaigning activities are supported by our public relations, political, and policy teams.

The Alliance is a membership organisation with incorporated company status and has over 107,000 members. The Alliance is politically non-aligned and acts in partnership and cooperation with many other rural groups including the British Association for Shooting and Conservation, the Country Land and Business Association, the Farmers' Union of Wales, The Game Conservancy Trust and the National Farmers' Union. The Alliance distributes a free weekly e-bulletin called the grass e-route. The grass e-route is open to all members and supporters and brings all the Alliance's latest news, views, events and plans straight to your inbox.

Source: adapted from www.countryside-alliance.org.uk

Your answers should refer to the extract as appropriate, but you should also include other relevant information.

(a) Identify **two** ways in which the internet aids campaigning. *(5 marks)*

(b) To what extent is the Countryside Alliance an outsider pressure group? *(10 marks)*

Taken from AQA specimen paper

2 (a) *Briefly* examine, using examples, why some groups are more successful than others when campaigning to influence a political decision. *(5 marks)*

(b) Using examples, assess the view that direct action campaigning is usually counter-productive to the cause it seeks to promote. *(10 marks)*

Taken from AQA papers June 2006 and June 2007, respectively

3 (a) Briefly examine, using examples, the argument that the media is too influential in setting the political agenda. *(5 marks)*

(b) Mass media coverage can make or break a campaign. Assess this statement with reference to any campaign designed to influence political decision making. *(10 marks)*

Taken from AQA papers, June 2006 and June 2005, respectively

4 (a) Briefly examine the case for **or** against devolving power to the nations and regions of the United Kingdom. *(5 marks)*

(b) How well has the devolution of power to the Scottish Parliament worked in practice *(10 marks)*

Part (a) taken from AQA paper, June 2005

13

Active citizenship skills and participation

Learning objectives:

- to gather information on the issue in question

- to analyse and evaluate the arguments for and against the issue

- to understand the implications of campaigns

- to consider the campaign methods used and media representation of the campaign

- to develop links with the local community.

The specifications for the AQA course build upon the ideas outlined above:

> A key element of Citizenship education is developing a student's skills, confidence and conviction to enable them to take action on citizenship issues in their communities to bring about change.

Central to this GCE Citizenship Studies Specification is active citizenship participation, allowing students to participate more effectively as citizens and take an active role in society. This specification builds on previous learning to enable students to move through three stages of citizenship development:

- becoming an *informed citizen*: developing citizenship knowledge
- becoming a *participating citizen*: developing citizenship skills and the ability to take part
- becoming an *active citizen*: using knowledge and skills to bring about change.

■ Tackling citizenship activities as part of your course: advice to students

When planning active citizenship projects, it is desirable that they be as youth-led as possible. This ensures that the issue is relevant and of interest to the key people involved, you, the students. It also fulfils the requirements of the Report of the Advisory Group on Citizenship for 16–19-year-olds in Education and Training (2000) namely that in post-16 Citizenship education young people should assume responsibility for a cause themselves.

Planning the activity

The first stage is to devise a list of issues that are of concern to you and your colleagues. A brainstorming session might find out what makes any of you upset/angry or what you feel is wrong in the local community or society at large. Issues currently in the news might offer other possibilities. If you feel that you have little knowledge about them, then the answer might be to think about how individually and collectively you could become more informed.

Other students will have different concerns to you. You will need to justify your choice, in the same way that others will also need to do. You will need to demonstrate that it is a matter of public importance and listen to the rival claims made by those around you. In so doing, you will have a chance to consider whether or not the issues under discussion are really citizenship issues. Are they really 'good works' or are they actually schemes of active citizenship? If they are the former, might they be capable of adaptation to become the latter?

Resolving such issues will enhance your skills of negotiation and compromise. Such deliberations encourage you to develop and exhibit the ability to mount a persuasive argument and to work as part of a team. Your tutor will be able to advise on what are and are not appropriate topics (perhaps pointing out potential pitfalls), in the light of his or her experience.

Some possible subjects for projects

■ Some issues provide the basis for activity that can take place in school or college, such as the creation of a School or College Council if there is not one already, or the improvement of an existing council. School or college policies in a variety of areas might be reviewed, from anti-bullying to help for slower-learning pupils, from the quality of sex education to treatment of pupils with a disability. In some cases, there may be a chance to consider the ways in which the school or college caters for new arrivals from overseas, be they members of families seeking asylum or who are economic migrants.

■ Others may be more community-based, such as clean-up campaigns of some part of the neighbourhood, recycling schemes, raising funds for some local charity or organising an inter-faith event.

■ Finally, some may be concerned with issues of national or international controversy, perhaps British government policy on GM (genetically modified) crops, energy sources or support for the Arts, or matters affecting the developing world, such as global inequality, the promotion of fair trade or protest against the treatment of political prisoners in support of Amnesty International.

Remember that in planning your activities, there are three dimensions in the AQA specifications:

■ *Becoming an informed citizen:* This may involve finding out about some issue on which you and other members of the group lack an adequate understanding (the extent of prejudice against immigrants in the local community or the complexities of the Palestinian question in the Middle East for example). Sometimes, important national or international issues in the news can be given a local focus, perhaps an issue of environmental concern such as conservation of resources.

■ *Becoming a participative citizen:* In school or college, this could involve participating in a class debate on some agreed topic, taking part in a school, college or local (if you are eligible) election, helping to run a student newspaper or being an active student mentor. In the local community, it might involve acting as a blood donor or joining some local action group. Nationally, it might involve being a part of some national pressure group campaign or writing to show support of some cause of importance to members of your group.

■ *Being an active citizen:* More than being a useful but passive participant, you might become involved in organising a school or college event, standing as the candidate for the School or College Council, promoting the case for fair trade. Locally, you might contact a councillor about the need to clear a run-down area of the community or the lack of amenities for young or elderly people and organise an action group to bring about change. Nationally, you might attend your MP's surgery to make known your views on anything from the war on terror to climate change, or you might take part in some national demonstration.

Each activity that you choose might involve all the stages of active citizenship mentioned above – informed, participating and active. Alternatively, activities might highlight a single area of active citizenship, such as acquiring a detailed knowledge and understanding of a key issue.

Drawing up an action plan

Having decided upon an issue or issues to investigate further, discussion can take place over the way ahead. This involves considering the means by which information might be gathered, the people to interview and the allocation of tasks. In particular, it involves further reflection upon the nature of the change you wish to bring about and how this might be achieved. Will it require the involvement of other people outside the group, perhaps in the school, neighbourhood or wider community? Will it necessitate bringing together and coordinating other groups within the vicinity? Will it involve organising a meeting? Should local councillors or your MP be invited? Will it require publicity?

Recording and evaluating what has been done

When the activity has been completed, there will be a need for writing up conclusions and, where necessary, making recommendations for action to whatever authority is involved, for instance the school management team, the local council or even to an MP.

Bearing in mind the need for any activity or enterprise to be evaluated and related to the needs of society (so that it fulfils the requirements of active citizenship), there needs to be an opportunity for reflection and discussion. To what extent have the aims of the exercise been achieved? Have they succeeded in bringing about desirable change? What could have been done differently? What more is left to do?

Finally, there is the need to record findings and conclusions in your Active Citizenship Profile (ACP), which will help you when you take your examination (see the Box on page 315).

Some of the means of developing participation and responsible action ia your activities were summarised in the Ofsted Report, *Towards Consensus*, as quoted in the AQA specifications:

- participation in class debate, exercising knowledge and understanding about becoming informed citizens, with pupils making responsible suggestions
- written and other class and home work arising from work in citizenship, taken to sensible conclusions and containing responsible suggestions
- where appropriate, recommendations, delivered in a responsible way to the management of the school, local authorities and other bodies, on policies and practice (for example, via the school council)
- where appropriate, recommendations, delivered responsibly, to the public at large in school publications and on school internet sites.

The importance of the AQA's Active Citizenship Profile in answering examination questions

The Active Citizenship Profile (ACP) provides an opportunity for students to record their involvement in a number of citizenship activities that may take place in the classroom, school/college or the wider community and be linked to local, national or global issues, as appropriate. The whole of the compulsory section B of the examination paper links to the work carried out for the ACP. It will be available in the exam room whilst students tackle this paper. It will provide examples to be drawn upon in offering responses to the questions set. Questions will require students critically to assess Active Citizenship with reference to work they have completed in this area.

The specimen question on Active Citizenship illustrates this approach well:

> 'Active citizenship is just about helping others'. Using examples from your own active citizenship participation critically assess this claim. *(25 marks)*

Key words or phrases in the question are 'active citizenship', 'examples' and 'critically assess':

- 'Active citizenship' is the essential theme of the piece of extended writing. It needs to be carefully defined, the distinction between 'active citizenship' and 'helping others' being clearly made.
- 'Examples' requires a selection of well-chosen cases to illustrate the quotation, certainly more than one, preferably a selection of types of issue
- 'Critically assess' means evaluate in a critical way, examining the 'for' and 'against' points relevant to the quotation.

Getting involved in community life

Citizenship involves people being active within their communities. They can do this in several ways, some on an individual basis; others in concert with other people. For instance, you might get involved in:

- doing good works (e.g. being neighbourly)
- doing voluntary work (e.g. taking part in collections or working in a charity shop)
- letter-writing (e.g. as part of an **Amnesty International** campaign on behalf of a suffering individual)
- joining a political party or pressure group (e.g. paying a subscription and perhaps attending meetings)
- being active within a party or pressure group (e.g. canvassing, producing a newsletter or organising meetings)
- standing for public office (e.g. as a councillor or parliamentary candidate)
- voting in various levels of elections
- planning and organising a campaign on a matter of importance to you (e.g. a clean-up of your locality).

Such things will enable you to use your influence to bring about change. Read the case study below on making a difference to see how individuals can become involved in helping the cause of elderly people.

> ### Key terms
>
> **Amnesty International:** a worldwide movement of people who campaign for internationally recognised human rights for all. It seeks to mobilise the 2.2 million members in more than 150 countries to put pressure on governments, armed groups, companies and intergovernmental bodies, for example by mass letter-writing.

Case study

Making a difference in the community

- **Support Help the Aged; together we can make a difference to the lives of older people**

There are many ways you can get involved with Help the Aged. Whether you raise money, make a donation, run a marathon or help in one of our shops, your support is vital to improve the lives of older people in the UK and overseas.

- **The Myanmar (Burma) Cyclone Appeal**

Tens of thousands of people have died and up to 1 million are believed to be homeless. We urgently need your help.

Activities

1 Refer back to page 267 on participation and in particular Crick's reasons for it. Write down a few ideas to say why voluntary activity is a) good for the individuals who engage in it and b) good for democracy.

2 Using the examples given by Help the Aged of how people might get involved in its work, list those you think might be of interest to young people.

– Make a donation.

■ **The Leeds Abbey Dash 2008**

The Dash is back, and registration has just opened!

– Sign up for the Leeds Abbey Dash.

■ **Overseas treks and cycle challenges**

Enjoy the adventure of a lifetime while raising money for Help the Aged.

– Cycle London to Amsterdam.

– Trek India.

■ **Run for Help the Aged**

– Have fun, get fit and raise money for older people.

■ **Be a volunteer**

Develop your skills and help older people.

– Work in our shops.

– Work in the community.

■ **Volunteer collectors**

– We need volunteers to collect money for Help the Aged outside B&Q stores on 14 and 15 June.

■ **Join us on Facebook**

Together we can make a difference to the lives of older people.

■ **Turn clutter into cash**

Clear your home and help support our charity shops.

■ **Regular gifts are vital to Help the Aged**

With your regular gifts, we can plan and commit to long term projects and campaigns.

– Set up a regular donation.

– Payroll giving.

■ **Recycling**

You can recycle all sorts of things to help us raise money.

– Recycle your mobile.

– Recycle old stamps.

– Schools recycling scheme.

Source: www.helptheaged.org.uk

Further information

A *How to organise an activity* guide is available from www.unitedagainstracism.org

For the publication *Organising a campaign* see www.myd.govt.nz

Planning and organising a campaign

The ways in which campaigners organise their activities depends on the type of campaign involved, be it individual, group or community-based. We have already seen some of the ways in which local and group campaigns go about their tasks (see pages 283–6). The Further information feature opposite gives some useful ideas on how to approach the task of planning a campaign.

Imagine that you are organising a campaign to encourage the use of Fairtrade goods (e.g. chocolate, coffee and tea) at your school or college. If so, you might plan along these lines:

■ *Your first objective is to raise awareness*, so that people recognise the Fairtrade 'brand' and understand what Fairtrade does and why it is important. To do this, you might give talks in assemblies and tutorials, run a poster campaign and run stalls at break-times – to let people taste Fairtrade products and give out information about them and the cause in general.

■ *Your second objective is to make it easier for people to buy Fairtrade products*, by getting them stocked in the school canteen, vending machines and canteen. To get Fairtrade stocked, ask students coming to your tasting stall to sign a petition to the canteen manager, write to ask your school or college governors for their support and meet with your head-teacher.

How your activities will benefit you: the skills acquired

In an appendix, the authors of the 2000 Advisory Group report drew attention to the ideal characteristics of young people who had undergone a course in post-16 Active Citizenship. As a result of your studies, you should become as follows:

■ *independent enquirers* who can plan and carry out research, identify key issues, view events or problems from different perspectives and appreciate the consequences of actions and decisions.

■ *creative thinkers* who can ask questions to extend your own thinking, generate ideas and explore possibilities and connect your own and others' ideas and experiences in inventive ways.

■ *reflective learners* who can establish goals and criteria for their development and work, assess yourself and others, review progress and act upon the outcomes.

■ *team workers* who can collaborate with others to work towards common goals, reach agreements, manage discussions, take responsibility and provide constructive support and feedback to colleagues.

■ *self- managers* who can seek out challenges or new responsibilities, show flexibility when priorities change, work towards goals, organise time and resources, prioritise actions and respond positively to change.

■ *effective participators* who can discuss issues of concern, present a persuasive case for action, propose practical ways forward and identify improvements that would benefit others as well as yourself.

Towards an informed and participative democracy

We have seen in Chapter 11 that there are some indications of apathy and alienation within the population as a whole. Some of them apply to young adults, for example the reluctance to vote. Yet there are many examples of voluntary involvement by young people in working with the community that demonstrate what can be done. While individuals may opt in and out of membership of political parties and pressure groups, we all face the challenge of living and working in the increasingly complex world of the 21st century. We can either allow others to make the decisions for us or, via the knowledge and skills we have developed, take some control over our own lives and influence decisions that affect us.

There is plenty of evidence to show that many young people wish to have a role in making informed choices and contributing to society. The skills you acquire from the opportunities presented in A/S Citizenship will hopefully equip you to be informed, participating and active members of your school or college, neighbourhood, country and world.

Further information

Key points to bear in mind when planning a campaign

■ Thought, planning and effort are essential

■ Decide on your issue or theme – something you feel strongly about

■ Define the issues – be clear on your objective

■ Brainstorm for ideas on techniques of persuasion and publicity

■ Be realistic – ensure that the goals and methods are achievable

■ Make a plan of action – allocate responsibilities, set a time-scale

■ As you proceed, keep records e.g. meeting notes, copies of media releases and photographs

■ At the end evaluate your campaign – ask yourselves what went well and, if you were repeating the exercise, what you might do differently.

Activities

1 Using the advice from Earth First! on page 294 as a guide, write a couple of paragraphs on what you regard as the essentials of a good, well-organised campaign. As you contemplate your answer, bear in mind the three Cs – commitment, contacts and creativity – and see how they assist you in your planning. You might list key points in order of priority.

2 If you were starting a national campaign to reintroduce capital punishment for those found guilty of murder, how would you go about it? List any things you could do that might make success more likely.

References

Allport G. (1954) *The Nature of Prejudice*, Cambridge, MA: Addison-Wesley.

Baggott R. (2000) *Pressure Groups and the Policy Process*, Sheffield: Sheffield Hallam University Press.

Baggott R. (1995) *Pressure Groups Today*, Manchester: Manchester University Press.

Bale T. (2005) *European Politics: A Comparative Introduction*, Basingstoke: Palgrave Macmillan.

Blondel J. (1965) *Voters, Parties and Leaders: The Social Fabric of British Politics*, Harmondsworth: Penguin Books.

Bogdanor V. (2003) *The British Constitution in the Twentieth Century*, Oxford: Clarendon Press.

Bowler S. and Farrell D. (1992) *Electoral Strategies and Political Marketing*, Basingstoke: Palgrave Macmillan.

Brecher J. et al. (2000) *Globalization from Below – the Power of Solidarity*, Cambridge, MA: South End Press

Bruce B. (1992) *Images of Power*, London: Kogan Page.

Budge I. et al. (1998) *The New British Politics*, London: Longman.

Coard B. (1971) *How the West Indian Child is Made Educationally Subnormal in the British School System*, London: New Beacon Books.

Crewe I. (1996) *Comparative Research on Attitudes of Young People*, London: Wiley.

Crick B. (1978) 'Basic concepts for political education' in B. Crick and E. Porter (eds), *Political Education and Political Literacy*, London: Longman.

(1998) 'Crick Report', Report on the Advisory Group on Education for Citizenship, QCA.

Dicey A. (1885) *Introduction to the Study of Law and the Constitution*, London: Macmillan.

Etzioni A. (1995) *The Spirit of Community: Rights, Responsibilities and the Communitarian Agenda*, London: Fontana.

Evans M. (1997) 'Political participation' in *Developments in Modern Politics 5*, London: Macmillan.

Farrell D. (1997) *Comparing Electoral Systems*, London: Harvester Wheatsheaf.

Finer S. (1967) *Anonymous Empire*, London: Pall Mall.

Gallie D., Marsh C. and Vogler C. (1993) *Social Change and the Experience of Unemployment*, Oxford: Oxford University Press.

Grant W. (2000) *Pressure Groups and British Politics*, Basingstoke: Palgrave Macmillan.

Gunther J. (1947) *Inside U.S.A.*, New York, NY: Harper and Brothers.

Hague R., Harrop M. (2004) *Comparative Government and Politics: An Introduction*, Basingstoke: Palgrave.

Hutton W. (1995) *The State We're in: Why Britain Is in Crisis and How to Overcome It*, London: Vintage.

Katz D. and Braly K. (1933) 'Racial stereotypes of one hundred college students', Journal of Abnormal and Social Psychology 28.

Kavanagh D. (1993) *Election Campaigning: The New Marketing of Politics*, Oxford: Blackwell.

Kavanagh D. and Butler D. (2005) *The British General Election of 2005*, Basingstoke: Palgrave.

Lippman W. (1922) 'Public opinion' in *Stereotypes*, New York, NY: Macmillan.

Macionis J. and Plummer K. (2005) Sociology: *A Global Introduction*, London: Pearson.

Marshall T. (1950) 'Citizenship and social class' in T. Marshall, *Sociology at the Crossroads*, London: Heinemann.

McNaughton N. (2001) 'Populist movements', *Talking Politics* 4:1.

Meehan D. (1983) *Ladies of the Evening: Women Characters on Prime-Time Television*, Metuchen, NJ: Scarecrow Press.

Milbrath L. and Goel M. (1977) *Political Participation: How and Why Do People Get Involved in Politics?*, Chicago, IL: Rand McNally.

Milne K. (2005) *Manufacturing Dissent: Single-Issue Protest, the Public and the Press*, London: Demos.

Morris G. (1999) 'The European Convention on Human Rights and Employment: to which acts does it apply?', *European Human Rights Law Review*, (i).

Osborne D. and Gaebler T. (1992) *Reinventing Government*, Reading, MA: Addison-Wesley.

Ouseley H. 'Community pride not prejudice', Bradford Vision (formed by Bradford Council and other local organisations), 7.3.05.

T. Paine, pamphlet (1995) 'Commonsense' (1776) and book *The Rights of Man* (1791) included in Collected Works, Library of America.

Parry G. et al. (1992) *Political Participation and Democracy in Britain*, Cambridge: Cambridge University Press.

Rauscher L., McLintock M. (1997) 'Ableism in curriculum design' in M. Adams. et al. (eds), *Teaching for Diversity and Social Justice*, London: Routledge.

Rush M. (1990) *Parliament and Pressure Groups*, Oxford: Clarendon Press.

Sampson A. (1971) *The New Anatomy of Britain*, London: Hodder & Stoughton.

Starmer K. (2003) 'Two years of the Human Rights Act', *European Human Rights Law Review*, (i.)

Stewart J. (1958) *British Pressure Groups*, Oxford: Oxford University Press.

Stoker G. (1996) *Talking Politics*, London: Palgrave.

Trowler P. (1999) *Investigating Mass Media*, London: Collins Educational.

Weber M. (1947) *The Theory of Social and Economic Organisation*, New York, NY: Free Press (re-issue of 1922 original).

Wedell E. (1968) *Broadcasting and Public Policy*, London: Joseph Books.

Weeks J. (1991) *Against Nature: Essays on History, Sexuality and Identity*, London: Rivers Oram Press.

Index

A

ableism 47, 50
absolute poverty 57, 57–9
abstainers 260
ACAS (Arbitration, Conciliation and Arbitration Service) 134
  case study 134
access points 271
accession countries 27
action plan, active citizenship 300
active citizenship 2
  action plan 300
  campaigning 302–3
  case study 6–7, 301–2
  citizen participation 298–303
  evaluating 300–1
  planning 298
  project subjects 299
  recording 300–1
  skills 298–303
administrative devolution 221
administrative law 135, 135–6
ADR see alternative disputes resolution
Advertising Standards Agency 205
advocacy 128
affirmative action programmes 71
age discrimination 50
ageism 47, 50, 71
agenda-setting 207
Airport Watch
  campaigning 283–5
  case study 283–5
al Qaeda 164
alienation 253
alternative disputes resolution (ADR) 133–7
American Declaration of Independence (1776) 65
Amitai Etzioni 4
Amnesty International 301
anti-discrimination policies 67–74
  case study 69
  policies instituted 70–4
anti-globalisation 294–5, 295
  case study 295
anti-smoking campaign, case study 3
antilocution 51
apathy 253
arbitration 133–4
ASBOs 121
assimilation, race relations 37

Asylum and Immigration Tribunal, case study 136
asylum seekers 22
asymmetric devolution 210
Athenian democracy 1, 2
Atlanticist 237
authoritarian regimes 161
autonomy 229

B

bail-out 179
balance of payments (BOP) 182–3
balancing conflicting interests 139–40
bandwagon effect 266
Bank of England 166, 184–5
banks
  Bank of England 166, 184–5
  clearing banks 179
  merchant banks 179, 180
  Northern Rock Bank 179, 180–2
The Bar 129
barristers 128–9
Basque nationalists 164
Best Value 230
bicameral legislatures 214
big tent 175
Birmingham Six 201
birth rate 23
black performance, case study 54
Blackpool, case study 58–9
Blackshirts 94
Blair, Tony, media 202–3
blasphemy 89
  case study 89–90
blogging 191
BME (black and minority ethnic) 124
boomerang effect 266
bovine spongiform encephalopathy (BSE) 273
BRC see British Retail Consortium
Britain see United Kingdom
British dependent territories 9
British overseas citizens 9
British Retail Consortium (BRC) 269, 269–70
Britishness 12–15
broadsheets 191
BSE see bovine spongiform encephalopathy
bullying 48, 49
by-elections 260

C

Cabinet 165, 217–18
Cabinet committees 218
Campaign for Nuclear Disarmament (CND) 288, 296
campaigning 283–97
  see also lobbying; pressure groups
  active citizenship 302–3
  Airport Watch 283–5
  anti-smoking campaign 3
  case study 283–6, 289–96
  election campaign 262–3
  Examination-style questions 297
  negative campaigning 264
  popular movements 289–96
  radical protest campaigning 293–4
  successful 286–8
canvassing 263
CAP see Common Agricultural Policy
capital punishment 120
capital value 230
capitalism 177
case law 116
case study
  ACAS (Arbitration, Conciliation and Arbitration Service) 134
  active citizenship 6–7, 301–2
  Airport Watch 283–5
  anti-discrimination policies 69
  anti-globalisation 295
  anti-smoking campaign 3
  Asylum and Immigration Tribunal 136
  black performance 54
  Blackpool 58–9
  blasphemy 89–90
  campaigning 283–6, 289–96
  celebrities 119–20
  child poverty 64
  citizen participation 257
  civil law 117, 118–20
  community cohesion 69
  councillors 232–3
  Countryside Alliance 288, 290
  damages 119–20
  defamation 118, 119–20
  democracy 254–5, 257
  Department of Work and Pensions (DWP) 213–14
  direct action 277–8
  disability 80

Earth First! 294
equality 75–6, 80
European Court of Human Rights (ECHR) 150–1
European Union (EU) 246–7
Fathers4Justice (F4J) 278
FOIA 108–9, 110–11
Freedom House 254–5
fuel protests (2000) 288, 291–2
General Medical Council (GMC) 135
Get Set Community Project 285–6
glorifying terrorism 95–6
government 213–14
harassment 51
homophobia 49
indirect discrimination 46
judicial review 153, 155–6
jury system 123
legal representation 128, 129, 131–2
life chances 54
lobbying 274–5
magistrates' courts 143–4
Make Poverty History (MPH) 288, 289
Martin, Tony 113–14
media 199, 202–3
MEPs 246–7
MPs 215
MRSN 75–6
multinational companies (MNCs) 185
Northern Rock Bank 180–2
participation 257
poverty 58–9
power 167–8, 170
prejudice 51
racial prejudice 45
Relate 133
restorative justice 126
RIAC Project 6–7
rights 89–90, 113–14
RSPB 274–5
RSPCA 274
self-defence 113–14
terrorism 119, 155
Toyota 185
catch-all parties 175
CCT *see* **compulsory competitive tendering**
CEHR see Commission for Equality and Human Rights
celebrities
    case study 119–20
    defamation 119–20
Chancellor of the Exchequer 178
Charter of Fundamental Rights 100

chief whip 216
Child Poverty Action Group (CPAG) 60
child poverty, case study 64
citizen participation 298–303
    active citizenship 298–303
    case study 257
    democracy 255–8
    local government 231–4
citizens 1–10, 3
economic power 187–90
Citizens Advice Bureaux 131
citizenship 1–10, 2
    law 122–7
Citizenship Test 9
City of London 166
civil courts 145
civil disobedience 86
civil law 116
    case study 117, 118–20
    punishment or compensation? 117–20
civil service 162
class ladder 19, 19–21
clearing banks 179
CND *see* **Campaign for Nuclear Disarmament**
co-decision procedure 245–6, **246**
coercion 162
Cold War 97, 98
commercialisation 197, 197–8
Commission for Equality and Human Rights (CEHR) 70
Commission for Racial Equality (CRE) 39, 70, 78–9
Common Agricultural Policy (CAP) 245–6, **246**
communitarian thinking 4, 61
community charge (poll tax) 61
community cohesion, case study 69
community punishment orders 121
community rehabilitation orders 121
companies
    see also **multinational companies (MNCs)**
    economic power 185–7
compensation or punishment? *see* punishment or compensation?
compulsory competitive tendering (CCT) 230
conciliation 133–4
conditional fee scheme 130
Confederation of British Industry 179, 180
conflicting interests, balancing 139–40
consensus 162
conservatism 175

constituency 172
constitution 82
consumer protection 189–90
consumer rights 112
Contempt of Court 89, **90**
conurbations 24
convergence criteria 243, 243–4
conveyancing 129
corporal punishment 120
Corporation of the City of London 220
Council of Europe 83
Council of Ministers 100, 247
councillors 231–4
    see also local government
    case study 232–3
    role 232–3
Countryside Alliance, case study 288, 290
courts
    civil courts 145
    court structure 142
    criminal courts 143–4
    crown courts 144–5
    European Court of Human Rights (ECHR) 72, 100–4, 148–51
    European Court of Justice 99
    Human Rights Act (1998) 147–51
    magistrates' courts 142–4
    powers 142–7
    protecting rights 138–57
    Supreme Court 140, 148
CPAG *see* Child Poverty Action Group
CRE *see* Commission for Racial Equality
credit crunch (or squeeze) 179
criminal courts 143–4
criminal law 116
    punishment or compensation? 120–2
    sanctions 120–2
cronyism 234
Crown 162
crown courts 144–5
culture 10
cycle of poverty 60

D

DA-Notices 89, **90**
damages 117–18
case study 119–20
personal injury 119
Data Protection Act (DPA) 105–7
de Gaulle (1890-1970), General 236
Dean Clough 69
death rate 23

decentralisation 210
defamation 89, 116
  case study 118, 119–20
  celebrities 119–20
  terrorism 119
democracy 159, 160, 161, 249–55
  case study 254–5, 257
  citizen participation 255–8
  criticisms 252–4
  democratic values 251–4
  electoral process 259–67
  Freedom House 254–5
  media 200–3
  participation 255–8
  taking part in the democratic
    process 249–55
  worldwide recogntion 251
Democratic Unionists 227
Department of Work and Pensions
  (DWP)
  case study 213–14
  services 213–14
dependency culture 61
deregulation 178, 178–9
deregulation of the media 192
devolution 11
  Scotland 222–5
  Wales 225–6
devolved government 169, 221–9
direct action
  case study 277–8
  electoral process 275–8
direct democracy 249, 250
direct discrimination 46
directives 239
directly-elected mayor (of London)
  220
disability 50, 71–2
  case study 80
  legislation 72
Disabled People's Council (DPC)
  71–2
discrimination 44
  see also equality
  age discrimination 50
  anti-discrimination policies
    67–74
  direct discrimination 46
  indirect discrimination 46
  positive discrimination 71
  racial discrimination 46
DPA see Data Protection Act
DPC see Disabled People's Council
duties 5
  rights relationship 84–7
DWP see Department of Work and
  Pensions

E

e-democracy 292, 292–3

Earth First! 294
  case study 294
ECHR see European Convention
  on Human Rights ; European
  Court of Human Rights
economic migrants 22
economic power
  citizens 187–90
  companies 185–7
economic power and control 175–9
ecotage 277
EHRC see Equality and Human
  Rights Commission
elected hereditaries 216
election campaign 262–3, 263
electoral process
  democracy 259–67
  direct action 275–8
  focus groups 266
  media role 263–5
  negative campaigning 264
  opinion polling 265–6
  pressure groups 268–82
  range of elections 259–60
  referendums 266–7
  turnout patterns 261–2
  value of elections 259
electorate 88, 250
elite 38
elitism 250
Englishness 10–12
entrapment 205
equal opportunities, government
  bodies 74
equality 65–7, 159, 160
  see also discrimination
  case study 75–6, 80
  legislation 70–4, 78–80
  women 73–4, 77–8
Equality Act (2006) 73
Equality and Human Rights
  Commission (EHRC) 74–5, 132
  equality before the law 82
  equality of opportunity 65
  equality of outcome 65
  Establishment 168
  ethnic cleansing 25, 52
ethnic groupings, United Kingdom
  33
  ethnic minorities
  age 34–5
  employment 34–5
  influence on national character
    36–7
  religious diversity 35–6
  stereotypes 43
  United Kingdom 32–7
Ethnic Minority Employment Task
  Force (2004) 76
ethnicity 14

European Commission 99
European Convention on Human
  Rights (ECHR) 83, 100–4, 147–8
European Council 247–8
European Court of Human Rights
  (ECHR) 72, 100–4
  case study 150–1
  role 148–51
European Court of Justice 99
European Economic Area 105, 242
European Parliament 99
European Social Charter 99
European super-state 237
European Union (EU) 169
  case study 246–7
  enlargement 235–6
  impact 235–48
  intergovernmental bodies 247–8
  legislative process 245
  lobbying 272–5
  MEPs 246–7
  rights 98–100
  supranational bodies 245–7
europhobes 239
eurosceptics 239
Eurozone 176
evaluating, active citizenship
  300–1
Examination-style questions 157–8
  campaigning 297
executive 161
government 216–18

F

F4J see Fathers4Justice
Factortame 239
Falklands dispute (1982) 199
fascism 174
Fathers4Justice (F4J), case study
  278
federal government 209, 210
female stereotypes 42
Financial Services Authority (FSA)
  181
fiscal policy 177, 177–8, 183–4
fiscal stimulus 179
floating voters 263
focus groups 266
FOIA see Freedom of Information
  Act
Fourth of July 12
FPTP (first past the post) 174
fragmentation 197, 197–8
franchise (or suffrage) 88
free market 178
free speech 88–9, 93
  glorifying terrorism 95–6
Freedom House
  case study 254–5
  democracy 254–5

Freedom of Information Act (FOIA) 107–11
case study 108–9, 110–11
FSA *see* **Financial Services Authority**
fuel protests (2000), case study 288, 291–2
funding, civil and criminal disputes 130–1

G

G8 218
de Gaulle (1890-1970), General 236
GCHQ 163
General Medical Council (GMC), case study 135
Geneva Conventions 97
genocide 52
Get Set Community Project, case study 285–6
ghettoes 38
Glasgow University Media Group (GUMG) 196, 207
glass ceiling 73
global citizenship 22
globalisation 17
media 197–8
glorifying terrorism 95
case study 95–6
GMC *see* General Medical Council
God-given law 115
Good Friday Agreement 226, 226–7, **266**
government 159, 160
Cabinet 165, 217–18
case study 213–14
devolved government 169, 221–9
DWP 213–14
executive 161, 216–18
forms of 208–9
impacts on citizens 212–14
judiciary 218
local government 218–21
MPs 215
power 168–70, 209–10
regional government in England 227–8
role 208–11
services 211, 213–14
structure 214–18
tiers 168–70, 211
United Kingdom 210–11
government bodies, equal opportunities 74
Government Equalities Office 75
government policies
anti-discrimination policies 67–74
effectiveness 76–7

green-belt land 276
guiding principles, **rule of law** 138–9
GUMG *see* **Glasgow University Media Group**

H

Habeas Corpus 87, 87–8
harassment, case study 51
Heath, Edward (1916-2005) 236
hereditary peerages 216
HM Treasury 168
homogeneity 32
homophobia 47–9, **48**
case study 49
Honeywell Centre 68
House of Commons 165, 214–16
roles 216
House of Lords 148, 150, 151
court structure 142
judicial independence 140
judicial review 155
law lords 140
rulings 155
structure 216, 217
HRA *see* **Human Rights Act (1998)**
Huguenots 25
human rights 5
see also rights
Human Rights Act (1998) 4, 4–5, 101–4
courts 147–51
terrorism 103–4
hung Parliament 265
Hutton Inquiry 141, 146, 199

I

ICCPR *see* **UN International Covenant on Civil and Political Rights**
identity 15
defining 15–22
ideologues 174
ideology 36
inalienable rights 81
income 19
indictable offences 143
indirect democracy 249–50, **250**
indirect discrimination 46
case study 46
individualism 4
Industrial Revolution 19
inflation 178
influence 159, **160,** 161
infrastructure 222
initiatives 249, **250**
injunction 93, 117
institutional (or structural) racism 52
integration 38, **237**

race relations 38
intergovernmental bodies, **European Union (EU)** 247–8
intergovernmental union 235
intergovernmentalism 237
International Labour Organisation (1919) 97
international law 116
International Monetary Fund 176
Irish Republican Army (IRA) 164
Islamicism 238

J

JAC *see* Judicial Appointments Commission
Jarrow marchers 293
Joint Intelligence Committee (JIC) 163
Joseph Rowntree Foundation 60
judges, role 145–7
judicial activism 83
Judicial Appointments Commission (JAC) 140, 146
judicial independence 140
judicial process 140–2
judicial review 151, 151–7
case study 153, 155–6
criticisms 154–5
difficulties 156–7
House of Lords 155
natural justice 152–3
terrorism 155
judiciary 102, 161
junta 209
jurisprudence 129
jury system 122–3
case study 123
justice 115

K

Keynes (1883-1946), John Maynard 177
Kilmuir Guidelines 141

L

labelling 40
Labour's initiatives, regional government in England 228–9
laissez-faire **177**
law
citizenship 122–7
meaning of 115
Law Centres 132
law lords 140
lay magistrates 124–7
leader of HM opposition 216
legal aid 66
legal framework 115–37
legal issues, equality 66
legal representation 127–32

case study 128, 129, 131–2
legal rights 5
examples 87–96
legislation
disability 72
equality 70–4, 78–80
race relations legislation 70, 89
racial harassment 70
legislative devolution 222
legislative process, **European Union (EU)** 245
legislature 161, 214–16
legitimacy 161
legitimate system of government 259
liberal democracies 5, 250
life chances 21
case study 54
distribution 53–7
life expectancy 23, 57
life peers 216
Lisbon (Reform) Treaty 100
list system 224
lobbying 271, 271–5
see also campaigning; pressure groups
case study 274–5
European Union (EU) 272–5
RSPB 274–5
RSPCA 274
local authorities 221
revenue sources 231
local democracy 219
local government 218–21
citizen participation 231–4
councillors 231–4
local authorities 221, 231
powers 229–35
structure 220–1
London bombings 22
lynching 52

M

Maastricht Treaty on European Union 14
magistrates' courts 142–4
case study 143–4
magistrates, lay 124–7
Magna Carta 87
Major (1943-), John 167
Make Poverty History (MPH), case study 288, 289
maladministration 136, 136–7
managing the media 198
Manchester Refugee Support Network (MRSN), case study 75–6
mandarin power 165
mandate 161
manifesto 162

marginal constituencies 263
Martin, Tony, case study 113–14
mass media 160
see also media
media 190–207
Blair, Tony 202–3
case study 199, 202–3
cross-media ownership 197
democracy 200–3
deregulation of the media 192
globalisation 197–8
influence 190–207
Market model 204
ownership/control 193–7
political attitudes 207
political spin 206–7
public opinion 193
Public service model 203
regulation 203–6
spin 206–7
media minders 198, 198–200
media role, electoral process 263–5
mediation 133–4
melting-pot 37
MEPs, case study 246–7
merchant banks 179, **180**
migration
case study 28–31
factors influencing 24–31
militant 276
Miners' Strike (1984-5) 94, 280
ministers 162
minor party 173
minority government 165
MNCs see **multinational companies**
monetary policy 177, 177–8
Monetary Policy Committee (MPC) 184, 184–5
morality 115
MPC see **Monetary Policy Committee**
MPH see Make Poverty History
MPs
case study 215
roles 215
MRSN see Manchester Refugee Support Network
mullahs 159, **160**
multi-ethnic society 32
multi-level governance 169
multi-level government 169
multi-party systems 259
multicultural society 18, 18–19
United Kingdom 31–9
multiculturalism 18, 18–19
race relations 38–9
multinational companies (MNCs) 166–7, 167, 185–7
case study 185

Toyota 185
multiple deprivation 58

N

National Health Service (NHS) 214
national sovereignty 244, 244–5
nationalisation 176
nationalism 221, 221–2
nationalists 222
nationality 8
NATO (North Atlantic Treaty Organization) 166, **167**
natural law 115
naturalised 8
Nazi party 45
negative campaigning, electoral process 264
negligence 116
net migration 23
New Commonwealth 19
New Deal 179
new democracies 237
New Labour 4
New Right 178
NHS (National Health Service) 214
NIMBY ('not in my back yard') 276
Northern Rock Bank 179
case study 180–2
numbers game 67

O

oath of allegiance 9
Obscene Publications Act (1959) 89, **90**
offences triable either way 143
Office for National Statistics 57
Office of Fair Trading (OFT) 189
Official Secrets Act (1989) 89, 108
OFT see **Office of Fair Trading**
oligarchy 250
OPEC see Organisation of Petroleum Exporting Countries
opinion polling, electoral process 265–6
order for specific performance 117
Orders in Council 226
Organisation for Security and Cooperation in Europe 97
Organisation of Petroleum Exporting Countries (OPEC) 176
Oxbridge 169, 169–70

P

paparazzi 205
Parliament 162
Parliamentary Commissioner for Administration (PCA) 136–7
parliamentary lobby system 200

Parliamentary Sovereignty 101
participation 161
   active citizenship 298–303
   case study 257
   citizen participation 255–8,
   298–303
   democracy 255–8
   electoral participation 261–2
Party Political and Party Election
   broadcasts 204
party system 173
party whips 171
PCA *see* Parliamentary
   Commissioner for Administration
peak organisations 269
penetration rate 191
persuasion 160
photo opportunities 264
planning, **active citizenship** 298
pluralist democracy 167
pogroms 25, 52
policies, government see
   government policies
political attitudes, media 207
political correctness 79
political Left 5, 5–6
political parties 170
   power 170–5
   role 170–5
political power, nature of 164–8
political Right 5
political spectrum 174
political spin 206–7
politics 159, 160
polity 5
popular movements
   campaigning 289–96
   common themes 292–3
population, United Kingdom 24
positive discrimination 71
poverty 57
   case study 58–9
   United Kingdom 57–64
poverty trap 61
power 159–207
   case study 167–8, 170
   concept of 159–61
   courts 142–7
   economic power and control
   175–9
   government 168–70, 209–10
   local government 229–35
   nature of 159–61
   political parties 170–5
   political power 164–8
   and the **state** 161–4
prejudice 44
   bases 47–50
   case study 51
   forms 44–5

hierarchy 51–3
pressure groups 250
see also campaigning; **lobbying**
   electoral process 268–82
   successful 278–80
pressure points 271
prime minister 165, 217–18
prime minister's questions (PMQs)
   216
Private Members' Bill 272
privatisation 176
pro bono publico 130
probate 129
progressive (taxation) **230**
project subjects, active citizenship
   299
protecting rights, courts 138–57
public corporation 194
public opinion 193
public service broadcasting 194
Public service model, media 203
punishment or compensation?
   117–22
   civil law 117–20
   criminal law 120–2
   push and pull factors 25

Q
al Qaeda 164
QMV *see* qualified majority voting
qualified majority voting (QMV)
   236
quangocracy 226
quangos 203

R
race 32
race relations 37–9
   assimilation 37
   integration 38
   multiculturalism 38–9
race relations legislation 70, 89
racial discrimination, forms 46
racial harassment, legislation 70
racial prejudice 44, 44–5
   case study 45
racial **stereotypes** 43
racism 39
   institutional (or structural)
   racism 52
radical protest campaigning 293–4
recession 178
recording, **active citizenship** 300–1
referendums 166
referendums, electoral process
   266–7
Refugee and Migrant Forum
   Manchester (RMFM) 75–6

Refugee Integration and Active
   Citizenship (RIAC) Project, case
   study 6–7
refugees 25
regional government in England
   227–9
   Labour's initiatives 228–9
regulation, media 203–6
regulations 239
Relate, case study 133
relative poverty 57, 57–9
representative democracy 249, **250**
reserved powers 223
restorative justice 125, 125–7
   case study 126
RIAC Project see Refugee Integration
   and Active Citizenship Project
right to know 104–11, 105
right to privacy 82
right to silence 88
rights 1, **2**, 81–114
   see also **human rights; Human**
   Rights Act (1998)
   accorded by law 81–2
   case study 89–90, 113–14
   courts protecting rights 138–57
   duties relationship 84–7
   European Union (EU) 98–100
   examples of **legal rights** 87–96
   legal rights examples 87–96
   South African Constitution 87
   UDHR 81
   United Nations 97–8
rights consciousness 83
rights culture 4
RMFM *see* Refugee and Migrant
   Forum Manchester
Roma peoples 44
Royal Society for the Protection of
   Birds (RSPB)
   case study 274–5
   lobbying 274–5
RSPCA
   case study 274
   lobbying 274
rule of law 115
   guiding principles 138–9
Runnymede Trust 47

S
scapegoating 45
Scarman Report (1981) 68
Scotland, **devolution** 222–5
section 28; 293
secular society 13
sedition 89
selective universality 62, 62–3
self-defence, case study 113–14
sexism 49–50
Single European Act (1986) 98

single issue groups 270
Sinn Fein ('We ourselves') 226
six counties 266
sleaze 234
smacking 92–3
Snowdrop 270, 288
Social Chapter 99, 236
social citizenship 5
social class 11
social engineering 66
social exclusion 63
Social Fund 61
social levelling 20
social mobility 20, 53
socialisation 16
socialists 8
society 16
solicitors 128–9
soundbites 200
South African Constitution, rights 87
sovereign power 161
Soviet bloc 97, 98
special relationship 237
spin, media 206–7
state 2
  power and the 161–4
statute law 116
stereotypes 18, 40–3
  ethnic minorities 43
  female 42
  racial 43
Stock Exchange 179
Stonewall 49
Stop the War Coalition 288, 296
sub-national administrations 209
sub-prime mortgage market 180
subjects 3, 3–4
subsidiarity 248
summary offences 143
supranational 210
Supreme Court 140, 148
surgeries 231
sustainable development 183

T

tabloids 191
taking part in the democratic
  process 249–55
'tarring and feathering' 52
tax credits 62
television
  bias 195–6
  ownership/control 194–6
television licence fee 194, 195
terrorism 163, 163–4
  case study 119, 155
  defamation 119
  glorifying terrorism 95–6
  Human Rights Act (1998) 103–4
  judicial review 155
Thatcher, Margaret 237
Thatcherism 178
The Bar 129
The Troubles 52
theocracies 209
think tanks 269
third party 173
totalitarian regimes 209
town meetings 249, 250
Toyota, case study 185
trades unions 166
trading standards departments 189
Treaty of Rome (1957) 98
tree-hugging stereotypes 284
trickle-down effect 66
turnout patterns, electoral
  participation 261–2
two-party system 173
Twyford Down 93
typology 270, 270–1
tyranny 159, 160

U

UDHR see Universal Declaration of
  Human Rights
umbrella organisations 269

UN Charter (1945) 97, 98
UN International Covenant
  on Civil and Political Rights
  (ICCPR) 83, 97
underclass 61
unitary councils 220
unitary system of government 169
United Kingdom 10–15
  constituent parts 10–15
  ethnic groupings 33
  ethnic minorities 32–7
  government 210–11
  multicultural society 31–9
  population 24
  poverty 57–64
United Nations 81
  rights 97–8
Universal Declaration of Human
  Rights (UDHR) 81, 83, 85

V

values 1, 2
VAT (value added tax) 183
veto 239

W

Wales, devolution 225–6
watchdog 189
wealth 19
welfare rights 112
Welfare State 6, 212
West Lothian Question (WLQ) 225
Whitehall 210
Winterval 39
women
  equality 73–4, 77–8
  in politics 78
wordsmiths 200

Y

YouTube 191

Acknowledgements

The publishers would like to thank the author where appropriate for use of images and drawings. We have attempted to contact all copyright holders and controllers. If any items are not fully credited this will be corrected in future editions. The author and publishers wish to thank the following for permission to use copyright material:

Text

pp6–7 Exeter CSV case study, with grateful thanks to Gabi Recknagel of Exeter CVS for help and assistance. Reprinted with permission; p10 'Englishness' within the UK, adapted from article by Nicholas Wade, New York Times: March 6, 2007. See www.nytimes.com/2007/03/06/science/06brits.html?scp=51&sq=march%206%202007&st=cse; p11 Table of UK population, from 2001 census figures, National Statistics online www.statistics.gov.uk/census2001/ © Crown Copyright reprinted under Crown Copyright PSI License C2008000256; p15 Boris Johnson quote from What does it mean to be British? by David Smith and Vanessa Thorpe, The Observer 31 July 2005. http://www.guardian.co.uk/uk/2005/jul/31/britishidentity.july7, reprinted with permission; p17 Stats of centenarians in the UK, National Statistics online www.statistics.gov.uk/census2001/ © Crown Copyright reprinted under Crown Copyright PSI License C2008000256.

p23 Fertility rates, Office of National Statistics, National Statistics online www.statistics.gov.uk/census2001/ © Crown Copyright reprinted under Crown Copyright PSI License C2008000256: p27 Home office figures, Immigration Research and Statistics Service © Crown Copyright reprinted under Crown Copyright PSI License C2008000256; p28–9 Case study of Poles in Crew, Tim Whewel, adapted from Newsnight, BBC Television, 20.1.2006; p31 Brits Abroad: Mapping the scale and nature of British emigration by Danny Sriskandarajah and Catherine Drew, 2006, Study conducted by IPPR 11 December 2006. See www.ippr.org.uk/publicationsandreports/publication.asp?id=509; p31 Table of UK net migration – Population Division of the Department of Economic and Social Affairs of the United Nations Secretariat, World Population Prospects: The 2006 Revision and World Urbanization Prospects. Public domain; p36 Table of reactions to London bombings adapted from Populus poll, June 05, Living in Britain Today, Populus, February 2006; p37 Attitudes to multiculturalism – BBC/MORI poll August 2005; p43 Case study: Lenny Henry on the British broadcasting media, Where are all the black new faces? by Owen Wilson, The Guardian, 11 February 2008, www.guardian.co.uk/media/2008/feb/11/television.race?gusrc=rss&feed=media copyright Guardian News & Media Ltd 2008.

p44 Levels of prejudice in British society, adapted from Rothon, C. and Health, A. (2003), 'Trends in racial prejudice', in Park, A., Curtice, J., Thomson, K., Jarvis, L. and Bromley, C. (eds.), British Social Attitudes: the 20th report, London: Sage http://www.natcen.ac.uk/natcen/pages/news_and_media_docs/2003bsa_pr.pdf; p46 Case study of Aina v Employment Service, 2002, adapted from the Equality and Human Rights Commission website; p48–9 Case studies from Stonewall website reproduced by kind permission of Stonewall; p51 Case study of Anisetti v Tokyo Mitsubishi International: extract taken from the Equality and Human Rights Commission website: www.equalityhumanrights.com; p54 Case study: Raising Black performance, adapted from article by Mike Baker, BBC Education Correspondent, BBC News, 16 March 2002; p58 Health in Blackpool – Health and Well-being Improvement Plan, Blackpool Council, 2006. see http://www.blackpool.gov.uk/NR/rdonlyres/FA3AF1F3-6534-4BD8-B6CB-3FBADEA7305C/0/HealthandWellbeingImprovementplan.pdf, reprinted with kind permission from the Policy and Communications Department, Blackpool Council www.blackpool.gov.uk; p58 Case study: poverty in Blackpool – Crime, Disorder & Drugs Audit, A profile of Blackpool, 2004: see www.bsafeblackpool.com; p59 Case study: poverty in Blackpool – Sigrún Davídsdóttir, Combined social support and health care in deprived areas, the Citizens Advice Bureau in Blackpool, 2007 Blackpool CAB Charity no. 511537; p59 Beyond the pleasure beach by Julie Bindel, The Guardian 30 May 2008. See www.guardian.co.uk/uk/2008/may/30/ukcrime.childprotection copyright Guardian News & Media Ltd 2007; p60 Mind the gap The Guardian 18 July 2007. See www.guardian.co.uk/commentisfree/2007/jul/18/socialexclusion.politics, copyright Guardian News & Media Ltd 2007.

p67 Department of Communities and Local Government publications, Consultation paper: An Action Plan for Community Empowerment: Building on Success, 2008; p75 Case study: The role of charities in bringing about improvement: Manchester Refugee Support Network – adapted from page 7 of a report of the Manchester Refugee Support Network, entitled The Skills Audit Community Project, authored by Shahida Sidduqe and Zoë Speekenbrink. See www.nwtwc.org.uk/library/downloads/Skills-Audit-Report.pdf; p78 Women in political office in the UK, from Government Equalities Office © Crown Copyright reprinted under Crown Copyright PSI License C2008000256; p78 Government Equalities Office – extract from the Equality and Human Rights Commission website; p80 Case study: How individuals can campaign for equal treatment, by Megan Murphy, Financial Times, 13 May 2008, reprinted with permission.

p88 Betjeman poem 'In Westminster Abbey' from Faith and doubts of John Betjeman, reprinted with permission from Aitken Alexander; p96 Making bad law worse. Louise Christian, 16 February 2006. See www.guardian.co.uk/politics/2006/feb/16/terrorism.uk copyright Guardian News & Media Ltd 2006.

p104 Belmarsh – Britain's Guantanamo Bay? BBC News 5 October 2004. See http://news.bbc.co.uk/1/hi/magazine/3714864.stm (c) bbc.co.uk; p106 Case study: Questions and responses taken from office of Information Commissioner website: www.ico.gov.uk; p108–9 Case study: Report of the release of Cabinet records on the proposed military action against Iraq by David Byers Timesonline 26 February 2008. See www.timesonline.co.uk/tol/news/politics/article3438974.ece; pp110–11 What freedom of information? By Robert Verkaik, 28 December 2006 The Independent, reprinted with permission.

p119–20 Sweet and Maxwell research, July 2007, available at their online legal information service, www.sweetandmaxwell.co.uk; p122 The case for juries, www.direct.gov.uk © Crown Copyright reprinted under Crown Copyright PSI License C2008000256; p123 Case study: Trial by jury in complex and technical cases, Paul Mcmillan, Chronicle Live, The Evening Chronicle, 19 May 2007. See www.chroniclelive.co.uk/north-east-news/; p126 Case study: Home Office research on the impact of restorative justice projects, justice.gov.uk/docs/Restorative-Justice.pdf © Crown Copyright reprinted under Crown Copyright PSI License C2008000256; p131 Case study: Citizens Advice Bureaux, extract from website www.citizensadvice.org.uk; p132 Law centres case study, extract from website www.lawcentres.org.uk; p132 Case study: Equality and Human Rights Commission, www.equalityhumanrights.com © Crown Copyright reprinted under Crown Copyright PSI License C2008000256; p133 The role of Relate case study, extract from website www.relate.org.uk; p134 Case study: ACAS www.acas.org.uk © Crown Copyright reprinted under Crown Copyright PSI License C2008000256; p135 Case study: the General Medical Council, Extract from website www.gmc-uk.org; p136 Case study: the Asylum & Immigration Tribunal, extract from website www.ait.gov.uk © Crown Copyright reprinted under Crown Copyright PSI License C2008000256.

p144 Case study: we must hold on to local justice, by Andrew Phillips, The Observer, 2 December 2001. See http://www.guardian. co.uk/politics/2001/dec/02/britainand911.humanrights copyright Guardian News & Media Ltd 2001; p146 First 10 high court judges under new diversity rules, by Clare Dyer The Guardian 28 January 2008. See www.guardian.co.uk/politics/2008/jan/28/ uk.immigrationpolicy1 copyright Guardian News & Media Ltd 2008.

p172 Getting involved in the Conservative Party, www.conservatives.com; p191 Table of daily newspaper sales, ABC. Public domain; p193 MORI survey for Electoral Commission, June – Sources of political knowledge in 2001 election campaign; p202–3 Tony Blair's speech on the media, 12 June 2007 www.number10.gov.uk/Page11923 © Crown Copyright reprinted under Crown Copyright PSI License C2008000256; p203 What's wrong with TV? By Jeremy Paxman in Guardian Media 25 August 2007. See http://image. guardian.co.uk/sys-files/Media/documents/2007/08/24/MacTaggartLecture.pdf copyright Guardian News & Media Ltd 2007; p215 Alan Meale case study, from www.alanmeale.co.uk.

p215 Sian James case study, from www.sianjamesmp.co.uk; p224 Alex Salmond quote, 2005, from Politics Association journal, Citizenship 3:3, April 2005; p228 William Hague quote, Speech to Policy Exchange, 21.2.2006, Public domain; p232–3 A Councillor? Who ... me? From www.scarborough.gov.uk/PDF/A%20councillor%20who%20me1.pdf, reprinted with kind permission from Scarborough Borough Council; p234 Local Government in the United Kingdom, 4th Revised Edition by David Wilson and Chris Game, reprinted with permission from Palgrave Macmillan; p240 A pro-European case, speeches by Tony Blair, 2000 and 2003, Public domain; p242 UKIP mission statement, Public domain; p242 Extract from Yes, Minister, Party Games, final episode of Yes Minister, BBC Television 1984; pp246–7 Case study – extract from website of Jean Lambert, MEP. See www.jeanlambertmep.org. uk/meet_jean_dayoflife.php, reprinted with permission; p254 Findings of the National Geographic-Roper 2002 Global Geographic Literacy Survey, based on information from www.nationalgeographic.com/geosurvey2002/download/RoperSurvey.pdf.

p254 Case study: three cheers for British democracy, The John Bull column, The Birmingham Post, 19.4.2006; p257 Electoral Commission report case study: Encouraging women's participation in public life, Gender and Political Participation, The Electoral Commission, April 2004; p258 Table: Some factors affecting in elections and via other means, Adapted from findings of Parry (1992) and Evans (1997); p278 F4J case study: F4J Storm Minister's House Extract from F4J website 10.6.2008 http://fathers-4-justice.org/ f4j//index.php?option=com_content&task=view&id=21&Itemid=42; p280 Biofuels quote, RSPB www.rspb.org.uk.

pp283–4 Case study: Airport Watch on resistance to airport expansion, adapted from a BBC report 2008; p285 Case study: Celebrity joins in Stansted Airport debate, BBC report 19 Feb 2007; pp285–6 Case study: Get Set Community Project, based upon an article by Anne Hazell of Magpie in Citizenship PA, vol 1:2, 2003; p295 Case study: the right to engage in anti-globalisation protest under the UNDHR, I have a right', BBC World Service website; p296 Case study: The Stop the War Coalition, reprinted with permission from the Stop the war coalition www.stopwar.org.uk; pp301–2 Case study: making a difference in the community, reprinted with kind permission from Help the Aged www.helptheaged.org.uk.

Photos

p10 Cate Gillon/Getty Images; p14 fish and chips, London bus and Henry VIII, Fotolia: police Elma Okic/Rex Features; p15 Boris Johnson courtesy of Greater London Assembly; p26 Douglas Miller/Keystone/Getty Images; p29 UKIP; p34 author's own; p48 Scott Olson/Getty Images; p50 Steve Finn/Capital Pictures; p57 William Campbell/Sygma/Corbis; p59 author's own; p62 Unite the Union; p65 Alamy; p68 Oldham Council; p73 Steve Finn/Capital Pictures; p74 Trevor Phillips courtesy of Equality and Human Rights Commission; p76 Tony Sapiano/Rex Features; p77 Alamy; p85 Electoral Commission; p89 Paul Brown/Rex Features; p95 News International; p100 public domain; p104 Gareth Fuller/ PA Archive/PA Photos; p113 PA Archive/PA Photos; p142 Lord Phillips courtesy of Ministry of Justice; p143 Annabel Ossel; p148 Alamy; p149 The Court of Human Rights courtesy of Council of Europe; p166 Alessandro Abbonizo/Getty Images; p169 José Barroso courtesy of European Commission; Shami Chakrabarti courtesy of Liberty/ Christopher Cox; p181 Gareth Fuller/PA Archive/PA Photos; p183 Andy Rain/epa/Corbis; p186 Google, BP, Ford Motor Company, Tesco, Kellogg's logo with permission of Kellogg Marketing and Sales Company (UK) Limited; p199 Phil Loftus/Capital Pictures; p206 Jo Moore by Fiona Hanson/PA Archive/PA Photos, cartoon from CartoonStock.com; p212 By permission of Llyfrgell Genedlaethol Cymru/The National Library of Wales/Solo Syndication; p217 Stephen Hird/AFP/Getty; p223 Scottish National Parliament, Alex Salmond courtesy of Scottish Executive Office; p225 courtesy of National Assembly of Wales; p228 courtesy of Campaign for an English Parliament; p239 UKIP; p242 courtesy of author and Politics Association; p244 courtesy of European Central Bank; p246 external photo European Parliament, photo of parliament in session Yves Herman/Reuters/Corbis; p276 Kevin Lister; p277 courtesy of Plane Stupid; p278 author's own; p289 Scott Barbour/Getty ImagesNews; p290 Ian Waldie/Getty Images News; p294 Earth First! Britain.